**Remapping the World
in East Asia**

Remapping the World in East Asia

Toward a Global History of the "Ricci Maps"

Edited by
Mario Cams and **Elke Papelitzky**

UNIVERSITY OF HAWAI'I PRESS
Honolulu

This publication was made possible in part by an award from the James P. Geiss and Margaret Y. Hsu Foundation.

© 2024 University of Hawaiʻi Press
All rights reserved

Printed in the United States of America
First printed 2024

Library of Congress Cataloging-in-Publication Data

Names: Cams, Mario, editor. | Papelitzky, Elke, editor.
Title: Remapping the world in East Asia : toward a global history of the "Ricci maps" / edited by Mario Cams and Elke Papelitzky.
Description: Honolulu : University of Hawaiʻi Press, [2024] | Includes bibliographical references and index.
Identifiers: LCCN 2023007279 (print) | LCCN 2023007280 (ebook) | ISBN 9780824895044 (hardback) | ISBN 9780824895051 (pdf) | ISBN 9780824895068 (epub) | ISBN 9780824896195 (kindle edition)
Subjects: LCSH: World maps, Manuscript. | Early maps. | Cartography—East Asia—History.
Classification: LCC GA300 .R46 2024 (print) | LCC GA300 (ebook) | DDC 912.09—dc23/eng20230823
LC record available at https://lccn.loc.gov/2023007279
LC ebook record available at https://lccn.loc.gov/2023007280

University of Hawaiʻi Press books are printed on acid-free paper and meet the guidelines for permanence and durability of the Council on Library Resources.

Designed by Mardee Melton

Contents

Acknowledgments   vii

Introduction: Remapping the World in East Asia
MARIO CAMS AND ELKE PAPELITZKY   1

PART I

Intertextuality, Locality, and Materiality in Ming-Era Artifacts

1 World Maps as Spaces of Intercultural Communication
NICOLAS STANDAERT   21

2 A Late Ming Terrestrial Globe
RICHARD A. PEGG   56

3 Explaining European Geography: The *Zhifang waiji* and Its Editions
WANG YONGJIE   79

4 From the Wall onto the Screen: Reframing World Maps in East Asia
CHENG FANGYI   103

5 Circling the Square: Encompassing Global Geography on Large Commercial Maps
MARIO CAMS   124

PART II

Beyond Ming China: Wider Circulation and Global Pathways

6 World Maps from China Reimagined in Japan
ELKE PAPELITZKY   159

7 From China to Korea: Kim Suhong's *Cheonha gogeum daechong pyeollam do*
YANG YULEI   188

8 Utopia and Dystopia: *Cheonha do* and the Reception of Renaissance
   Geography in Late Joseon Korea
   SOH JEANHYOUNG   **206**

9 A Manuscript Map of East Asia Assembled by Jesuits in Nagasaki and Macao
   MARCO CABOARA   **229**

10 China Translata: *The 1555* Map of Advantageous Terrain Then and Now
   FLORIN-STEFAN MORAR   **245**

11 Beyond Translation: Michele Ruggieri's Manuscript Atlas of China
   LIN HONG   **271**

   Postscript: Remapping Map History from East Asia
   MATTHEW H. EDNEY   **295**

   Glossary of Titles   **303**

   Contributors   **309**

   Index   **311**

Acknowledgments

This volume was produced during the height of the global pandemic that first engulfed the world in the winter of 2020. Its origins lie in a workshop organized at the University of Macau (UM) in the summer of that year, which eventually took place online two months behind schedule. When this book entered its final editing stage, the lingering effects of pandemic control policies still made it impossible for the authors of this volume to gather in person. This reality contrasted with the focus of our work, which highlights the global mobility of individuals in the sixteenth and seventeenth centuries. Given this context, we are particularly pleased to present the collected essays of twelve scholars active in western Europe, East Asia, and North America. It was not easy to bring together scholarship born of different academic traditions for such a tightly construed edited volume and so, as editors of this volume, we would first and foremost like to thank all the authors for their patience and enthusiasm. Special thanks go to Matthew H. Edney for agreeing to write a postscript at short notice during the final stages of manuscript preparation.

We are also indebted to several colleagues, students, and friends. Isa Chan and Su Lei helped to navigate the red tape at UM, facilitating the organization of the workshop. Eszter Csillag agreed to participate in the workshop and to share her research. Vera Dorofeeva-Lichtmann took up the role of discussant and provided her valuable insights to many of the presenters, and Charlie Zhang Xinyu, then an undergraduate student in the UM Department of History, provided technical assistance. John Cirilli helped with language editing of the initial papers during the preparation of this volume, while Robert Parkin and Wendy Lawrence were involved in a later stage, and Carlos Gonzalez Balderas assisted in checking Spanish transcriptions. As the team at University of Hawai'i Press took over, Masako K. Ikeda, Gianna Marsella, and Mary Mortensen prepared the book for production. Lim Jongtae, finally, provided his generous help in contacting Korean university libraries and museums to obtain images.

Financial support for the workshop came from the UM Faculty of Arts and Humanities. The university also provided an initial subvention for the publication of this volume (grant number MYRG2020–00051–FAH), and both the Geiss-Hsu Foundation and the MacLean Collection generously agreed to fund further subventions that allowed the inclusion of the nearly one hundred color images. We would like to thank Masako K. Ikeda and Richard A. Pegg for their role in making this possible. Finally, while editing this volume, Elke Papelitzky received funding from the European Research Council Advanced Grant project TRANSPACIFIC (grant number 833143) under the European Union's Horizon 2020 Research and Innovation Programme.

Introduction

Remapping the World in East Asia

MARIO CAMS and **ELKE PAPELITZKY**

THIS VOLUME TELLS THE STORY OF AN early modern meeting of worldviews expressed in maps, globes, atlases, and geographical treatises. In each case these artifacts resulted from individual conversations about cosmology and world geography that not only involved two global centers of learning and print culture but also received guidance and support from myriad global pathways. These conversations were supported and bolstered by European maritime expansion in Asia, which first brought Iberian traders and Catholic missionaries to the coasts of southern China and Japan in the mid-sixteenth century. It is along these routes of expansion and trade, and in the first proselytizing stations set up in China and Japan, that our story begins. Especially in Ming China (1368–1644), Jesuit missionaries started engaging with an intellectual culture they considered to be on a par with that of Renaissance Europe: both shared a strong moral code, Christian or Confucian, both deployed a unifying script, Roman or Chinese, and both maintained an advanced system of schooling with a relatively high mobility of teachers and students, as well as a print culture that allowed for the effective expression and circulation of information across regional and state boundaries.[1]

Modern historical scholarship has not always reflected the belief that these two societies shared much in common. Historians once ascribed the material products of the encounter with East Asian scholars almost entirely to the intellect and genius of Jesuit missionaries. When studying maps, they paid disproportionate attention to Matteo Ricci (1552–1610) and the "Ricci map." Usually, only the large 1602 *Kunyu wanguo quantu* 坤輿萬國全圖 (Complete map of all countries on earth; figure 1.1) serves to illustrate this "Ricci map," a world map in Chinese script centered on the Pacific and prominently presenting the five continents of Asia, Europe, Libya (Africa), the Americas, and the antipodal southern continent of Magellanica. Besides place-names, the map itself contains numerous annotations and large blocks of text, and margins containing diagrams and texts explaining the cosmological bearings of Renaissance world geography surround it.

Rather than referring to a single artifact, however, the term "Ricci map" is commonly used to cover a series of maps in Chinese script that drew inspiration from Renaissance wall maps. Although each map in this series differs greatly in aspects such as content, title, size, and format, historians continue to understand these maps as iterations of one and the same map. The "Ricci map" is, after all, a well-established symbol of a grand encounter—sometimes interpreted as a clash—between two civilizations or cultural blocs: China and Europe. In such narratives the mobile Jesuit missionaries quite naturally take center stage at the expense of their Chinese, Japanese, and Korean interlocutors. This imbalance in turn reinforces the lack of appreciation for the many extant material expressions of the meeting of worldviews under discussion, each dependent on social networks and material cultures across East Asia. In contrast, more recent scholarship seems fully committed to steering the conversation in new directions by discussing the contexts in which concrete artifacts were produced within complex local realities, thereby giving voice to more non-European actors.[2]

While this volume intends to bolster these new directions, it also aims to push the conversation one step further by making two coordinated interventions. The first insists on a more global perspective by explicitly casting off the shadows of the civilizational approach. Rather than taking over and thereby confirming the conceptual boundaries between such imagined communities as "East and West" or "China and Europe," we aim to tell the many stories of collaboration among individual actors in Chinese, Japanese, and Korean cities and en route across maritime Asia. What emerges is a long and multidirectional process of knowledge formation, with several instances not even involving European actors. Second, the successive chapters transcend cultural or state boundaries within East Asia and beyond as they connect artifact production and circulation throughout the region. This extended frame not only furthers the global agenda of this volume by crossing cultural boundaries but also achieves a historiographical conversation between different academic and linguistic skill sets. Thus, by crossing boundaries and emphasizing process, this volume ultimately presents a case study in the global history of knowledge formation.

Toward a Global Approach

While historians have been working to give voice to more non-European actors in the meeting of Renaissance and Ming-era worldviews, the idea that Matteo Ricci's world map was a singular act of mapmaking that "gave the Chinese their first glimpse of what the world looked like" still reverberates today.[3] Among works of popular history, at times Ricci becomes something of a missionary-hero who single-handedly adapted a European world map for a Chinese audience, thus bringing a "correct" understanding of world geography to the Middle Kingdom. This interpretation does not match what historians have found over the last decades: we not only have a long list of artifacts from across East Asia that borrow and repackage selected elements from Renaissance cosmology and geography but have also discovered that, in turn, East Asian maps and atlases shaped and defined European knowledge of world geography.[4] This leaves the "Ricci map" and its history, a static symbol of contact between the intellectual cultures of western Europe and East Asia, in dire need of revision.

Two grand narratives that long ago reached their expiry date provided the fertile ground in which the popular imagination surrounding the "Ricci map" thrived and continues to thrive. The first is that modern mapmaking has its immediate roots in the Renaissance, after which it developed into modern cartography along a linear trajectory of improved accuracy facilitated by European expansion. A second and related grand narrative is the idea that science developed solely within Europe, from where it spread across the globe in the footsteps of early modern empire. Based on this understanding of science as foundational to Europe's unique path of progress, the field of cartography emerged in the nineteenth century, just as history became a separate discipline at European universities. Nineteenth-century intellectuals understood cartography as the science of mapmaking and, as Matthew H. Edney explains, as a "necessarily timeless and universal endeavor."[5] They were only concerned with geometrical mapping, identified by such devices as projection, map scale, and numerical ratios, and in tracing "rational" or "universal" tendencies in cartography back to the Renaissance.[6] As the triumphant narrative went, Europeans started measuring the Earth during the Renaissance, putting them on a path that would gradually lead them to perfect the world map. In this history of cartography, the maps at issue were overwhelmingly produced by white men and fit comfortably within this narrow math-based straitjacket of European progress in mapping the world.

After World War II, these views were gradually problematized as historians started to explore how other major civilizations, such as those of East Asia, had contributed to world history. This focus led to a comparative turn as historians sought to provide a historical explanation for European hegemony in the sciences. The (in)famous "Needham question" captures this: "The essential problem [is] why modern science had not developed in Chinese civilization (or Indian) but only in Europe."[7] The man who raised this question, Joseph Needham (1900–1995), initiated the publication of the *Science and Civilization in China* series,[8] in which he and his collaborators shifted the focus from China's early modern failure to its contribution to science in the period preceding the "meteoric rise . . . in the West."[9] In the decades that followed, slowly but surely the focus shifted, and sociocultural critiques of these strongly Eurocentric histories became more prevalent.

The earliest scholarly works to feature the world map series attributed to Matteo Ricci show a similar trajectory that generally follows this paradigm shift. Nicolas Standaert has analyzed these works in a theoretical essay that uses scholarship on the "Ricci map" as a lens through which to discuss historical approaches to the study of contact between cultures.[10] It suffices here to mention two of these scholarly works in light of the more general shift toward sociocultural critique. An article by Kenneth Ch'en, "Matteo Ricci's Contribution to, and Influence on, Geographical Knowledge in China," published in 1939, takes the missionary as the only active element in a straightforward exchange between China and Europe.[11] As Standaert points out, in both the title and the narrative as a whole, it is the missionary who "contributes" and "influences," whereas the Chinese appear only as passive subjects unable to comprehend the superior incoming knowledge of astronomy and world geography. In this "transmission framework," the historian constructs two cultural-civilizational blocs that come not only with a clear bias—looking over the shoulders of the European missionary, who brought a global geography to the passive and rather ignorant Chinese—but also with an often explicit opposition between "rational science" and the "traditional thought" of the Chinese.

This bias toward the European missionary's transmission of a superior science remained prevalent in works that featured the "Ricci map" until at least the 1990s and is responsible for how the story is still told as part of popular history today.[12] When scholars trained in Asian languages slowly started making their mark, they contributed to a burgeoning field that took the agency of non-European peoples in history much more seriously. As part of a general wave of social critiques in the discipline of history, they made a point of studying East Asian science within its own historical context. Cordell D. K. Yee's chapter "Traditional Chinese Cartography and the Myth of Westernization" in the *History of Cartography* series is a case in point.[13] In the discussion of the "Ricci map," the Eurocentric bias makes room for the exact opposite: the story is told from the perspective of "Chinese cartography" and dismisses the agency of the European missionary. While this "reception framework" was a welcome intervention that helped correct Eurocentric approaches, the new narrative did not question two of its most basic premises—namely, that the story is one of a straightforward exchange between two cultural blocs and that an essential difference existed between European and Chinese cartographies. In their fervor, scholars working within this framework of reception thus created a cartography of the *other* that differed so completely from the cartography of the *self* that the two clashed and inevitably led to a failure of communication.[14]

With few exceptions, much anglophone scholarship produced over the last two decades still largely subscribes to the reception framework, in which the formation of scientific knowledge in East Asia is studied "on its own terms."[15] On the other hand, recent studies have studied specific "Ricci maps" more attentively while working on a deeper sociocultural contextualization and a wider set of connections across East Asia.[16] This historiographical change now makes clear that the geographical books, maps, and globes produced as a result of contact between western Europe and East Asia do not simply reflect the successful or unsuccessful transmission of European cartography into another world of Chinese or East Asian cartography. Rather, we increasingly come to understand that knowledge and information were circulated in complex ways and multiple directions and that, in the first place, we are studying artifacts shaped by a highly contextual (or local) negotiation of knowledge between individual actors. This process in effect repackages existing worldviews, or certain elements thereof, within new scholarly discourses and print cultures. Seen in this light, the maps produced with the assistance of Matteo Ricci are only one small part of a larger dynamic.

In this book we build on these insights by presenting a globally inspired history of what was in reality a connected series of artifacts produced in East Asia, each uniquely capturing different moments in the early modern contact between two open systems of cosmological and geographical knowledge. As successive acts of mapping throughout the late sixteenth, seventeenth, and eighteenth centuries, maps, atlases, globes, and books on geography literally created spaces for new ideas from faraway lands to enter the Sinographic sphere, where the Chinese script linked communities across state and cultural boundaries.[17] This was achieved gradually, through consultation with patrons; discussions and coauthorship with scholars; inclusion within new intellectual discourses; and incorporation into the material cultures of China, Japan, and Korea. It is therefore time—high time—to leave behind the idea of a single-authored map by a European missionary and appreciate the complex processes and conditions that enabled selected Renaissance ideas to be refracted in the intellectual and material worlds of Sinographic Asia. The chapters in this volume therefore focus not on Matteo Ricci per se or the world maps attributed to him but on the process of recontextualizing and encompassing the Renaissance worldview through the production of artifacts. As part of this approach, we intend to offset the grand narratives of civilizational or cultural encounters by making two interventions: the first to emphasize the long process of remapping the world as represented by a series of material artifacts and the second to firmly contextualize this process within a wider global framework.

Remapping the World from China

The extended process of mapping and remapping the world in East Asia discussed in this volume constitutes part of a global integration of worldviews and material cultures. More concretely, various artifacts, not limited to large maps, each bridged the distance between western European and East Asian systems of knowledge in their own ways and connected the social, intellectual, and material worlds that maintained these systems. Since trying to pin down the sixteenth-century European worldview in contrast to the East Asian worldview may lead us back to the contact between two "imagined civilizations,"[18] it suffices to note that the artifacts produced in both world regions in the sixteenth century share a few crucial aspects that facilitated their complex interactions at the cognitive, social, and material levels. First, world geography was seldom divorced from textual elaborations, even on large-sheet maps; second, geometrical accuracy and topographical precision were not of primary concern, with images of the world primarily functioning as narrative, expansive devices; and third, a visualization of terrestrial geography (a spatial representation of the world of humankind) was central, enabling mental traveling or, in Chinese, *woyou* 臥遊 (literally, wandering while lying down). This common ground further informed and shaped the meeting of worldviews of the sixteenth and seventeenth centuries and facilitated the networked and material production of new artifacts. As such, describing this extended process of mapping the world in shifting local contexts emerges as the only viable alternative to the idea of a single-authored "Ricci map."

"Ricci map" as a singular generic term is usually used to describe a series of maps produced in the late sixteenth and early seventeenth centuries, the best known of which is certainly the *Kunyu wanguo quantu* printed in 1602 in Beijing. While in 1917 and 1918 John F. Baddeley and Lionel Giles still referred to the maps as "Father Matteo Ricci's Chinese World-Maps" and "Ricci's Series of World Maps,"[19] subsequent studies came to understand them as different editions of one and the same map. Hong Weilian (William Hung), in one of the earliest detailed discussions, distinguishes eight different editions.[20] Soon afterward, Pasquale D'Elia published a facsimile and an Italian translation of the *Kunyu wanguo quantu* held by the Vatican Library, explicitly identifying it as the third edition of the "Ricci map." In a follow-up study published decades later, D'Elia established the contours of a consensus in the field—namely, that "the world map in Chinese of Father Matteo Ricci SJ" existed in four editions: the first edition, produced in 1584 in Zhaoqing; the second, made in 1600 in Nanjing; the third, the 1602 *Kunyu wanguo quantu* printed in Beijing; and the fourth, titled *Liangyi xuanlan tu* 兩儀玄覽圖 (Mysterious visual map of the two forms) and printed one year later, also in Beijing.[21] Only prints of the *Kunyu wanguo quantu* and the *Liangyi xuanlan tu* are extant (figures 1.1 and 1.2), some having been reprinted during the Qing (1644–1911), the successor to the Ming state.[22]

Hong's and D'Elia's two ways of counting do not necessarily contradict each other but do present different views on what constitutes an edition. Hong was foremost concerned with the content of the artifacts and included a wide range of prints and stone carvings that did not all involve the missionary; D'Elia, on the other hand, aimed to reconstruct the versions Ricci himself had produced. Over the decades, both ways of counting were revised multiple times. For example, building on Hong's study, Ayusawa Shintarō and John D. Day proposed a set of twelve maps and a set of eight.[23] Following D'Elia's categorization, Unno Kazutaka added a fifth edition, possibly made in 1604 in Beijing, to which Huang Shijian and Gong Yingyan further added, arguing that Ricci also produced a map during his stay in Nanchang between 1595 and 1598.[24] Both approaches, however, are problematic in their own way. Day's study, for example, includes a wide range of maps (building on the lists by Hong and Ayusawa) but distinguishes between those made during Ricci's lifetime, assuming that Ricci exerted some control over them, and later or related iterations. Huang and Gong, Unno, and D'Elia, on the other hand, assume that a limited number of main editions together constitute one single "Ricci map" and that Ricci constantly "improved" it in step with his personal "ascent to Beijing," reinforcing the mythical aura surrounding the missionary.

There are certainly good reasons to group certain artifacts together when pursuing specific inquiries. Studying Ricci's interaction with Chinese scholars, for example, yields a list very close to what D'Elia envisaged, not because they are editions of a single map but because they are the products of interactions directly involving the missionary. Yet, as artifacts, the four maps are rather different: they do not share the same coauthors, printers, patrons, places of production, contents, size, or even titles. If we consider them simply as iterations of the same map, the idea that one man—Matteo Ricci—kept perfecting its contents persists and further bolsters the narrative that Ricci showed the Chinese what the world really looked like. Moreover, this line of thinking obscures the agency of many other artifacts (not limited to large maps) produced across Ming and Qing China, Joseon Korea, and Edo Japan. With this volume we therefore propose to leave behind discussion of the different editions and to recontextualize the production processes of individual artifacts instead.

Following this reasoning, the first part of this volume emphasizes intertextuality, locality, and materiality. Chapter 1, by Nicolas Standaert, and chapter 2, by Richard A. Pegg, set the stage for unpacking the myth of just the one "Ricci map" by looking at the intertextuality of a wide range of extant material and thereby tracing a long process of communication, negotiation, and production. As Standaert shows, the term "Ricci map" in fact refers to a series of coauthored artifacts produced over a period of more than two decades. Even though several maps are directly linked to the missionary, each constitutes a snapshot in an evolving web of communication and interaction. In chapters 2 and 3, Pegg and Wang Yongjie extend this web by focusing on a globe and a book project, respectively, that, after Ricci's death, were both realized by a shifting network of Jesuit missionaries and Chinese scholar-officials who connected the capital with the intellectual center of the lower Yangtze region. Through the analysis of successive acts of mapping and their multiple authorships, the artifacts emerge as networked spaces of negotiation and communication. They are canvases that express various interpretations and tensions, in effect testing how new forms of knowledge may or may not relate to preexisting ones. As a result, these successive artifacts were only one stage in a larger process, as evidenced by many visual and textual references to them in other Ming-era printed materials.

This networked process of mapping and remapping was thoroughly shaped by the localities in which it took place. After Ricci's death, the city of Hangzhou emerged as a hot spot in the 1620s, as Pegg and Wang suggest. It was there that several Chinese patrons hailed and provided shelter from persecution to a new generation of Jesuits. Their protection and sponsorship resulted in the production of a book on world geography, the *Zhifang waiji* 職方外紀 (Record of everything beyond the administration), as well as a terrestrial globe. The locality of their production thoroughly shaped both artifacts: the lower Yangtze River region (with Hangzhou at the center) had been not only a central node of the late Ming book market but also a longtime center of lacquer-making and Christian book printing. As Wang points out, Giulio Aleni (1582–1649) subsequently proselytized and networked his way down to Fujian Province, another hot spot of a booming and increasingly commercialized book market.[25] As a consequence, the *Zhifang waiji* was reprinted in Fujian several years after its first printing in Hangzhou. In chapter 5, Mario Cams explores how the Fujian book market shaped the circulation of large commercial maps to Europe and how the city of Nanjing and its socioeconomic environments motivated a provincial scholar and a printer to produce new imbricated artifacts.

This brings us to the material aspects that shaped this extended process. While Pegg focuses on the techniques involved in globe production, both Wang and Cams zoom in on the late Ming printing technologies that defined the commercial book market. Books on geography were widely available for purchase and included the coedited *Zhifang waiji*. The book contains six maps, two of which also circulated as separate artifacts (figures 2.8, 2.9, 3.1, 3.2, and 5.9). As Cams shows, books containing maps, as well as large commercial maps, circulated widely across East Asia and ultimately to Europe. Cheng Fangyi, in chapter 4, further explores the role of material culture by considering how the presentation and framing of large maps fashioned their contents, as well as how aesthetic cultures and modes of presentation affected the reception of these artifacts. Materiality thus surfaces as a crucial element in our focus on the process of mapping: print culture, production techniques, book markets, material framing, and modes of presentation defined how knowledge was expressed and therefore also how knowledge and information were distributed, appreciated, and digested.

By exploring intertextuality, locality, and materiality, the authors of part I focus on processes of mapping across different artifacts and within particular social networks and localities. This flattens out the civilizational-cultural divide that historians have so often taken for granted. It also helps to illustrate how learned individuals confronted with a new global imaginary never simply chose between resolute rejection and full acceptance due to cultural barriers but individually judged new ideas against the systems of knowledge familiar to them. In some cases, intellectual curiosity enticed them to interweave and combine elements into an entirely new compound artifact. Thus, although cultural backgrounds and worldviews thoroughly shaped the individuals involved in these mapping processes, it is the individuals themselves, not abstract cultural or civilizational entities, who produced these maps, books, and globes. As a result, rather than describing a missionary's singular act of mapmaking that simply transposed scientific European cartography into China, the chapters in part I provide insights into a long process of mediation by groups or individuals and the resulting repackaging of ideas on the cognitive, social, and material levels. As Pegg, Wang, Cheng, and Cams suggest in their chapters, this process extended well beyond Ming China in both time and space: it continued into Qing China, the state that succeeded it, extended its impact to Edo Japan and Joseon Korea, and rippled back to Europe. The chapters of part II explore these wider connections.

To Japan, Korea, and Beyond

The book market in sixteenth- and seventeenth-century China was not isolated but had close ties to neighboring regions. Printed and manuscript materials circulated widely, especially between China, Korea, Japan, the Ryukyu Kingdom, Vietnam, and the Philippines. A common written language enabled this peacetime exchange: officials and scholars in Korea, Vietnam, and Ryukyu used Chinese as their primary written language, and the learned elite in Japan and the Chinese diaspora across East and Southeast Asia could read and write Chinese. The history of geographical knowledge in these regions is intertwined with the history of the book and the circulation of artifacts between different regions in East Asia.[26] Despite a rich exchange, only a few scholars explicitly address these connections in the history of mapmaking.[27] When they do, it is often in the context of bilateral exchange, without considering the wider connections across East Asia and beyond. The second part of this volume explicitly highlights this wider framework by considering artifact production in the local contexts of Japan and Korea and by addressing the global pathways that took East Asian artifacts across the Pacific and Indian Oceans.

All kinds of artifacts were part of the rich cross-border circulation throughout Sinographic Asia. Merchants, envoys, travelers, pilgrims, and missionaries transported books and maps along various routes of travel, including diplomatic missions between Beijing and Hanyang (Seoul) and maritime trade between Ningbo, Nagasaki, and other port cities. But it was not only peaceful contact among China, Japan, and Korea that led to the cross-border mobility of artifacts. In the last decade of the sixteenth century, when Japan tried to conquer Korea during the Imjin War (1592–1598), which also involved China, maps and books on geography were taken from Korea to Japan. All these routes combined resulted in Japanese artifacts making their way to China and Korea, Korean artifacts to Japan and China, and Chinese artifacts to Korea and Japan. The well-known *Kangnido*, for example, a map usually understood as the first Korean world map but actually the culmination of Islamicate, Mongol, Chinese, and Korean acts of mapping, arrived in Japan because of the Imjin War.[28] Given these close connections, it seems natural that artifacts such as the *Kunyu wanguo quantu* and other materials that borrowed from Renaissance mapping circulated outside China within the context of a wider Sinographic sphere.[29]

World maps produced in Japan have been categorized as either "Nanban," "Ricci-type," or "Dutch" world maps, in contrast to "Buddhist."[30] These categories reflect the familiar cultural-civilizational divide between East Asia and western Europe upheld by historians but in many cases obscure their multilayered origins. "Nanban" world maps often represent the earliest adaptations of the Renaissance worldview by Japanese artists and mapmakers and emerged after the arrival of Iberian traders and missionaries called "Nanban" (southern barbarians) in the mid-sixteenth century. "Ricci-type" maps, on the other hand, were adaptations of artifacts arriving from China, mainly the

Kunyu wanguo quantu, but also included a range of maps appearing in Chinese books. "Dutch" maps, finally, originated in the late eighteenth century from contact zones with mainly Dutch traders in Nagasaki. In recent years, scholars have come to recognize that these categories restrict our understanding of the diverse set of artifacts they intend to catalogue.[31] Individual artifacts often combine elements from multiple categories and share similarities that clearly run across these categories.[32] For example, Kinda Akihiro and Uesugi Kazuhiro have argued that the difference between the maps arriving directly from Europe (the "Nanban" maps) and those arriving via China (the "Ricci-type" maps) is in the first place chronological.[33] By tracing processes of circulation between China and Japan, chapter 6 by Elke Papelitzky brings more complexity to this categorization: the censorship of Christianity in late seventeenth- and early eighteenth-century Japan resulted in mapmakers removing any traces of the Jesuits' involvement and identifying many of the world maps as Chinese. It goes on to show that this well-established categorization of world maps, partly inspired by a familiar cultural-civilizational divide, obscures some of the intraregional connections that link artifacts together.

In contrast, Joseon Korea did not have direct relations with Iberian traders or Jesuits and maintained a close connection to China. This permitted the consumption of new modes of mapping the world, including the *Kunyu wanguo quantu* and the *Zhifang waiji*. Each year, the Korean court sent several tribute missions overland to Beijing, so its envoys had ample opportunity to examine Chinese texts and maps, which they often acquired and took back to Korea.[34] For the most part, the artifacts that Yang Yulei and Soh Jeanhyoung discuss in chapters 7 and 8, respectively, came to the attention of Korean scholars through these official diplomatic channels. This fundamental relationship with China became an issue of concern for Korean scholars during the transition from the Chinese-ruled Ming to the Manchu-led Qing state in the mid-seventeenth century. Essentially, the Manchu were considered "barbarians" within a worldview that was popular with Chinese and Korean scholars, based on a strict separation between the civilized Chinese and the non-Chinese "barbarian" worlds. Since Korean scholars and mapmakers regarded the Qing as "barbarians" and thus illegitimate rulers of the central state, they continued to depict the Ming administrative structure well into the eighteenth century. One example of such a map is that of Kim Suhong 金壽弘 (1601–1681), discussed by Yang. Soh, on the other hand, focuses on Korean scholars for whom the *Zhifang waiji* and *Kunyu wanguo quantu* were reliable sources, even after the Qing had become an insurmountable reality, precisely because they originally hailed from Ming China. The *Kunyu wanguo quantu* and the maps from the *Zhifang waiji*, in contrast to maps that depict an enlarged (Chinese) central state at the center, even served to offset the idea that China was the center of civilization, giving Koreans a chance to take over the Ming's civilizing mission and thereby according them a more central role in the world.

When artifacts arrived in Japan and Korea from China, they met with distinct intellectual environments, material cultures, and publishing markets. Chinese and

Japanese artifacts had much in common in terms of materiality: screens, globes, large commercial maps, and books circulated widely and included various visions of world geography and cosmology. While in China the publishing boom took place in the late sixteenth century, similar processes can be observed in late seventeenth-century Japan with the emergence of a thriving and increasingly diverse market in large cities. Much of what we know about the Edo-period map market is informed by the eighteenth and nineteenth centuries, when selling maps as single sheets was very lucrative. Yet the foundations for publishing world maps that accommodate a variety of worldviews were laid in the seventeenth century, as Papelitzky explains in chapter 6. In Korea the market was considerably smaller and geared toward an elite audience, especially during the seventeenth century. Kim Suhong's map, as Yang discusses, is an example of this and one of the few Joseon-period maps that is both dated and signed. In contrast, popular Korean atlases circulated mostly in manuscript form, without indicating the author, time, or place of production. This smaller publishing market also meant that artifacts from China shaped Korean acts of mapping more directly when compared to the Japanese context. It was also a more elite reception compared to Japan, which by the late seventeenth century saw world maps circulating in several popular encyclopedias published in Japanese instead of Chinese.[35]

In all, the artifacts produced in China and introduced in the first part of this volume were extensively adapted, reconfigured, and borrowed from in various ways in Korea and Japan. Numerous copies of the *Kunyu wanguo quantu* and other artifacts were replicated, sometimes colored, translated, or slightly amended, without changing their overall geographical scope or context when compared to their Chinese precursors. At the other end of the spectrum, the name Li Madou 利瑪竇 (the Chinese name that Ricci adopted) was enough to suggest a wider view of the world, as Yang outlines in chapter 7. In another example, Soh reminds us that Wi Baekgyu 魏伯珪 (1727–1798) used Ricci's Chinese name in the title of a map that has no relation to any of the maps discussed in this volume, although he later recognized his mistake. This approach by Korean scholars thus propagated the idea that there was in fact a singular "Li Madou map," in a striking similarity to the imagined and highly static "Ricci map" created by twentieth-century historians.

As European traders and missionaries from a wide variety of backgrounds entered this intellectually and materially connected Sinographic sphere in the sixteenth century, they started acquiring maps and atlases created in East Asia. During and even before Matteo Ricci and his coauthors' remapping of the world in East Asia, artifacts produced in East Asia also traveled to Europe. On the way there, the information they contained went through similar transitions, from simple annotations and translations to combinations and adaptations, creating new compound artifacts. Marco Caboara, for example, elaborates on a newly produced combination of Chinese, Korean, and Japanese materials in chapter 9, while Florin-Stefan Morar describes the partial annotations in Spanish on the *Gujin xingsheng zhi tu* 古今形勝之圖 (Map of advantageous terrain then and now, 1555; figure 10.1) in chapter 10, and Lin Hong traces various stages of adaptation of a Chinese book on geography in chapter 11. The different approaches discussed by Caboara, Morar, and Lin come from the desire of European intellectuals to understand Chinese, Japanese, and Korean artifacts and, in many cases, to make them accessible to their contacts and patrons. Once in Europe, this amended or recontextualized knowledge entered distinct book and print cultures. These processes were thus no different than those described in the preceding chapters: individuals and groups adapted unfamiliar knowledge and information and brought it into more familiar systems of knowledge, intellectual discourses, and material cultures.

While it is certainly true that this volume addresses processes of mapping in Asia beyond China, artifact production in Ming and Qing China constitutes the central connection of the chapters on Japan, Korea, and beyond: part I focuses on acts of mapping within a relatively connected Chinese intellectual culture, while part II builds on these artifacts, extending the scope of their circulation and afterlives, first within East Asia, and later reflecting on a wider set of global pathways. This is a reminder that this volume necessarily engages with just one part of a connected story of knowledge formation supported by an intricate web of global connections without clear demarcations in time and space. Similar and deeply related processes took place earlier, when the works of Greek antiquity were recontextualized and adapted in Islamicate centers of learning before finding their way into European and East Asian systems of knowledge. At the same time, as suggested by most of the chapters in this volume, the processes and artifacts discussed here went on to lead their own social lives, influencing later engagements with the liminal worldviews they express. As with a stone that hits the water and causes large and small ripple effects across a pond, early modern contact between Europe and Asia led to a web of networked and highly contextual adjustments, adaptations, and reinterpretations of what the world could possibly look like, without a clear beginning or end. As such, the early modern meeting of worldviews partially covered in this volume cannot be captured by one "Ricci map" crossing a major civilizational divide. Rather, it constitutes an extended and global process of entanglement that was highly contingent yet deeply structural all at once.

Notes

1. Standaert, *Methodology*, 2–3. For a comparison of European and East Asian print cultures, see Chow, *Publishing, Culture, and Power*; and McDermott and Burke, *Book Worlds of East Asia and Europe*.
2. Morar, "Relocating the Qing"; Cheng, "Pleasing the Emperor"; Moerman, *Japanese Buddhist World Map*.
3. Ch'en, "Matteo Ricci's Contribution," 326.
4. For examples, see Akin, *East Asian Cartographic Print Culture*; Batchelor, *London*; and Brook, *Completing the Map*.
5. Edney, *Cartography*, 5.

6. Ibid, 4–6.
7. Needham, *Grand Titration,* 16.
8. Needham et al., *Science and Civilization in China.* More volumes are planned.
9. Needham, *Grand Titration,* 16.
10. Standaert, *Methodology.*
11. Ch'en, "Matteo Ricci's Contribution."
12. Examples in English are Wallis, "Influence of Father Ricci"; Foss, "Western Interpretation of China"; Foss, "Jesuit Cartography"; and the chapter "Jesuit Contributions to Chinese Cartography" in Smith, *Chinese Maps,* 42–49.
13. Yee, "Traditional Chinese Cartography." Richard J. Smith takes a similar approach in *Mapping China and Managing the World* in a chapter titled "Mapping China's World: Cultural Cartography in Late Imperial China," 47–88.
14. Standaert also distinguishes a third invention framework in which a postmodern quest for the missionary's colonization of Chinese thought is set up. An example is Mignolo, *Darker Side of the Renaissance,* 219–226. Here, too, the dichotomy between "European science" and "Chinese tradition" remains.
15. To quote the title of a book by Benjamin Elman.
16. Huang and Gong, *Li Madou shijie ditu yanjiu;* Zhang, *Making the New World Their Own;* Morar, "Relocating the Qing"; Cheng, "Pleasing the Emperor."
17. Most notably in China, Korea, Japan, Vietnam, and the Ryukyu Kingdom. The concept of "Sinography" is explored in Handel, *Sinography.*
18. Hart, *Imagined Civilizations.*
19. Baddeley, "Father Matteo Ricci's Chinese World-Maps"; Giles, "Translations," 367.
20. Hong, "Kao Li Madou de shijie ditu," 28. Hong's contribution was part of a special issue of the journal *Yugong,* which laid the foundations in Chinese for further studies on the "Ricci map."
21. D'Elia proposed the title of the Zhaoqing map to be *Yudi shanhai quantu* 輿地山海全圖 (Complete map of lands, mountains, and seas) and the title of the Nanjing map to be *Shanhai yudi quantu* 山海輿地全圖 (Complete map of mountains, seas, and lands). D'Elia, *Il Mappamondo Cinese;* D'Elia, "Recent Discoveries."
22. For a list of extant prints, see the appendix in chapter 1.
23. Ayusawa, "Ri Matō no sekai chizu ni tsuite," 267; Day, "Search for the Origins," 97. Although Day claims that his list only includes maps Ricci himself made, the maps he includes make it conceptually much more similar to Hong's. Roderich Ptak has attempted to consolidate some of Hong's and Day's editions (Ptak, "Sino-European Map").
24. Unno, "Min, Shin ni okeru Mateo Ricchikei sekaizu," 71; Huang and Gong, *Li Madou shijie ditu yanjiu,* 12–20. Huang and Gong further propose that the title of the Nanchang map might have been *Yudi shanhai quantu* and that the title of the 1584 Zhaoqing map instead might have been *Shanhai yudi tu* 山海輿地圖 (Map of mountains, seas, and lands). Recently, at least one of these titles has been called into question. Tang Kaijian and Zhou Xiaolei propose the Zhaoqing map's title to be *Daying quantu* 大瀛全圖 (Complete map of the great ocean). Tang and Zhou, "Mingdai Li Madou shijie ditu chuanboshi siti," 297.

25. For more on the late Ming book market, see Brokaw and Kornicki, *History of the Book in East Asia.*
26. Ibid.
27. This is especially true for studies in English. A general framework has been set by Nathan Sivin and Gari Ledyard in the volume on East Asia in *The History of Cartography* (Sivin and Ledyard, "Introduction"). Two further examples are Akin, *East Asian Cartographic Print Culture;* and Pegg, *Cartographic Traditions in East Asian Maps.* Many of Unno Kazutaka's articles also take the East Asian connection into account, as, for example, in Unno, *Tōyō chirigakushi kenkyū.*
28. The full title of the map is *Honil gangni yeokdae gukdo ji do* 混一疆理歷代國都之圖 (Map of integrated lands and regions of historical countries and capitals). See Park, "World Map Produced in Korea"; Miya, *Mongoru teikoku ga unda sekaizu,* especially 255–272.
29. It would not be hard to imagine some of the artifacts discussed in this volume having circulated in Vietnam as well. On mapping in Vietnam, see Whitmore, "Cartography in Vietnam."
30. Unno, "Nanbankei sekaizu no keitō bunrui," 117; Kinda and Uesugi, *Nihon chizushi,* 247.
31. Leca, "Maps of the World in Early Modern Japan"; Kaida, *Zusetsu zōran.*
32. For the combining of material across categories in the case of Buddhist maps, see Muroga and Unno, "Buddhist World Map in Japan"; Moerman, *Japanese Buddhist World Map.*
33. Since Japanese scholars described "Ricci-type" maps as "European." Kinda and Uesugi, *Nihon chizushi,* 251.
34. Clark, "Sino-Korean Tributary Relations," 281; Seth, *Concise History of Korea,* 206–207.
35. Japanese publishers made maps using a mixture of Chinese and Japanese scripts, depending on their audience, while the Korean market was overwhelmingly in Chinese script despite the existence of a Korean alphabet. Ledyard describes one eighteenth-century map in Hangeul instead of Chinese, the only such known map before the mid-nineteenth century (Ledyard, *Unique 18th-Century Korean Map,* 11). A few earlier books written in Hangeul exist, although they are primarily vernacular fiction and poetry, not scholarly works. Baker, "Science, Technology, and Religion."

References

Akin, Alexander. *East Asian Cartographic Print Culture: The Late Ming Publishing Boom and Its Trans-Regional Connections.* Amsterdam: Amsterdam University Press, 2021.

Ayusawa Shintarō 鮎澤信太郎. "Ri Matō no sekai chizu ni tsuite" 利瑪竇の世界地圖に就いて. *Chikyū* 地球 26, no. 4 (1936): 261–277.

Baddeley, John F. "Father Matteo Ricci's Chinese World-Maps, 1584–1608." *Geographical Journal* 50, no. 4 (1917): 254–270.

Baker, Don. "Science, Technology, and Religion in Chosŏn Korea." In *Oxford Research Encyclopedia of Asian History,* 2017. oxfordre.com/asianhistory, 10.1093/acrefore/9780190277727.013.192.

Batchelor, Robert K. *London: The Selden Map and the Making of a Global City, 1549–1689.* Chicago: University of Chicago Press, 2014.

Brokaw, Cynthia, and Peter Kornicki, eds. *The History of the Book in East Asia.* Farnham: Ashgate, 2013.

Brook, Timothy. *Completing the Map of the World: Cartographic Interaction between China and Europe.* Taipei: Institute of Modern History, Academia Sinica, 2020.

Ch'en, Kenneth. "Matteo Ricci's Contribution to, and Influence on, Geographical Knowledge in China." *Journal of the American Oriental Society* 59, no. 3 (1939): 325–359.

Cheng, Fangyi. "Pleasing the Emperor: Revisiting the Figured Chinese Manuscript of Matteo Ricci's Maps." *Journal of Jesuit Studies* 6, no. 1 (2019): 31–43.

Chow, Kai-wing. *Publishing, Culture, and Power in Early Modern China.* Stanford, CA: Stanford University Press, 2004.

Clark, Donald N. "Sino-Korean Tributary Relations under the Ming." In *The Cambridge History of China.* Vol. 8, *The Ming Dynasty, 1368–1644,* edited by Denis C. Twitchett and Frederick W. Mote, pt. 2, 272–300. Cambridge: Cambridge University Press, 1998.

Day, John D. "The Search for the Origins of the Chinese Manuscript of Matteo Ricci's Maps." *Imago Mundi* 47 (1995): 94–117.

D'Elia, Pasquale. *Il mappamondo cinese del P. Matteo Ricci S. I. Terza ed., Pechino, 1602.* Vatican City: Biblioteca Apostolica Vaticana, 1938.

———. "Recent Discoveries and New Studies (1938–1960) on the World Map in Chinese of Father Matteo Ricci SJ." *Monumenta Serica* 20, no. 1 (1961): 82–164.

Edney, Matthew H. *Cartography: The Ideal and Its History.* Chicago: University of Chicago Press, 2019.

Elman, Benjamin A. *On Their Own Terms: Science in China, 1550–1900.* Cambridge, MA: Harvard University Press, 2005.

Foss, Theodore. "Jesuit Cartography: A Western Interpretation of China." *Review of Culture* 21, no. 4 (1994): 133–156.

———. "A Western Interpretation of China: Jesuit Cartography." In *East Meets West: The Jesuits in China, 1582–1773,* edited by Charles E. Ronan and Bonnie B. C. Oh, 209–251. Chicago: Loyola University Press, 1988.

Giles, Lionel. "Translations from the Chinese World Map of Father Ricci." *Geographical Journal* 52, no. 6 (1918): 367–385.

Handel, Zev. *Sinography: The Borrowing and Adaptation of the Chinese Script.* Leiden: Brill, 2019.

Harley, J. B., and David Woodward, eds. *The History of Cartography.* Vol. 2, bk. 2, *Cartography in the Traditional East and Southeast Asian Societies.* Chicago: University of Chicago Press, 1994.

Hart, Roger. *Imagined Civilizations: China, the West, and Their First Encounter.* Baltimore: Johns Hopkins University Press, 2013.

Hong Weilian 洪煨蓮. "Kao Li Madou de shijie ditu" 考利瑪竇的世界地圖. *Yugong banyuekan* 禹貢半月刊 5, no. 3–4 (1936): 1–50.

Huang Shijian 黃時鑒, and Gong Yingyan 龔纓晏. *Li Madou shijie ditu yanjiu* 利瑪竇世界地圖研究. Shanghai: Shanghai guji chubanshe, 2004.

Kaida Toshikazu 海田俊一. *Zusetsu zōran: Edo jidai ni kankō sareta sekai chizu* 図説総覧: 江戸時代に刊行された世界地図. Tokyo: Ars Medica, 2019.

Kinda Akihiro 金田章裕, and Uesugi Kazuhiro 上杉和央. *Nihon chizushi* 日本地図史. Tokyo: Yoshikawakō bunkan, 2012.

Kornicki, Peter. *The Book in Japan: A Cultural History from the Beginnings to the Nineteenth Century.* Leiden: Brill, 1998.

Leca, Radu. "Maps of the World in Early Modern Japan." In *Oxford Research Encyclopedia of Asian History,* 2020.

Ledyard, Gari. "Cartography in Korea." In Harley and Woodward, *History of Cartography,* vol. 2, bk. 2, 235–345.

———. *A Unique 18th-Century Korean Map: East Asia Institute Special Report.* Seoul: East Asia Institute, 2013.

Lee, Chan. *Old Maps of Korea.* Translated by Kim Sarah. Paju: Bumwoo, 2005.

McDermott, Joseph P., and Peter Burke, eds. *The Book Worlds of East Asia and Europe: Connections and Comparisons.* Hong Kong: Hong Kong University Press, 2015.

Mignolo, Walter. *The Darker Side of the Renaissance: Literacy, Territoriality, and Colonization.* Ann Arbor: University of Michigan Press, 1995.

Miya Noriko 宮紀子. *Mongoru teikoku ga unda sekaizu: Chizu ha kataru* モンゴル帝国が生んだ世界図: 地図は語る. Tokyo: Nihon keizai shinbun shuppansha, 2007.

Moerman, D. Max. *The Japanese Buddhist World Map: Religious Vision and the Cartographic Imagination.* Honolulu: University of Hawai'i Press, 2022.

Morar, Florin-Stefan. "Relocating the Qing in the Global History of Science: The Manchu Translation of the 1603 World Map by Li Yingshi and Matteo Ricci." *Isis* 109, no. 4 (2018): 673–694.

Muroga, Nobuo, and Unno Kazutaka. "The Buddhist World Map in Japan and Its Contact with European Maps." *Imago Mundi* 16 (1962): 49–69.

Needham, Joseph. *The Grand Titration: Science and Society in East and West.* Toronto: University of Toronto Press, 1969.

———, et al. *Science and Civilization in China.* 7 vols. Cambridge: Cambridge University Press, 1954–2015.

Park, Hyunhee. "The World Map Produced in Korea in 1402 and Its Possible Sources from the Islamic World." *Journal of Asian History* 52, no. 2 (2018): 209–234.

Pegg, Richard A. *Cartographic Traditions in East Asian Maps.* Honolulu: MacLean Collection, University of Hawai'i Press, 2014.

Ptak, Roderich. "The Sino-European Map (*Shanhai yudi quantu*) in the Encyclopaedia *Sancai tuhui.*" In *The Perception of Maritime Space in Traditional Chinese Sources,* edited by Angela Schottenhammer and Roderich Ptak, 191–207. Wiesbaden: Harrassowitz, 2006.

Seth, Michael J. *A Concise History of Korea: From Antiquity to the Present.* 3rd ed. Lanham, MD: Rowman and Littlefield, 2019.

Sivin, Nathan, and Gari Ledyard. "Introduction to East Asian Cartography." In Harley and Woodward, *History of Cartography,* vol. 2, bk. 2, 23–31.

Smith, Richard J. *Chinese Maps: Images of "All under Heaven."* Hong Kong: Oxford University Press, 1996.

———. *Mapping China and Managing the World: Culture, Cartography and Cosmology in Late Imperial Times.* London: Routledge, 2013.

Standaert, Nicolas. *Methodology in View of Contact between Cultures: The China Case in the Seventeenth Century.* Hong Kong: Chinese University of Hong Kong, 2002.

Tang Kaijian 湯開建, and Zhou Xiaolei 周孝雷. "Mingdai Li Madou shijie ditu chuanboshi siti" 明代利瑪竇世界地圖傳播史四題. *Ziran kexueshi yanjiu* 自然科學史研究 34, no. 3 (2015): 294–315.

Unno Kazutaka 海野一隆. "Min, Shin ni okeru Mateo Ricchikei sekaizu: Shutoshite shinshiryō no kentō" 明・清におけるマテオ・リッチ系世界図: 主として新史料の検討. In *Tōzai chizu bunka kōshōshi kenkyū* 東西地図文化交渉史研究, 33–92. Osaka: Seibundō, 2003.

———. "Nanbankei sekaizu no keitō bunrui" 南蛮系世界図の系統分類. In *Tōzai chizu bunka kōshōshi kenkyū* 東西地図文化交渉史研究, 117–175. Osaka: Seibundō, 2003.

———. *Tōyō chirigakushi kenkyū: Tairiku hen* 東洋地理学史研究: 大陸編. Osaka: Seibundō, 2004.

Wallis, Helen. "The Influence of Father Ricci on Far Eastern Cartography." *Imago Mundi* 19 (1965): 38–45.

Whitmore, John K. "Cartography in Vietnam." In Harley and Woodward, *History of Cartography*, vol. 2, bk. 2, 478–508.

Yee, Cordell D. K. "Traditional Chinese Cartography and the Myth of Westernization." In Harley and Woodward, *History of Cartography*, vol. 2, bk. 2, 170–202.

Zhang, Qiong. *Making the New World Their Own: Chinese Encounters with Jesuit Science in the Age of Discovery.* Leiden: Brill, 2015.

PART I

Intertextuality, Locality, and Materiality in Ming-Era Artifacts

1

World Maps as Spaces of Intercultural Communication

NICOLAS STANDAERT

Autrui is "man without horizon," he who, coming from no land and errant, is dispossessed of any belonging and he who, in his dispossession—and herein lies the chance of this encounter and also of speech—dispossesses me. Since *autrui* is a stranger, also the guest, "the one who is coming," the encounter with *autrui* opens the space in which the unknown is encountered *as* unknown. *Autrui* "cites," calls up, the site of a between-two, between appearing and disappearing.

WORLD MAPS MAY SUPPLY A TEST CASE for the study of the communication of knowledge between cultures. Here I will limit myself to one case: the "Ricci map," the Chinese-language maps associated with the Jesuit Matteo Ricci (1552–1610). In fact, as already pointed out in the introduction to this book, this is not one single map but a series of at least four different maps, produced in the cities of Zhaoqing (1584), Nanjing (1600), Beijing (1602), and again Beijing (1603). Each of these comes with its own characteristics, but only the last two remain extant: the *Kunyu wanguo quantu* 坤輿萬國全圖 (Complete map of all countries on earth; figure 1.1) and the *Liangyi xuanlan tu* 兩儀玄覽圖 (Mysterious visual map of the two forms; figure 1.2).[1] This chapter focuses on these maps, all of which involved Ricci personally, discussing them as a whole yet identifying particular maps when appropriate. Since others have already studied these maps extensively, it is not my purpose to reveal new information about the different versions but to show how the study of these "Ricci maps" may contribute to the historiography of contacts between China and Europe.

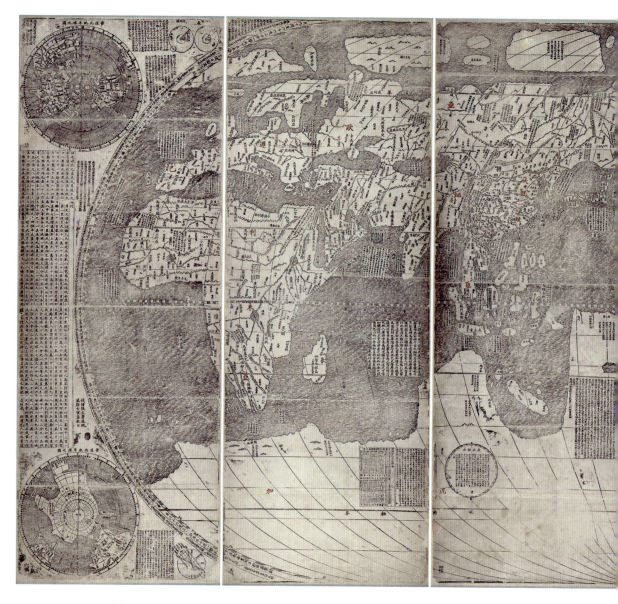

FIGURE 1.1.

The *Kunyu wanguo quantu*. Printed by Zhang Wentao in six parts and dated fall 1602. Approx. 161 × 371 cm when assembled. Miyagi Prefectural Library, Sendai.

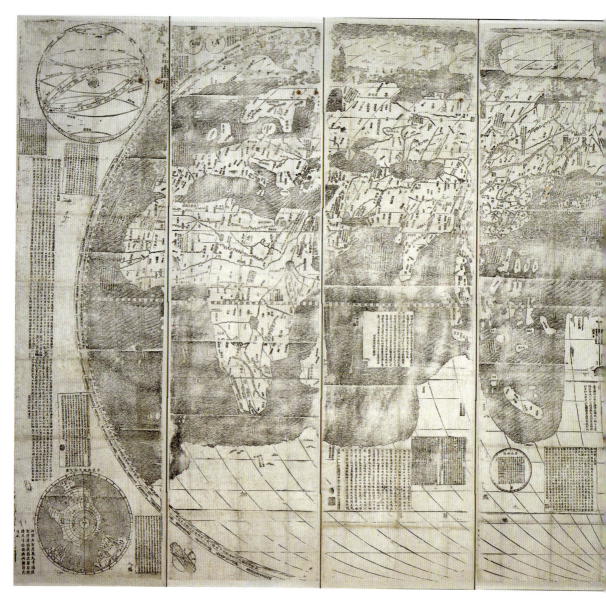

FIGURE 1.2.

The *Liangyi xuanlan tu*. Printed in eight parts and dated 1603. Compared to the *Kunyu wanguo quantu*, it amends place-names and annotations, adds more textual insets and printed seals, and presents a revised diagram of the universe (*in the top right corner*, including eleven rather than nine layers). Approx. 198 × 444 cm when assembled. Korean Christian Museum of Soongsil University, Seoul.

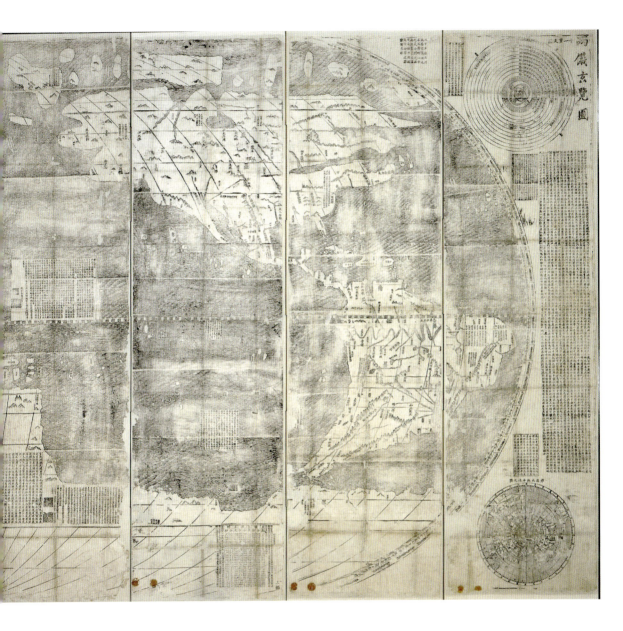

Earlier I confronted this historiography via a more theoretical approach involving four different frameworks useful in the study of contacts between cultures, taking the communication model of transmitter, receiver, and message as a basis.[2] In that overview I laid out the major approaches to studying the "Ricci maps" thus far: the first framework takes the missionary as primary agent in the transmission and investigates the influence and contribution of the "Ricci maps" in the Chinese context (transmission framework);[3] the second framework starts with the Chinese scholars, explores the ways in which they received the map or not, and often concludes that they misunderstood the cartographical knowledge that was transmitted (reception framework);[4] the third framework exposes how the map functioned as a means of constructing the world and colonizing Chinese imagination (invention framework).[5]

Here I wish to consider the "Ricci maps" from the point of view of communication and interaction, the fourth framework, an approach this earlier overview merely sketches.[6] This framework stresses the reciprocity in the interaction between transmitter and receiver and centers around the notion of "in-betweenness." This approach does not reject prior approaches but applies some of the notions discussed in the theoretical exposition of the frameworks to consider the same map in a new way.[7] It illuminates a single facet of the ubiquitous idea that there is something fundamental about a map: "It is a basic form of human communication."[8] This approach thus shows how, based on the numerous prefaces in Chinese, the map clearly originated within, entered into, and created a space of intercultural communication and that it remains a continuous "source" of communication today. The map thus becomes a subject that displaces and dislocates historians. By allowing them to enter into it, the map dislocates historians' ordinary views, forcing us to meet that liminal world of maps wherein Chinese and Europeans communicated during the seventeenth century.

Before discussing the "Ricci maps" and the prefaces written on them, we should consider their genesis. Right from the beginning, it appears these world maps were spaces for communication. One can discern this in Ricci's own account, written originally in Italian, then edited and revised in Latin by Nicolas Trigault SJ (1577–1628) as *De Christiana expeditione apud Sinas*.[9] In it, Ricci/Trigault recount the origins of the first map, produced in Zhaoqing:

> Hanging on the wall of the reception room in the Mission House there [in Zhaoqing] was a cosmographical chart of the universe, done with European lettering. The more learned among the Chinese admired it very much and, when they were told that it was both a view and a description of the entire world, they became greatly interested in seeing the same thing done in Chinese. Of all the great nations, the Chinese have had the least commerce; indeed, one might say that they have had practically no contact whatever with outside nations, and consequently they are grossly ignorant of what the world in general is like. . . . When they learned that China was only a part of the great east, they considered such an idea, so unlike their

own, to be something utterly impossible, and they wanted to be able to read about it, in order to form a better judgment. So the Governor consulted with Father Matteo Ricci and asked him, as he expressed it, if he, with the help of his interpreter, would make his map speak Chinese, assuring him that such a work would bring him great credit and favour with everyone. Ricci had had considerable training in mathematics, which he studied for several years at Rome under Father Christophorus Clavius, Doctor of Science and Prince of Mathematicians of his day. In answer to the Governor's request, he went to work immediately at this task, which was not at all out of keeping with his ideas of preaching the Gospel. According to the disposition of Divine Providence, various ways have been employed at different times, and with different races, to interest people in Christianity. In fact this very attraction was to draw many of the Chinese into the net of Peter.[10]

This quotation about the origin of the first Chinese map in the series refers to a process of continuous communication: from the anonymous visitors to the governor and his interpreter to Ricci and back again. It explicitly shows how Chinese scholars, impelled by curiosity (i.e., the impulse to know),[11] wanted to read more about it and how the governor instructed Ricci to make a Chinese version because he wanted to have it printed and "communicate it with the whole of China."[12] This quest on the part of the Chinese, which preceded the map's production, is a key aspect of the process of intercultural communication. This was no well-planned unilateral communication from Ricci as transmitter to the Chinese as receivers. There are no indications, for instance, that Ricci deliberately carried a map with him to China in order to show the Chinese what the world "really" looked like. It was rather the complete intellectual environment of the late Ming, with its stress on concrete studies (*shixue* 實學), that created the space for this exchange between these Chinese and European scholars. The story of this map in fact confirms an important aspect of (intercultural) communication: a message is more easily accepted when there is a preceding quest for it. This quest by the Chinese enabled this communication concerning maps and encouraged Ricci to pique their interest with the maps he happened to have with him. The map he created was without doubt a situated artifact, "the product of a place,"[13] specifically of China—or better, Ming China—exemplified by the central position accorded the Unified Great Ming (Da Ming Yitong 大明一統) on the map (figure 1.3).[14]

Multiple Authorship

The first question concerning the maps concerns authorship: Who is their author? The modern secondary literature identifies each map unambiguously as a "Ricci map," and not without good reason. Chinese primary sources, such as the prefaces and dedications to the maps, also identify each with Ricci.[15] We may note, however, that the maps bear no signature, unlike maps by certain other missionaries.[16] While Ricci's signature

FIGURE 1.3.

Detail of the *Kunyu wanguo quantu* (figure 1.1), showing the four large characters Da Ming Yitong 大明一統 (Unified Great Ming) on land and the smaller Da Ming Hai 大明海 (Great Ming Sea) in the ocean arranged vertically.

is absent from all versions of the map per se, it does close the adjunct explanatory texts concerning general notions of cosmography and geography on the *Kunyu wanguo quantu* and *Liangyi xuanlan tu*.[17] The *Liangyi xuanlan tu*, however, omits his signature on one of these adjunct texts, tracking fluctuations in the signature's significance.

The matter of signatures bears upon the entire question of authorship.[18] Matthew Edney has highlighted the idealized view of mapmaking as wholly individual: "The individualist preconception emphasizes the work of the map-maker's own intellect, which selects the data, abstracts the world, and encodes the map's symbols."[19] Such preconceptions imagine the individual author and, in this case, his cultural background, wholly defining the map and its meanings. In contradistinction with such preconceptions, the interaction framework considers a text or a map to be the result of interaction between several individuals who through communication and common collaboration select data, abstract the world, and encode symbols. Especially given the absence of Ricci's signature, one may even wonder whether we ought truly to keep calling each version a "Ricci map." While we must not minimize Ricci's key role in its production, which he himself mentions in his explanation of the two extant Beijing maps, we must also rediscover the map as the collaborative result of efforts, Ricci's included, within a web of relationships. As in the above quotation concerning the Zhaoqing map, these explanatory texts refer clearly to Ricci's collaborators and to the map's origination in response to their quests, questions, and requests.[20] The main purpose, then, is to reinstall the role of the other in producing the map. If we still consider Ricci the map's "author," we must also remember his multiple collaborators as, in some manner, "coauthors." This stress on the role of the multiple (not singular) other in the map's creation has implications for how researchers look at the map itself. Most publications treat Ricci as the map's sole author, therefore often calling it the "Ricci map," and thus a product solely of European knowledge, subsequently contrasted in opposition to Chinese knowledge. Acknowledging Chinese participation in its production lends the dichotomy between European versus Chinese interpretations far greater nuance.

Certain textual hints implicitly suggest such collaboration. For example, when Ricci translated European terms and place-names into Chinese, in some cases he selected Chinese characters employed earlier to approximate the sounds of (foreign) Buddhist terminology, indicating his indebtedness to his Chinese collaborators.[21] In other cases he explicitly appropriated specific Chinese names for particular foreign regions.[22] Moreover, as with many of Ricci's Chinese texts, we may presume a Chinese collaborator who must have corrected his annotations on the map, indirectly renegotiating Ricci's expressions. Ricci/Trigault acknowledge the role of Chinese collaborators (or interpreters) from their first mention of the map in *De Christiana expeditione*: the Italian version mentions Ricci made the map "with the help of a *literatus,* who was his friend,"[23] and the Latin version reports: "So the Governor [of Guangdong] consulted with Father Matteo Ricci and asked him, as he expressed it, if he, *with the help of his interpreter,* would make his map speak Chinese."[24] As I shall show below, this interpreter may well have played an active role since he provided Chinese source materials Ricci included in "his" map.

More explicit indications of multiple authorship include the names of scholars known as editors: Wang Pan 王泮 (*jinshi* 1574) for the Zhaoqing map, Wu Zhongming 吳中明 (d. 1608) for the Nanjing map, (Leo) Li Zhizao 李之藻 (1565–1630, *jinshi* 1598; baptized 1610) for the *Kunyu wanguo quantu,* and (Paul) Li Yingshi 李應試 (1559–1620?, baptized 1602) for the *Liangyi xuanlan tu*. Ricci refers frequently to their active roles,[25] not only in requesting the map and financing its printing but also—to a significant extent—in taking charge of its production (e.g., selecting the printed map's dimensions).

No indication of the engravers' names has survived. One note on the *Kunyu wanguo quantu* identifies its printer: "Zhang Wentao 張文燾 of Qiantang 錢塘 (Hangzhou) passed the paper [over the blocks] on a day in the first month of autumn, 1602."[26] A note on the *Liangyi xuanlan tu* by the editor, Li Yingshi, most explicitly evinces collaboration, acknowledging that six or seven Chinese, in fact the first Chinese Jesuits, participated in its preparation: Zhong Boxiang 鍾伯相 (or Zhong Mingren 鍾鳴仁, Sébastien Fernandes; 1562–1621), Huang Fangji 黃芳濟 (or Huang Mingsha 黃明沙, Francisco Martins; ca. 1569–1606), You Wenhui 游文輝 (or Manuel Pereira; 1575–1633), Ni Yicheng 倪一誠 (or Jacques Niva, Japanese origin; 1579–1638), Qiu Liangbing 丘良稟 (or Pascoal Mendes; 1584–1640), Xu Bideng 徐必登 (or António Leitão; ca. 1578–1611), and possibly Wang Xin 王莘.[27] Thus the "Ricci maps" were products of collaborative cultural negotiation, appropriating and incorporating knowledge from multiple sources.[28]

Map Production as a Process

Any production of text entails a process. Readers generally see only the final version, obscuring somewhat the text's progress, inevitably, through multiple iterations. There are indications that the maps Ricci and his collaborators were involved with changed continuously, cycling through recurrent interplays of communication and negotiation. As mentioned in the introduction, modern scholars generally agree there were at least four different maps: Zhaoqing (1584), Nanjing (1600), Beijing (1602), and Beijing (1603). Only the two Beijing maps survive.[29]

Comparing the maps with information from both Ricci's own reports and the prefaces by Chinese authors confirms the maps' continual evolution, including in title, layout, and content. First, the titles: Chinese sources indicate the title of the Zhaoqing map was *Daying quantu* 大瀛全圖 (Complete map of the great ocean);[30] that of the Nanjing map was *Shanhai yudi quantu* 山海輿地全圖 (Complete map of mountains, seas, and lands).[31] The latter two make explicit reference to the classical Chinese text *Shanhai jing* 山海經 (Classic of mountains and seas). This mythogeography, composed piecemeal between the fifth century BCE and the fifth century CE, describes the entire world as then known. The mention of *Shanhai* indicates this map contained information congruent with some descriptions of the *Shanhai jing*.[32] The 1602 map's title of *Kunyu wanguo quantu* stresses "all the countries" (*wanguo* 萬國) because it depicts many more countries than the previous versions. Contrast is also clear in the 1603 map's title, *Liangyi xuanlan tu* (figure 1.2): "Two forms" (*liangyi* 兩儀) is a classical expression referring to heaven and earth. "Mysterious vision" or "mysterious mirror" (*xuanlan* 玄覽) is from the Taoist classic *Daode jing* 道德經 (Classic of the way and the power).[33] In this regard we may note the map contains not only geographical explanations and visual representations of the earth but also cosmological explanations and astronomical representations of heaven (the nine heavens and the solar and lunar eclipses).[34] Several prefaces and dedications describe how the map, via its broad vision, evoked a mysterious (*xuan* 玄) sensation. It is also important to note what is absent from these titles: any reference to the West (*taixi* 泰西, *xiyang* 西洋, or *xiguo* 西國), an expression both Jesuit and Chinese scholars used in other texts' titles in reference to the West.[35] Likewise, the titles of the reproduction of the map within Chinese works lack the reference to the West. This absence underlines the map's presentation as not a specifically European vision but a map of the world tout court.

The second change is in layout, including each map's size, which indirectly mediates the content of the map via the close relation between the two. The greater the size, the more detailed information, in both textual and visual representation, the maps could convey.[36] Here one may also observe the important role of the editor. Li Zhizao, in conjunction with his friends, for instance, had the *Kunyu wanguo quantu* printed on six leaves, quadruple the size of the previous map.[37] Ricci acknowledges that its larger size allowed him to add "the names of many hundred new kingdoms" and that "wherever a space happened to be left on the paper, I inserted notes on the customs and products of the various countries."[38] Space also played a role in the preface to the *Liangyi xuanlan tu:* "[Because the description] of the peoples, of their products and of their customs had to follow the size of the paper, it was hardly possible to put everything down,"[39] reflecting the reality that greater detail requires more space.

The third variety of change concerned the maps' content and the various ways information becomes knowledge. The maps combine visual representation with text. The visual representation contains geographical devices, geographical delineation, the nine heavens, and solar and lunar eclipses; some later manuscript versions whose production Ricci may not have been involved in even contain representations of fish, animals, and ships. The text can be divided into three types, each consisting of separate text blocks: first, text passages in the map's margins to explain the work to the reader, as a whole, while others detail specific features, including general notions of calculations of heaven and earth, the armillary sphere, and descriptions of various peoples; second, the aforementioned short legends or vignettes annotating the countries on the map; and, finally, the "prefaces." Each of these changes with every successive map.

All these changes followed various communications.[40] In addition to the aforementioned personal communications, intertextual communications also produced changes by interweaving information from European and Chinese sources. Specialized analysis shows that the different versions utilized information fresh from Europe, including European maps by Abraham Ortelius (1527–1598), Gerard Mercator (1512–1594), and Peter Plancius (1552–1622).[41] Ricci found that the European maps he had brought with him depicted East Asia quite inaccurately. Mercator, for instance, had confused the river of Canton in China with the classical Ganges and included a northwest passage to Cathay.[42] Ricci or his collaborators partly used their own observations, as well as, more importantly, Chinese maps and atlases in correcting this misinformation.[43]

The maps also contain textual information in addition to geographical depictions: short legends provide basic information about most of the countries shown. Ricci primarily employed European sources for the legends concerning Europe, Africa, and the Americas but acknowledged having also consulted Chinese official histories and geographical documents.[44] While Ricci and his collaborators did not credit all their accounts, he certainly did not discard the information of places that at least in the eyes of the modern reader are a surprise: the Land of Dwarfs (Airen Guo 矮人國), the Land of Women (Nüren Guo 女人國), and the ox-hoofed Turks (Niuti Tujue 牛蹄突厥).[45] To the north of China lay the Land of Ghosts (Guiguo 鬼國): "In this region the inhabitants wander about during the night and hide during the day. They wear deerskin for clothing. Their eyes, ears, and nose are like those of human beings, but their mouth is on their neck. They eat deer and snakes." This description, possibly drawn from Ma Duanlin's 馬端臨 *Wenxian tongkao* 文獻通考 (Comprehensive study of documents, 1280), appears in ancient Chinese texts, including the *Shanhai jing* (available in numerous editions during Ricci's time).[46] All these elements show that intercultural communication brought about multiple changes and that Ricci and his collaborators had no single fixed vision of the world but combined various forms of contemporary European and Chinese knowledge in creating their maps.

Maps as Spaces of Dialogue

Communication and interaction appear even more obvious in the text blocks visible on the maps. The prefaces merit particular attention. As a preliminary remark, I use the word "preface" as it is deployed in modern Chinese publications, although it may not be the perfect term to denote the text passages by different authors that appear without a title on the maps. In the strictest sense, maps do not contain "prefaces," since this term usually refers to a preliminary text that goes before the main text (such as an introduction or foreword to a book) and maps are present all at once. Still, from the earliest times these texts were included in anthologies of prefaces and postfaces, where they appear as dedications (*ti* 題) and prefaces (*xu* 序/敘) to the maps included in other works.

Such prefaces are "intertexts" because as individual utterances they stand in relation to other utterances and often respond to them or echo them.[47] Moreover, in this case, this dialogical exchange visually takes place within the same space. They can literally be considered intertexts because they appear *within* the map itself, in the open areas of the oceans or the southern continent of Magellanica. They figuratively occupy a space "in between" the different continents and therefore refer to the in-betweenness of the interaction between scholars born on these different continents.

Seventeen different authors wrote the sixteen known prefaces to the series of maps (apart from those by Ricci)—the greatest number of prefaces to any known text produced by Jesuits in the seventeenth or eighteenth centuries—clearly demonstrating the web of relationships established amid the mapmaking (figure 1.4).[48] Simply considering how and where these prefaces or dedications appear reprinted leads one easily to conceptualize an extended "communication web of prefaces." For instance, the preface to the Nanjing map (itself now lost) survives in the apparatus of the two extant Beijing maps, which underscores the link between the maps. The prefaces specific to those later versions are all different on each map. Yet they are joined together in two anthologies of prefaces and postfaces compiled by Chinese scholars: Yang Tingyun's 楊廷筠 (1557–1627) *Juejiao tongwen ji* 絕徼同文紀 (Collected essays from distant lands, 1615/1616, enlarged ca. 1629) and Liu Ning's 劉凝 *Tianxue jijie* 天學集解 (Collected explanations on heavenly studies, ca. 1680, completed ca. 1715; 284 texts).[49] These collections also contain further prefaces: those composed for maps based on the "Ricci maps" but produced by Chinese scholars. Thus, within these compilations, prefaces and dedications that never accompanied the same map share the same textual space of communication.

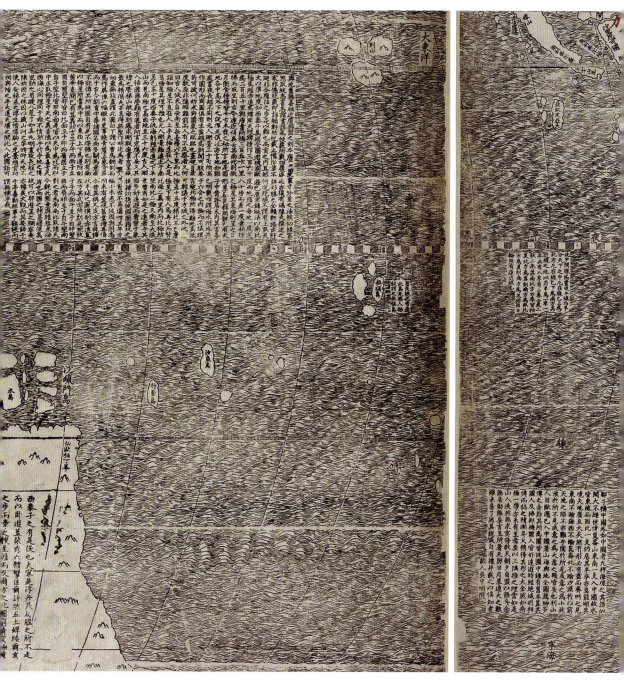

FIGURE 1.4.

Detail of the *Kunyu wanguo quantu* (figure 1.1) showing two prefaces placed in the central Pacific Ocean as blocks of text (*top-left and bottom-right corners*).

Prefaces:

Zhaoqing map: Zhao Kehuai 趙可懷 (1541?–1604).

Nanjing map: Wu Zhongming and Feng Yingjing 馮應京 (1555–1606, *jinshi* 1592).

Kunyu wanguo quantu: Ricci, Wu Zhongming (= Nanjing map), Li Zhizao, Chen Minzhi 陳民志 (*jinshi* 1592), Qi Guangzong 祁光宗 (*jinshi* 1598), and Yang Jingchun 楊景淳 (*jinshi* 1589).

Liangyi xuanlan tu: Wu Zhongming (= Nanjing map), Ricci: new plus one note; five new prefaces: (Paul) Li Yingshi, (Louis) Ruan Taiyuan 阮泰元 and Zou Yanchuan 鄒衍川, Feng Yingjing, Chang Yinxu 常胤緒, and Hou Gongchen 侯拱宸.

Other prefaces:

Guo Zizhang 郭子章 (Jingluo 青螺, 1543–1618): preface (1604) to his own reproduction of the Nanjing map.

Cheng Bai'er 程百二: preface to his own world map he credits to Ricci in the *Fangyu shenglüe*: this work also contains the prefaces of Wang Xijue 王錫爵 (*jinshi* 1562), Xu Guangqi 徐光啟 (1562–1633, *jinshi* 1604), Zhang Jingyuan 張京元 (*jinshi* 1604), and Xu Shijin 徐時進 (*jinshi* 1595).

Through the inclusion of prefaces, the maps themselves thus become spaces of communication and dialogue. These texts interact with each other indirectly simply because they coexist on the same map. But they also enter into more direct dialogue, referring to other prefaces' authors by name, sometimes addressing one another collegially, or sometimes discussing similar subjects or leveling personal commentary.[50] This dialogue occurs entirely in the present. As with the prefaces Chinese scholars wrote for their colleagues, prefaces extol both the work and Ricci himself in lofty words (in highly classical language) of praise, expressing at times their writers' exhilaration while gazing over the map.[51] Prefaces and dedications are a specific rhetoric genre in which writers rarely expressed open or strong disagreement with author's opinions. Yet, in terms of a relationship to the other, they can be analyzed from the praxeological level: the rapprochement or distancing of the other. They show that the relationship of these scholars was not simply indifferent or neutral but that a certain level of closeness existed among them, in this case toward Ricci and the mode of mapping the world he had brought with him. But the dialogue on these maps is not only one of praise, harmony, and agreement; it is also one of tension.

The new spaces opened by the maps caused the tension. Chang Yinxu explains how a group of nine scholars had the *Liangyi xuanlan tu* engraved "so that those of our group might know what they had never known before and might see what they had never seen before."[52] Through the map he became aware that "there are places where no boat or cart has yet gone, here our book knowledge reveals its limits; and there are places to which mind and eye have not penetrated, here our empirical knowledge may be deficient."[53] This concession of ignorance creates a space for new knowledge, but by calling into question the knowledge currently available and reaching new places, the new knowledge necessarily causes displacement.[54]

As a result, this dialogue among Chinese scholars concerns not only European knowledge or questions of science and exact measurement but also, primarily, a discourse regarding China's own past. The spaces these maps created spawned multiple tensions. One such tension emerged between the information on the map and that within the Chinese classics and other knowledge from Chinese tradition. Hou Gongchen, for instance, observes that no document of previous eras in Chinese history, whether during the Zhou (1046–256 BCE), Han (206 BCE—220 CE), Tang (618–907), or Song (960–1279), mentions Europe.[55] Feng Yingjing and Guo Zizhang point out that the texts of the Zhou supposedly contain an entire description of all "barbarians" in existence.[56] Others emphasize the fact that the form and size of the earth given in classical texts differs from what the present map claims. According to the *Huainan zi* 淮南子 (second century BCE), for instance, the earth was a perfect square of 233,500 *li* and 75 paces, while Ricci taught that the earth was a globe with a diameter of 28,600 and more *li* and a perimeter of 90,000 *li*.[57]

The tension related to this knowledge is that between ancient information, which states that China's fame and teachings are widespread, and the new maps, which indicate that this is no longer the case. Feng Yingjing expresses it thus: "The fame and teaching [of China] was [during the Ming] still greater than in ancient times, but if we look at this map, we see that it only reached to one fifth [of the earth]. And so the saying 'There is no place so far that [the fame and teaching of China] has not yet arrived there,' is it still true or not?"[58] A further tension arises due to the fact that the information arrives with a foreigner. Guo Zizhang makes this question very explicit: "Some people might perhaps say: 'But Mr. Ricci is a foreign barbarian; his chart and its explanation do not necessarily and exactly conform to heaven and earth; why do you, doctor [Guo], attribute so much importance to it?'"[59]

These tensions can both promote further communication and obstruct communication. One example is Wei Jun 魏濬 (*jinshi* 1604), the author not of a preface but of a text critical of Ricci: *Li shuo huangtang huoshi* 利說荒唐惑世 (The theories of Ricci are incoherent and deceive the world). In one passage he plainly rejects the map: "The map of the world which [Ricci] made, extends into vast and mysterious places, it is a downright attempt to deceive people with what their eyes cannot see and their feet cannot reach, so that it cannot be verified. It is just like a painter who paints ghosts and demons."[60]

In virtue of these tensions, the maps also become sites for negotiation, for testing knowledge. The prefaces not only discuss the tensions already mentioned; they also make choices in addressing the different options opened up and provide (temporary) solutions to the questions raised. In these negotiations, authors use commentarial strategies previously employed with other texts, offering new knowledge from the other. One important strategy involves showing the new knowledge to be coherent with and congruent to tradition.⁶¹ "Their teaching is in the same path as that of the Duke of Zhou and of Confucius."⁶² A common strategy in reaching such a conclusion is identifying historical precedent, arguing that the new information was already present in one form or another in classic Chinese texts.

The references by several authors to Zou Yan 鄒衍 (305–240 BCE) are a clear example. Traditional sources claim Zou was of the opinion

> that the Central Region [= Zhongguo 中國], which scholars spoke of, occupied just one of the eighty-one parts of the world. The Central Region he called "the Sacred Township of the Red County" (Chixian shenzhou 赤縣神州). The Sacred Township of the Red County itself contained nine lands, the nine which Yu ordered, but these could not be counted as "lands." Outside the Central Region there were nine places like the Sacred Township of the Red County and these were what he called the "nine lands" (Jiuzhou 九州). There was a small ocean around each of them and men and animals could not travel between them, each located as if placed in the midst of a sphere. There were nine places like this and then a great ocean (daying 大瀛) surrounding them. Heaven and Earth met there. His methods were all like this.⁶³

Sima Tan 司馬談 (ca. 165–110 BCE) and Sima Qian 司馬遷 (ca. 145 or 135–86 BCE), the authors of the *Shiji* 史記 (The grand scribe's records) who wrote down this description, considered Zou Yan's words "extravagant and unconventional" (*hongda bujing* 閎大不經).⁶⁴ Texts such as the *(Hetu) kuodixiang* (河圖)括地象 (Comprehensive description of the features of the earth according to the map of the Yellow River) and the *Shanhai jing* contained other information considered equally extraordinary.⁶⁵ In the eyes of Wu Zhongming and Guo Zizhang, while the central region had never heard of some of Ricci's theories, they were congruent with the abovementioned works and thus proof of Zou Yan's theories:

> Guo Pu [276–324, author of the *Mu tianzi zhuan* 穆天子傳 (Biography of Mu, son of heaven)] said: "The bamboo books came to light after a thousand years just to back up what is said today." What wise words these are! And yet this was an authentication of a book by means of books. Would he not say today that Mr. Ricci, of the kingdoms of the Great West, with his bringing into the Central Region, four thousand years afterwards, a *Complete Map of Mountains, Seas, and Lands*, had shown himself a faithful disciple of Master Zou Yan? Yet, this would be to authenticate books through a man, something quite different from [Guo's biography of Mu], which hinges on the empty words of books written on bamboo slips.⁶⁶

By insisting on congruity between Ricci's new knowledge and Chinese tradition, these scholars explicitly assimilate the other into the self. They observe difference and work to render it identical with the self and so acceptable to their audience. However, this identification is not with the mainstream tradition but with the other within tradition: those theories that until then had been rejected.

This identification makes it possible to accept claims from someone completely other, one considered a "barbarian." In answer to the question of whether they may rely on Ricci since he is a foreigner, Guo Zizhang begins again from the classic strategy by drawing from tradition's reservoir, selecting in this case a story from the *Zuozhuan* 左傳, a Chinese classic, in which Confucius did not believe himself disgraced through having learned something from a "barbarian" (*yi* 夷).[67] In the eyes of Guo, Ricci is one such *yi* from whom one can learn. The reason was because China, as a moral-cultural sphere, had assimilated him: "Ricci has been in China for a long time. As a result, if while being a barbarian, he has been Chinese, then he has been made Chinese."[68] Guo here makes implicit reference to Han Yu's 韓愈 (768–824) famous text *Yuan Dao* 原道 (Essentials of the [moral] way): "When Confucius wrote the Spring and Autumn Annals, if the enfeoffed lords followed the rituals of the barbarians, he treated them as barbarians. If they progressed to [using the rituals] of the central states, then he treated them as central states."[69] As one desirous to restore tradition, Han Yu pleaded for a return to the teachings of the former kings and the ways of ancient saints, rather than following "barbarian" practices to become "barbaric."

Yet some information is not treated in the Chinese classics. What leads the prefaces' authors to accept such information as other? Here we encounter a foundational, if rarely expressed, aspect of communication: confidence. Several authors refer to the trust they have in Ricci himself, established through both their personal relationships with him and their own experiences confirming what he tells them, enabling them to respect the other as different without assimilation.[70] Ruan Taiyuan, for instance, relates how, when he was twenty, he sailed to the South Sea and reached the great ocean, where it seemed "he had come to the limits of the terrestrial globe and was about to ascend to the Milky Way" but ultimately found this was not the case. Later, when he saw Ricci's explanation that while the heaven surrounds the outside and the earth is suspended in the center of heaven and air fills the space in between, he realized that his "former guess had not been far from the truth but it had not been deep enough."[71] This confidence established, the authors consider the map trustworthy because it is based on books written in Ricci's country,[72] using direct observations by European travelers and by Ricci himself,[73] or on the calculations and the mathematical methods Ricci used.[74] Thus, the maps open a space where they may encounter the unknown as known.[75]

The exchange established by the maps leads not only to assimilation of the other within tradition, or to respect for the other as other, but also to communication and dialogue in complementarity, in some cases leading to new identity. Feng Yingjing, for instance, insists on this complementarity: "Just as the western countries have certainly never heard the teaching of the saints of the Middle Kingdom, so we too have never heard speak of the books of the saints from the West, which they are spreading.

But now both enlighten each other, both benefit each other. In this way the whole world has become a single family and minds have interpenetrated, and so there is no longer a difference [between the people in the countries] spreading to the east and [those] extending to the west."[76]

The idea this quotation expresses seems to presume a certain fusion. In fact, it derives from a key saying by Lu Jiuyuan 陸九淵 (1139–1192), which, according to seventeenth-century interpreters, emphasizes that despite the many differences separating two worldviews, communication remains possible because the same moral principles are present in all human beings from the East and the West: "If sages appear in the eastern seas, they have the same mind and the same principle; if sages appear in the western seas, they have the same mind and the same principle" (東海有聖人出焉, 此心同也, 此理同也; 西海有聖人出焉, 此心同也, 此理同也). Several authors employed this sentence in connection to Ricci's maps as well as to many other texts within the exchanges between China and Europe in the seventeenth century. In the eyes of Li Yingshi, for instance, "Despite the fact that the Westerners have sounds in their languages and a writing so different from those of the Central Region, they can be the same, for the mind is the same and the principle is also the same (*xintong litong* 心同理同)."[77] And in the eyes of Li Zhizao, "in the past literati were of the opinion that the best was to speak about Heaven. Now when one looks at this map one realizes that it corresponds with this idea in a concealed way. Would it be possible then not to trust that in the eastern sea and in the western sea, people have the same mind and the same principle?"[78]

Partners in Map Dialogue

Thus far we have seen how the maps themselves created spaces for dialogue. There is also, however, an external intertext: while Ricci's maps present some new information, and even new visions on the world, the maps did not initiate the dialogue but entered a dialogue already begun. As such, the maps joined a map dialogue that continued after the maps' publication, as evinced by the other chapters in this volume. As mentioned above, Ricci and his Chinese collaborators availed themselves of preexisting Chinese maps, while some subsequent Chinese maps combined traditional knowledge with some information from Ricci's maps, as with Liang Zhou's 梁輈 *Qiankun wanguo quantu gujin renwu shiji* 乾坤萬國全圖古今人物事跡 (Complete map of all countries in the universe, with famous persons and important events then and now; figure 5.7) and Cao Junyi's 曹君義 *Tianxia jiubian fenye renji lucheng quantu* 天下九邊分野人跡路程全圖 (Complete map of all under heaven, the nine frontiers, astral allocations, human traces, and route itineraries, 1644; figure 5.8), discussed in detail by Mario Cams in chapter 5.[79]

More significant in terms of map dialogue is the Chinese authors' inclusion of maps within numerous compilations on various subjects. The maps Ricci helped to produce (unlike some later maps produced by Jesuits) appeared first not as part of a book but as stand-alone sets of scrolls. Such separate maps, however, were "too large to be easily studied,"[80] so some Chinese scholars had them reduced in size and incorporated into books, creating new contexts wherein the map is no longer singular but one among several illustrations. Such maps appear in geographical works such as *Fangyu shenglüe* 方輿勝略 (Complete survey of the earth, 1609–1612) by Cheng Bai'er and others, a work of eighteen *juan* (chapters) containing a geographical description of Ming territories arranged according to the provinces, as well as seven additional *juan* on "outer barbarians" (*waiyi* 外夷). The first *juan* contains the description of the world and a depiction of the two hemispheres according to the "Ricci maps"; the others treat places such as Tartary, Korea, Hami, Turfan, Annam, and Nanzhong (Sichuan-Yunnan area) based on earlier Chinese books, thus juxtaposing different geographical approaches in the same work (figure 1.5).[81]

The immediate context for a map derived from one of the "Ricci maps," however, does not necessarily concern geography. Feng Yingjing's *Yueling guangyi* 月令廣義 (Extended meaning of the monthly proceedings, 1602), for instance, discusses the "extended meaning" of the "Yueling" 月令 (Monthly proceedings) chapter of the *Liji* 禮記 (Record of rites), which describes the seasons, the weather, and the government proceedings according to the twelve months of the year. Feng's work in twenty-four *juan* is preceded by an additional *juan* containing explanations of charts (*tushuo* 圖說). These include charts on topics ranging from *Luoshu* 洛書 (Inscription of the River Luo), *Hetu* 河圖 (Yellow River chart), the Mingtang 明堂 (Bright Hall), astronomical, geographical, musical, and medical charts to the world map "Shanhai yudi quantu" as the final chart (figure 1.6). The astronomical charts also include a chart of the nine-layered heaven (*jiuzhongtian tu* 九重天圖) with an explanatory text. The appearance of the geographical map among these other charts symbolizes the map's entry into a web of communication not limited solely to the domain of geographical knowledge. Here the metaphor of textile/texture is most apt: as one thread in a broader texture, the map interweaves with textiles of various kinds. This is even more apparent concerning reproductions of the map in encyclopedias. The world maps in both Wang Qi's 王圻 (*jinshi* 1565) *Sancai tuhui* 三才圖會 (Illustrated compendium of the three powers, completed in 1607 and printed in 1609; figure 1.7) and Zhang Huang's 章潢 (1527–1608) *Tushu bian* 圖書編 (Compendium of illustrations and writings, originally compiled between 1562 and 1577 and reprinted with addenda in 1613 and 1623; figure 1.8) appear arranged under the category of geography (*dili* 地理), itself figuring alongside a much wider range of categories, such as astronomy, human and moral qualities of the human being, directives for times and seasons, buildings, utensils, clothing for official and private use, and more. This map dialogue shows how the map entered into a wider context of texts reflecting the culture of the time, becoming in its multiple forms a communicated cultural reality.

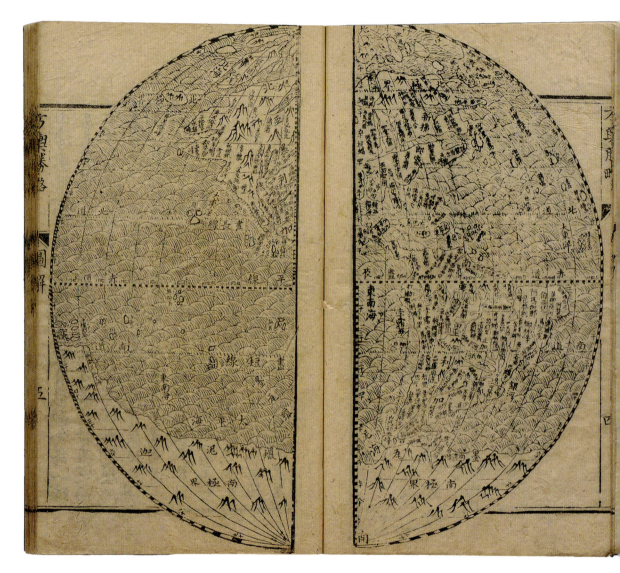

FIGURE 1.5.

The two hemispheres included in the *Fangyu shenglüe* (1612). Height of print area, approx. 20.4 cm. Naikaku Bunko, Tokyo.

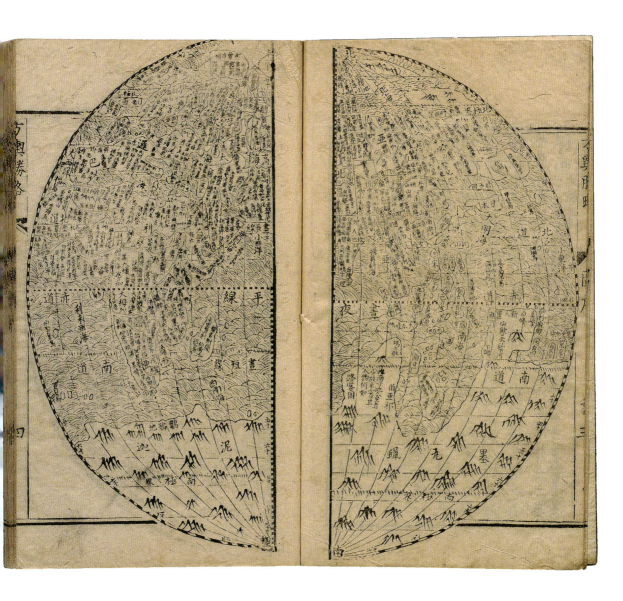

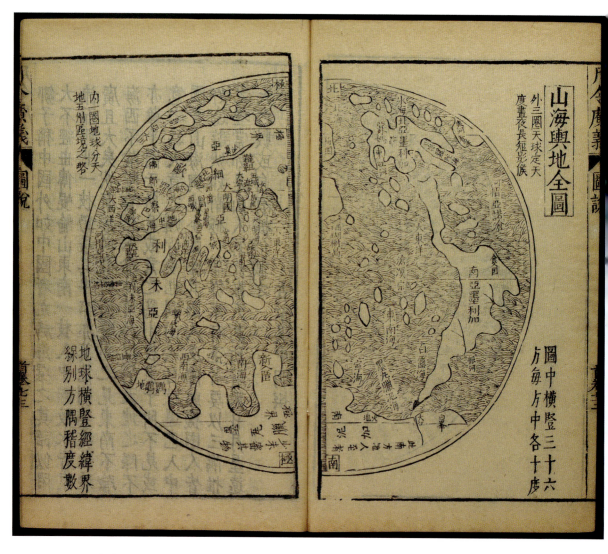

FIGURE 1.6.

The "Shanhai yudi quantu" included in the *Yueling guangyi* (1602). Height of print area, approx. 22.5 cm. Harvard-Yenching Library.

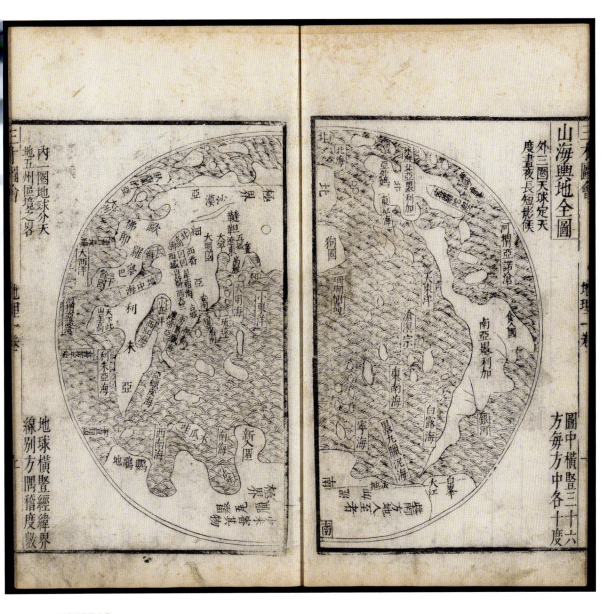

FIGURE 1.7.

The "Shanhai yudi quantu" included in the *Sancai tuhui* (1609). Height of print area, approx. 20.4 cm. Harvard-Yenching Library.

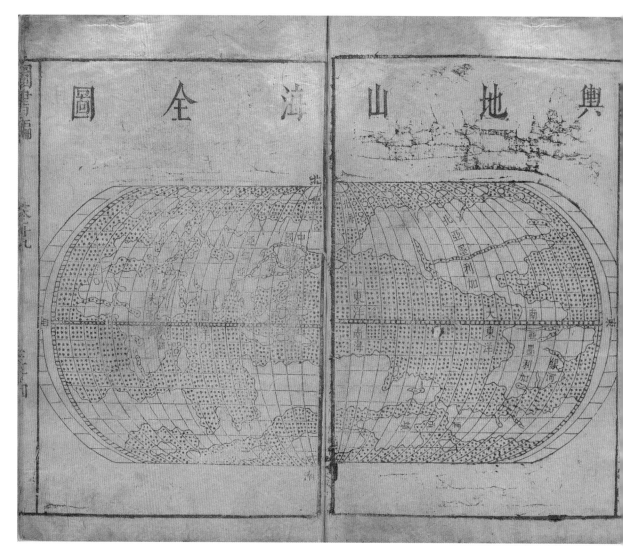

FIGURE 1.8.

The "Yudi shanhai quantu" included in the *Tushu bian* (1613). Height of print area, approx. 22 cm. Harvard-Yenching Library.

Dislocation through Mental Traveling

Thus far I considered the maps as passive objects, as exemplars of some characteristics of the communication and interaction framework. Within this theoretical frame, I pointed out how a historical text such as a map may also become, for the modern historian, a subject,[82] capable in its turn of affecting the person looking upon it. This is exemplified by maps' various functions. Maps can be a means for finding one's way from one place to another, a means to exert and extend political power, or wondrous objects to unfurl for the pure joy of imagining other places to travel. In his preface, Feng Yingjing gives a good description of these multiple uses: "Many are those who will see this map in China, some will get from it the pleasure of traveling while reclining at their ease (*woyou zhi xing* 臥遊之興); others will enlarge their administrative plans; others will rid themselves of petty sentiments of excessive provincialism; still others will thrust away vain ideas of worthless gossip. And will there be any one who will take from it to go forward in the way (*dao* 道)?"[83]

We can follow the thread of imaginary travel several of these Chinese scholars describe. "Would this undertaking by Mr. Ricci not be like traveling by boat through the world? While lying down one can travel (*woyou* 臥遊) to places one's legs have never walked on."[84] In the words of Qi Guangzong: "Thus it was made possible for the spectator, sitting at his ease, to survey the whole world at a glance—a feat that would never have been accomplished except by one who carried the map about in his own brain. May we not say that the author is a man who has penetrated the arcana of the universe?"[85] It is noteworthy how, for several of these Chinese scholars, the maps are a springboard for mental travel, which "opens up one's mind."[86] This possibility of traveling explains, some believe, the title "mysterious vision" (*xuanlan*): "The universe has no limits, and yet when so many eyes look at this map, without peering through the door or window, all the countries are within reach as if [one has all places] on one's palm like balls which one juggles. The appellative 'mysterious vision' is truly appropriate."[87]

While a traveler may undoubtedly function as a subject, deciding whither to roam, we may also consider traveling as a passive process, entailing for the transported traveler displacement and dislocation. Claude Lévi-Strauss gave a good description of the multiple displacements experienced while traveling: "Travel is usually thought of as a displacement in space. This is an inadequate conception. A journey occurs simultaneously in space, in time and in the social hierarchy." He claims one may relate each impression of arriving in another place jointly along these three axes. After describing differences in space (trees, houses, climate), Lévi-Strauss continues:

> But I noticed other changes too; from being poor I had become rich, first because my material circumstances had changed, and secondly because the prices of local produce were incredibly low. . . . Finally the state of open-mindedness which accompanies arrival at a new port of call, and the unsolicited opportunities that one feels obliged to take advantage of, create an ambiguity conducive to the suspension of one's usual self-discipline and produce an almost ritual outburst of prodigality. . . . Not only does a journey transport us over enormous distances, it also causes us to move a few degrees up or down in the social scale. It displaces us physically and also—for better and for worse—takes us out of our class context, so that the colour and flavour of certain places cannot be dissociated from the always unexpected social level on which we find ourselves in experiencing them.[88]

As with the multiple modes of dislocation through physical or mental traveling Lévi-Strauss describes, the coauthors of the "Ricci maps" also experienced dislocation to some extent. Due to the communication established through the maps, they received new identities shaped through their encounters with the other. Their visions of China and of the world changed.

In this chapter I attempted to present an approach to the "Ricci maps" as a locus for communication and interaction. In addition to discussing authorship and consideration of mapmaking as a process, I focused on the prefaces, which appear, tellingly, in the maps' open spaces—its interstices. These spaces are profoundly important because often precisely such interstices—spaces *in between* cultures—foster the reformulation and reinvention of concepts and ideas. Since the maps concern not only visual but also linguistic representations, the term "dialogue" has often been used in this regard. I focused on one aspect: how these maps entered into a web of communication or, even better, originated within a web of communication, concluding that even today, the maps remain a site for communication.

The "Ricci maps" and other maps discussed above are still a continuous source of communication. Maps are then not only objects of construction but a subject that displaces and dislocates historians. By allowing historians to enter the map, the map dislocates their preexisting views. The maps compel us to meet another world, the world in which Chinese and Europeans of the seventeenth century communicated.

The preface by Hou Gongchen on the *Liangyi xuanlan tu* expresses this idea well: "Indeed, when this map is spread out, one finds oneself in an instant in contact with all the countries of the world, situated in the space of a few inches, and an 'Assembly of Princes' is displayed on the table [in front of one's] sitting-mat."[89] "Assembly of Princes" refers to a meeting of envoys from faraway countries at the court of King Wu in the distant Zhou past, a significant symbolic pivot from geographical descriptions of countries to interaction and communication between people of different cultures in the past and at present.[90]

Appendix

Extant printed versions of the *Kunyu wanguo quantu* 坤輿萬國全圖 (Complete map of all countries on earth, 1602) in six panels:

- Vatican Library, Rome. 179 × 414 cm. Intact.
- Miyagi Prefectural Library, Sendai. 171 × 361 cm. Intact (figure 1.1). The names of the continents are colored in red.
- Private collection in France. 168.7 × 380.2 cm. Formerly in the collection of Philip Robinson, auctioned by Sotheby's in 1988. Intact.
- Kyoto University Library. 166.5 × 366 cm. Three Jesuit seals cut out. The mountains and waterways of Africa were hand colored in green and blue.

- James Ford Bell Library, University of Minnesota. 182 × 365 cm. Three Jesuit seals and Matteo Ricci's name are cut out.
- Japanese National Archives, Naikaku Bunko, Tokyo. Only the central, oval world map. Cut into ten strips and attached to the backside of a map of East Asia titled *Huangyu tu* 皇輿圖 (figure 6.3).
- Museo della Specola, Bologna. First and last panel only. Each panel 180 × 70 cm (figure 4.8).

Later prints:

- Austrian National Library, Vienna. Six panels. 165 × 365 cm. The character "Ming" 明 used to refer to "China" (Da Ming Yitong 大明一統) has been replaced in manuscript by "Qing" 清. Unknown print date. Gifted to the Austrian emperor by Prospero Intorcetta in 1672.
- Royal Geographical Society, London. Six panels. 182 × 365 cm. Printed after 1644 as "China" is called "Qing" (Da Qing Yitong 大清一統). Title: *Chengyu wanguo quantu* 城輿萬國全圖.

Extant printed versions of the *Liangyi xuanlan tu* 兩儀玄覽圖 (Mysterious visual map of the two forms, 1603) in eight panels:

- Korean Christian Museum of Soongsil University, Seoul. 198 × 442 cm. Previously in the possession of Hwang Byeongin 黃炳仁 (figure 1.2).
- Liaoning Provincial Museum, Shenyang. 200 × 442 cm. Includes handwritten translations in Manchu.

World maps in seventeenth-century printed Chinese books:

1. A map in an oval projection in Zhang Huang's 章潢 (1527–1608) *Tushu bian* 圖書編 (1613, 2nd ed. 1623), 29.33b–34a (figure 1.8). Title: "Yudi shanhai quantu" 輿地山海全圖.
2. A map in two hemispheres with no place-names in *Tushu bian,* 16.47ab. Title: "Haotian hunyuan tu" 昊天渾元圖.
3. Two polar views in *Tushu bian,* 29.36b–38a; one view each of the Northern and Southern Hemisphere. Title: "Yudi tu shang" 輿地圖上 and "Yudi tu xia" 輿地圖下.
4. A circular map in the following:
    a. Feng Yingjing's 馮應京 *Yueling guangyi* 月令廣義 (1602), *shoujuan* 首卷 60b–61a. Title: "Shanhai yudi quantu" 山海輿地全圖 (figure 1.6).
    b. Wang Qi's 王圻 (fl. 1565–1614) *Sancai tuhui* 三才圖會 (1609), *dili* 地理 1.2ab. Title: "Shanhai yudi quantu" (figure 1.7).
    c. Cao Xueci's 曹學賜 *Xingli bicheng jiyao* 性理筆乘集要 (1612), *tushuo shoujuan* 圖說首卷 9b–10a. Title: "Shanhai yudi quantu."
    d. You Yi's 游藝 (1614–1684) *Tianjing huowen* 天經或問 (1675), *qianji* 前集 1.20b–21a. Title: "Dadi yuanqiu zhuguo quantu" 大地圓球諸國全圖.
5. A map in two hemispheres:
    a. Cheng Bai'er 程百二 (fl. 1606–1615) et al.'s *Fangyu shenglüe* 方輿勝略 (latest preface: 1612), *waiyi* 外夷 1.3b–5a. Title: no title on the map, but title given as "Shanhai yudi quantu" in the preface to the map (figure 1.5).
    b. Pan Guangzu 潘光祖 (1625 *jinshi*) and Li Yunxiang's 李雲翔 *Huiji yutu beikao quanshu* 彙輯輿圖備考全書 (prefaces: 1633), 1.1b–3a. The authors list the *Fangyu shenglüe*

as one of their sources. Title: "Chandutu" 纏度圖 on the map and "Tianwen chandu sida buzhou tu" 天文纏度四大部洲圖 according to the table of contents.

6. A section showing East and Southeast Asia from a polar view, related to the northern polar view of the *Kunyu wanguo quantu* in Wang Zaijin's 王在晉 (1564–1643) *Haifang zuanyao* 海防纂要 (1613), inserted before the first *juan*. Title: "Zhoutian geguotu sifen zhi yi" 週天各國圖四分之一.

7. A map in Giulio Aleni (1582–1649) and Yang Tingyun's 楊廷筠 (1557–1627) *Zhifang waiji* 職方外紀 (1st ed., 1623) (figure 2.9). Title: "Wanguo quantu" 萬國全圖.

8. A map that, apart from its title, is unrelated to the 1602 *Kunyu wanguo quantu* in Xiong Mingyu's 熊明遇 (1579–1649) *Gezhi cao* 格致草, 152b. Included in the 1648 *Hanyu tong* 函宇通. Title: "Kunyu wanguo quantu."

9. A map in Xiong Renlin's 熊人霖 (1604–1666) *Diwei* 地緯, 186a. Included in the 1648 *Hanyu tong*. Title: "Yudi quantu" 輿地全圖.

Notes

Epigraph: Hanson, foreword to *The Infinite Conversation*, xxxi.

1. For an extensive bibliography on the maps, see the four versions of the *Kunyu wanguo quantu* 坤輿萬國全圖, in Ad Dudink and Nicolas Standaert, Chinese Christian Texts Database (CCT-Database), http://www.arts.kuleuven.be/sinology/cct. One will find the link to secondary sources in the same records.
2. Standaert, *Methodology*.
3. See, e.g., Ch'en, "Matteo Ricci's Contribution"; D'Elia, *Il mappamondo cinese,* 121–168: "Capo X. Il contributo del Ricci alle conoscenze geografiche e cartografiche dei Cinesi"; Wallis, "Influence of Father Ricci on Far Eastern Cartography."
4. See, e.g., Yee, "Traditional Chinese Cartography": He focuses on the "Chinese responses" but still argues that the Chinese reproductions "betray an incomplete understanding of Ricci's maps," "mislabel certain countries," "misinterpret Ricci's notes as place-names," etc. His general approach is in line with Cohen's "China-centered approach." Cohen, *Discovering History in China*.
5. See, e.g., the section on "Father Ricci's Move" in part 3, "The Colonization of Space," in Mignolo, *Darker Side of the Renaissance*, 219–226.
6. These ideas were first developed in 2001 and presented at a conference in Cambridge in January 2005. For recent alternative approaches to the map, see, e.g., Zhang, "Matteo Ricci's World Maps"; Zhang, *Making the New World Their Own;* Morar, "Relocating the Qing"; Morar, "Westerner."
7. Standaert, *Methodology,* 23ff.
8. Wilford, *Mapmakers,* 13.
9. For a modern English translation, see Gallagher, *China in the Sixteenth Century* (original Italian version in *Fonti Ricciane*). The differences between the Italian manuscript and the Latin translation have been the object of various studies. See the CCT-Database for references.

10. Gallagher, *China in the Sixteenth Century,* 165–166; see Trigault, *De Christiana expeditione,* 182–183; compare with D'Elia, *Fonti Ricciane,* 1.207–208.
11. On curiosity, see Burke, *What Is the History of Knowledge?,* 17–18.
12. D'Elia, *Fonti Ricciane,* 1.207.
13. Michel de Certeau in *The Writing of History* (1975; English trans. 1988), quoted by Burke, *What Is the History of Knowledge?,* 33.
14. Standaert, "Making of 'China' out of 'Da Ming.'"
15. One of the earliest mentions of the term "Ricci map" in Chinese primary sources is the reference to *Li Madou ditu* 利瑪竇地圖 as a rubbing of a stele (*bei tie* 碑帖) in the private library catalogue *Zhao Dingyu shumu* 趙定宇書目 of the scholar-official Zhao Yongxian 趙用賢 (1535–1596; *hao:* Dingyu 定宇; from Changshu 常熟). This may refer to a rubbing of the stone edition of the map by Zhao Kehuai in Suzhou in 1597. Tang and Zhou, "Mingdai Li Madou shijie ditu chuanboshi siti," 299–304.
16. One example is the world map produced by Ferdinand Verbiest (1623–1688) in the early 1670s titled *Kunyu quantu* 坤輿全圖 (figure 5.1).
17. As included in D'Elia, *Il mappamondo cinese,* Ricci's preface, table 17.
18. A signature is not the only way to demark authorship; in Chinese tradition the seal often plays a more central role. Moreover, a preface or postscript to a map may link it to an author or the patronage of an edition to its patron. One example is *Yudi tu* 輿地圖 (1512–1513, 1526), with a postscript by Yang Ziqi 楊子器, called *Yang Ziqi ba yudi tu* 杨子器跋輿地圖. Cao et al., *Zhongguo gudai ditu ji: Mingdai,* map 12.
19. Edney, *Cartography,* 64.
20. See, Giles, "Translations," Ricci's preface, 367–370; D'Elia, *Il mappamondo cinese,* table 17; D'Elia, "Recent Discoveries," Ricci's preface, 153–155: "In order to respond to the good intention of my friends."
21. Foss, "Cartography," 754.
22. The *Chouhai tubian* 籌海圖編 (1562) provided the basis for the names of the regions of Japan. Lin, "Li Madou de shijie ditu," 328.
23. D'Elia, *Fonti Ricciane,* 1.207–208.
24. Trigault, *De Christiana expeditione,* 182; Gallagher, *China in the Sixteenth Century,* 166.
25. For references to Li Zhizao, see Giles, "Translations," 308; for references to Li Yingshi, see D'Elia, "Recent Discoveries," 155.
26. D'Elia, *Il mappamondo cinese,* table 25; Giles, "Translations," 372. For punctuated versions, see also Huang and Gong, *Li Madou shijie ditu yanjiu,* 165–167, 170–171.
27. D'Elia, "Recent Discoveries," 145–146; Wang, "Lun Li Madou Kunyu wanguo quantu," 109. This is their earliest mention in a Chinese document.
28. Cf. Burke, *What Is the History of Knowledge?,* 37.
29. One may gain a rough indication of the first two versions' appearance by considering reproductions of certain Chinese maps we know to be based on them. Unno, "Min Shin ni okeru Mateo Ritchi kei sekaizu"; Huang and Gong, *Li Madou shijie ditu yanjiu.*

30. Tang and Zhou, "Mingdai Li Madou shijie ditu chuanboshi siti," 295–298. "Daying" is a term used in the passage on Zou Yan in the *Shiji*; see below.

31. D'Elia ("Recent Discoveries," 86, 89) points out that the former is more correct: "His learned friends had evidently been helping the author to polish his work." It is unclear whether an actual printed map ever bore this title. On the history of its use, see Tang and Zhou, "Mingdai Li Madou shijie ditu chuanboshi siti," 304.

32. These similarities are referred to in D'Elia, "Recent Discoveries," Guo Zizhang's preface, 100–101.

33. Lau, *Lao Tzu*, 66: "Can you polish your mysterious mirror, and leave no blemish?" Or, in the translation by James Legge (in the Chinese Texts Project, https://ctext.org/dao-de-jing/ens?filter =530871): "When he has cleansed away the most mysterious sights (of his imagination), he can become without a flaw."

34. On this title, see Wang, "Lun Li Madou Kunyu wanguo quantu," 111. D'Elia, "Recent Discoveries," Ruan Taiyuan's preface, 143–144, refers to it; see also ibid., Hou Gongchen's preface, 151, Feng Yingjing's preface, 136, and Chang Yinxu's preface, 137–138.

35. Consider, for example, texts such as *Xiguo jifa* 西國記法, *Taixi shuifa* 泰西水法, *Taixi renshen shuogai* 泰西人身說概, and *Xiyang huogong tushuo* 西洋火攻圖說.

36. See also the remark in D'Elia, "Recent Discoveries," Ruan Taiyuan's preface, 144.

37. D'Elia, *Il mappamondo cinese*, Li Zhizao's preface, table 12; Giles, "Translations," 372.

38. Giles, "Translations," Ricci's preface, 369; D'Elia, *Il mappamondo cinese*, table 17.

39. D'Elia, "Recent Discoveries," Ricci's preface, 155.

40. There were several other changes—e.g., the presence of the seals of the Society of Jesus (D'Elia, "Recent Discoveries," 124); the number of heavens (eleven rather than nine: ibid., 125–126); and changes in the hemispheres: compare *Kunyu wanguo quantu* (printed 1602; figure 1.1), *Kunyu wanguo quantu* (manuscript; figure 4.3), and *Liangyi xuanlan tu* (1603; figure 1.2).

41. D'Elia, "Recent Discoveries"; Lin, "Li Madou de shijie ditu"; Huang and Gong, *Li Madou shijie ditu yanjiu*. Ricci presented Abraham Ortelius's *Theatrum orbis terrarum* to the emperor in Beijing in 1601. D'Elia, *Fonti Ricciane*, 2.114.

42. Foss, "Cartography," 754.

43. Such as Luo Hongxian's 羅洪先 (1504–1564) *Guang yutu* 廣輿圖 (Extended territorial maps). See, e.g., D'Elia, *Il mappamondo cinese*; D'Elia, *Fonti Ricciane*, 1.14–15n3, 209n1; Foss, "Cartography," 754ff.

44. See Ricci's note to the *Liangyi xuanlan tu* (D'Elia, "Recent Discoveries," 156). In his journal Ricci mentions that he utilized the 1579 print of a work titled *Descrittione della Cina* (L. *Sinarum Regni descriptio*), identifiable as Luo Hongxian's *Guang yutu*. See D'Elia, *Fonti Ricciane*, 1.14; Trigault, *De Christiana expeditione*, 7; Gallagher, *China in the Sixteenth Century*, 9. D'Elia suspected it was *Guang yutu* but, unable to consult the text, could not confirm it. D'Elia, *Fonti Ricciane*, 1.14–15n3. See also Unno, *Chizu bunkashi-jō no Kōyozu*.

45. Ch'en, "Matteo Ricci's Contribution," 330, 333–334; D'Elia, *Il mappamondo cinese*, tables 15 and 19.

46. D'Elia, *Il mappamondo cinese*, tables 15–16; see also Ch'en, "Possible Source for Ricci's Notices." For supplementary remarks, see D'Elia, "Recent Discoveries," 117–118. See also Lin, "Li Madou de shijie ditu," 322ff., 326ff. for the different Chinese sources and Huang and Gong, *Li Madou shijie ditu yanjiu*, 75. Ricci, however, remained critical of other descriptions, such as those of

"people with three heads, with a single arm, people without thighs or without bellies, with eyes in the rear, with bodies joined, people who do not die." He chose not to include them because they "would be insults to the Creator." D'Elia, "Recent Discoveries," 157–158.

47. Julia Kristeva introduced the term "intertextuality" in her presentation of Bakhtin, and Todorov adopted it. Todorov, *Mikhail Bakhtin,* 60ff.
48. In the late Ming, the trend was to include more prefaces in a book. The sixteen prefaces associated with the "Ricci maps" are among the higher number of prefaces to works of the time. Chow, *Publishing, Culture, and Power,* 114.
49. For a brief description of these two anthologies, including their table of contents, see the CCT-Database. A punctuated version of the prefaces to the maps is included in Xie Hui, *Ming Qing zhiji xixue hanji xuba mulu ji,* 30–47, 267–268. Note that the version of a particular preface preserved in one collection may exhibit multiple differences from that in another and may also differ from its first appearance on the map or on other versions of Chinese works. For another punctuated version with different (modern) titles, see Huang and Gong, *Li Madou shijie ditu yanjiu,* 163–182.
50. A clear example of this network is the list in Chang Yinxu's preface. See D'Elia, "Recent Discoveries," 138–139. Nine authors of prefaces are given, and three are the authors of prefaces to the *Kunyu wanguo quantu* of 1602. References to other authors of prefaces are included, for example, in D'Elia, "Recent Discoveries," Ruan Taiyuan's preface, 138; D'Elia, *Il mappamondo cinese,* Qi Guangzong's preface, table 22, and Yang Jingchun's preface, table 14; see also Giles, "Translations," 372.
51. Examples of explicit comments on Ricci personally: D'Elia, "Recent Discoveries," Wu Zhongming's preface, 94, Li Yingshi's preface, 146–147, Hou Gongchen's preface, 151; D'Elia, *Il mappamondo cinese,* Li Zhizao's preface, table 12, and Chen Minzhi's preface, table 14.
52. D'Elia, "Recent Discoveries," Chang Yinxu's preface, 139.
53. Ibid, 140.
54. Cf. Burke, *What Is the History of Knowledge?,* 20: "Innovation is a kind of displacement."
55. D'Elia, "Recent Discoveries," Hou Gongchen's preface, 151; on Europe, see ibid., Li Yingshi's preface, 147. For a reference to *Zhouli* 周禮, which supposedly contained information about all the different "barbarians," see ibid., 98.
56. Ibid., Feng Yingjing's preface, 130–131, Guo Zizhang's preface, 98.
57. Ibid., Guo Zizhang's preface, 99, 105, Chang Yinxu's preface, 138–139. For an illustration of the square earth and round heaven, see Zhang, *Tushu bian,* 28.2a. For other references to classical works, see D'Elia, "Recent Discoveries," Ruan Taiyuan's preface, 141; and D'Elia, *Il mappamondo cinese,* Yang Jingshun's preface, table 14.
58. D'Elia, "Recent Discoveries," Feng Yingjing's preface, 131.
59. Ibid., Guo Zizhang's preface, 105–106.
60. Ch'en, "Matteo Ricci's Contribution," 348; Xia, *Shengchao poxie ji,* 183.
61. Zürcher, "Jesuit Accommodation," 36.
62. D'Elia, "Recent Discoveries," Li Yingshi's preface, 149.
63. *Shiji,* 74.2344; Ssu-ma, *Grand Scribe's Records,* 7.180–181.
64. The reference to Zou Yan appears in D'Elia, "Recent Discoveries," prefaces of Wu Zhongming, 92, and Guo Zizhang, 100.

65. D'Elia, "Recent Discoveries," Guo Zizhang's preface, 99ff., 105: "These are some of the theories of which the Middle Kingdom had never, from the most ancient times onward, heard, and which are secretly in accordance with the *Comprehensive Description of the Features of the Earth* and with the *Classic of the Mountains and the Seas.*"
66. Ibid., Guo Zizhang's preface, 103–104. Not all agreed. Li Weizhen (1547–1626), for example, believed that Ricci, like Zou Yan, depreciated China. See Lin, "Li Madou de shijie ditu," 362. In another example of congruity, the map was considered a new proof of the parable of the puddle and the marsh in the *Zhuangzi*. See D'Elia, "Recent Discoveries," Hou Gongzhen's preface, 152. A third example is that Ricci's theories and ideas were thought to correspond to *Zhoubi suanjing* 周髀算經 and other texts. See D'Elia, *Il mappamondo cinese,* Li Zhizao's preface, table 12.
67. "If the son of Heaven were to lose [the names of] his functionaries, they might be learned again from the four barbarians (*yi* 夷)." Cf. *Zuozhuan,* seventeenth year of Duke Zhao. Legge, *Chinese Classics,* vol. 5, pt. 2, 666–667.
68. D'Elia, "Recent Discoveries," Guo Zizhang's preface, 106–107.
69. Ibid.
70. For the theme of trust, see ibid., Chang Yinxu's preface, 139, Wu Zhongming's preface, 95.
71. Ibid., Ruan Taiyuan's preface, 142–143.
72. Ibid., Wu Zhongming's preface, 94, Li Yingshi's preface, 147.
73. Ibid., Chang Yinxu's preface, 137–138; D'Elia, *Il mappamondo cinese,* Li Zhizao's preface, table 12; Giles, "Translations," 371–372; D'Elia, *Il mappamondo cinese,* Qi Guangzong's preface, table 22; and Lin, "Li Madou de shijie ditu," Zhang Yuanjing's preface, 355.
74. See, e.g., D'Elia, "Recent Discoveries," Wu Zhongming's preface, 95, Chang Yinxu's preface, 137–138, Ruan Taiyuan's preface, 143–144; and D'Elia, *Il mappamondo cinese,* Li Zhizao's preface, table 12.
75. Cf. Hanson, Foreword, xxxi.
76. D'Elia, "Recent Discoveries," Feng Yingjing's preface, 134–135.
77. Ibid., Li Yingshi's preface, 149. For the idea that the mind is the same throughout the universe, see also ibid., Feng Yingjing's preface, 132. See a reference to *tongxin* in the conclusion of D'Elia, *Il mappamondo cinese,* Yang Jingshun's preface, table 14.
78. D'Elia, *Il mappamondo cinese,* Li Zhizao's preface, table 12. On the topic of *xintong litong,* see also Ge, "Yige pubian zhenli guannian de lishi lüxing."
79. Cao et al., *Zhongguo gudai ditu ji: Mingdai,* maps 145, 146.
80. D'Elia, "Recent Discoveries," Guo Zizhang's preface, 105. In 1604, Guo Zizhang reproduced Ricci's Nanjing map in booklet form; this version is lost, but the preface survives in his *Qiancao* 黔草 (Weeds from Guizhou). See ibid., 98n49. During the years 1595–1598, Zhao Kehuai initiated the map's reproduction on stone for easy copying through rubbings.
81. On this and the following reproductions, see, e.g., Unno, "Min Shin ni okeru Mateo Ritchi kei sekaizu"; Huang and Gong, *Li Madou shijie ditu yanjiu.*
82. Standaert, *Methodology,* 49.
83. D'Elia, "Recent Discoveries," Feng Yingjing's preface, 129–130. The expression *woyou* also occurs in Ricci's preface to *Kunyu wanguo quantu:* Giles, "Translations," 369–370; D'Elia, *Il mappamondo cinese,* table 17 ("The map becomes a means to travel while reclining at ease in one's studio").

84. D'Elia, *Il mappamondo cinese,* Chen Minzhi's preface, table 14.
85. Ibid., Qi Guangzong's preface, table 22; Giles, "Translations," 372.
86. D'Elia, "Recent Discoveries," Chang Yinxu's preface, 140.
87. Ibid., Ruan Taiyuan's preface, 144; the expression *nongwan* 弄丸 (juggling balls) refers to a passage from the *Zhuangzi* in which Yi Liao 宜僚 was able to juggle nine balls at a time.
88. Lévi-Strauss, *Tristes tropiques,* 85–86; reference found in Ge, "Gu ditu yu sixiang shi," 162.
89. D'Elia, "Recent Discoveries," Hou Gongchen's preface, 152.
90. Ibid., 130n20. The same analogy is present in ibid., Feng Yingjing's preface, 130.

References

Burke, Peter. *What Is the History of Knowledge?* Cambridge: Polity Press, 2016.

Cao Wanru 曹婉如, Zheng Xihuang 鄭錫煌, Huang Shengzhang 黃盛璋, Niu Zhongxun 鈕仲勳, Ren Jincheng 任金城, Qin Guojing 秦國經, and Hu Bangbo 胡邦波, eds. *Zhongguo gudai ditu ji: Mingdai* 中國古代地圖集: 明代. Beijing: Wenwu chubanshe, 1994.

CCT-Database: Ad Dudink and Nicolas Standaert, Chinese Christian Texts Database (CCT-Database), http://www.arts.kuleuven.be/sinology/cct.

Ch'en, Kenneth. "Matteo Ricci's Contribution to, and Influence on, Geographical Knowledge in China." *Journal of the American Oriental Society* 59 (1939): 325–359. Originally published in Chen Guansheng 陳觀勝. "Li Madou dui Zhongguo dilixue zhi gongxian jiqi yingxiang" 利瑪竇對中國地理學之貢獻及其影響. *Yugong* 禹貢 5, no. 3–4 (1936): 51–72.

———. "A Possible Source for Ricci's Notices on Regions near China." *T'oung Pao* 34 (1938): 179–190.

Chow, Kai-Wing. *Publishing, Culture, and Power in Early Modern China.* Stanford, CA: Stanford University Press, 2004.

Cohen, Paul A. *Discovering History in China: American Historical Writing on the Recent Chinese Past.* New York: Columbia University Press, 1984.

D'Elia, Pasquale, ed. *Fonti Ricciane: Documenti originali concernenti Matteo Ricci e la storia delle prime relazioni tra l'Europa e la Cina (1579–1615).* 3 vols. Rome: La Libreria dello Stato, 1942–1949.

———. *Il mappamondo cinese del P. Matteo Ricci, S.I.* Vatican City: Biblioteca Apostolica Vaticana, 1938.

———. "Recent Discoveries and New Studies (1938–1960) on the World Map in Chinese of Father Matteo Ricci S.J." *Monumenta Serica* 20 (1961): 82–163.

Edney, Matthew H. *Cartography: The Ideal and Its History.* Chicago: University of Chicago Press, 2019.

Foss, Theodore N. "Cartography." In *Handbook of Christianity in China.* Vol. 1, *635–1800,* edited by Nicolas Standaert, 752–770. Leiden: Brill, 2001.

Gallagher, Louis J., trans. *China in the Sixteenth Century: The Journals of Matthew Ricci (1583–1610).* New York: Random House, 1953.

Ge Zhaoguang 葛兆光. "Gu ditu yu sixiang shi" 古地圖與思想史. *Ershiyi shiji* 二十一世紀 61 (2000): 154–164.

———. "Yige pubian zhenli guannian de lishi lüxing: Yi Lu Jiuyuan 'xin tong li tong' shuo wei li tan guannian shi de yanjiu fangfa" 一個普遍真理觀念的歷史旅行：以陸九淵"心同理同"說為例談觀念史的研究方法. *Dongyue luncong* 東岳論叢, no. 4 (2004): 5–15.

Giles, Lionel. "Translations from the Chinese World Map of Father Ricci." *Geographical Journal* 52 (1918): 367–385; 53 (1919): 19–30.

Hanson, Susan. Foreword to *The Infinite Conversation,* by Maurice Blanchot. Translated by Susan Hanson. Minneapolis: University of Minnesota Press, 1993.

Huang Shijian 黃時鑒, and Gong Yingyan 龔纓晏. *Li Madou shijie ditu yanjiu* 利瑪竇世界地圖研究. Shanghai: Shanghai guji chubanshe, 2004.

Lau, D. C., trans. *Lao Tzu: Tao Te Ching.* Harmondsworth: Penguin Books, 1963.

Legge, James, trans. *The Chinese Classics.* Vol. 5, *The Ch'un Ts'ew, with the Tso Chuen.* Hong Kong: Lane, Crawford; London: Trübner, 1872.

Lévi-Strauss, Claude. *Tristes tropiques.* Translated by John and Doreen Weightman. New York: Atheneum, 1974.

Lin Dongyang (Lin Tong Yang) 林東陽. "Li Madou de shijie ditu ji qi dui Mingmo shiren shehui de yingxiang" 利瑪竇的世界地圖及其對明末士人社會的影. In *Collected Essays of the International Symposium on Chinese-Western Cultural Exchange in Commemoration of the 400th Anniversary of the Arrival of Matteo Ricci S.J. in China,* edited by Lo Kuang, 311–378. Taipei: Fujen University Press, 1983.

Mignolo, Walter D. *The Darker Side of the Renaissance: Literacy, Territoriality, and Colonization.* Ann Arbor: University of Michigan Press, 1995.

Morar, Florin-Stefan. "Relocating the Qing in the Global History of Science: The Manchu Translation of the 1603 World Map by Li Yingshi and Matteo Ricci." *Isis* 109, no. 4 (2018): 673–694.

———. "The Westerner: Matteo Ricci's World Map and the Quandaries of European Identity in the Late Ming Dynasty." *Journal of Jesuit Studies* 6, no. 1 (2019): 14–30.

Shiji 史記. Beijing: Zhonghua shuju, 1985.

Ssu-ma, Ch'ien. *The Grand Scribe's Record.* Edited by William H. Nienhauser. Bloomington: Indiana University Press, 1994.

Standaert, Nicolas. "The Making of 'China' out of 'Da Ming.'" *Journal of Asian History* 50, no. 2 (2016): 307–328.

———. *Methodology in View of Contact between Cultures: The China Case in the 17th Century.* Hong Kong: Chinese University of Hong Kong, 2002.

Tang Kaijian 湯開建, and Zhou Xiaolei 周孝雷. "Mingdai Li Madou shijie ditu chuanboshi siti" 明代利瑪竇世界地圖傳播史四題. *Ziran kexueshi yanjiu* 自然科學史研究 34, no. 3 (2015): 294–315.

Todorov, Tzvetan. *Mikhail Bakhtin: The Dialogical Principle.* Minneapolis: University of Minnesota Press, 1984.

Trigault, Nicolas. *De Christiana expeditione apud Sinas.* Augsburg: Christoph Mang, 1615.

Unno Kazutaka 海野一隆. *Chizu bunkashi-jō no Kōyozu* 地図文化史上の広輿図. Tokyo: Tōyō bunko, 2010.

———. "Min Shin ni okeru Mateo Ritchi kei sekaizu: Shu toshite shin shiryō no kenkyū" 明清における マテオ・リッチ系世界図: 主として新史料の検討. In *Shin hatsugen Chūgoku kagakushi shiryō no kenkyū: Ronkō hen* 新発現中国科学史資料の研究. 論考篇, edited by Yamada Keiji 山田慶兒, 507–580. Kyoto: Kyōto daigaku jinbun kagaku kenkyūjo, 1983.

Wallis, Helen. "The Influence of Father Ricci on Far Eastern Cartography." *Imago Mundi* 19 (1965): 38–45.

Wang Mianhou 王綿厚. "Lun Li Madou Kunyu wanguo quantu he Liangyi xuanlan tu shang de xuba tishi" 論利瑪竇坤輿全圖和兩儀玄覽圖上的序跋題識. In Cao et al., *Zhongguo gudai ditu ji: Mingdai,* 107–111.

Wilford, John Noble. *The Mapmakers.* Rev. ed. New York: Vintage, 2001.

Xia Guiqi 夏瑰琦, ed. *Shengchao poxie ji* 聖朝破邪集. Hong Kong: Jiandao shenxueyuan, 1996.

Xie Hui 謝輝, ed. *Ming Qing zhiji xixue hanji xuba mulu ji* 明清之際西學漢籍序跋目錄集. Shanghai: Shanghai guji chubanshe, 2021.

Yee, Cordell D. K. "Traditional Chinese Cartography and the Myth of Westernization." In *The History of Cartography.* Vol. 2, bk. 2, *Cartography in the Traditional East and Southeast Asian Societies,* edited by David Woodward and J. B. Harley, 170–202. Chicago: University of Chicago Press, 1994.

Zhang Huang 章潢. *Tushu bian* 圖書編. 1613. http://nrs.harvard.edu/urn-3:FHCL:28553803.

Zhang, Qiong. *Making the New World Their Own: Chinese Encounters with Jesuit Science in the Age of Discovery.* Leiden: Brill, 2015.

———. "Matteo Ricci's World Maps in Late Ming Discourse of Exotica." *Horizons* 1, no. 2 (2010): 215–250.

Zürcher, Erik. "Jesuit Accommodation and the Chinese Cultural Imperative." In *The Chinese Rites Controversy: Its History and Meaning,* edited by David E. Mungello, 31–64. Nettetal: Steyler, 1994.

2

A Late Ming Terrestrial Globe

RICHARD A. PEGG

IN LATE MING CHINA, A MATRIX OF European Jesuits and Chinese scholars created platforms for meaningful spiritual and intellectual discourse, exchange, and collaboration via "contact zones."[1] Within these contact zones, the Jesuits, Christian scholars expert in various scientific and mathematical disciplines, introduced elite Confucian intellectuals to European scientific, mathematical, and geographical knowledge. A singular nexus can be understood as emerging in the 1620s around the fabrication of an important (yet little-known) and still extant Chinese-made, four-color lacquer terrestrial globe. Through first examining globes and globe production of the period in western Europe and East Asia and then considering the different collaborators, together with others such as the skilled Chinese lacquer artisans, we can better understand how overcoming historically challenging circumstances in a complex collaborative exchange of knowledge and technologies culminated in the creation of China's first known terrestrial globe.

The Materiality of Globes

In premodern times, the ostensibly simple, straightforward idea of the world as a globe required a tremendous intellectual and spiritual leap in time and space. How should one make this idea manifest? Flat maps of the world attempt to depict in two dimensions a three-dimensional world. Viewing or "reading" a globe requires intellectual combinations of abstract concepts similar to those necessary to interpret flat world maps. A globe, however, facilitates and requires a haptic/kinetic and optic/static interaction between viewer and object. One must physically rotate a globe to view the world in its entirety, and yet never in a single glance, necessitating an imaginative spatial response that enables a three-dimensional imagined cartography possible only when using a globe. The globe is the best format for presenting visually the concepts of a terraqueous spherical world. A globe is also considerably more expensive to manufacture than a sheet map, requiring greater fabrication time, special materials, and additional craftsmen of various skill sets. As Matteo Ricci (1552–1610) himself notes in a text on the 1602 *Kunyu wanguo quantu* 坤輿萬國全圖 (Complete map of all countries on earth; figure 1.1): "Originally I should have announced making a globe, but because it was an inconvenient form for a map, I was obliged to convert the sphere into two dimensions and turn circles into lines."[2]

The earliest known terrestrial globe in China likely arrived there in 1267 with Jamāl al-Dīn (known as Zhima Luding 紮馬祿丁 in Chinese) as one of seven astronomical instruments presented to the Great Khan in Beijing.[3] Instrument number six was a terrestrial globe.[4] Joseph Needham states: "The new instrument [was] 'a globe made of wood, upon which seven parts of water are represented in green, three parts of land in white, with rivers, lakes, etc. Small squares are marked out so as to make it possible to reckon the sizes of regions and the distances along roads.'"[5]

The earliest known—and still extant—Chinese terrestrial globe in the world, however, was produced in 1623 and is currently in the collection of the British Library (BL; figures 2.1 and 2.2).[6] One of the featured texts on the globe is dated and signed by Yang Manuo 楊瑪諾 (Manuel Dias Jr., 1574–1659) and Long Huamin 龍華民 (Niccolò Longobardo, 1559–1654). It measures fifty-nine centimeters in diameter, at a scale of 1:21,000,000.[7] The current mount, probably fabricated in Europe in the early twentieth century, sets it on a vertical axis (as discussed in the note to the reader on the globe itself) and thus differs both from European globes of the period (figure 2.3) and from a later Palace Museum globe (figure 2.6).

Locating the BL globe within the paradigm of European globe production provides comparative and contextual understanding of its fabrication requirements. Construction of the first terrestrial globe may date back to 150 BCE, and various surviving records describe celestial and terrestrial globes in India, China, and Persia in the fifth, eighth, and ninth centuries CE, respectively.[8] In Europe the earliest center for globe production was Nuremberg, where Martin Behaim (1450–1506) made a large (fifty-one centimeters in diameter) terrestrial globe showing the latest Portuguese discoveries while Martin Waldseemüller (1470–1520) created the first globe using printed gores in 1509.[9] In Flanders, Gerard Mercator (1512–1594) was the first to scale up production, making globes from 1536 until his death.[10] Meanwhile, in Amsterdam the Dutch families of Jodocus Hondius (1563–1612) and Willem Janszoon Blaeu (1571–1638) became the preeminent globe makers of the 1590s to 1650s.[11] Blaeu had studied under Tycho Brahe (1546–1601), the Danish astronomer, in 1595 and produced his first globes in 1599. By the turn of the seventeenth century, the preferred method of globe manufacture in Europe was cutting and gluing sets of copperplate-printed paper gores onto a core (made using a variety of techniques).[12] Using printed gores enabled and motivated multiple copies of any given globe. The core, if made from wood, was cut, shaped, and dried to ensure minimal warping over time; coated with plaster or gesso for final shaping and to ensure a good

FIGURE 2.1.

The British Library globe showing the Pacific Ocean. The introductory text is signed Manuel Dias Jr. and Niccolò Longobardo (see figure 2.7) and dated 1623. Diameter, approx. 59 cm. British Library Board, Maps.G.35.

FIGURE 2.2.

The same British Library globe showing the Americas. British Library Board, Maps.G.35.

substrate onto which to glue the gores; and, finally, varnished. Brass pins at the poles were typically fixed to a flat brass ring secured in turn to a mount so the globe could rotate freely, facilitating haptic interaction.

A terrestrial globe of this type produced in 1632 by Matthäus Greuter (1564–1638), a German etcher and engraver then working in Rome, now resides in the MacLean Collection (figure 2.3).[13] This globe, fifty centimeters in diameter, consists of two sets of twelve copperplate-printed paper gores with two polar calottes. Each gore extends from the equator to eighty degrees latitude on a scale of 1:26,000,000. Its date, size, and scale all resemble the BL globe.[14] Its lightweight interior structure is of unknown construction. The present modern table-style mount sets the globe on a 23.5-degree tilt/axis of rotation relative to the orbital plane.[15] The original mount would likely have taken the form of a floor stand, the typical presentation at that time for globes of this size.

Greuter, born in Strasbourg, worked in France until moving to Rome in 1606, where he began producing works for the Papal Court. Greuter dedicated his terrestrial globe, an update of a Blaeu globe of 1622, to Jacobo Boncompagni, an Italian lord and major patron. Latin text panels dot the sphere, including a dedication: "To the most illustrious and excellent Prince Lord Jacobo Boncompagni, Duke of Sora and Arce, Marquis of Vignola and Count of Aquino, his most worshipful Lord, Matthäus Greuter

FIGURE 2.3.

A terrestrial globe by Matthäus Greuter, dated 1632. Diameter, approx. 50 cm. MacLean Collection, Illinois, MC16373.

with humble obedience dedicates."[16] The address to the reader, also in Latin, nearly identical to Blaeu's, and likewise located southeast of New Guinea, reads:

> In this representation of the terrestrial globe, which we show, you will find all the lands and islands which have been seen and reported by sailors from Portugal as well as from other sea-faring nations, set out in their own longitude and latitude with the highest care and industry, which should be not only a delight to students of geography, but also of the utmost usefulness for those who frequent remote places, warming under another sun. And so, I hope that you may receive our work with as much gratitude as the care we bestowed on it. Matthäus Greuter, the author, 1632.

Two standing navigators flank the ovoid colophon, one bearing a quadrant, the other a cross-staff, gazing upon a globe between them. Several additional colophons address issues such as locating the prime meridian in the Fortunata (Blessed, today's Canary) Islands.[17] In addition, two mermen, seven other sea creatures, thirteen ships, one compass, and two wind roses—all typical for an early seventeenth-century European globe—adorn the oceans.

On the BL globe, lacquer in four colors—black, white, red, and brown—covers the wooden core. It is a manuscript globe, made without printed paper gores. Both the BL and Greuter globes center around meticulously prepared cores, and the progress of each until completion likely took quite a bit of time.[18] In East Asia, large lacquered objects typically started with a core shaped and dried from blocks of wood, taking a year or more to treat and cure for lacquering. Each color and layer of lacquer, following application, needed to dry over months before additional colors and layers repeated the process. In Europe, gores were etched on copperplate, printed, trimmed, and glued to the core before the application of a final coat of varnish. Both methods of manufacture involved multiple specialized craftsmen and, from core fabrication to the final clear finish, were probably equally time-consuming.

The center of lacquer-making in China had been the city of Hangzhou, once named Lin'an 臨安 as the capital of the Southern Song dynasty (1138–1279). At that time it became an important production center for many fine arts and crafts, including lacquer-making. During the succeeding Yuan dynasty (1279–1368), lacquerers founded major schools just north of Hangzhou in the city of Jiaxing 嘉興 (in the northern part of today's Zhejiang Province), and by the Ming dynasty (1368–1644) the Jiaxing area had become one of the two great centers in all of China for lacquer-carving.[19] In the late Ming, the most important book on lacquer-making, *Xiushi lu* 髹飾錄 (Records of lacquer décor), compiled during the Longqing reign (1567–1572) by Huang Cheng 黃成, was published in Jiaxing.[20] This annotated version bears a preface (dated 1625) by Yang Ming 楊明, scion of a family involved in lacquer-making from the Southern Song period onward.[21] The BL globe emerged from this active area of Hangzhou and nearby Jiaxing lacquer-making.

The specialized manufacture of lacquer globes in China may have begun with the BL globe, but it continued evolving over the seventeenth century. The 1636 *Huntian yishuo* 渾天儀說 (Exposition on the armillary sphere) by Johann Adam Schall von Bell (1592–1666), Giacomo Rho (1593–1638), Li Tianjing 李天經 (1579–1659), and several of their students has a section titled "Method for globe manufacture" (Zhiqiu fa 制球法). Liu Baojian has paraphrased it as follows: "Take some pieces of wood of one *cun* square for the length of the radius, have them intersect at the globe's center. After they are fixed, fill them up until they assume the shape of a sphere, which is then polished, painted, drawn with a map, written with explanatory notes, and finally coated with a thin layer of clear lacquer. If one wants to make a globe this should probably be the method."[22] The manual also includes woodblock-printed gores for globe manufacture (figures 2.4 and 2.5). Further, the section on instruments for calendar regulation in Xu Guangqi 徐光啟 (1562–1633) and Li Tianjing's *Xinfa suanshu* 新法算書 (Books on calculations according to new methods, 1645) includes a list of ten needed instruments: seven to be made in bronze, one in stone, and two in wood and lacquer (a celestial and a terrestrial globe). We can speculate Xu may have specifically had the BL globe in mind as a prototype.[23]

The next-known extant Chinese-made globe hails from the Qing court, perhaps from the late Kangxi period (1661–1722; figure 2.6).[24] The globe, now in Beijing's Palace Museum, is molded wood pulp covered in painted gesso. Mounted in its original red sandalwood framework as a standing floor globe, the globe measures sixty-four centimeters in diameter.[25] The Palace Museum example was likely prepared following Schall von Bell's "Method for Globe Manufacture" of 1636.[26] This globe also provides some idea of the type of mount that likely originally accompanied the BL globe.

Although in terms of contents Japanese and Chinese globes resemble each other, Japan followed its own trajectory in the manufacture of globes, preferring paper rather than lacquer for fabrication. The archives of the Spanish settlement of Manila contain a report presented in April or May of 1593 by Antonio López regarding the second Spanish embassy to Japan (in 1592), including a reference to a globe in Japan.[27] López was a Chinese Christian convert who, with Juan Cobo (1546–1592), envoy of the governor-general in Manila, met with Toyotomi Hideyoshi 豊臣秀吉 (1537–1598) in Nagoya and showed him a globe with Chinese characters. The earliest-known Japanese globemaker, Shibukawa Harumi 渋川春海 (1639–1715), appointed first Court Astronomer to the shogun in 1685, created the first Japanese-based calendar using his own calculations to reform preexisting calendars.[28] He fabricated terrestrial and celestial globes in a variety of materials, including a still-extant paper-on-wood manuscript terrestrial globe in 1690, measuring twenty-four centimeters, based on the 1602 *Kunyu wanguo quantu*.[29]

The BL globe's visual and textual components draw from various sources. Many short inscriptions in red lacquer, copied from the 1602 *Kunyu wanguo quantu*, describe trade and natural resources such as "good fishing off Africa's West coast" or physical

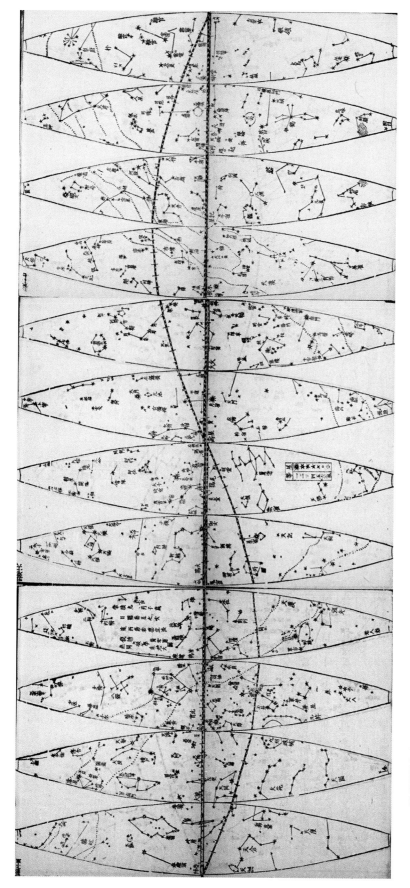

FIGURE 2.4.

Globe gores inserted in the *Huntian yishuo* (1636) to explain the manufacture of a celestial globe. Printed across three folios, digitally assembled. Bibliothèque nationale de France, gallica.bnf.fr.

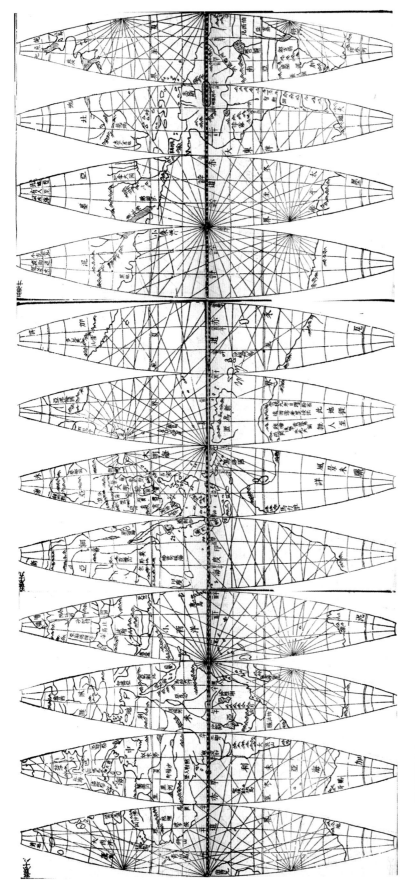

FIGURE 2.5. Globe gores inserted in the *Huntian yishuo* (1636) to explain the manufacture of a terrestrial globe. Printed across three folios, digitally assembled. Bibliothèque nationale de France, gallica.bnf.fr.

FIGURE 2.6.

Undated terrestrial globe produced at or for the Qing court. Diameter, approx. 64 cm. Palace Museum, Beijing.

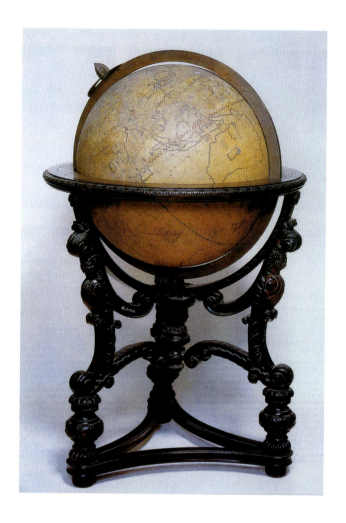

characteristics such as Japan's "one main long island 3200 *li* long and 600 *li* wide, sixty-six provinces, resources, and minerals."[30] The globe also includes supplemental descriptions of Korea, China, India, Melaka, Patani, and others. Updated geographical information absent from earlier collaborative maps produced in China includes coastlines in Asia (e.g, those of India, Ceylon, Japan, Korea, Borneo, and the East Indies), plus a dramatic alteration in the shape given New Guinea (figure 2.1).[31]

The largest block of text, located below China inside an ornate border with eight fleurs-de-lis on each side, is the note to the reader, in black characters on a light brown background, titled "Globe Explanation" (Diqiu shuo 地球說; figure 2.7). The text, signed by Yang Manuo (Manuel Dias Jr.) and Long Huamin (Niccolò Longobardo), is laid out unpunctuated in fifteen long columns (twenty-five to twenty-seven characters each) alternating with fourteen short columns (ten to eleven characters each) running parallel with the lines of longitude, allowing visually uniform character size.[32] It presents some general principles of European geophysics and celestial science, refuting the

64   CHAPTER 2

FIGURE 2.7.

Detail of the British Library globe (figures 2.1 and 2.2), showing cracks in the lacquer and the introductory text signed by Manuel Dias Jr. and Niccolò Longobardo. Photograph by Richard A. Pegg.

world-as-flat theory through both the text and the globe's own physicality, described as "upright and plumb"—in other words, on a vertical axis (perhaps the reason it is presently so mounted). The discussion of time discrepancies in eclipses points to recent errors in the Chinese calendar. This also hints at the upcoming effort at court to correct such errors, among others, by Xu Guangqi, Li Zhizao 李之藻 (1565–1630), and Longobardo. The text joins the concepts of yin and yang with hot and cold, attempting to shift the Chinese constructs so the North and South Poles can both be cold, thus leading to the five temperate zones. The analogy of the yolk of an egg was first introduced in China by the Later Han scholar Zhang Heng 張衡 (78–139) to compare the relationship between earth and the celestial sphere with the structure of an egg, with earth as the yolk and the celestial sphere as the shell. This analogy was a cosmological construct for the world's place in a larger universe that also worked quite well within a European Ptolemaic geocentric view. Copernicus and Galileo's geoheliocentric view was certainly known but not yet integrated by the Jesuits at that time. Chinese scholars engaged with all this "new" knowledge willingly—despite its introduction by Europeans—simply as new knowledge to incorporate syncretically. The text here integrates several specifically Chinese scientific concepts and advances, as does the description of the lodestone and the gravitational effects of terrestrial magnetism, the egg-yolk metaphor, and the use of yin and yang as methods and opportunities to join the known to the new knowledge.

Collaboration between Beijing and Hangzhou

Amid this apparent fusion of Chinese and European cosmological and geographical knowledge, numerous individuals already mentioned, including several Chinese scholar-officials such as Yang Tingyun 楊廷筠 (1557–1627), Xu Guangqi, and Li Zhizao, as well as several European Jesuits, including Niccolò Longobardo, Manuel Dias Jr., and Giulio Aleni (1582–1649), contributed in various ways to the globe's manufacture. These scholars' biographies indicate the extent of their cosmological and metaphysical interests and, more importantly, the numerous intersections among them, and for the 1620s collectively, within the historical matrix of the late Ming contact zones that gave rise to the globe's production.

The pursuit of faith and knowledge as well as the constant intersection and comingling of their personal, intellectual, and professional lives linked Yang Tingyun, Xu Guangqi, and Li Zhizao.[33] All three, born during the same eight-year span and dying within the same six, were highly accomplished scholar-officials, each having passed the prestigious *jinshi* 進士, or metropolitan examination in Confucian doctrines and methodologies, and achieving the examination system's utmost degree in 1592, 1604, and 1598, respectively. In 1611, when Li Zhizao's father died, Yang Tingyun journeyed from Beijing to Hangzhou (their shared hometown) to mourn with Li and there began conversing with Lazzaro Cattaneo (1560–1640) and Nicolas Trigault (1577–1628), the two Jesuits Li had brought along to perform Christian funerary rites for his deceased father.[34] Soon afterward they baptized Yang, and later Li and Yang would together found a Jesuit mission in Hangzhou. During the 1616–1622 persecutions of Christians led by Grand Secretary Shen Que 沈㴶 (died 1624), Li Zhizao and Yang Tingyun stayed at Hangzhou, and they eventually retired from official life to Hangzhou at different times.

Yang, Xu, and Li were all acutely aware of the daily deterioration of social, political, and intellectual practices amid the late Ming, and all three believed Jesuit teachings offered pathways to spiritual and intellectual enlightenment. They yearned to participate in a community of like-minded intellectuals of their choosing, in line with their shared syncretic relationship with religion. Yang, trained in the orthodox neo-Confucian doctrine of civil service preparation, followed the teachings of Wang Yangming's 王陽明 (1472–1529) idealist school. Yang's publications of 1592–1611, exploring the *Yijing* 易經 (Book of changes),[35] indicate ambivalence toward Confucianist, Daoist, and Buddhist teachings, although, following his retirement from civil service in 1609, he studied Buddhist texts closely for two years. Yang welcomed and appropriated in turn Ricci's appropriation of his religious faith, considering himself to be a Confucian Christian and his Jesuit friends and colleagues to be "Western Confucians" (*Xiru* 西儒).[36] While Yang never fully accepted the Jesuit's Sinicized Christianity or Christianized Confucianism, he did support Christian works publicly, building churches, chapels, and cemeteries and providing Jesuits sanctuary in his home.[37]

Xu, critical of Buddhist and Daoist practices early in his career, remained approachable via other intellectual and spiritual paths.[38] While Xu also did not agree with everything the Jesuits stated, they lived in, according to Liu Yu's book namesake, "harmonious disagreement" (*he'er butong* 和而不同).[39] Li wrote prefaces for Ricci's 1603 *Tianzhu shiyi* 天主實義 (True meaning of the Lord of heaven) critical of both Buddhism and Neo-Confucianism and for his 1608 *Jiren shipian* 畸人十篇 (Ten essays on an extraordinary man), which addressed religious and moral questions.[40] We must understand Yang, Li, and Xu's relationship with the Christian Church as far more nuanced than elevating one religion above all others. All considered themselves first and foremost scholars and, like many of the Jesuits with whom they kept in contact, simultaneously embraced Confucian and Christian practices. Shared intellectual as well as spiritual curiosity bound together their relationships.

All three, tied to the Ming court in Beijing, met Matteo Ricci in the early years of the seventeenth century. Yang became an imperial censor (*yushi* 御史) in 1601, and it is likely he met Ricci then, as well as subsequently (in 1606 or 1607), leading to his baptism, probably in 1611. Xu first met Ricci in Beijing in 1600 and was baptized in 1603.[41] Li, appointed to the Ministry of Works (Gongbu 工部) in Nanjing around 1599, met Ricci in Beijing in 1601. Ricci immediately impressed Li as an ethical and intelligent man promoting a virtuous harmony among heaven, man, and oneself.[42] According to Ricci's recollections, Li, who wished to learn astronomy, mathematics, and geometry from him, was interested particularly in geography (Li had in younger years published a geographical description of China but realized after seeing a world map in Ricci's residence that he had much to learn).[43] Li, who saw no conflict between Confucian and Catholic teachings and practices (he was baptized in 1610), learned to maintain a balance between the two and soon began collaborating with Ricci to publish his works, for which he wrote several prefaces.

All three became Christian converts, supportive both of the Jesuit mission in China and (enthusiastically) of Jesuit publications of all kinds. Li was a sponsor and Zhang Wentao 張文燾—another Hangzhou native—the printer for the 1602 *Kunyu wanguo quantu* (figure 1.1), while Xu sponsored the 1603 *Liangyi xuanlan tu* 兩儀玄覽圖

(Mysterious visual map of the two forms; figure 1.2). From 1604 to 1607, Xu worked with Ricci in Beijing, extensively translating books on the European sciences, such as the first six books of Euclid's *Elements* (known in Chinese as *Jihe yuanben* 幾何原本, 1607) and the *Celiang fayi* 測量法義 (Principles of measurement, 1607–1617).[44] In studying Euclid's *Elements,* Xu learned how mathematics and geometry could aid military logistics and, in 1621, contributed (aided by Li and Yang) to the purchase and demonstration of European cannon for defense against Manchu-Qing incursions.

Ricci's studies at the Collegium Romanum during the 1570s had included working with Christopher Clavius (1538–1612), from 1579 a key figure in the Gregorian calendrical reform (Pope Gregory XIII enacted Clavius's revisions in 1582, whence they remain in use today). Undoubtedly, Ricci's presentation of Clavius's work facilitated the Jesuits' crucial involvement in late Ming and early Qing calendar reform. It was Li who first petitioned the Wanli emperor (r. 1572–1620) to recruit Jesuit assistance in reforming the Chinese calendar. In 1629, Xu, along with Li and Longobardo, helped to fulfill the imperial request to correct the existing Chinese calendar using the new mathematical practices. Xu was editor in chief of seventy-two chapters of translations and lists of related materials on astronomical subjects, titled *Chongzhen lishu* 崇禎曆書 (Calendar book of the Chongzhen era, 1635). Following Xu's death, Li Tianjing combined these chapters with 55 of his own, amounting to 137 chapters, to finish his *Xinfa suanshu.*[45]

Li was keen on translating European books, composing throughout his career numerous memorials to the Wanli emperor on the Jesuits' behalf in order to get books on the European calendar, irrigation, mathematics, geography, and geometry translated and to gain information not covered in their Chinese counterparts. Like Xu, Li also published translated works by Ricci's teacher Clavius—for example, his 1585 *Epitome arithmeticae practicae* (Selected arithmetic methods) as *Tongwen suanzhi* 同文算指 in 1614, for which Yang wrote a preface mentioning his conversations with Ricci.[46] Like Li and Xu, Yang enthusiastically supported scientific and technical learning.[47] Yang also wrote a preface for Aleni's *Xixue fan* 西學凡 (Summary of Western learning, 1623), and the men coauthored the *Zhifang waiji* 職方外紀 (Record of everything beyond the administration, 1623), both printed in Hangzhou. Xu continued, following Ricci's death in 1610, to translate European books on science. The lives of Li, Xu, and Yang thus intersected in Beijing and Hangzhou and comingled personally, intellectually, spiritually, and professionally, first with Ricci and then with the Jesuits that followed in his footsteps.

Of the missionaries, Niccolò Longobardo and Manuel Dias Jr., both signatories to the introductory text on the globe, and perhaps Giulio Aleni, worked on the globe project. Longobardo, a Sicilian Jesuit who arrived in China in 1597, is best known today for building a church in the Guangdong city of Shaozhou, reputedly the oldest Catholic Church in China.[48] He also published a number of books on religion, but beyond his work on the globe, he only produced one other scientific work: *Dizhen jie* 地震解

(Treatise on earthquakes, 1626). He arrived in Beijing in 1609 and succeeded Ricci as superior-general of the China mission in 1610 following Ricci's death. As Li had done within the Wanli court, Longobardo petitioned Rome to dispatch books to create libraries and train Jesuit recruits to teach mathematics and astronomy. The pope thereupon sent Giacomo Rho, Johann Adam Schall von Bell, and Johann Terrenz (1576–1630), all subsequently vital to calendar reform and intellectual exchange.[49] Longobardo also resided in the dwelling Ricci had acquired in 1605 and succeeded in gaining the support of Li and Xu. In 1617, Longobardo and Francesco Sambiasi (1582–1649), forced to leave Beijing in order to avoid the persecution of Christians, sheltered in the house of Yang Tingyun in Hangzhou. It was not until 1623 that Longobardo returned to Beijing.

Manuel Dias Jr. was a Portuguese Jesuit who arrived in Macao in 1605 and in 1611 reached Shaozhou, as did Ricci and Longobardo before him. He entered Beijing in 1621, living first in Xu's home.[50] Together with Longobardo, he was persuaded to serve at the Ministry of War around the year 1623, which may well have provided the context for producing the globe under discussion.[51] Later, in 1627, with Yang's support, he founded a church with which he continued his missionary work throughout China until his death. Besides his work on the globe, Dias Jr.'s *Tianwen lüe* 天問略 (Outline and questions about heaven), commonly known by its Latin title *Explicatio sphaerae coelestis* and first published in 1615 (Xu, Li, and Yang all appear listed as proofreaders for the text),[52] did not present mathematical astronomy but the latest in European descriptive cosmology.[53] This was the first Jesuit text devoted exclusively to the exposition of European astronomical theories and to the latest discoveries, including those of the Pisan mathematician and astronomer Galileo Galilei (1564–1642), whose *Siderius nuncius* (Sidereal, or starry, messenger) had been published in 1610.

A third possible collaborator is not mentioned on the globe itself. Giulio Aleni was an Italian Jesuit who arrived in Macao in 1609 and around 1614 reached Beijing, where he met Xu Guangqi. Aleni, with Yang Tingyun, set out for Hangzhou after Grand Secretary Shen Que's Christian persecution of 1616.[54] In 1625 Aleni became the first Jesuit to enter Fuzhou, and from 1641 to 1648, he served as vice-provincial of Jesuit missions in southern China.[55] Best known among Aleni's thirty-some works on varying topics, including biographies of both Matteo Ricci and Yang Tingyun, is the *Zhifang waiji*.[56] Two Jesuits in Beijing, Diego de Pantoja (1571–1618) and Sabatino de Ursis (1575–1620), began the later book project, as Wang Yongjie explains in chapter 3, to explain a set of maps.[57] After Pantoja's death in 1618, Aleni expanded and completed the explanation in a collaboration with Yang Tingyun while Li wrote one of the prefaces. The exposition was printed as five chapters in 1623 in Hangzhou and was therefore produced during the exact same period as the BL terrestrial globe.[58]

Aleni also printed a single-sheet *Wanguo quantu* 萬國全圖 (Complete map of all countries), of which a Qing-era copy with added color survives in Milan's Braidense Library (figure 2.8). The composition visually combines, on a single sheet, the text block above along with two maps that are also in the *Zhifang waiji*. The title of the text, "Wanguo tu xiaoyin" 萬國圖小引 (Brief introduction to the map of all countries), appears at the top right, diagonally opposite the prominent signature: "Aleni from the western seas" as well as his seal and the Jesuits' IHS (monogram for the name Jesus in ancient Greek) seal, both carved. The text begins by declaring the "King of creation made the twelve heavens," then recounts the world's physical properties. Inside the neat line of the world map below is the title of the map in four characters arrayed prominently in the four corners while the strikingly colored map fills the rest of the space. Below the world map is the double map of the Northern and Southern Hemispheres, with diagrams explaining solar eclipses and lunar occultations in the margins. This design creates an effective overall layout in a single-sheet format that is visually more compelling than the maps' alternative context, as embedded in the *Zhifang waiji*'s larger, more in-depth, textual discussion of the world (figure 2.9).

Both formats present the main world map in an oval projection with a simple grid similar to Ortelius's world map. The minimal textual information on the map proper includes labels for the five known continents of Asia, Europe, Libya (Africa), America, and Magellanica, as well as for oceans, several countries, Chinese provinces, mountains, and major rivers. These maps effectively convey in two dimensions the two principles of the earth as a terraqueous sphere. Aleni's collaboration on this project with Yang and Li is similar to the collaboration of Yang, Li, Xu, Dias, and Longobardo on the terrestrial globe in that both projects heavily relied on the mobility of Jesuits and their scholar-official friends between Beijing and the city of Hangzhou. The overall composition of the BL globe, moreover, combines elements from the *Zhifang waiji* (printed in Hangzhou in 1623), as well as texts taken from large-format collaborative maps such as the *Kunyu wanguo quantu,* as another act in forging a new mode of mapping the world. Thus, in the early 1620s, Jesuit "Western Confucians" and Chinese scholar-official Christian converts came together, after a period of persecution, and produced at least two important acts of mapping between Beijing and Hangzhou—one of them a geographical treatise with maps, the other a globe.

Within late Ming contact zones, the Jesuits, Christian scholars expert in various scientific and mathematical disciplines, introduced elite Confucian intellectuals to European scientific, mathematical, and geographical knowledge. Certain ideas, such as the Ptolemaic geocentric cosmos or—soon to follow—the geoheliocentric construct of Tycho Brahe, each fundamentally presupposing the earth to be a terraqueous sphere,

FIGURE 2.8.

(*Opposite page*) The *Wanguo quantu*. Stand-alone Qing-era print with added color, signed Giulio Aleni, not dated. Approx. 115 × 60.5 cm. Ministry of Culture, Pinacoteca di Brera, Biblioteca Nazionale Braidense, Milan.

萬國圖小引

造物主化成十二重天而火氣水土四行從輕至重漸次相裹地在天之中形圓而德方永不遷移東西南北之名上下中外之分人昔從厥所居以定實則無往非中也地與天同一圓體度數相應故畫地必取規於天天有黃赤二道南北二極冬夏二至經緯之度各三百有六十地圖赤做此以成然地既形圖則畫之以氊最能像象惟是畫之平而回不免展為長形如劑柑皮而伸之者然天下萬方總分為五大州曰亞細亞曰歐邏巴曰利未亞曰墨瓦蠟泥加又此各州中分大小無算之國小圖不能盡其於上天不過逝其大約五耳億五州之大萬國之眾篤於上天不過逝其中之一點亦吾所居之邦又五州之一點也吾之所駐足又大邦之一點也今我比天地何如乎我比大地又大主又為何如乎則我正儗蟻中之一點而無處可覓我矣我之在天地蠢蠢甚微而一點云才焉 造物主所賦自能包括天地而明天地萬物之眞主所謂人身一小天地也信爾以此形軀之至小則何處可生倨傲之情以此靈心之至大則無可自棄自賤之理果知乎此則天地在目登徒然哉

西海艾儒略敬題

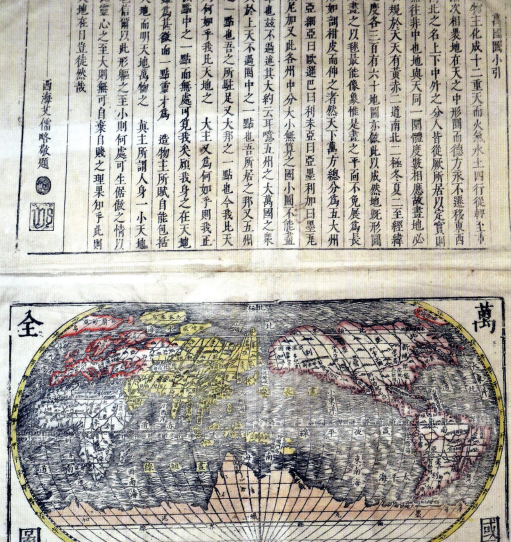

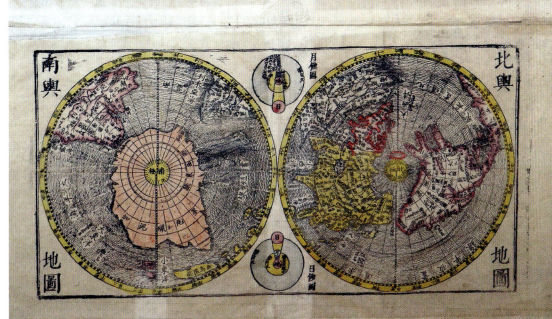

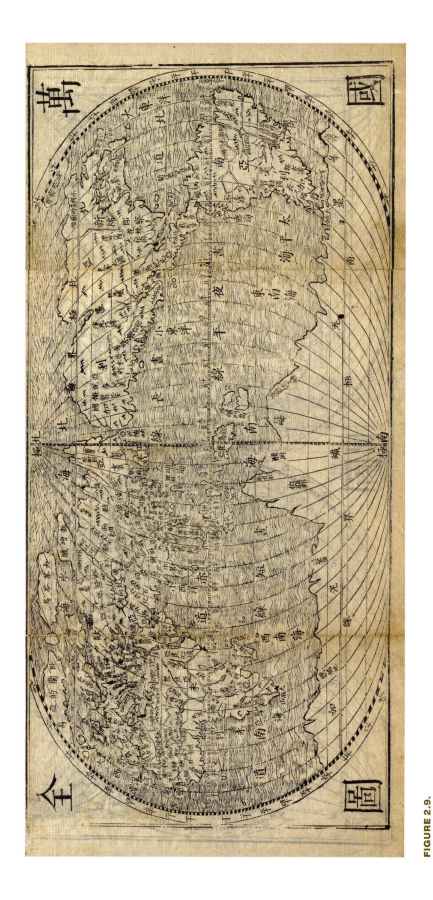

FIGURE 2.9.

The "Wanguo quantu" bound as a foldout sheet in the *Zhifang waiji* (1620s). Height of paper, approx. 26 cm. Naikaku Bunko, Tokyo.

presented ideas in distinct contrast to the traditional Chinese constructs of a "round heaven, square earth" (*tianyuan difang* 天圓地方) and "square earth, four seas" (*fangdi sihai* 方地四海").[59] Bound through their mutual pursuit of faith and knowledge, these actors were willing collaborators in promoting and publishing works on a range of terrestrial and celestial matters. For one moment, European Jesuits comingled ideas with Chinese scholar-official Christian converts passionate about exchanging knowledge and publications in collaboration with lacquer craftsmen in a complex exchange resulting in the fabrication of a lacquered terrestrial globe.

As already noted, Xu Guangqi states in his *Xinfa suanshu* that calendrical regulation required fabricating a wood-and-lacquer pair of globes, terrestrial and celestial. Although it does seem likely that Xu had the terrestrial BL globe in mind as perhaps the prototype and that its celestial mate was lost, if it was ever made at all, there is no evidence the BL globe was made as part of Xu's list. Although the date of in or around 1629 has been suggested for the globe's fabrication, the note to the reader signed by Dias Jr. and Longobardo in the BL globe is dated to 1623, providing a specific date without ambiguity.[60] It would be highly unusual for an object as costly and time-consuming to produce as the BL globe to have a fabrication date separate (later) from the date inscribed on the globe itself. Separately, the actual place of the BL globe's production is not recorded. It has been suggested here, given the importance of the mobility between Beijing and the Yangtze River delta for our list of collaborators, that it is likely that a wood-and-lacquer project as large and materially complex as a terrestrial globe would have involved expert know-how linked to the lacquer-making Hangzhou area.

Notes

1. For "contact zones" in China, see Zhang, *Making the New World Their Own*; Liu, *Harmonious Disagreement*.
2. On the 1602 printed version of the *Kunyu wanguo quantu*, this excerpt is included on the first scroll's (*far right*) introductory text, at the bottom of the seventh line from the right.
3. Needham and Wang, *Science and Civilisation* 3:372–376, cites *Yuanshi* (History of the Yuan), 48.10b.
4. Needham and Wang, *Science and Civilisation* 3:374.
5. Ibid.
6. The globe's provenance begins about 1938 when the son of a Parisian antiques dealer discovered it in Beijing. Sir Percival David, on viewing its photograph while visiting Paris, immediately ordered the globe, which reached his home in Henley just after the outbreak of World War II (Wallis and Grinstead, "Chinese Terrestrial Globe," 90). It was gifted to the British Museum in 1961 and transferred to the BL upon its creation in 1973.
7. The globe's condition (some crazing and minor losses to the lacquer) is surprisingly good given its age.

8. Stevenson, *Terrestrial and Celestial Globes* 1:8, 26, 33.
9. Van der Krogt, *Old Globes in the Netherlands,* 18.
10. Ibid., 19.
11. Ibid., 20–21.
12. One variant core, a "Papier-mache ball, of very light construction," is in the Hispanic Society of America Collection (Stevenson, *Terrestrial and Celestial Globes* 2:55). The description for another instructs: "To make the sphere, a round wooden stick is used serving as the axis of the globe. Then a great number of felt-like segments are nailed to the ends of the axis. A great number of these moistened segments are layered on top of each other and modelled into a firm ball. On this ball a layer of plaster is cast; the plaster is scoured till it forms a perfect sphere." Van der Krogt, *Old Globes in the Netherlands,* 7.
13. MC16373. The MacLean Collection also has the celestial globe mate of 1636 (MC35337).
14. The MacLean Collection also has a partial set of twenty (from twenty-four) original gores (MC22645).
15. The MacLean Collection commissioned two stands in 2011 for the restored terrestrial and celestial globes (acquired in 2000).
16. For the Latin, see Van der Krogt, *Old Globes in the Netherlands,* 132–133.
17. For the Latin transcription and translation, see Stevenson, *Terrestrial and Celestial Globes* 2:89–90. Claudius Ptolemy's (ca. 100–170) *Geography* is the first to cite the Fortunata Islands as the prime meridian.
18. A series of scientific tests on the BL globe to glimpse the wooden block configuration—or other sort of support system—hidden within the core would prove fascinating.
19. Zhu, *Zhongguo qiqi quanji.*
20. Ibid., 1.
21. Chan, "Yang Hsüan."
22. In Cao et al., *Zhongguo gudai ditu ji: Qingdai,* 1, 24. For the original, see Schall von Bell et al., *Huntian yishuo,* 5.21b–23a.
23. This would also imply a celestial globe of wood and lacquer of similar vintage (Xu, *Xinfa suanshu,* 1.24ab).
24. Cao et al., *Zhongguo gudai ditu ji: Qingdai,* entry 2–3. A similar globe in the Palace Museum (Gu141917) in Beijing, likely the same globe, measures seventy centimeters in diameter and has a different *zitan* wood mount. See Rawski and Rawson, *China, the Three Emperors,* entry 153.
25. Another globe on an ornate floor stand appears in the *Huangchao liqi tushi* 皇朝禮器圖式 (Illustrations of imperial ritual paraphernalia) of 1766. Chapter 3, "Scientific Instruments" (*Yiqi* 義器) includes entry 37, which is titled "Imperially Made Globe Apparatus" (*Yuzhi diqiu yi* 御製地球儀) with explanatory text and a drawing. Its circumference is forty-five *cun* (for a diameter of some forty-eight centimeters, smaller than the present globe). Perhaps the text mentions this globe elsewhere. In addition, their mounts are very different. Cao et al., *Zhongguo gudai ditu ji: Qingdai,* 1, 24.
26. Cao et al., *Zhongguo gudai ditu ji: Qingdai,* 1, 24.
27. Blair and Robertson, *Philippine Islands,* 11:45. The official record reads: "Antonio Lopez declares that Father Fray Juan Cobo showed the king of Japan the kingdoms of our king on a globe. He gave

this to the king, with the names of kingdoms written in Chinese characters, with the distances between them. The occasion for this arose, because when the king of Japan read the letter written from this country, he saw so many kingdoms, whereupon he asked to have them pointed out to him in detail, with their size and the distances between them." This reference to the globe is itself open to considerable interpretation, as it includes nothing of its physical characteristics or place of origin. It could have been a Chinese-made globe manufactured in Manila in a manner similar to the Selden map or perhaps a European-made globe annotated in Chinese characters prior to its presentation to Hideyoshi.

28. Known as the Jōkyō calendar after the Jōkyō reign period (1684–1688), it ended the previous reliance on Chinese-made calendars. Miyajima, "Japanese Celestial Cartography," 588–592.
29. Unno, "Cartography in Japan," 391, color plate 24.
30. For all forty inscriptions and a list of all toponyms on the globe, see Cao et al., "Xiancun zuizao zai Zhongguo zhizuo de yijia diqiu yi."
31. New Guinea was discovered and mapped by Luis Vaez de Torres in 1606. The globe calls it "Little Java" (Wallis and Grinstead, "Chinese Terrestrial Globe," 88–89). Additional comparisons to various geographical details have been noted elsewhere (ibid., 86–89).
32. This alternation of long and short columns, common in calligraphy on the folding fan format in East Asia, allows the top row of characters and the bottom row of characters on the fan to be uniform in size. As the fan—or, in this case, globe—tapers toward the bottom, the surface area decreases, making descending uniform lines of characters impossible. The ratio of three-to-one generally permits a full but not crowded presentation of the text body.
33. Peterson, "Why Did They Become Christians."
34. Ibid., 132.
35. Liu, *Harmonious Disagreement,* 172–174.
36. Ibid., 178.
37. Ibid., 191.
38. Ibid., 133.
39. Ibid., 142.
40. Peterson, "Why Did They Become Christians," 138.
41. Yang, "Hsü Kuang-ch'i."
42. Liu, *Harmonious Disagreement,* 155.
43. Ibid., 150; Peterson, "Why Did They Become Christians," 137.
44. Only with the translation by English Protestant missionary Alexander Wylie (1815–1887) and the Chinese mathematician Li Shanlan 李善蘭 (1811–1882), published in 1857, did the last nine books join the first six. Athanasius Kircher (1602–1680) immortalized the relationship between Ricci and Xu through a well-known illustrated plate depicting the two in his 1667 *China Illustrata*.
45. This appeared reprinted many times under varying titles, such as *Xiyang xinfa lishu* 西洋新法曆書 (Calendar book of new methods from the western ocean). The *Siku quanshu* 四庫全書 (Complete library of the four treasuries) employs the latter title. Yang, "Hsü Kuang-ch'i," 319; Yang, "Li T'ien-fu."
46. Liu, *Harmonious Disagreement,* 178–179.
47. Ibid., 185.

48. Goodrich, "Longobardo, Nicolo."
49. Ibid., 986.
50. Goodrich, "Dias, Manuel."
51. Leitão, "Contents and Context," 99–103.
52. Goodrich, "Dias, Manuel," 415.
53. The locus classicus of the book's Chinese title, *Tianwen lüe*, originated from *Tianwen*, the Chu poetry anthology by poet Qu Yuan 屈原 (ca. 340–278 BCE). Whereas Qu Yuan believed in nine spheres of heaven, Dias introduced twelve divisions. Following Ricci's method of explaining Christian concepts in terms familiar to the Chinese and taking into consideration their familiarity with the nine spheres of heaven, Dias repackaged and promoted the unfamiliar astronomy and religion by placing God in the twelfth division, called the Mountain of Paradise, and thus in a visual and symbolic way strengthening the Chinese reader's knowledge of God and paradise. Dias's fifteen other works relate to religious topics.
54. Goodrich, "Aleni, Giulio."
55. Ibid., 4.
56. Aleni dictated both Matteo Ricci's biography, *Daxi Xitai Li xiansheng xingji* 大西西泰利先生行蹟 (Biography of Mr. Xitai Li from the great West, published in 1630) and Yang Tingyun's biography *Yang Qiyuan xiansheng chaoxing shiji* 楊淇園先生超性事蹟 (Supernatural biography of Mr. Yang Qiyuan, 1627–1644).
57. Cheng Fangyi has suggested that two decades earlier, Jesuits Diego de Pantoja and Sabatino de Ursis created pictorial versions of Ricci's world map for the Wanli emperor, seeking thereby to impress the emperor and so save the China mission (following prior Jesuit expulsions from court). Cheng, "Pleasing the Emperor," 42–43.
58. Chapter 3 in this volume explores the genesis and printed editions of the *Zhifang waiji* in detail.
59. These two concepts, describing the earth as both a sphere and terraqueous (multiple land masses surrounded by multiple bodies of water), particularly challenged Chinese notions of a flat earth consisting of a single large square continent surrounded by four oceans, as captured in the traditional "round heaven square earth" and "square earth four seas" constructs (Yee, "Taking the World's Measure," 117–124; Zhang, *Making the New World Their Own*, 355–360).
60. Cao Wanru, He Shaogeng, and Frances Wood suggest 1629 as a possible date of creation. Cao et al., "Xiancun zuizao zai Zhongguo zhizuo de yijia diqiu yi," 117.

References

Aleni, Giulio (Ai Rulüe 艾儒略), and Yang Tingyun 楊廷筠. *Zhifang waiji* 職方外紀. Annotated edition as *Zhifang waiji jiaoshi* 職方外紀校釋, by Xie Fang 謝方. Beijing: Zhonghua shuju, 2000.

Blair, Emma Helen, and James Alexander Robertson, eds. *The Philippine Islands, 1493–1898*. Vol. 11, *1599–1602*. Cleveland: Arthur H. Clark, 1904.

Cao Wanru 曹婉如, He Shaogeng 何紹庚, and Wu Fangsi 吳芳思 (Frances Wood). "Xiancun zuizao zai Zhongguo zhizuo de yijia diqiu yi" 現存最早在中國製作的一架地球儀. In Cao Wanru et al., *Zhongguo gudai ditu ji: Mingdai*, 117–121.

Cao Wanru 曹婉如, Zheng Xihuang 鄭錫煌, Huang Shengzhang 黃盛璋, Niu Zhongxun 鈕仲勳, Ren Jincheng 任金城, Qin Guojing 秦國經, and Hu Bangbo 胡邦波, eds. *Zhongguo gudai ditu ji: Mingdai* 中國古代地圖集:明代. Beijing: Wenwu chubanshe, 1994.

Cao Wanru 曹婉如, Zheng Xihuang 鄭錫煌, Huang Shengzhang 黃盛璋, Niu Zhongxun 鈕仲勳, Ren Jincheng 任金城, Qin Guojing 秦國經, and Wang Qianjin 汪前進, eds. *Zhongguo gudai ditu ji: Qingdai* 中國古代地圖集:清代. Beijing: Wenwu chubanshe, 1997.

Chan, Albert. "The Scientific Writings of Giulio Aleni and Their Context." In *"Scholar from the West": Giulio Aleni S.J. (1582–1649) and the Dialogue between Christianity and China,* edited by Tiziana Lippiello and Roman Malek, 455–478. Brescia: Fondazione Civiltà Bresciana; Sankt Augustin: Monumenta Serica Institute, 1997.

Chan, Hok-lam. "Yang Hsüan." In Goodrich and Fang, *Dictionary of Ming Biography,* 1508–1510.

Cheng, Fangyi. "Pleasing the Emperor: Revisiting the Figured Chinese Manuscript of Matteo Ricci's Maps." *Journal of Jesuit Studies* 6, no. 1 (2019): 31–43.

Goodrich, L. Carrington. "Aleni, Giulio." In Goodrich and Fang, *Dictionary of Ming Biography,* 2–6.

———. "Dias, Manuel." In Goodrich and Fang, *Dictionary of Ming Biography,* 414–416.

———. "Longobardo, Nicolo." In Goodrich and Fang, *Dictionary of Ming Biography,* 985–989.

Goodrich, L. Carrington, and Chaoying Fang, eds. *Dictionary of Ming Biography, 1368–1644.* New York: Columbia University Press, 1976.

Harley, J. B., and David Woodward, eds. *The History of Cartography.* Vol. 2, bk. 2, *Cartography in the Traditional East and Southeast Asian Societies.* Chicago: University of Chicago Press, 1994.

Hummel, Arthur W., ed. *Eminent Chinese of the Ch'ing Period (1644–1912).* Washington, DC: U.S. Government Printing Office, 1943.

Leitão, Henrique. "The Contents and Context of Manuel Dias's *Tianwenlüe.*" In *The Jesuits, the Padroado and East Asian Science (1552–1773),* edited by Luís Saraiva and Catherine Jami, 99–121. Singapore: World Scientific, 2008.

Liu, Yu. *Harmonious Disagreement: Matteo Ricci and His Closest Chinese Friends.* New York: Peter Lang, 2015.

Luk, Bernard Hung-kay. "A Study of Giulio Aleni's 'Chih-Fang Wai Chi' 職方外紀." *Bulletin of the School of Oriental and African Studies, University of London* 40, no. 1 (1977): 58–84.

Miyajima, Kazuhiko. "Japanese Celestial Cartography before the Meiji Period." In Harley and Woodward, *History of Cartography,* vol. 2, bk. 2, 579–603.

Needham, Joseph, and Ling Wang. *Science and Civilisation in China.* Vol. 3, *Mathematics and the Sciences of the Heavens and the Earth.* Cambridge: Cambridge University Press, 1959.

Peterson, Willard J. "Why Did They Become Christians? Yang T'ing-Yün, Li Chih-Tsao, and Hsü Kuang-Ch'i." In *East Meets West: The Jesuits in China, 1582–1773,* edited by Charles E. Ronan and Bonnie B. C. Oh, 129–152. Chicago: Loyola University Press, 1988.

Rawski, Evelyn Sakakida, and Jessica Rawson. *China, the Three Emperors, 1662–1795.* London: Royal Academy of Arts, 2005.

Schall von Bell, Adam (Tang Ruowang 湯若望), Giacomo Rho (Luo Yagu 羅雅谷), and Li Tianjing 李天經. *Huntian yishuo* 渾天儀說. 1636. ark:/12148/btv1b9002837q.

Standaert, Nicolas, ed. *Handbook of Christianity in China.* Vol. 1, *635–1800.* Leiden: Brill, 2001.

Stevenson, Edward Luther. *Terrestrial and Celestial Globes: Their History and Construction, Including a Consideration of Their Value in the Study of Geography and Astronomy.* New Haven, CT: Yale University Press, 1921.

Unno, Kazutaka. "Cartography in Japan." In Harley and Woodward, *History of Cartography,* vol. 2, bk. 2, 346–477.

Van der Krogt, Peter. *Old Globes in the Netherlands.* Utrecht: H&S, 1984.

Wallis, Helen M., and E. D. Grinstead. "A Chinese Terrestrial Globe, A.D. 1623." *British Museum Quarterly* 25, no. 3/4 (1962): 83–91.

Xu Guangqi 徐光啟. *Xinfa suanshu* 新法算書. Jingyin Wenyuange Siku quanshu 景印文淵閣四庫全書. Taipei: Taiwan shangwu yinshuguan, 1983.

Yang, J. C. "Hsü Kuang-ch'i." In Hummel, *Eminent Chinese,* 316–319.

———. "Li T'ien-fu." In Hummel, *Eminent Chinese,* 488–489.

Yee, Cordell D. K. "Taking the World's Measure: Chinese Maps between Observation and Text." In Harley and Woodward, *History of Cartography,* vol. 2, bk. 2, 96–127.

Zhang, Qiong. *Making the New World Their Own: Chinese Encounters with Jesuit Science in the Age of Discovery.* Leiden: Brill, 2015.

Zhu Jiajin 朱家濳. *Zhongguo qiqi quanji: Mingdai* 中國漆器全集:明代. Fuzhou: Fujian meishu chubanshe, 1995.

3

Explaining European Geography

The Zhifang waiji *and Its Editions*

WANG YONGJIE

The *Zhifang waiji* 職方外紀 (Record of everything beyond the administration) is a Chinese book of geography describing the five continents of Asia, Europe, Libya (Africa), America, and the antipodal southern continent known as Magellanica, as well as the world's oceans, based mainly on European works of geography. Edited collaboratively by the Italian Jesuit missionary Giulio Aleni (1582–1649) and the Chinese scholar-official Yang Tingyun 楊廷筠 (1557–1627), it was the first work systematically introducing European world geography to late Ming audiences. Due to the book's frequent reprinting, it enjoyed far wider dissemination and reading than large maps such as the *Kunyu wanguo quantu* 坤輿萬國全圖 (Complete map of all countries on earth, 1602; figure 1.1). Modern scholars have discussed its publication process, its various versions, its source materials, and other matters. Among them, the annotated edition by Xie Fang 謝方 makes full use of Chinese materials for comparison and annotation, especially concerning the sections covering Southeast Asia and the Indian Ocean region, for which Chinese sources are abundant.[1] In contrast, the Italian scholar Paolo De Troia set out to analyze its European source materials, and his annotated Italian translation is particularly detailed on the sections describing Europe, Africa, and America.[2] This chapter will build on their scholarship to discuss the book's source materials, its production processes, and the printed editions widely available to Ming readers.

The Origins of the Project

In one of the book's prefaces, titled "Preface for the Engraving of *Zhifang waiji*," Li Zhizao 李之藻 (1565–1630) begins by recounting Matteo Ricci's (1552–1610) presentation of an atlas in a European language to the emperor as a gift in 1601, along with a world map mounted on a screen. The European atlas has been identified as Abraham Ortelius's (1527–1598) *Theatrum orbis terrarum* (Display of the lands of the globe).³ Aleni confirms this in his own preface to the *Zhifang waiji*. As a result, scholars often assume that the source material for this work of geography must have been the atlas Ricci presented to the emperor, an idea that found further confirmation in a catalogue entry written more than a century later for the eighteenth-century imperial collection known as the *Siku quanshu* 四庫全書 (Complete library of the four treasuries), which included the *Zhifang waiji:* "The preface of Aleni records that Ricci presented the *Wanguo tuzhi*, then Pantoja [Diego Pantoja (1571–1618)] was ordered to translate it, and finally Aleni himself supplemented and finished it. This book is mainly a revised edition of Ricci's and Pantoja's old versions, not a work completely written by Aleni."⁴ In this excerpt, scholars have often found confirmation that the *Zhifang waiji* was based on a translation of Ortelius's atlas, referred to here as *Wanguo tuzhi* 萬國圖志 (Maps and treatises on all countries), and some even argue it was a supplement for the *Kunyu wanguo quantu*.⁵

Other elements, however, seem to contradict this thesis. Notes in one Ming edition concerning the book's authorship claim it was "translated and annotated by Giulio Aleni of the Western Ocean and written by Yang Tingyun of the Eastern Ocean."⁶ A close translation of Aleni's own preface, moreover, yields further detail of the production process prior to Aleni and Yang's editorial collaboration:

> In the reign of Shenzong [the Wanli emperor, r. 1572–1620] . . . my friend Ricci presented the *Wanguo tuzhi* to the emperor and by the order of the emperor my friend Pantoja translated maps carved in Europe into a geographical treatise according to what he saw and heard . . . but it was not printed and distributed. In the reign of the present emperor . . . I, Aleni . . . accidentally saw the early translation of Pantoja, then went through the draft of world geography compiled by myself and carried from the West, and supplemented it with Pantoja's work. In this way, I compiled the book and called it *Zhifang waiji*. . . . I dedicate this book to my companions, who traveled through the world and shared their knowledge.⁷

Aleni here illustrates that the text of *Zhifang waiji* depended partially on Pantoja's manuscript of the translation of unspecified "European maps" supplemented with a "draft of world geography which was compiled by me" and with information from Jesuit companions.⁸

Several copies of the printed book now housed in the Biblioteca Apostolica Vaticana, the National Library of China, and the Naikaku Bunko (as well as various Japanese manuscript copies) include two memorials to the throne written in 1612 by Pantoja and Sabatino de Ursis (1575–1620). These documents record the translation and annotation of certain European maps that had reached the court from Fujian Province and Pantoja and de Ursis's request to consult a European atlas that the missionaries had previously presented to the emperor.⁹ We can deduce from this statement that Pantoja and de Ursis requested to examine the copy of Ortelius's *Theatrum orbis terrarum* that Ricci had presented in order to make sense, and to produce an annotated translation, of a separate set of European maps that had reached the court. However, the same document clearly indicates that their request was unsuccessful. If this holds true, then neither Pantoja's annotated description nor the *Zhifang waiji* (based partly on Pantoja's work) referred to Ortelius's atlas.

Thus, the process of creating the *Zhifang waiji* most likely began not from Ortelius's atlas but from a set of European maps from Fujian Province presented to the court, which the emperor then ordered Pantoja and others to translate. In another preface, Li Zhizao elaborates:

> The Min *shuidang* 閩稅璫 [the eunuch tax collector in Fujian] presented two maps which are in European characters and gotten from a ship. At that time, Ricci had passed away and two friends, Pantoja and de Ursis, were staying in Beijing and began to translate them by the emperor's order. . . . They also made eight screen panels to write down hearsay, customs, and products of each area, detailed and in standard handwriting. I went there to fill an official position in the 42nd year of Wanli [1614], so I was lucky to see it.¹⁰

In addition, one of the two memorials of Pantoja and de Ursis records:

> On the 2nd day of the 9th month of the 40th year of Wanli [1612], a eunuch close to the emperor, Pang Cheng 龐成, who is in charge of the clock in the Forbidden City's observatory, came with others by the emperor's decree to send two printed European maps titled *Wanguo dihai quantu* 萬國地海全圖 (Complete map of all countries, lands, and seas) and ordered us [Pantoja and de Ursis] to check the details of the maps.¹¹

From this, we can further reconstruct that the maps arrived from Fujian Province between 1610 and 1612 and that Pantoja and de Ursis translated and annotated the maps onto screens for presentation to the throne between 1612 and 1614. If their translation was indeed the basis for the *Zhifang waiji*, it is important to note that these initiatives dated from the period following Ricci's death.

Further investigation of this link with the eunuch tax collector in Fujian is possible through a close reading of the local records from Fujian collected in Zhang Xie's 張 燮 (1574–1640) *Dongxiyang kao* 東西洋考 (Study on the eastern and western oceans) printed around 1618. This work includes the "Records of the Eunuch Tax Collector" for the period from 1599 to 1614. At first, Gao Cai 高寀 was the eunuch officer for shipping taxes and mining in Fujian until his removal from that post in 1615. According to "Tax Records" elsewhere in the same work, during Gao Cai's residence in Fujian "the shipping tax was collected by the eunuch officer himself." He not only collected taxes in currency but also solicited gifts. This position allowed Gao Cai to control and tax the two largest ports in the province. In 1604, moreover, the Dutch, operating from neighboring Taiwan, bribed Gao Cai and offered him a series of gifts, after which he wrote a memorial to the throne arguing that the Dutch should be allowed to trade at Fujian's ports.[12] Gao Cai must have been the official, therefore, who procured the two maps from a ship in Fujian and presented them to the Wanli emperor.

In addition, some European sources record the arrival of European maps from Fujian Province and Pantoja's translation work at the court in Beijing. According to the 1612 annual report of the Jesuits in China, the eunuch sent to Fujian to collect taxes got his hands on two maps in Latin and printed in Europe.[13] The report states, further, that these maps, probably carried from Manila, depicted Europe and the Americas. The eunuch presented the maps to the emperor, who then ordered the Qintianjian 欽天監 (Bureau of Astronomy) to explain and annotate them. When they found they could not, they turned to Pantoja. Pantoja, whom the bureau had consulted before, annotated the two maps and drew maps of Asia and Africa in the same manner (based possibly on European atlases in the Jesuit library at Beijing).[14] This was the context of Pantoja's request to consult Ortelius's *Theatrum orbis terrarum* (presented to the throne by Ricci) in order to improve his annotations,[15] although, as noted above, he never received authorization to do so.

All these sources demonstrate that the *Zhifang waiji* project originated not from the Ortelius atlas Ricci presented to the throne but from two European printed maps the eunuch Gao Cai presented to the emperor in 1612. The emperor then ordered Pantoja and de Ursis to translate and annotate these maps and to add depictions of Asia and Africa. While the work remained unprinted, Li Zhizao notes that it "circulated as handwritten copies between scholars in Beijing."[16] After both men passed away (Pantoja in 1618, de Ursis in 1620), the manuscript reached Hangzhou, possibly in the hands of Aleni, where it was edited, augmented, and finally printed (figures 3.1 and 3.2). Around the same time and within the same network, a Chinese-language terrestrial globe was produced, as discussed by Richard A. Pegg in chapter 2 of this volume (figures 2.1 and 2.2).

The Production and Printing Process

According to the two prefaces to the *Zhifang waiji* by Aleni and Li Zhizao, Aleni supplemented the manuscript work of Pantoja and de Ursis with a "draft world geography . . . compiled by me and carried from the West" and information from Jesuit companions.[17] From 1621 to 1624, Giulio Aleni stayed in several cities in the lower Yangtze River region, spending considerable time at Yang Tingyun's house in Hangzhou. In the summer of 1623, Aleni worked with Yang Tingyun to annotate Pantoja's manuscript (it went to print by autumn).[18] In 1623, Li Zhizao was transferred to Nanjing but soon dismissed, after which he returned home to Hangzhou, where he lived until 1629. Thus, in 1623 this collaborative work was carved and printed for the first time in Hangzhou in five chapters with the title *Zhifang waiji*.[19] Several years later, when Li Zhizao printed the collection *Tianxue chuhan* 天學初函 (First collection on heavenly learning; before 1630), he also included the *Zhifang waiji*, again in five chapters and even using the same woodblocks.[20]

Hangzhou was then an important center for Jesuit missionaries, having become a refuge from the Nanjing persecution (1616–1617) under the protection of Yang Tingyun and Li Zhizao. Other missionaries living in Hangzhou from 1620 to 1623 included Manuel Dias Jr. (1574–1659), Nicolas Trigault (1577–1628), and Francisco Furtado (1587–1653).[21] As a result, Hangzhou also became a publication center for works initiated by Jesuits. According to a study by Wang Shen, between 1583 and 1753, missionaries in China turned out more than 243 books in Chinese, at least 53 of them printed in Hangzhou, with forty Chinese scholars recorded as cocompilers, thirty-eight as authors of prefaces, and twelve as sponsors.[22] Among them, Yang Tingyun and Li Zhizao were the most important.

Fuzhou, the capital of Fujian Province, was another important center for the missionaries, especially for Aleni, who lived there during the last twenty-five years of his life. In 1624, former grand secretary and Fuzhou native Ye Xianggao 葉向高 (1559–1627), retired from his post and passing through Hangzhou en route to Fujian Province, invited Aleni to accompany him.[23] This helps explain the reprinting of the *Zhifang waiji* in Fujian. In the preface to this reprint, Ye Xianggao notes: "This book was printed in Zhejiang province, and the people of Fujian asked for it, so Aleni re-printed it."[24] The reprint included an important adjustment: the contents dealing with the southern continent Magellanica (Mowalanijia 墨瓦臘泥加) now occupied a separate sixth chapter. Due to the centrality and importance of these two Ming-era printing sites (Hangzhou and Fuzhou), the *Zhifang waiji* enjoyed wide circulation. The Hangzhou edition was included in the eighteenth-century imperial collection *Siku quanshu* and later recarved and included in collectanea.[25] Various Japanese handwritten copies also exist, most based on the six-chapter Fuzhou edition. Its printing and dissemination over several centuries throughout East Asia had a significant impact on readers in late imperial China as well as in Japan and Korea.

Since the five-chapter Hangzhou edition and the six-chapter Fuzhou edition each broadly reflects the production process of the *Zhifang waiji*, scholars generally divide all surviving Ming-printed editions into one Hangzhou and one Fuzhou edition.[26] However, a close study of a wide range of surviving copies, both printed and manuscript, adds significantly greater complexity to this framing. An analysis of eleven original copies of Ming-era prints, four electronic scans on library portals, three modern photocopies, editions included in Qing-era collectanea, and a series of Japanese manuscripts has enabled the reconstruction of a full genealogy explicating the relationships among all these prints and manuscripts (figure 3.3; table 3.1).[27]

FIGURE 3.1.

The "Yaxiya tu" 亞細亞圖 (Map of Asia), bound as a foldout sheet in the *Zhifang waiji* (1620s). Height of paper, approx. 26 cm. Naikaku Bunko, Tokyo.

FIGURE 3.2.

The "Nanbei Yamolijia tu" 南北亞墨利加圖 (Map of North and South America), bound as a foldout sheet in the *Zhifang waiji*. Height of paper, approx. 26 cm. Naikaku Bunko, Tokyo.

Table 3.1. Nomenclature of Ming prints and select Japanese manuscripts

ABBREVIATION	LIBRARY	CALL NUMBER	TITLE ON COVER	PRINT OR MANUSCRIPT	REPRODUCTION/SCAN
A.	Biblioteca Ambrosiana, Milan	S. Q. V. VIII 15/3	*Zhifang waiji*	Print	
B.	Beijing Normal University Library	善6926	*Zhifang waiji*	Print	
C.	Library of Congress	B686 A25	*Zhifang waiji*	Print	hdl.loc.gov/loc.asian/lcnclscd.2012402472
F.	Bibliothèque nationale de France	Chinois 1519–1520	*Fengzhi fanyi, Zhifang waiji*	Print	ark:/12148/btv1b90060999 ark:/12148/btv1b9006100h
I.19	Archivum Romanum Societatis Iesu	Jap. Sin. II 19	*(Feng)zhi fanyi, Zhifang waiji*	Print	
I.20	Archivum Romanum Societatis Iesu	Jap. Sin. II 20	No cover	Print	
N.14114	National Library of China	14114	*Zhifang waiji*	Print	*Zhonghua zaizao shanben*, Beijing tushuguan chubanshe, 2009
N.15551	National Library of China	15551	*Zhifang waiji*	Print	
N.5200	National Library of China	5200	No cover	Print	
N.T4528	National Library of China	T4528	No cover	Print	
Nai.	Naikaku Bunko, National Archives of Japan	292-0171	*Zhifang waiji*	Print	www.digital.archives.go.jp/img/3668962
NK.	Previously in University of Nanking Library, then Rome, now in Taiwan		No cover	Print	Xuesheng shuju, 1965
O.	Bodleian Library, University of Oxford	Sinica 977	*Zhifang waiji*	Print	
P.	Peking University Library	SB/980.4/4426	*Zhifang waiji*	Print	
P. ms.	Peking University Library	LSB/534	*Zhifang waiji*	Manuscript	

Table 3.1. Nomenclature of Ming prints and select Japanese manuscripts (continued)

ABBREVIATION	LIBRARY	CALL NUMBER	TITLE ON COVER	PRINT OR MANUSCRIPT	REPRODUCTION/SCAN
R.	Biblioteca Nazionale Centrale di Roma	72. C. 494	Zhifang waiji	Print	De Troia (2009)
T.	Tōyō Bunko	V-5-A-28-0	Zhifang waiji	Print	
VB.	Biblioteca Apostolica Vaticana	Borgia Cinese, 512, 1°-2°	Zhifang waiji	Print	
W.	Waseda University Library	文庫08 C0488	Zhifang waiji	Print	www.wul.waseda.ac.jp/kotenseki/html/bunko08/bunko08_c0488
W.B0138	Waseda University Library	文庫08 B0138	Zhifang waiji	Manuscript	www.wul.waseda.ac.jp/kotenseki/html/bunko08/bunko08_b0138
W.B0139	Waseda University Library	文庫08 B0139	Zhifang waiji	Manuscript	www.wul.waseda.ac.jp/kotenseki/html/bunko08/bunko08_b0139
W.C0489	Waseda University Library	文庫08 C0489	Zhifang waiji	Manuscript	www.wul.waseda.ac.jp/kotenseki/html/bunko08/bunko08_c0489
W.01068	Waseda University Library	ル02 01068	Zhifang waiji	Manuscript	www.wul.waseda.ac.jp/kotenseki/html/ru02/ru02_01068
Unknown	Unknown	Unknown	No cover	Print	Five-chapter edition, in Ye (2011)

Note: Each copy is named according to the library collecting it; if a library contains multiple collections, they are distinguished by their call numbers.

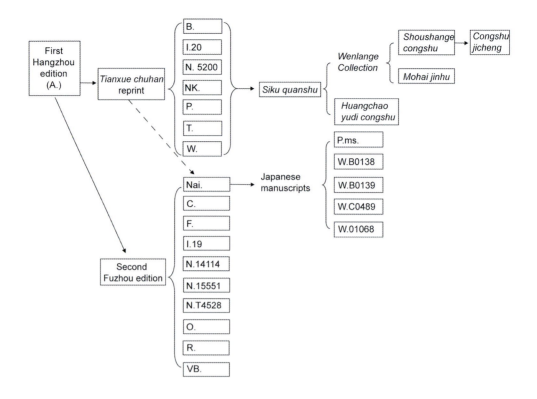

FIGURE 3.3.

Genealogy of extant print and manuscript copies of the *Zhifang waiji*. For an explanation of the abbreviations, see table 3.1.

A Genealogy of Ming-Era Editions

The genealogy shown in figure 3.3 confirms the *Zhifang waiji* was divided into a Hangzhou and a Fuzhou edition, according to their structuring into five and six chapters, respectively, and reflects Aleni and Ye's move from Hangzhou to Fuzhou. In general, we can also observe the primary itineraries of each: the Hangzhou edition went on to circulate through later Qing collectanea, whereas the Fuzhou edition circulated in Japan. At the same time, within each edition important differences exist. To ascertain the precise relationships among these versions, we must analyze them in greater detail.

The covers of the various prints bear two different titles. Most copies display the title *Zhifang waiji* on the cover, but the two six-chapter Fuzhou copies in the Bibliothèque nationale de France and at the Archivum Romanum Societatis Iesu have a more elaborate title: *Fengzhi fanyi Zhifang waiji* 奉旨翻譯職方外紀 (Record of everything beyond the administration as translated by the emperor's order), referring directly to the Wanli emperor's order to Pantoja and de Ursis to translate European maps (figure 3.4). Despite the title these two copies lack the two missionaries' memorials reporting the translation of European maps for the emperor.

The totality of known versions of the book, print and manuscript alike, includes prefaces to the *Zhifang waiji* written by a total of nine men, but the quantities and combinations of those prefaces vary from version to version (see table 3.2). All extant prints contain the prefaces of the two authors, Yang Tingyun and Aleni, and that of the Hangzhou sponsor Li Zhizao. Only the print at Beijing Normal University Library is missing Li Zhizao's preface (probably lost at a later stage). The prefaces of Qu Shigu 瞿式穀, Xu Xuchen 許胥臣, and Xiong Shiqi 熊士旂 appear in most prints of both the Hangzhou and Fuzhou editions. All prints of the six-chapter Fuzhou edition also include Ye Xianggao's preface.[28] The two memorials of Pantoja and de Ursis are in only a few of the prints (but in all manuscripts) of the six-chapter Fuzhou edition.

FIGURE 3.4.

Cover pages of the *Zhifang waiji* held at Waseda University Library (*left*) and the Bibliothèque nationale de France (*right*), gallica.bnf.fr. The latter carries the alternative title *Fengzhi fanyi Zhifang waiji* (Record of everything beyond the administration as translated by the emperor's order).

Table 3.2. Prefaces of the *Zhifang waiji*

AUTHOR	TITLE	COPIES INCLUDING IT
Giulio Aleni 艾儒略	"Zhifang waiji zixu" 職方外紀自序	All
Yang Tingyun 楊廷筠	"Zhifang waiji xu" 職方外紀序	All
Li Zhizao 李之藻	"Ke Zhifang waiji xu" 刻職方外紀序	All except B.
Ye Xianggao 葉向高	"Zhifang waiji xu" 職方外紀序	C., F., I.19, N.14114, N.15551, N.T4528, Nai., O., P.ms., R., W.01068, WB.0138, WB.0139, WC.0489
Qu Shigu 瞿式谷	"Zhifang waiji xiaoyan" 職方外紀小言	A., F., I.19, N.14114, N.15551, N.T4528, Nai., NK., O., P.ms., R., W., W.01068, WB.0138, WB.0139, WC.0489
Xu Xuchen 許胥臣	"Zhifang waiji xiaoyan" 職方外紀小言	A., F., I.19, N.14114, N.15551, N.T4528, Nai., NK., O., P.ms., R., W., W.01068, WB.0138, WC.0489
Xiong Shiqi 熊士旂	"Ba" 跋	A., N.5200, I.19, N.14114, N.T4528, Nai., P.ms., R., W.01068, WB.0138, WB.0139, WC.0489
Li Zhizao 李之藻	"Ke Tianxue chuhan tici" 刻天學初函題辭	Nai.
Lü Tunan 呂圖南	"Du Taixi zhushu xu" 讀泰西諸書叙	Nai.
Diego Pantoja 龐迪我	"Zoushu" 奏疏	N.15551, VB., Nai., P.ms., W.01068, WB.0138, WB.0139, WC.0489
Diego Pantoja 龐迪我, Sabatino de Ursis 熊三拔	"Zoushu" 奏疏	N.15551, VB., Nai., P.ms., W.01068, WB.0138, WB.0139, WC.0489

Note: The abbreviations for each copy follow table 3.1.

Moreover, among the copies I could personally consult, only three of the five-chapter Hangzhou editions have exactly the same prefaces in the same order.[29] None of the other copies are completely identical with regard to the prefaces and their order. Comparing the prefaces of the Hangzhou and Fuzhou editions shows that the texts of the prefaces and postscripts are essentially identical, with only minor differences among them. For example, in Li Zhizao's preface the "two maps" the eunuch tax collector in

Fujian allegedly presented became "four maps" in all consulted five-chapter prints. As noted above, the two memorials of Pantoja and de Ursis and the annual report of the Jesuits only mention "two maps," so the six-chapter edition's record of two maps is correct.

The contents and arrangement of the five-chapter Hangzhou and the six-chapter Fuzhou editions are essentially the same. The main change, as mentioned above, is that the Fuzhou edition spins the last section of chapter 4 in the five-chapter Hangzhou edition ("Mowalanijia zongshuo" 墨瓦蠟尼加總說 [General description of Magellanica]), together with Wang Yiqi's 王一錡 "Shu Mowalanijia hou" 書墨瓦蠟泥加後 (Postscript on Magellanica) into a fifth chapter. In consequence, the former fifth chapter, "Sihai zongshuo" 四海總說 (General description of the four seas) became the sixth.[30] The five- and six-chapter editions differ, therefore, not so much in their content as in their structural arrangement into chapters. Moreover, each chapter in the Fuzhou edition adds a column at the beginning articulating the roles of Aleni and Yang: "Translated and expanded by Ai Rulüe 艾儒略 [i.e., Aleni] of the Western Ocean, Collected and recorded by Yang Tingyun of the Eastern Ocean (figure 3.6)." This note, following the usual practices of Chinese bookmaking, states clearly the authorship of the text, which is less obvious in the five-chapter Hangzhou edition that omits such statements of authorship. On the other hand, the latter includes printed circles and dots accentuating key phrases for readers, whereas the red circles and dots on some pages of Fuzhou edition copies are later handwritten additions.

Moving beyond the differences in paratext between the editions, the content of the texts themselves also bears discrepancies—for example, in the section on Judea (Rudeya 如德亞). All extant *Tianxue chuhan* reprints (using the blocks of the Hangzhou edition) note interlineally under the section title of Judea: "The ancient name [of Judea] is Fulin 拂菻 (Forūm, Byzantium), or Daqin 大秦 (the Roman Empire). In the reign of Zhenguan 貞觀 (627–650) during the Tang dynasty, people came from there and presented Nestorian scriptures and images/statues. A Nestorian tablet survives, which confirms this."

The "tablet" is the famous Nestorian stele, dated between 635 and 781 and rediscovered around Xi'an 西安 in 1623, the year *Zhifang waiji* was first printed. Although news of the discovery spread quickly among the Jesuits and Chinese Christians, Li Zhizao would have had no time to include the news from Xi'an in the 1623 print. The Biblioteca Ambrosiana copy of *Zhifang waiji* is the only known original print from Hangzhou, but it unfortunately does not preserve the first part of the book, including the section on Judea. In *Tianxue chuhan*, however, Li Zhizao contextualized the tablet in an addendum to Aleni's book *Xixue fan* 西學凡 (Summary of Western learning) titled "Du jingjiao bei shu hou" 讀景教碑書後 (After reading the Nestorian stele, 1625). Li Zhizao, as the main sponsor of the *Tianxue chuhan* in 1625–1630, must have had the note carved on the original Hangzhou printing blocks. The fact that this note on Judea is also missing from the later Fuzhou edition substantiates this thesis (figure 3.5).[31]

Despite these differences in content, all extant copies are basically identical in layout, even when comparing the Hangzhou and Fuzhou editions. Each chapter and preface has the same folio numbers (even when the ordering of the prefaces differs, Chinese books number the pages for each preface and chapter separately), and each folio has basically the same content and typesetting (nine columns per half folio, nineteen characters per column). Not even the insertions described above alter the overall layout. The insertion of signatures at the beginning of each chapter in the six-chapter Fuzhou edition also did not change the overall typesetting of that folio: the first column,

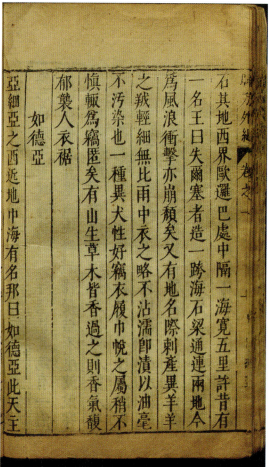

FIGURE 3.5.

In the five-chapter Hangzhou edition of the *Zhifang waiji* kept at Waseda University Library (*left*), the smaller characters under the name "Judea" (*second column from the left*) give additional information. These two rows are missing from the six-chapter Fuzhou edition kept at the Library of Congress (*right*).

 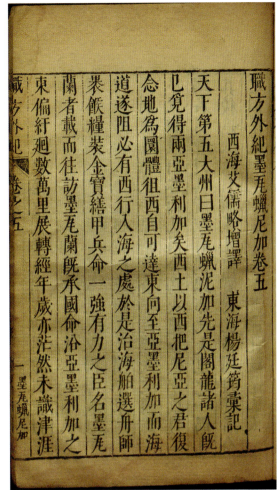

FIGURE 3.6.

The first page of chapter 5 "General Statement on the Four Seas" in the five-chapter Hangzhou edition of the *Zhifang waiji* kept at the Waseda University Library (*left*) and the same page in the six-chapter Fuzhou edition kept at the U.S. Library of Congress (*right*). To keep the same layout while adding the signature to the beginning of each chapter (*in the second column from the right*), the six-chapter edition simply merged the number and title of each chapter. The fishtails are visible at the far left of each page.

stating the chapter number, and the second column, stating the chapter title, of the five-chapter Hangzhou edition merge into the first column for the Fuzhou edition, enabling the author to be named in the second column (figure 3.6). This means that while having the blocks for their edition carved in Fuzhou, Aleni and his collaborators deliberately imitated the original print of the Hangzhou edition closely.

All extant prints of both editions bear single-sided sidelines on all four margins and a blank center strip. The main difference between the two editions is the so-called fishtail, a symbol consisting of one or two triangles in the center strip to align the folio in bookbinding, printable either with just the outlines or in solid black. On every print within each edition, the fishtails are identical, but between the two the design of the fishtails differs. The Naikaku Bunko print presents yet another type: the preface by Li Zhizao has no fishtail, while the preface by Lü Tunan 呂圖南 has black fishtails (in the style of the Hangzhou *Tianxue chuhan* edition in five chapters), although all other pages of this copy have the same fishtails as in the six-chapter Fuzhou edition. Further, all extant copies within each edition have the same characters and even share similar small gaps and defects on the folio sidelines (figures 3.7 and 3.8).

As this close comparison of layout illustrates, all five-chapter copies and all six-chapter copies were printed from the same blocks. This means that all extant five-chapter copies used the printing blocks that Li Zhizao had made in Hangzhou, while all six-chapter prints used the printing blocks that Aleni and his collaborators had made in Fuzhou. However, as the number and the order of the prefaces differ in most prints, even within the same edition, the actual printing of each copy probably occurred at different times. In other words, the main variation between different copies of the same edition is the addition or subtraction of prefaces and their order. For example, the three copies of the five-chapter Hangzhou version mentioned above, with the identical number and ordering of prefaces, were probably printed and bound at the same time. However, even these three versions differ in the number of maps.[32] This means no two extant prints of the *Zhifang waiji* are identical.

Repeated printings at different times entail replacing or repairing printing blocks. Minor differences between prints of the same edition corroborate this. Further, comparing each collection by print quality reveals—to some extent—the order of their printing. The quality of paper in the six-chapter Naikaku Bunko copy is comparatively good, its characters' edges sharply printed, so it is probably an earlier print. The copies in the Library of Congress and the Bibliothèque nationale de France, on the other hand, have heavy ink marks and poor printing quality, so their printing probably occurred later, after repeat printings had worn down the printing blocks.

Therefore, we may summarize the general division of editions discussed thus far as follows: first came the Hangzhou five-chapter edition under the sponsorship of Li Zhizao, which he later included in his collection *Tianxue chuhan*. The Fuzhou edition followed—with Ye Xianggao's preface—in six chapters. However, two prints extant today, one held by the Naikaku Bunko and one by the Bodleian Library, include elements from both editions, suggesting further creation and distribution practices of the *Zhifang waiji*.

The Naikaku Bunko copy contains six chapters, including Ye Xianggao's preface, and thus shares most characteristics with the six-chapter Fuzhou edition, but its first two prefaces appear only in the *Tianxue chuhan* (one preface even refers to the

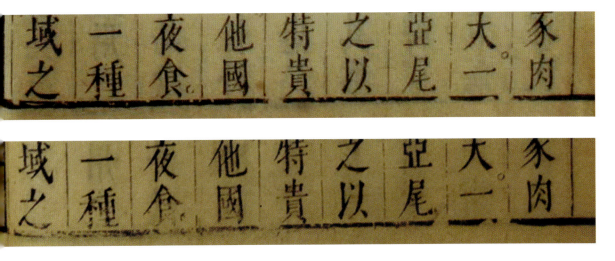

FIGURE 3.7.

Similar gaps in the printed sidelines in different copies of the five-chapter Hangzhou edition of the *Zhifang waiji*. Waseda University Library, Tokyo (*top*) and Veneranda Biblioteca Ambrosiana, Milan (*bottom*).

FIGURE 3.8.

Similar defects in the printed sideline in different copies of the six-chapter Fuzhou edition of the *Zhifang waiji*. U.S. Library of Congress (*left*) and National Library of China (*right*).

collection by name).³³ Moreover, the back side of the front cover bears the title *Tianxue chuhan* in large printed characters while the title page also includes a list of books in this collection. Two books on the list are in no other extant print of the *Tianxue chuhan*, but the list demarks them as "to be carved later" (*si ke* 嗣刻),³⁴ indicating this is the title page of an earlier edition of the *Tianxue chuhan*, prior to the collections' completion. Since one of the prefaces in the Naikaku Bunko copy dates to the eighth month of 1626,³⁵ its printing must have occurred after that date but before Li Zhizao's death in 1630.

There are two possible explanations for the creation process behind the Naikaku Bunko copy. Aleni, Li Zhizao, Yang Tingyun, and Ye Xianggao had an opportunity to discuss the carving and printing of *Zhifang waiji* and *Tianxue chuhan* in Hangzhou in 1624. Thus, when Aleni and Ye Xianggao produced the Fuzhou edition and Li Zhizao had the *Tianxue chuhan* carved, they might have helped one another, with the Naikaku Bunko copy resulting from their cooperation. Another possibility is that someone not originally involved in the process mistakenly combined the prefaces of the *Tianxue chuhan* with the six-chapter Fuzhou edition, producing the Naikaku Bunko copy.³⁶ In other words, the Naikaku Bunko copy shows that the early forms of both the *Tianxue chuhan* reprint and the Fuzhou editions coexisted, as well as that the two editions have a complicated relationship we will only understand fully when further evidence emerges.

The collection of Alexander Wylie's (1815–1887) books at the Bodleian Library in Oxford holds another mixed copy made up of three different parts. Wylie took it to England and sold it to the University of Oxford in 1881 or 1882. It contains six prefaces, including Ye Xianggao's. These prefaces, as well as some of the printing details in the first chapter, identify these parts as originating from a six-chapter Fuzhou edition. Chapter 2 and the final folios of chapters 1 and 5 are handwritten, while chapters 3 to 5 are consistent with the five-chapter Hangzhou edition.³⁷ Perhaps this mixed copy was bound before Wylie bought it in China (it is possible that in the late nineteenth century, it was difficult to obtain a complete Ming-era edition). Wylie's copy also shows us that although the five-chapter *Siku quanshu* edition was available from the mid-eighteenth century onward, the six-chapter Fuzhou edition still circulated.

From a detailed analysis of the textual content and format of the Ming-era copies, we see that the printing of the five-chapter Hangzhou edition and that of the six-chapter Fuzhou edition involved two separate sets of printing blocks. The differences in prefaces and in the printing quality of each copy printed from the same blocks clearly show that the *Zhifang waiji* underwent many printings and therefore enjoyed a wide circulation. Moreover, the fact that Aleni lived in both cities and took part in both printing processes—ever in touch with Li Zhizao and Yang Tingyun in Hangzhou—explains the clearly close relationship in format between the different editions and their many extant printed copies and manuscript versions.

As charted in this chapter, the *Zhifang waiji* first originated from a project by Pantoja, Aleni, Yang Tingyun, and their collaborators to translate and annotate European maps presented to the emperor by a eunuch tax collector from Fujian. In Beijing in 1612, Pantoja and de Ursis started the project and generated a manuscript, which Aleni then took over and carried to Hangzhou, where he supplemented it with his collaborator Yang Tingyun. This project's first printing took place in 1623. Li Zhizao in Hangzhou supervised the carving and printing of both the first edition and its reprint in the *Tianxue chuhan*. Aleni and Ye Xianggao later led the publication of a six-chapter edition in Fuzhou, carved from different printing blocks. Save for a section on Magellanica set aside in its own chapter, the note on Judea, and the inclusion of the preface of Ye Xianggao in the six-chapter edition, the two editions are identical in their textual contents and in their arrangements of such contents. While the format of every chapter is the same within each of the two editions, numerous notable differences (regarding the cover page and the prefaces) clearly demonstrate that the book was printed many times with the same printing blocks.

These multiple printings of both editions signify a wide distribution of the *Zhifang waiji*. The five-chapter Hangzhou edition became well known during the Qing due to book collectors and scholars in Jiangsu and Zhejiang, so it was later included in the *Siku quanshu* imperial library.[38] The many Japanese handwritten copies evidently relied upon the six-chapter format printed in Fuzhou (probably due to Fujian Province having been a center for trade between China and Japan in the late Ming and early Qing periods). In Korea, the five-chapter Hangzhou edition became popular, as elaborated by Soh Jeanhyoung in chapter 8. The book's differing impacts in China, Korea, and Japan to some extent reflects the diversity in their attitudes toward the incoming worldview. When European and American imperial ambitions, powered by the Industrial Revolution, targeted China in the nineteenth century, Chinese intellectuals and officials took renewed interest in the *Zhifang waiji*, and the book once again became a resource for scholars seeking to understand the wider world.[39]

Notes

Wang Yongjie would like to thank Prof. Chen Cunfu of Zhejiang University, Dr. Pier Francesco Fumagalli of the Biblioteca Ambrosiana, and Prof. Paolo De Troia of Sapienza Università di Roma for their help with historical materials and Prof. Zou Zhenhuan of Fudan University, Dr. Chen Huaiyu of Arizona State University, Prof. Hsu Kuang-Tai of National Tsing Hua University, Prof. Gong Yingyan of Ningbo University, and Dr. Lin Hong of Shanghai Normal University for their valuable comments.

1. Xie, *Zhifang waiji jiaoshi*.
2. De Troia, *Giulio Aleni*.
3. Ricci writes the name of this atlas as *Theatrum orbis* in his Italian memoirs (1608–1610) and *Orbis theatrum Ortelij* in its published edition (1615) by Nicolas Trigault. Trigault, *De Christiana expeditione*, 443; D'Elia, *Fonti Ricciane*, 2.114; Huang, *Donghai xihai*, 224–228.

4. Ayusawa, "Shokuhō gaiki no genhon ni tsuite," 291–294.
5. Luk, "Study of Giulio Aleni's *Chih-fang wai chi*," 60, 77; Pfister, *Zaihua Yesu huishi,* 141; Chan, *Chinese Books and Documents,* 300; De Troia, "Zhongxi dili xue zhishi," 70.
6. This excerpt appears only in the Fuzhou six-chapter edition.
7. Aleni and Yang, *Zhifang waiji,* 1–2.
8. Giulio Aleni claimed that since the *Da Ming yitong zhi* 大明一統志 (Gazetteer of the unified Great Ming) recorded China and its tributary states, such as "Tartary" and Annam, he would write not about them but only about those countries "which are not recorded in geography works of China." In fact, some of the records in the book do refer to Chinese writings. Xie, "Ai Rulüe," 132–139; Xie, *Zhifang waiji jiaoshi,* Xie's preface, 1–11; Aleni and Yang, *Zhifang waiji,* 32–34.
9. The maps are usually referred to in the Chinese texts as *Wanguo quantu* 萬國全圖 or *Wanguo dihai quantu,* whereas the European atlas is referred to as *Wanguo tuzhi* or *Wanguo zhi* 萬國志. To the best of my knowledge, the two memorials to the throne do not occur in other Ming and Qing copies. Xie Fang found them only in the Japanese manuscript in the Peking University Library and argues that they should have been in the original printed edition but not in the *Tianxue chuhan.* Xie Fang included them in his annotated edition and pointed out that "the last paragraph seems to be not the words of Pantoja and de Ursis, but the comments of the first memorial." Xie, *Zhifang waiji jiaoshi,* 19n1.
10. Aleni and Yang, *Zhifang waiji,* 6. Matteo Ricci died on May 11, 1610 (Wanli 38). The statement that Li Zhizao "fill[ed] in the official position in the year Wanli 42" attests that "in the beginning of Wanli 42 (1614), Li Zhizao finished his mourning period and went to Beijing to join in the revision of the calendar." Gong and Ma, "Guanyu Li Zhizao shengping," 92.
11. Xie, *Zhifang waiji jiaoshi,* 17–18.
12. According to "Records of the Eunuch Tax Collector," Gao Cai was born in Wen'an 文安 County, Shuntian 順天 (now Wen'an County, Hebei Province). He served the emperor from childhood and was gradually promoted to assistant supervisor of the Imperial Horse Guard. In 1599 he was sent to Jingkou 京口 (now Zhenjiang, Jiangsu Province) to collect taxes and was also relocated to Fujian, where he lived until 1614. During his official term in Fujian, he grew corrupt. In 1614 the people rebelled because they believed he had committed murders, and he was called back to Beijing. When he refused, "The emperor was angry, gave an order to send him back to the capital under escort." "Records of the Eunuch Tax Collector" contains more detailed records on these events. Zhang, *Dongxiyang kao,* 134–135, 155–169.
13. Nicolo Longobardo (1559–1654), superior of the Jesuit China mission, wrote his annual report on February 20, 1613, in "Nanhium" (today's Nanxiong, Guangdong Province) and sent several copies (by different routes for security) to Europe. The Portuguese copy in the Archivum Romanum Societatis Iesu (ARSI; Jap-Sin, 113, ff. 215–264), the fourth copy, refers to the two maps in ff. 224v–226r. "Nanhium" is misspelled as "Namyung" by D'Elia (D'Elia, *Il mappamondo cinese,* 223–224n358). According to Paolo De Troia, the European atlas carried to China and used as a supplement by Aleni may be the *Moderne tavole di geografia* (Modern geographic atlas) of the Italian geographer Giovanni Antonio Magini (1555–1617). The *Catalogue of the Pei-T'ang Library* contains European books brought to China from the end of the Ming period. The catalogue lists Magini's 1598 Italian edition of *Moderne tavole di Geografia,* which still resides in the National Library

of China. In a letter dated January 28, 1611, addressed to Magini in Macao, Aleni said he came to China with two books of Magini, one being the "tavole." De Troia also found many similarities and connections between the two books. De Troia, "Zhongxi dili xue zhishi," 68, 74–75.

14. The map of Asia is referred to as *Zhongguo tu* 中國圖 (Map of China) and the map of Africa as *Xinan fangguo tu* 西南方國圖 (Map of countries to the southwest) in Pantoja and de Ursis's memorials to the Wanli emperor.

15. The 1612 Annual Report names this atlas as *Theatrum orbis,* exactly as in Ricci's manuscript memoirs.

16. Aleni and Yang, *Zhifang waiji,* 6.

17. Aleni and Yang, *Zhifang waiji,* 1–2, 7.

18. Yang's work apparently focused mainly on revising the Chinese text. Ibid., 1–2, 6–8.

19. This first print, long thought lost, is now identifiable as the print held by the Ambrosiana Library in Milan. Huang, *Donghai xihai,* 273–280; Wang, "Yidali Angbuluoxiu tushuguan," 74–77.

20. Regarding the date of the *Tianxue chuhan*'s printing, the 1965 facsimile edition published by Xuesheng shuju in Taipei presents two different opinions: Luo Guang's "Preface to the photocopy edition of *Tianxue chuhan*" (p. 1) points to 1628; Fang Hao's "Study on the Printing of *Tianxue chuhan* by Li Zhizao" (p. 2) to 1630. Xie Fang indicates it was prior to 1629. See Xie, *Zhifang waiji jiaoshi,* Xie's preface, 6.

21. Pan, *Xilai Kongzi Ai Rulüe,* 26–28.

22. Wang, "Mingmo Qingchu chuanjiao shi," 99, 102–103.

23. Ye's hometown was Fuqing 福清, a county subordinate to Fuzhou Prefecture. In his preface, Ye signed as "Ye Xianggao of Futang 福唐," the latter an old name for Fuqing.

24. On the twentieth day of the eleventh month (December 29, 1624), Ye Xianggao and Aleni "came by the same boat" to Fuzhou. Ye Xianggao died on the twenty-ninth day of the eighth month of 1627 (October 7, 1627). Louis Pfister, Xie Fang, and Erik Zürcher attributed the wrong dates to Aleni's arrival in Fujian, but since Aleni came to Fuzhou at the end of 1624, Xie Fang's date of 1625–1627 for the carving and printing of the Fujian edition is still more appropriate. Pfister, *Zaihua Yesu huishi,* 134; Xie, *Zhifang waiji jiaoshi,* Xie's preface, 1–11; Lin, "Ye Xianggao zhishi."

25. It was included in the *Mohai jinhu* 墨海金壺 by Zhang Haipeng 張海鵬 (1755–1816), the *Shoushange congshu* 守山閣叢書 by Qian Xizuo 錢熙祚 (1800–1844), and the *Huangchao fanshu yudi congshu* 皇朝藩屬輿地叢書 compiled by Mr. Pu 浦 during the Guangxu reign (1875–1908). The *Shoushange congshu* edition was later inserted into the *Congshu jicheng* 叢書集成 published by Shangwu yinshuguan.

26. Enoki, "Shokuhō gaiki no kanpon ni tsuite"; Xie, *Zhifang waiji jiaoshi,* Xie's preface, 1–11.

27. For the details, see Wang, "*Zhifang waiji* chengshu guocheng."

28. In his introduction to *Zhifang waiji jiaoshi* (p. 6), Xie Fang wrote: "Besides those prefaces of the original printed edition, the edition printed in Fujian added the preface of Ye Xianggao and put it ahead of all other prefaces." The copy of the Fujian edition used by Xie Fang is in the National Library of China, but according to my inquiry, all three copies of the six-volume edition in that library bear Ye Xianggao's preface after Yang Tingyun's; regarding copies at other libraries, only I.19, O., and R. bear Ye Xianggao's preface first.

29. These three copies include one from the former University of Nanking Library, one at Waseda University Library (文庫08 C0488), and a reproduction in *Ai Rulüe Hanwen zhushu quanji*.
30. The six-chapter edition confuses the character for *ni* 尼 in Mowalanijia with 泥 several times. This chapter quotes according to the original texts.
31. Some records give the date of the stele's unearthing as 1625, but Manuel Dias Jr. recorded the year as 1623 in a preface dated 1641 in a book about the stele itself published in 1644. The date 1625 from Li Zhizao's preface is only the year when he wrote the preface; perhaps some scholars misinterpreted this date. Xie, *Zhifang waiji jiaoshi*, Xie's preface, 5–7.
32. Of course, it remains possible that missing maps (e.g., in the Naikaku Bunko copy) are merely lost.
33. As only a few elements of the Naikaku Bunko copy (the cover page and the first two prefaces) belong to the five-chapter Hangzhou edition, Enoki Kazuo considers it a six-chapter Fuzhou edition (Enoki, "Shokuhō gaiki no kanpon ni tsuite").
34. The two books are *Qike* 七克 (Seven victories) and *Lingyan lishao* 靈言蠡勺 (*De anima*).
35. Lü Tunan's "Du Taixi zhushu xu."
36. Xie, "*Zhifang waiji* zai Ming Qing de liuchuan," 112. In addition, it seems the bookbinder made a mistake on this copy, as two pages are missing without any indications of damage or rebinding, suggesting the bookbinder simply skipped these two pages (folios 3 and 4 of chapter 5). All five Japanese manuscripts at Waseda University Library and Peking University Library have the same omissions, so their copyists must all have employed this Naikaku Bunko print.
37. We cannot be sure, however, whether chapters 3–5 belong to the original first-edition print or the *Tianxue chuhan* reprint, as the key indicators (the note on the Nestorian tablet and the postface of Xiong Shiqi) appear in other chapters.
38. Wu, *Siku caijin shumu*, 33, 120, 271; Xie, "*Zhifang waiji* zai Ming Qing de liuchuan," 111–116.
39. At that time, Wei Yuan's *Haiguo tuzhi* 海國圖志 (Illustrated record of the sea countries) and *'Dzam gling rgyas bshad* (World geography) in Tibetan quoted from and referred extensively to the *Zhifang waiji*. Xu and Chen, "*Haiguo tuzhi* yu *Zhifang waiji*," 65–69; Wei, "*Shijie guangshuo* yu *Zhifang waiji*," 297–316.

References

Aleni, Giulio (Ai Rulüe 艾儒略), and Yang Tingyun 楊廷筠. *Zhifang waiji* 職方外紀. Annotated edition as *Zhifang waiji jiaoshi* 職方外紀校釋, by Xie Fang 謝方. Beijing: Zhonghua shuju, 2000.

Ayusawa Shintarō 鮎澤信太郎. "Jurio Arēni no Shokuhō gaiki ni tsuite" 艾儒略の職方外紀に就いて. *Chikyū* 地球 23, no. 5 (1935): 244–256.

———. "Shokuhō gaiki no genhon ni tsuite: Shiko zensho zōmoku teiyō kaisetsu no ayamari wo tadasu" 職方外紀の原本に就いて：四庫全書總目提要解說の誤りを正す. *Rekishi chiri* 歷史地理 79, no. 4 (1937): 291–294.

Chan, Albert. *Chinese Books and Documents in the Jesuit Archives in Rome. A Descriptive Catalogue: Japonica-Sinica, I–IV*. New York: M. E. Sharpe, 2002.

D'Elia, Pasquale, ed. *Fonti Ricciane: Documenti originali concernenti Matteo Ricci e la storia delle prime relazioni tra l'Europa e la Cina (1579–1615)*. 3 vols. Rome: La Libreria dello Stato, 1942–1949.

———. *Il mappamondo cinese del P. Matteo Ricci, S.I.* Vatican City: Biblioteca Apostolica Vaticana, 1938.

De Troia, Paolo, trans. *Giulio Aleni. Geografia dei paesi stranieri alla Cina: Zhifang waiji* 職方外紀. Brescia: Fondazione Civiltà Bresciana, 2009.

———. "Zhongxi dili xue zhishi ji dili xue cihui de jiaoliu: Ai Rulüe *Zhifang waiji* de xifang yuanben" 中西地理學知識及地理學詞彙的交流：艾儒略《職方外紀》的西方原本. *Wakumon* 或問 67, no. 11 (2006): 67–75.

Enoki Kazuo 榎一雄. "Shokuhō gaiki no kanpon ni tsuite" 職方外紀の刊本について. In *Iwai hakase koki kinen tenseki ronshū* 岩井博士古稀記念典籍論集, 136–147. Tokyo: Tōyō bunko, 1963.

Gong Yingyan 龔纓晏, and Ma Qiong 馬瓊. "Guanyu Li Zhizao shengping de xin shiliao" 關於李之藻生平的新史料. *Zhejiang daxue xuebao (renwen shehui kexue ban)* 浙江大學學報 (人文社會科學版), no. 3 (2008): 89–97.

Huang Shijian 黃時鑑. *Donghai xihai: Dongxi wenhua jiaoliu shi (Dahanghai shidai yilai)* 東海西海：東西文化交流史 (大航海時代以來). Shanghai: Zhongxi shuju, 2011.

Huang Zhengqian 黃正謙. *Xixue dongjian zhi xuzhang—Mingmo Qingchu Yesu huishi xinlun* 西學東漸之序章——明末清初耶穌會史新論. Hong Kong: Zhonghua shuju, 2020.

Li Zhizao 李之藻. *Tianxue chuhan* 天學初函. Taipei: Xuesheng shuju, 1965.

Lin Jinshui 林金水. "Ye Xianggao zhishi yu Ai Rulüe rumin zhi yanjiu" 葉向高致仕與艾儒略入閩之研究. *Fujian shifan daxue xuebao (zhexue shehui kexue ban)* 福建師範大學學報 (哲學社會科學版), no. 2 (2015): 115–124, 170.

Luk, Bernard Hung-kay. "A Study of Giulio Aleni's *Chih-fang wai chi*." *Bulletin of the School of Oriental and African Studies* 40, no. 1 (1977): 58–84.

Pan Fengjuan 潘鳳娟. *Xilai Kongzi Ai Rulüe* 西來孔子艾儒略. Tianjin: Tianjin jiaoyu chubanshe, 2013.

Pfister, Aloys. *Zaihua Yesu huishi liezhuan ji shumu* 在華耶穌會士列傳及書目. Translated by Feng Chengjun 馮承均. Beijing: Zhonghua shuju, 1995.

Trigault, Nicolas. *De Christiana expeditione apud Sinas suscepta ab Societate Jesu. Ex. P. Matthaei Riccii eiusdem Societatis Commentarijs.* Cologne, 1617.

Wang Shen 王申. "Mingmo Qingchu chuanjiao shi zai Hangzhou kanke shuji huodong tanze" 明末清初傳教士在杭州刊刻書籍活動探賾. *Guji zhengli yanjiu xuekan* 古籍整理研究學刊, no. 3 (2016): 51, 99–103.

Wang Yongjie 王永傑. "Yidali Angbuluoxiu tushuguan cang *Zhifang waiji* yanjiu" 意大利昂布羅修圖書館藏《職方外紀》研究. *Waiguo wenti yanjiu* 外國問題研究, no. 3 (2018): 74–77.

———. "*Zhifang waiji* chengshu guocheng ji banben kao" 《職方外紀》成書過程及版本考. *Shilin* 史林, no. 3 (2018): 100–110.

Wei Yi 魏毅. "*Shijie guangshuo* yu *Zhifang waiji* wenben guanxi kao" 《世界廣說》與《職方外紀》文本關係考. *Lishi dili* 歷史地理 29 (2014): 297–316.

Wu Weizu 吳慰祖. *Siku caijin shumu* 四庫采進書目. Beijing: Shangwu yinshuguan, 1960.

Xie Fang 謝方. "Ai Rulüe jiqi *Zhifang waiji*" 艾儒略及其《職方外紀》. *Zhongguo guojia bowuguan guankan* 中國國家博物館館刊 15–16 (1991): 132–139.

———, ed. *Zhifang waiji jiaoshi* 職方外紀校釋. Beijing: Zhonghua shuju, 2000.

Xie Hui 謝輝. "*Zhifang waiji* zai Ming Qing de liuchuan yu yingxiang" 《職方外紀》在明清的流傳與影響. *Guangxi shehui kexue* 廣西社會科學, no. 5 (2016): 111–116.

Xu Xuya 許序雅, and Chen Xianghua 陳向華. "*Haiguo tuzhi* yu *Zhifang waiji* guanxi kaoshu" 《海國圖誌》與《職方外紀》關系考述. *Fujian luntan: Renwen shehui kexue ban* 福建論壇: 人文社會科學版, no. 7 (2004): 65–69.

Ye Nong 葉農, ed. *Ai Rulüe Hanwen zhushu quanji* 艾儒畧漢文著述全集. Guilin: Guangxi shifan daxue chubanshe, 2011.

Zhang Xie 張燮. *Dongxiyang kao* 東西洋考. Edited by Xie Fang 謝方. Beijing: Zhonghua shuju, 1981.

4

From the Wall onto the Screen

Reframing World Maps in East Asia

CHENG FANGYI

THE WORLD MAP SERIES INITIATED BY MATTEO RICCI (1552–1610) and his scholarly collaborators includes several artifacts produced in China. These include printed maps, like the *Kunyu wanguo quantu* 坤輿萬國全圖 (Complete map of all countries on earth, 1602; figure 1.1) and the *Liangyi xuanlan tu* 兩儀玄覽圖 (Mysterious visual map of the two forms, 1603; figure 1.2), as well as manuscripts (based on the former) such as the so-called figured manuscripts that included images of ships, animals, and monsters. Later replications produced in Japan, as discussed by Elke Papelitzky in chapter 6, and in Korea are also extant. As significant points of intersection in the history of encounters between western Europe and East Asia, these maps have attracted tremendous scholarly attention. Studies have focused on far-flung aspects of that history: the accuracy of the maps' geographical information, Chinese responses to the new geographical knowledge, and possible reasons why the maps did not displace Chinese mapping traditions. These last inquiries have particularly been concerned with whether these collaborative mapping methods were more "universal," "accurate," or "useful" than the traditional Chinese ones. Moreover, scholars' investigations into the impact of western European practices upon East Asian methods have taken early modern European world maps, tacitly, to be nearer their implicitly preconceived ideal cartography than their traditional Chinese counterparts. Matthew H. Edney, pointing out how modern culture only began to idealize cartography as "a modern myth" after 1800, admonishes us to reject "the entire ideal and all of its preconceptions."[1] Rather than beginning from such an idealized world map or the abovementioned world map series' geographical details, therefore, this chapter seeks to contextualize these world maps by analyzing the manners of displaying and viewing them.

By "reframing" the maps within East Asian mapping practices, this chapter first explores the adoption in China, Korea, and Japan of numerous mapping formats for the *Kunyu wanguo quantu* series.[2] "Format" here refers not only to maps' materiality but also to their modes of conveyance, such as various screens. The chapter then examines how multiple formats affected the content of the map series in their emphasis on and accumulation of texts and illustrative pictures. With the adoption of new formats for making world maps came new manners of displaying those maps. These modifications in format, contents, and manner of display relocated the *Kunyu wanguo quantu* series deeper within the context of East Asian mapping practices, enabling scholar-officials and social elites—whether in China, Korea, or Japan—to "appreciate" them more directly, greatly increasing the world maps' scope of distribution. These modifications, informed by East Asian mapping practices, gradually displaced these world maps' supposed "ideal" attributes over the course of the maps' dissemination. Even the maps' faithful copying and modeling became superfluous to later reproductions.

Format and Content

This section addresses the East Asian mapping convention's clear impact on the form of the *Kunyu wanguo quantu* world map series. Neither in Europe nor in Asia did mapping practices prior to 1800 match any idealized cartography. As Cordell D. K. Yee has noted, it is crucial that when considering Chinese maps, we take "a humanistic approach . . . in which the claims of value are recognized, in the hope of stimulating further investigation."[3] Scholarly discussions exploring possible connections between East Asia's mapping practices and other forms of art have not failed generally to compare the former with, for example, Chinese painting, calligraphy, and poetry. How, then, did East Asian mapping (or its sister disciplines) shape this collaborative, cross-cultural world map series, particularly with regard to format, including packaging, binding, and carriers?

In China, Matteo Ricci and his colleagues displayed in their residences at Zhaoqing and Beijing world maps printed in Europe. Recalling the map in Zhaoqing, Nicolas Trigault (1577–1628) wrote: "Hanging on the wall of the reception room in the Mission House there was a cosmographic chart of the universe, done with European lettering. The more learned among the Chinese admired it very much and, when they were told that it was both a view and description of the entire world, they became greatly interested in seeing the same thing done in Chinese."[4] As Li Zhizao 李之藻 (1565–1630), moreover, described in his preface to the *Zhifang waiji* 職方外紀 (Record of everything beyond the administration, 1623) upon first meeting Ricci (in Beijing in 1601): "There was a world map hanging on the wall, on which the lines drawn to show degrees were very clear."[5] These two records reveal that Ricci maintained the familiar European manner of displaying world maps hanging on walls while residing in China.

Scholars still debate which map Ricci displayed. Huang Shijian and Gong Yingyan claim that any map from an atlas, such as the world map from the *Theatrum orbis terrarum* (Display of the lands of the globe, first edition 1570), would be too small to display thus.⁶ In reality, however, the designs of many maps produced in Renaissance Europe, especially in Italy and the Low Countries, were often printed over several sheets of paper and then pasted together, specifically intended as wall displays. By the mid-sixteenth century, about fifteen hundred copies of wall maps approximately 200 × 300 cm in size were in existence, although only a few have survived—for example, the world maps of Giacomo Gastaldi (1500–ca. 1565; map, 1561, approximately 90 × 180 cm), Gerardus Mercator (1512–1594; map, 1569, 135 × 212 cm; figure 4.1), and Abraham Ortelius (1527–1598; map, 1569).⁷ These maps adorned the walls not only of European courts but also of courtiers, scholars, and merchants (figure 4.2).⁸

Following his first stop at Zhaoqing, Ricci began working with scholar-officials, drawing and printing world maps in Chinese. They had already produced several world maps prior to creating the *Kunyu wanguo quantu*, including the map produced in Zhaoqing in the 1580s and the map composed in Nanjing at the turn of the century (discussed by Nicolas Standaert in chapter 1). Those maps are no longer extant, save, as with many maps from imperial China, in significantly reduced woodblocks inside gazetteers, encyclopedias (*leishu* 類書), and geography books.⁹ Even though Guo Zizhang 郭子章 (1543–1618) considered the Nanjing map too large for a booklet version for his readers and so reduced its size further upon adapting it,¹⁰ Li Zhizao considered all the earlier world maps by Ricci and his Chinese collaborators to be of "small sizes without details" (*fuxiao weixi* 幅小未悉).¹¹ In his preface to the *Kunyu wanguo quantu*, Ricci mentions how Li Zhizao "dislikes the narrow and limited nature of the previous block-printed editions, which are not close to one tenth of the original maps from the West, and [he] plans to further expand and enlarge them."¹² Li Zhizao thus clearly wanted to make the maps as large as possible.¹³ From this we may first speculate that the maps Ricci hung on his wall should have been larger than the world map from the *Theatrum orbis terrarum*. How, then, to enlarge such a world map even further?

In Renaissance Europe, mapmakers assembling large wall maps would first print the different areas of maps onto several separate sheets of paper and then paste them together. The solution Li Zhizao gives is similar: print the 1602 *Kunyu wanguo quantu* (the most famous and copied print) onto six sheets of paper, forming a rectangle. To print each sheet, he used six woodblocks aligned together. Several later versions, such as the figured manuscripts, followed Li's model. Extant prints of the 1602 edition are all more or less the same size—approximately 168 × 374 cm—with each sheet measuring about 168 × 62 cm (table 4.1). The reasons for varying sizes may well have included occasional misaligned woodblocks for each sheet. The Biblioteca Vaticana Apostolica copy, while an original 1602 print, is larger than the other extant 1602 prints of the *Kunyu wanguo quantu*, possibly reflecting—in part—different measurement practices. The same is true for the *Kunyu wanguo quantu* in the Austrian National Library.¹⁴ The figured manuscripts are similar in height to the 1602 edition but vary in width due to differing numbers of constituent sheets. The manuscript held by the Nanjing

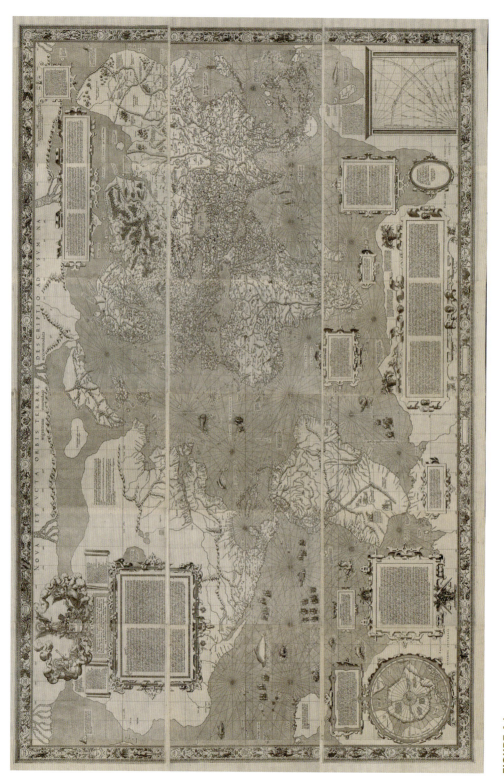

FIGURE 4.1.

Gerhard Cremers's (Gerardus Mercator) *Nova et aucta orbis terrae descriptio ad usum navigantium emendate accommodata* (New and more complete representation of the terrestrial globe properly adapted for use in navigation, 1569). 135 cm × 212 cm. Basel University Library.

FIGURE 4.2.

Johannes Vermeer's *Woman Reading a Letter* (ca. 1662–1663), featuring a large map on the wall in the background. 46.5 cm × 39 cm. Rijksmuseum Amsterdam.

Museum has a width of 380.2 cm across six pieces (figures 4.3 and 4.4), while those produced in Korea add panels, as explained below, and are thus wider: the Seoul University Museum manuscript measures 531 cm in width over eight pieces (figure 4.5), and the manuscript in the Kitamura Collection measures 530 cm in width across ten sheets. Later, in 1603, Ricci and Li Yingshi 李應試 (1559–1620?) produced another larger world map, the *Liangyi xuanlan tu*, at about 200 × 442 cm in size. Compared to the wall maps produced in Renaissance Europe (usually measuring about 200 × 300 cm),[15] Ricci's world maps ranged in size from as large as their European cousins to significantly larger.

Thus, the world maps made in Zhaoqing and Nanjing (prior to the 1602 Beijing print) were generally smaller in size—limiting their textual and pictorial content—and circulated only on a small scale. The 1602 print's larger size increased its capacity to accommodate textual descriptions, energizing in turn the textual emphasis of Chinese mapping practices.[16] Thus, in addition to toponyms labeling their namesakes on the map, there were also several interpretive texts providing geographical, celestial, calendrical, ethnological, or zoological information relevant to different places on the map. As Ricci explained in his preface, he and his collaborators had "added hundreds of country names and recorded their customs and local products in the empty area of the map."[17]

Table 4.1. Sizes of select prints and manuscripts of the *Kunyu wanguo quantu* and *Liangyi xuanlan tu* according to library catalogues and secondary literature

	HEIGHT × WIDTH IN CM (NUMBER OF PANELS)	SOURCE FOR MEASUREMENT/ COMMENT
Kunyu wanguo quantu, print, Miyagi Prefectural Library	167.9–169.0 × 374.4–377.4 (6)	Library catalogue
Kunyu wanguo quantu, print, Kyoto University Library	169 × 372 (6)	Library catalogue—measurements provided by the website are 214 cm × 408 cm (far larger than the other printed copy); website image of the map (alongside a ruler) shows its size is approximately 169 cm × 372 cm
Kunyu wanguo quantu, print, James Ford Bell Library	167.5 × 371.2 (6)	Library catalogue
Kunyu wanguo quantu, print, Biblioteca Vaticana Apostolica	183 × 396 (6)	Day (1995)
Kunyu wanguo quantu, print, Austrian National Library	165 × 365 (6)	Library catalogue
Kunyu wanguo quantu, figured manuscript, Nanjing Museum	168.7 × 380.2 (6)	Huang and Gong (2004), 147
Kunyu wanguo quantu, figured manuscript, Seoul University Museum	172 × 531 (8)	Seo (2019)
Kunyu wanguo quantu, figured manuscript, Kitamura Collection	172 × 530 (10)	Seo (2019)
Liangyi xuanlan tu, print, Liaoning Museum	200 × 442 (8)	Huang and Gong (2004), 156–157
Liangyi xuanlan tu, print, Korean Christian Museum of Soongsil University	198 × 444 (8)	Huang and Gong (2004), 156 Liaoning Provincial Museum and Korean prints of the *Liangyi xuanlan tu* may be the same size, as variances in the recorded dimensions may reflect differing measurement practices

FIGURE 4.3.

A so-called figured manuscript based on the 1602 *Kunyu wanguo quantu*. Images of animals, sea monsters, and ships feature prominently. 168.7 × 380.2 cm. Nanjing Museum. Photograph by Elke Papelitzky.

FIGURE 4.4.

Detail of figure 4.3, showing animals and a ship.

In *De christiana expeditione apud Sinas* (The Christian expedition among the Chinese), Trigault writes: "To complete this work, Father Matthew [Ricci] augmented it by adding other kingdoms, more places of note, and various observations. He also placed the sun and stars on the margins, with other decorations, in addition to descriptions of Christian customs and explanations of Christian belief. Several of the literati also ornamented this work [the world map] with elegantly written introductions."[18]

Ricci and his collaborators wanted to add further toponyms and other information to "perfect this work," necessitating a larger map with space sufficient for the additional text. Further, as with Chinese scroll paintings, they may have wanted to append various prefaces (*xu* 序/敘), postscripts (*ba* 跋), and dedications or colophons (*ti* 題; *shi* 識) to the world map, as Nicolas Standaert discusses in chapter 1 of this volume.

Five different individuals each contributed a preface or postscript to the 1602 *Kunyu wanguo quantu,* in addition to Ricci's three texts. Similarly, the later *Liangyi xuanlan tu* includes eleven pieces of writing in total. Later, at the Korean court, the artisans who created the figured manuscripts added panels to each side of the map for further colophons, perhaps believing the map proper already contained too much text. As a result, the figured manuscript at the Seoul University Museum covers eight sheets (figure 4.5), while ten constitute the Kitamura manuscript.

The map's increased size also rendered the world map to some extent a vector of Chinese art, enhancing the "pictorialism" of China's mapping practices, wherein mapmakers often added illustrative images (e.g., of buildings, people, mountains, and rivers) to the map.[19] The figured manuscripts of the *Kunyu wanguo quantu* and *Liangyi xuanlan tu* also reflect this approach. To the figured manuscript of the *Kunyu wanguo quantu* held by the Nanjing Museum (figures 4.3 and 4.4) and the Liaoning Museum's *Liangyi xuanlan tu,* the mapmakers introduced mountains painted in the manner of Chinese landscape art. Further, China's pictorialism had close contemporaneous analogues in Europe: land animals, especially from the Americas, marine creatures, human activities, and sailing ships all appeared on large European maps, such as Gerardus Mercator's multisheet maps (figure 4.1). The Chinese mapmakers adopted and adapted marine creatures, land animals, and vessels from European maps, a practice Francesco Sambiasi (1582–1649; figure 4.6), Ferdinand Verbiest (1623–1688; figure 5.1), and their respective collaborators perpetuated in their own later mapmaking.

The world maps' enlargement, by virtue of both the textualism and the pictorialism of Chinese mapping practices, undoubtedly shaped their textual and pictorial contents. The Jesuits' Chinese collaborators emphasized, and their readerships appreciated, the textual and pictorial details that corresponded with Chinese mapping methods, taking this series of world maps along a gradually divergent trajectory from their European Renaissance cousins. The mathematical aspect of the Jesuits' Renaissance-inspired mapping practices was often diminished, overlooked, and distorted via the world maps' copying and circulation, an effect in no way restricted to their content. The exhibitions and the websites of museums and libraries nowadays typically display the *Kunyu wanguo quantu* series as whole maps, like the world maps produced today. Did East Asian audiences consistently paste together the six, eight, or ten different sheets constituting each map, as contemporary Europeans did, or did some mount the sheets separately as hanging scrolls? Where and in what manner did they display the maps from this world map series?

Displaying and Viewing

Li Zhizao, in his preface to the 1602 *Kunyu wanguo quantu,* bemoans the "small sizes" and lack of details of its precursors and then describes how he "made six screen panels with people who had common interest with me."[20] This statement accords precisely

FIGURE 4.5.

Manuscript map based on the *Kunyu wanguo quantu* (figure 1.1) with two added side panels bearing adorning text as well as images of animals, sea monsters, and ships. Approx. 172 × 531 cm. Seoul National University Museum.

FIGURE 4.6.

A world map titled *Kunyu quantu* 坤輿全圖 (Complete map of the earth; ca. 1639), signed by Francesco Sambiasi. 72.5 × 108 cm. Sea monsters and ships feature prominently on the map. Ghent University Library.

with Ricci's remark in his own preface of producing "six big screen panels as a tool for spiritual travelling in one's study."[21] In his preface to *Zhifang waiji* some twenty years later, Li Zhizao recalled his experience working with Ricci on the world map, "engraved as screens of the *Wanguo tu* 萬國圖 (Map of all countries)."[22] This "Map of All Countries" screen was clearly the 1602 printed world map. It is therefore clear that both Li Zhizao and Matteo Ricci intended to make six-screen panels for the six pieces of the printed edition of *Kunyu wanguo quantu* in 1602. For what manner of screen, however, did they design their world maps?

Two key varieties of screens functioned as furniture in Ming (1368–1644) and Qing (1644–1911) China: the sitting screen (*zuoping* 座屏) and the surrounding

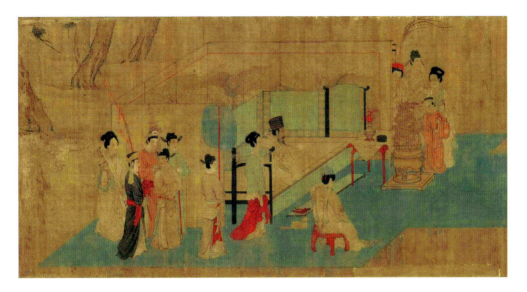

FIGURE 4.7.

A large *weiping* (surrounding screen) features in the left section of a Ming-era scroll painting once attributed to Zhou Wenju 周文矩 (917–975). 41.9 × 184.2 cm. Chicago Institute of Art.

screen (*weiping* 圍屏; figure 4.7).[23] The former consists of a pedestal with one, three, or five panels fixed or inserted. Most of the latter are coromandel screens: large folding screens with twelve leaves decorated using the "incised colors" (*kuancai* 款彩) technique. Apparently, the six panels of the *Kunyu wanguo quantu* could fit into six sitting screens (one panel apiece) or into two sitting screens of three panels each. This practice of setting multiple map sections into sitting screens was not uncommon during the Ming and the Qing. The twelve sections of a map titled *Jiubian tu* 九邊圖 (Map of the nine frontiers) produced in the sixteenth century, for example, occupied twelve sitting screens when discovered in the Imperial Palace at Shenyang in 1949.[24] Further, contemporary documents describe the *Liangyi xuanlan tu* held by the Liaoning Provincial Museum, found along with the *Jiubian tu* in 1949, similarly mounted on screens.[25] It seems likely, therefore, that the eight sheets of the *Liangyi xuanlan tu* were also mounted onto eight sitting screens when displayed in the Imperial Palace at Shenyang.

Interestingly, records of the discovery of the Nanjing Museum manuscript of the *Kunyu wanguo quantu* in Beijing in 1922 describe it as six *zhen* 幀, a term typically applied to paintings or works of calligraphy, not to screens. This use of *zhen* thus makes it clear that the panels were not on screens (the six pieces' precise manner of mounting remains unclear).[26] Meanwhile, the Qing-era manuscript *Kunyu wanguo quantu* in the Tōyō Bunko survives mounted as hanging scrolls (it is possible to roll up the six

CHENG 115

scrolls and place them in six small cases, which fit inside a bigger case).[27] The websites of the Miyagi Prefectural Library and the Kyoto University Library both record the six pieces of the 1602 print of each world map as mounted on six hanging scrolls (*kakejiku* 掛軸).[28] It seems likely many displayed their world maps as scrolls (only removed and remounted later). But how shall we understand the use of hanging scrolls in context? Where and how would contemporaries of Ricci and his collaborators have displayed and enjoyed the hanging scrolls that together made up a large world map?

From the late fifteenth century on, with economic strength and developments in architectural technology originating from the Jiangnan area (in the Yangtze River's lower reaches), the typical urban residence grew higher and brighter, particularly the halls and spaces for receiving visitors, ancestral sacrifice, recreation, and so on. Prior decades' sitting screens were thus too low for aesthetic display in such tall spaces. Screens of a new type, called "screen doors" (*pingmen* 屏門) or "back screens" (*beiping* 背屏), thus came to divide the spaces in these larger halls.[29] Back screens were wide and of sufficient height to reach the ceiling, providing abundant space within which to frame or upon which to hang large calligraphy artwork and paintings. Since the late Ming, large hanging scrolls had become popular for displaying calligraphy and paintings, and sets of four, six, or eight scrolls (called *pingtiao* 屏條, "screen strip," or *pingfu* 屏幅, "screen panel") might hang together on back screens.[30] This explains why Li Zhizao, who hailed from Hangzhou, referred to printing the *Kunyu wanguo quantu* as "six screen panels" (*zuo pingzhang liu fu* 做屏障六幅), hanging scrolls mounted on back screens. Therefore, the likely initial design and printing of the large world maps as sheets easily mounted as separate hanging scrolls or on screen panels probably presumed they would be displayed on back screens in the halls of urban residences.

Setting the map sheets on screen panels was not irrevocable: it was possible to remove and remount them in other ways for preservation or display. Scholars believe some hanging scrolls from imperial China were originally displayed in sitting screens.[31] Their target readerships, then, could have mounted the world map's six or more screen panels in various ways: within sitting screens, as hanging scrolls, on back screens, or otherwise. Their modern framing can likewise vary significantly, as illustrated by two parts of the *Kunyu wanguo quantu* kept at the University of Bologna (figure 4.8).[32] After such maps reached the Korean Peninsula and Japan, the map pieces often appeared mounted on the big folding screens popular in those countries (e.g., as the figured manuscripts produced there).[33] Based on markings and other damage to parts of the Miyagi Prefectural Library print where the sheets would meet if joined together, Huang Shijian and Gong Yingyan speculate that the sheets, later mounted on foldable screens, entered Japan as scrolls.[34]

These modifications regarding size, content, and manner of display also affected how one might experience these world maps. Printed wall maps in Renaissance Europe bore dedications to various patrons, including European royal families and diverse courtiers, scholars, and merchants, and contained various contexts when displayed. The wall maps displayed in a particular room might convey political or religious ideas or serve solely as decorative objects—for example, as status symbols for the upper-middle class.[35] In almost every context, visitors viewed, examined, and even learned and received geographical knowledge and other political or religious ideas the maps conveyed.

Although a decorative object, the screen map served a specific purpose within a room, first and foremost by subdividing the space. The screen then became a background for the partitioning of the living room, the study, or even the bedroom and thus provided a setting for the owner's activities therein. In this sense, the screen map acted at once as a decorative object and a piece of furniture, representing its owner's aesthetic and tastes. At the same time, the screen could also enclose an area, surrounding the occupants of that space to create a sense of immersion, as when contemplating the world map (or other content on the screen, ranging from calligraphic works to paintings to engravings).[36] Consequently, the screen map had a close relationship with the owner of the space.

The screen could even interact with onlookers. While contemplating the painting on a screen, viewers might pause and reflect and perhaps even add notations to one side or other of the screen to impart their experiences.[37] From this point of view, the viewers of a map thus made their own contributions to, and became part of, the process of mapmaking. The map would not only teach its readers about the world but also aid them in building their own worlds through "spiritual traveling" (*woyou* 卧游, literally, "wandering while lying down").[38] In his preface to *Kunyu wanguo quantu,* Matteo Ricci stated specifically and explicitly that he was "making six big screen panels as a tool for spiritual travelling in one's study," designed, in other words, to enclose a space within a study for spiritual travel.[39]

The furniture inside the enclosed space near the screen often included chairs and beds. The term "spiritual traveling," which Ricci's Chinese collaborators, such as Li Zhizao, may have provided, also referred to a manner of appreciating Chinese landscape painting. The artist Zong Bing 宗炳 (375–443 CE) first formulated this way of appreciating landscape paintings after age and illness restricted him to painting the natural places he had enjoyed traveling to in his youth and then practicing meditation before the paintings: "Emptying one's mind and beholding the *dao*,[40] it can be done through travelling while lying down."[41] Via spiritual traveling, viewers could then behold and appreciate the painted mountains and waters (*shanshui* 山水) spiritually, experiencing the harmony and the integration of humans with nature.[42] The literati could thus use the *Kunyu wanguo quantu,* Ricci and Li Zhizao claimed, to gain similar experiences. The additional texts and pictures, especially the sea creatures and land animals on the figured manuscripts, helped to make their "journeys" more informative and vivid.

Many of the maps discussed in this volume gradually gained greater aesthetic value, especially those that further adapted the world maps by Ricci and his Chinese collaborators to East Asian mapping practices and material cultures. These

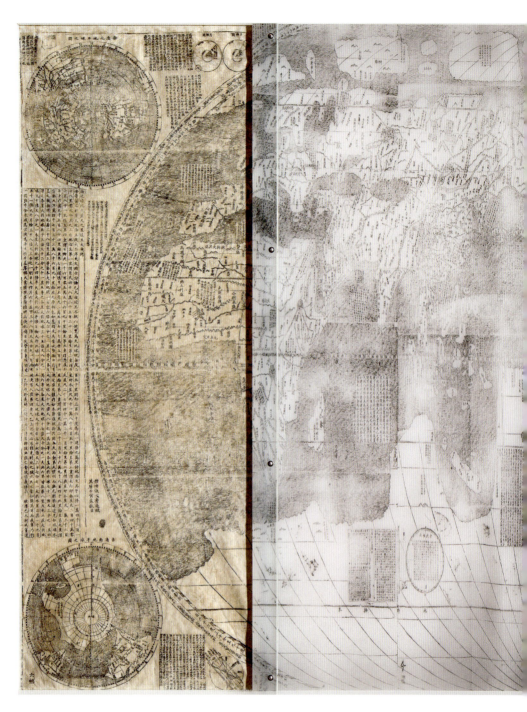

FIGURE 4.8.

The first (*right*) and the sixth (*left*) part of the 1602 *Kunyu wanguo quantu,* here in a modern framing with an attempt to replace the missing second to fifth sheets with a highly compressed black-and-white scan (compare to figure 1.1). Università di Bologna, Dipartimento di Astronomia, Museo della Specola.

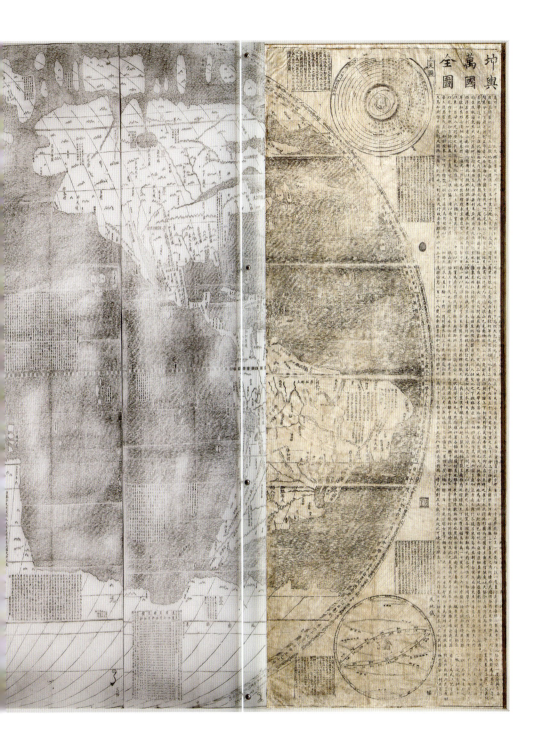

modifications—by, inter alia, the map readers themselves—precipitated a gradual loss of certain salient attributes these world maps had inherited from Europe's mapmaking practices.

Taking this series of world maps as an example, Nicolas Standaert has presented four different research frameworks (transmission, reception, invention, and interaction) for the history of contacts between cultures. By locating them within the context of East Asian mapping practices, this chapter has sought to show the processes behind the encompassment of these world maps in East Asian material cultures. The *Kunyu wanguo quantu* series increased in size, augmenting in turn the map's textual and pictorial contents. The world map's printing in sections led to its display alternately as sitting screens, as hanging scrolls, or on back screens or folding screens to facilitate map readers' spiritual traveling. Highlighting these modifications to the world maps casts questions of reception in a new light. Recovering the East Asian intellectual and material contexts of the world map series shows how the Chinese, Koreans, and Japanese—but especially Ming-era scholars—received the maps produced by the Jesuits and their Chinese collaborators, as well as how messages regarding the world maps changed significantly through that reception. The transition from wall display onto screens, however, was more than just a new meandering in a "dialogue of misunderstandings."[43] Locating the world maps within the contexts of Chinese art forms also reveals the screen maps' internal and external coherence. Their internal coherence included the practicing of textualism and pictorialism upon the enlarged screen world map, while their external coherence included the screen map's new role within the Ming scholars' practice of spiritual enjoyment. Between transmitter and receiver, the screen maps created yet another new space, another meeting place emerging amid seventeenth-century encounters between western Europe and East Asia.

Notes

1. Edney, *Cartography*, 8.
2. I adopt Edney's suggestion and use "mapping" and "mapping history" rather than "cartography" and "cartographic history." Ibid., 8.
3. Yee, "Chinese Cartography among the Arts," 165.
4. Gallagher, *China in the Sixteenth Century*, 165–166; Trigault, *De Christiana expeditione*, 182.
5. Aleni and Yang, *Zhifang waiji*, 6–8.
6. Huang and Gong, *Li Madou shijie ditu yanjiu*, 5.
7. Fiorani, "Cycles of Painted Maps in the Renaissance," 805–806.
8. Ibid.
9. Huang and Gong, *Li Madou shijie ditu yanjiu*, 3–29.
10. Guo, *Binyisheng qian cao*, 11.35b.
11. *Kunyu wanguo quantu*, Li Zhizao's preface.

12. *Kunyu wanguo quantu,* Matteo Ricci's preface.
13. Gallagher, *China in the Sixteenth Century,* 397; Trigault, *De Christiana expeditione,* 436.
14. Huang and Gong, *Li Madou shijie ditu yanjiu,* 5, 144–147.
15. Brotton, *Great Maps,* 110; Nurminen, *Mapmaker's World,* 215.
16. Regarding "textualism" in Chinese mapping, see Yee, "Taking the World's Measure."
17. *Kunyu wanguo quantu,* Matteo Ricci's preface.
18. Gallagher, *China in the Sixteenth Century,* 397–398; Trigault, *De Christiana expeditione,* 436.
19. For "pictorialism" in Chinese mapping, see Yee, "Chinese Cartography among the Arts."
20. *Kunyu wanguo quantu,* Li Zhizao's preface.
21. *Kunyu wanguo quantu,* Matteo Ricci's preface.
22. Aleni and Yang, *Zhifang waiji,* 6.
23. Wang Shixiang, *Mingshi jiaju zhenshang,* 32–33.
24. Wang Mianhou, "Ming caihui ben *Jiubian tu* yanjiu," 26–27.
25. Ibid. The two maps were dismounted from their screens for study and conservation following their initial discovery.
26. "Li Madou zhi Kunyu quantu."
27. Refer to the image on the website of the Tōyō Bunko, accessed January 14, 2020, http://124.33.215.236/gazou/index_img.php?tg=J1.
28. Kyoto University Library, accessed April 14, 2022, https://rmda.kulib.kyoto-u.ac.jp/item/rb00013547; Miyagi Prefectural Library, accessed April 14, 2022, https://eichi.library.pref.miyagi.jp/da/detail?data_id=040-61694.
29. Zhang Pengchuan, "Ming Qing shuhua zhongtang yangshi de yuanqi."
30. Wu Xiaoming, "Shufa pingtiao yuanliu kaoshu."
31. Li, *Neiwai zhijian,* 7. Michael Sullivan, however, says no recognizable screen paintings from ancient China exist today; see Sullivan, "Notes on Early Chinese Screen Painting," 239.
32. A figured manuscript map with a similar modern framing was sold at auction at Christie's in London on July 12, 2017, for £155,000. See Qin Xie, "Now THAT'S a Hidden Treasure! Rare Hand-Painted World Maps from the Seventeenth Century Are Discovered in a Garage and Auctioned for $24,000," *MailOnline,* October 26, 2016, accessed January 14, 2020, https://www.dailymail.co.uk/travel/travel_news/article-3871282/Now-S-hidden-treasure-Rare-hand-painted-world-maps-17th-century-discovered-garage-auctioned-24-000.html. Kaminski Auctions had previously sold the map segments at auction for US $24,000 on October 1, 2016.
33. Seo, "Joseon hugi chaesaeg pilsabon byeongpung *Gonyeo manguk jeondo.*"
34. Huang and Gong, *Li Madou shijie ditu yanjiu,* 156–157.
35. Fiorani, "Cycles of Painted Maps in the Renaissance," 805–806.
36. Landscape paintings were a very common theme on screen maps.
37. On the screen's function in ancient China, see Wu, *Double Screen,* 9–28; Li, *Neiwai zhijian,* 2–8.
38. Edney has pointed out that the ideal of cartography separated the map consumers from the map producers; Edney, *Cartography,* 234.
39. *Kunyu wanguo quantu,* Matteo Ricci's preface.
40. *Dao* 道, literally "way" or "path," is a fundamental concept in traditional Chinese thought.

41. Zhang Yanyuan, *Lidai minghua ji,* 161. As Edney has pointed out, similar expressions were in use in sixteenth-century Europe. In their works, George Braun and Robert Burton both discussed a map's function, which is to enable viewing the world without actual travel. However, "pre-1800 sentiments about maps as tools of visualization varied according to the mode of mapping"—e.g., the spiritual traveling. Edney, *Cartography,* 104–106.
42. Li, *Neiwai zhijian,* 187–194.
43. Standaert, *Methodology,* 14.

References

Aleni, Giulio (Ai Rulüe 艾儒略), and Yang Tingyun 楊廷筠. *Zhifang waiji* 職方外紀. Annotated edition as *Zhifang waiji jiaoshi* 職方外紀校釋, by Xie Fang 謝方. Beijing: Zhonghua shuju, 2000.

Brotton, Jerry. *Great Maps: The World's Masterpieces Explored and Explained.* London: Dorling Kindersley, 2014.

Day, John D. "The Search for the Origins of the Chinese Manuscript of Matteo Ricci's Maps." *Imago Mundi* 47 (1995): 94–117.

Edney, Matthew H. *Cartography: The Ideal and Its History.* Chicago: University of Chicago Press, 2019.

Fiorani, Francesca. "Cycles of Painted Maps in the Renaissance." In *The History of Cartography.* Vol. 3, bk. 1, *Cartography in the European Renaissance,* edited by David Woodward, 803–835. Chicago: University of Chicago Press, 2007.

Gallagher, Louis J., trans. *China in the Sixteenth Century: The Journal of Matthew Ricci: 1583–1610.* New York: Random House, 1953.

Guo Zizhang 郭子章. *Binyisheng qian cao* 蠙衣生黔草. Siku quanshu cunmu congshu 四庫全書存目叢書. Jinan: Qilu shushe, 1997.

Harley, J. B., and David Woodward, eds. *The History of Cartography.* Vol. 2, bk. 2, *Cartography in the Traditional East and Southeast Asian Societies.* Chicago: University of Chicago Press, 1994.

Huang Shijian 黃時鑒, and Gong Yingyan 龔纓晏. *Li Madou shijie ditu yanjiu* 利瑪竇世界地圖研究. Shanghai: Shanghai guji chubanshe, 2004.

"Li Madou zhi Kunyu quantu" 利瑪竇製坤輿全圖. *Dongfang zazhi* 東方雜誌 20, no. 9 (1923): n.p.

Li Xi 李溪. *Neiwai zhijian: Pingfeng yiyi de Tang Song zhuanxing* 內外之間：屏風意義的唐宋轉型. Beijing: Beijing daxue chubanshe, 2014.

Livieratos, Evangelos. "The Matteo Ricci 1602 Chinese World Map: The Ptolemaean Echoes." *International Journal of Cartography* 2, no. 2 (2016): 186–201.

Nurminen, Marjo. *The Mapmaker's World: A Cultural History of the European World Map.* London: Pool of London Press, 2015.

Seo Yoonjung. "Joseon hugi chaesaeg pilsabon byeongpung *Gonyeo manguk jeondo* wa *Gonyeo jeondo* ui dongmul sabhwa: Jisig gwa dosang ui jeonseung gwa byeonyong." *Misul sahag yeongu* 303 (2019): 131–169.

Standaert, Nicolas. *Methodology in View of Contact between Cultures: The China Case in the 17th Century.* Hong Kong: Chinese University of Hong Kong, 2002.

Sullivan, Michael. "Notes on Early Chinese Screen Painting." *Artibus Asiae* 27, no. 3 (1965): 239–264.

Trigault, Nicolas. *De Christiana expeditione apud Sinas*. Augsburg: Christoph Mang, 1615.

Wang Mianhou 王綿厚. "Ming caihui ben *Jiubian tu* yanjiu" 明彩繪本《九邊圖》研究. *Beifang wenwu* 北方文物, no. 1 (1986): 26–37.

Wang Shixiang 王世襄. *Mingshi jiaju zhenshang* 明式家具珍賞. Beijing: Wenwu chubanshe, 1985.

Wu, Hung. *The Double Screen: Medium and Representation in Chinese Painting*. Chicago: University of Chicago Press, 1996.

Wu Xiaoming 吳曉明. "Shufa pingtiao yuanliu kaoshu" 書法屏條源流考述. *Meishu guancha* 美術觀察, no. 8 (2011): 97–100.

Yee, Cordell, D. K. "Chinese Cartography among the Arts: Objectivity, Subjectivity, Representation." In Harley and Woodward, *History of Cartography,* vol. 2, bk. 2, 128–169.

———. "Taking the World's Measure: Chinese Maps between Observation and Text." In Harley and Woodward, *History of Cartography,* vol. 2, bk. 2, 96–127.

Zhang Pengchuan 張朋川. "Ming Qing shuhua zhongtang yangshi de yuanqi" 明清書畫中堂樣式的緣起. *Wenwu* 文物, no. 3 (2006): 87–96.

Zhang Yanyuan 張彥遠. *Lidai minghua ji* 歷代名畫記. Suzhou: Jiangsu meishu chubanshe, 2007.

5

Circling the Square

Encompassing Global Geography on Large Commercial Maps

MARIO CAMS

AN ALL-ENCOMPASSING CHRISTIAN COSMOGRAPHY UNDERLAY ALL TEACHING of geography in Catholic institutions of higher learning throughout sixteenth-century Europe. Under this umbrella, world geography played a significant role in the study of the physical world of humankind and, as such, stood in close relation with the pursuits of astronomy and geometry. These burgeoning but akin areas of knowledge shared a common foundation: works of Greek antiquity "recovered" by way of the Islamicate world.[1] Projection methods employing latitudes and longitudes, originally gleaned from Greek astronomy, bound the terraqueous and celestial worlds together mathematically and geometrically.[2] Nearly all world maps printed in Europe in the late sixteenth and seventeenth centuries evince that lineage, emphasizing that the world is a globe (an *orbis terrarum*) encompassed in finite spherical heavens (*caelum*). Unsurprisingly, Jesuit missionaries to East Asia and their scholarly collaborators perpetuated that emphasis in the large world maps they produced.

The different map, book, and globe projects discussed earlier in this volume by Nicolas Standaert, Richard A. Pegg, and Wang Yongjie in chapters 1–3, however, were clearly no mere slavish replications of European prototypes. The decidedly global geography they propounded had to find its own place within the print cultures and discourses of another intellectual universe, establishing the contours of new modes of mapping in East Asia. For the missionaries, the large world maps, books, and globes they helped to produce provided springboards for discussing central links between the terraqueous and the celestial, emphasizing the universal and its connection to the divine.[3] Late

Ming intellectuals, on the other hand, approached these works seeking access to a new and larger, if enigmatic, view of the world amid multiple territorial crises and societal unease. For these men, the global geography that the missionaries propounded, in sharp contrast to the state-based worldview informing most large commercial maps printed in China, provided an intriguing sounding board for addressing the increasingly central question of how to relate the unraveling Ming state to the threatening world beyond. These interests ensured this global mode of mapping's survival until at least the eighteenth century: the process of creating a new mode of mapping the world, in Chinese script and embedded in late Ming intellectual and material culture, gave rise to a robust genealogy of large maps produced by Jesuit missionaries and their many scholarly collaborators, including but not limited to the *Kunyu wanguo quantu* 坤輿萬國全圖 (Complete map of all countries on earth, 1602; figure 1.1), the *Liangyi xuanlan tu* 兩儀玄覽圖 (Mysterious visual map of the two forms, 1603; figure 1.2), and the world maps of Francesco Sambiasi (1582–1649; figure 4.6) and Ferdinand Verbiest (1623–1688; figure 5.1).

Such large maps, all produced with the assistance of Jesuit missionaries, dominate the scholarship. Other maps reflecting the same dynamics but steeped in a strong Ming tradition of printing large commercial maps are far less well known, perhaps because the missionaries, as far as we know, were not involved in their production. Taking such maps into account nevertheless not only illustrates the multiple receptions of the global worldview in East Asia but also unveils how the format of large maps, most of them printed for profit, emerged as a material common ground for dialogue between the global geography of the late Renaissance, encompassed in a broader Christian cosmology, and Ming world geography, centered on a civilized (*hua* 華) state administrative order. This chapter is dedicated to reconstructing such acts of mapping the global without the help of the Jesuits. I argue that, taken together, these maps constitute a second major new mode of mapping the globe that also survived for centuries and likewise circulated within East Asia and beyond.

Three Large Printed Maps

Although the great majority of extant maps produced in imperial China survive in books, a small number of extant large commercial maps originated not in books (although closely related to printed books of geography) but as separately printed large-sheet maps.[4] Not many such maps survive, due primarily to their delicate paper substrates, but the circulation of those extant suggest, paradoxically, a thriving trade. Large commercial maps first and foremost summarized at a glance the fine-grained information presented in the voluminous books of geography. They thus followed a more general tendency, manifesting especially in the final century of Ming rule, of increasing both printed works' audiences and their ease of use.[5] There are indications, further, that large maps may have been a preferred tool in teaching imperial geography

FIGURE 5.1.

Ferdinand Verbiest's *Kunyu quantu* 坤輿全圖 (Complete map of the earth, 1674) mounted on six scrolls. Each scroll measures approx. 51 × 172 cm. Bibliothèque nationale de France, gallica.bnf.fr.

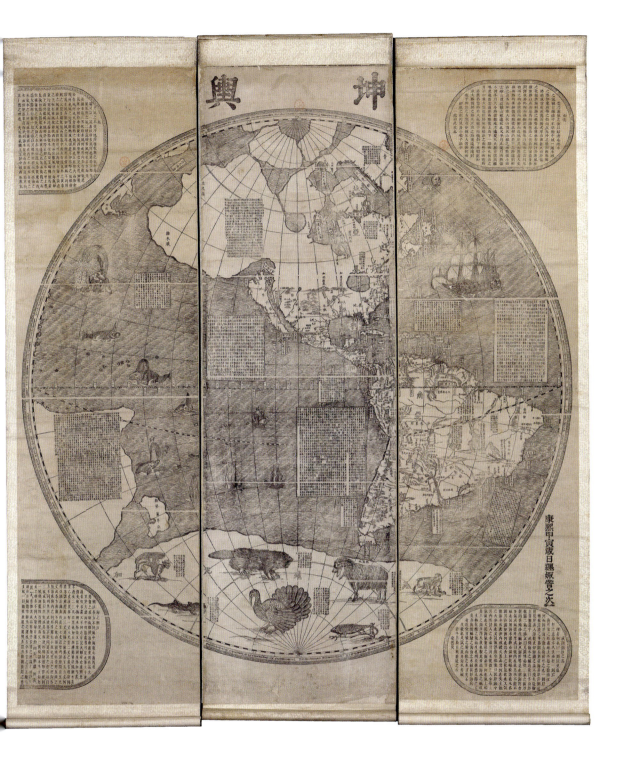

and administration to aspirant scholar-officials. Before delving into the impact of global geography on such large stand-alone maps, therefore, this chapter first explores how large commercial maps related to other late Ming works of geography and how they survived.

Works on geography constituted an important sphere of the thriving late-Ming book market. The demand for books grew as elites, concentrated in the lower Yangtze River delta, grew increasingly mobile and interconnected. By the mid-sixteenth century, the crossing of internal boundaries—between social classes as well as economically and between regions—was transforming Ming society, bolstering the commercial book trade. At the same time, a number of territorial threats along the state's maritime and northern frontiers naturally sent the empire's scholar-officials, in their common ambition to "order the world" (*jingshi* 經世), seeking works of state geography to better understand those threats and to formulate policy solutions.[6] Unfortunately, the official ninety-volume state geography, the *Da Ming yitong zhi* 大明一統志 (Gazetteer of the unified Great Ming, first printed 1461), proved thoroughly impracticable: its central project had sought to construct imperial space bottom-up, compiling locally negotiated geohistorical information through the co-optation of local elites. In fact, only the last two of the gazetteer's ninety chapters briefly outline neighboring regions, states, and peoples.[7] Scholar-officials' criticism of the state gazetteer spurred the production and printing of more user-friendly and abridged works of geography.

The printing of large maps appears related to this general demand for increased practicality and ease of use. Large overview maps followed quickly upon a popular new abridged edition of the gazetteer printed in Fujian Province. A certain Gan Gong 甘宮 compiled the oldest extant copy (printed in 1555 near Fuzhou), which bears the title *Gujin xingsheng zhi tu* 古今形勝之圖 (Map of advantageous terrain then and now; figure 10.1).[8] It literally maps out the state gazetteer, although demarcating only major administrative units and omitting the lower echelons.[9] Neighboring states and peoples appear about the margins, locked out as islands or textual insets in the seas to the east and south or separated from the state administration by the Great Wall or the upper reaches of the Yellow River to the north and west. Several short descriptive sentences, nearly all traceable back to the state gazetteer, appear in abridged form on the map itself. Its representations of major rivers and mountains likewise stylistically emulate the gazetteer's diagram maps. A small inset in the bottom-right corner confirms the mapmaker's heavy reliance on the *Da Ming yitong zhi:* "This map was compiled based on the *tong zhi* [short for *yitong zhi*, the comprehensive gazetteer] for the convenience of scholars to skim through history and easily understand the world's geographical features as well as strategic places old and new. Those places not mentioned by the classic [text] could not be fully listed." This short excerpt explicitly states that this large map answered a desire for *convenient* access to the ninety-chapter state gazetteer. By noting the impossibility of including all places, it even implicitly acknowledges scholarly critiques of the state gazetteer. The map survives in Spain, bearing annotations tracing its trajectory from Fujian to Spain via the Philippines, as Florin-Stefan Morar discusses in chapter 10 of this volume.

Around the time of the printing of this map, Luo Hongxian 羅洪先 (1504–1564), a prominent official, suffered dismissal from his post in the capital, having allegedly insulted the emperor. After journeying to his hometown in central Huguang Province, he turned his energies to producing a more practically inclined book on geography titled *Guang yutu* 廣輿圖 (Extended territorial maps, first printed 1556 or 1557) and counting only two chapters. Rather than focusing, as the gazetteer did, on historical-geographical information specific to each prefecture, Luo combined hands-on knowledge circulating within the central administration with information from a large map—sporting a distance-based grid system—dating back to the Mongol Yuan period (1271–1368). As a result, Luo's *Guang yutu* was able to (partially) break free from the constraints of state geography, reflected, for example, in the work's structuring into two equal parts: the first preserved for state administrative geography, the second devoted to what one might best describe as a transverse geography in the sense that it deals with issues reaching across and beyond the administrative structure (e.g., transport systems, frontier defenses, waterways, neighboring states, etc.). At the same time, the work also achieves balance between maps and text (statistics, administrative tables, and brief descriptions), both featuring important components that effectively answered the sixteenth-century demand for greater practicality. Unsurprisingly, Luo's work immediately became highly sought after, appearing in no less than seven editions in the two decades after its first printing.[10] In the wake of its success, more and more works on geography entered the market, some seeking to reconcile the state gazetteer with Luo's *Guang yutu* by recombining select information and maps into differing configurations.[11]

A second extant large map titled *Beizhi huang Ming yitong xingshi fenye renwu chuchu quanlan* 備誌皇明一統形勢分野人物出處全覽 (Overview of the origins of famous persons, astral allocations, and topographical features from the unified imperial Ming's complete records, printed in 1605; figure 5.2), kept today in the National Museum in Krakow, achieves precisely that. Printed, like the *Gujin xingsheng zhi tu* discussed earlier, in or near Fuzhou, this map compiles place-names from the entirety of Luo's atlas into one highly condensed map of Ming China, surrounded in its broad margins with abridged provincial descriptions derived from the *Da Ming yitong zhi*. This map fell into the hands of a British East India Company captain and merchant named John Saris, who passed it along to Richard Hakluyt (1553–1616). It later appeared as the China map in Samuel Purchas's *Pilgrimes,* a book printed in London in 1625 (figure 5.3).[12] The general shapes and outlines of the rivers and boundaries were carefully traced, and a projection grid was added. In lieu of place-names, the map bears empty squares (Purchas, presumably, could find no one in London able to transcribe Chinese script).

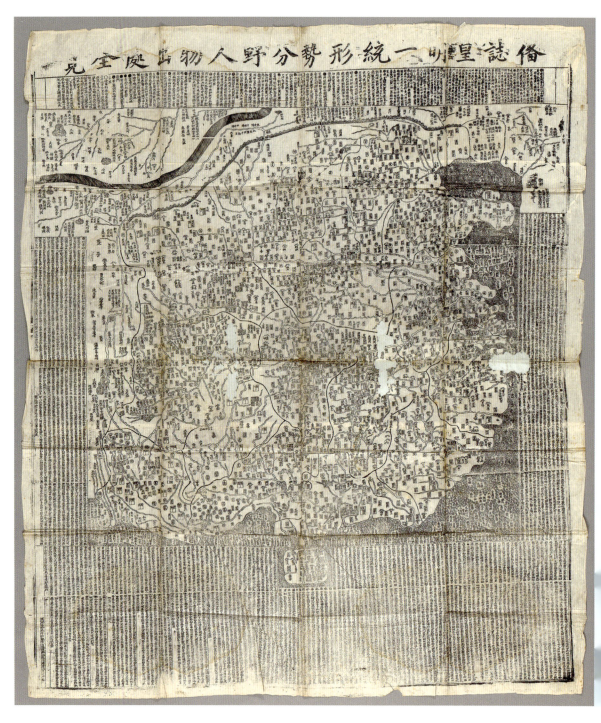

FIGURE 5.2.

The *Beizhi huang Ming yitong xingshi fenye renwu chuchu quanlan* (1605). Approx. 170 × 200 cm. Laboratory Stock National Museum in Krakow/Princes Czartoryski Museum.

FIGURE 5.3.

The map of China in Purchas's *Pilgrimes* (1625–1626) is a replication of the map in figure 5.2, with empty squares displacing place-names, an added projection grid, and three decorative figures, including a portrait of Matteo Ricci. Approx. 36.9 × 29.3 cm. Hong Kong University of Science and Technology Library, G7820 1625 P87.

The fact that the two oldest large commercial Chinese maps extant in Europe hail from Fujian Province may well give historians of China little pause: the Fujian coastline was a prime zone of contact with European traders, particularly the Spanish but later the Dutch as well. In this case, however, it seems both maps came into Europeans' possession indirectly. Fujian ports were also the main nodes connecting continental East Asia to maritime trade networks extending all the way to Japan and across Southeast Asia, including Spanish Manila and English-dominated Bantam on the western end of Java. Apart from its position within networks of trade and maritime contact across the region, the province was also home to Jianyang 建陽, a town in the mountains of the interior famous for its commercial book market, the main source of affordable prints—including works of geography—across the empire.

A third extant large map was composed in Nanjing in 1643 on the eve of the Manchu-Qing invasion of Ming China.[13] Its title, *Huang Ming fenye yutu gujin renwu*

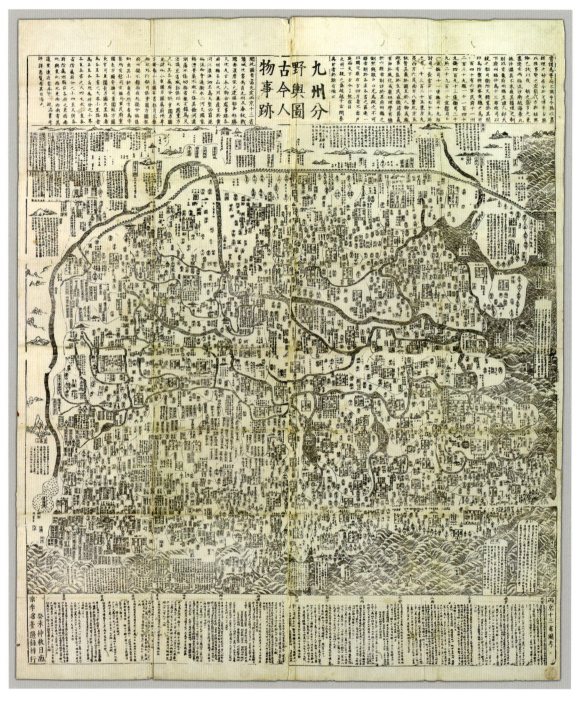

FIGURE 5.4.

Ji Mingtai's *Jiuzhou fenye yutu gujin renwu shiji*. Approx. 172 × 117 cm. University of British Columbia Library, Asian Rare-5 no.35.

shiji 皇明分野輿圖古今人物事跡 (Map of astral allocations of the imperial Ming, with famous persons and important events then and now; figure 5.4), refers to the concatenation of information from different origins characteristic of the production of geographies at the time. The map's bottom margin, moreover, contains statistical data in the tradition of Luo's *Guang yutu*. Signs of woodblock tampering on the print held at the Asian Library of the University of British Columbia, when compared to a manuscript copy of the map kept at the Harvard-Yenching Library, indicate that imprints were made both before and after the Qing takeover of the lower Yangtze delta in 1645 (the appendix lists both maps). One may glean this from the fact that all alterations gloss over the map's most obvious references to the Ming state. First, in the title, *Jiuzhou* 九州 (Nine regions) replaces *Huang Ming*. Second, a homonym character replaces the middle character in Ji Mingtai 季明臺, the compiler-printer's name identical to the name of the Ming state (his name now reading 季名臺). Third, the reign name of one of the last Ming emperors, Chongzhen 崇禎 (r. 1628–1644), is cut out. Since the administrative structures depicted date from 1575 to 1587,[14] this late Ming imprint may have been a near-exact copy of an earlier map. In 1679 a certain Lü Junhan 呂君翰 adjusted the map slightly before reengraving it in Beijing.[15]

Ji Mingtai's map also reached Europe, not in the hands of European traders but in those of a Jesuit missionary to China. Sicilian Jesuit Prospero Intorcetta (1626–1676) bore the map with him on his return to Rome in 1671. In the spring of that year, while Intorcetta visited his mother in Sicily, the Jesuits of Palermo commissioned a portrait depicting their colleague holding a map (figure 5.5). Examining its title confirms it is precisely Ji Mingtai's map (figure 5.6). Even though this is the only large commercial map known with certainty to have reached Europe in Jesuit hands, a series of other maps in the same tradition also bear links to the Jesuits. The remaining part of this chapter focuses on two extant maps that are highly similar to Ji Mingtai's map in form and content. At the same time, both maps also engage directly with the global geography first introduced to Ming audiences by Jesuit missionaries and their scholarly collaborators.

Discursively Global: The Liang Zhou Map

Central Fujian's location within important networks of the commercial printing and maritime trades, as well as European merchant and missionary mobility between western Europe and East Asia, thus facilitated the global circulation of Ming China's large commercial maps. The fact that such maps reached Europe early on in various ways testifies to their perceived value to men of diverse backgrounds, both as aids to understanding East Asia's geography and as exotica (as deployed in the Intorcetta portrait). In Europe, as in China, large commercial maps indeed functioned both as media of geographic knowledge and as objects of conspicuous consumption. At the same time, understandably, there were profound differences: whereas in Ming China most large commercial maps reflected a desire for convenient access to the otherwise voluminous

FIGURE 5.5.

Portrait of Prospero Intorcetta, April or May 1671. Oil on canvas, approx. 150 × 200 cm. Biblioteca Comunale "Leonardo Sciascia" di Palermo. Gift from the Fondazione Prospero Intorcetta Cultura Aperta.

FIGURE 5.6.

Detail of the map featured on the portrait of Prospero Intorcetta (figure 5.5). The map depicted here is Ji Mingtai's map (figure 5.4).

works of geography in support of the empire's state administrative order, in Catholic Europe their essential purpose was to facilitate readers' contemplation of humanity's relationship to the physical world and, by extension, to the divine. Beneath this divergence, however, lay common ground: the full display (*theatrum*) of terraqueous geography central to both practices became a springboard to the creation of two distinct genealogies in mapping the global in East Asia.

This common ground is fully engaged by the first genealogy of maps and geographical texts produced in Ming China by the Jesuits and their Chinese collaborators, as well as the later replications of these artifacts produced throughout East Asia. In the first place, their nomenclature—in which the terms constituting the title of the 1602 *Kunyu wanguo quantu* occupy a central position—distinguishes these niche works. The term *kun* 坤, the second hexagram of *Yijing* 易經 (Book of changes), demotes the earth to part of a wider cosmological whole, because it is associated with *qian* 乾, the first hexagram. *Qiankun* thus forms an expression referring to heaven and earth (which the Jesuits and their collaborators adopted early on to convey the Catholic vision of the "universe").[16] However, when *kun* is combined with *yu* 輿, a character originally representing a cart or chariot, the emphasis shifts to the physical earth. The term that follows, *wanguo* 萬國, is more political in meaning, denoting all countries, or states, in the world. Last, the term *quantu* 全圖 was adopted (which had appeared in at least one work published prior to Jesuit missionaries' arrival in the Chinese provinces) as a counterpart to the Renaissance *theatrum:* the comprehensive display enabling mankind to contemplate its relation to the physical world, the universe, and the divine.[17] Thus, the full title *Kunyu wanguo quantu* seemingly refers directly to the *Theatrum orbis terrarum* (Display of the lands of the globe, first edition 1570), Abraham Ortelius's (1527–1598) famous atlas, copies of which Matteo Ricci (1552–1610) repeatedly gifted to his contacts in China.[18] For the Jesuits, these works thus served as an entrée to broaching the divine with potential converts. At the same time, this newly established niche of world maps and the enigmatic global geography they illustrated also attracted Ming intellectuals, for whom relating the Ming state to the outside world constituted an increasingly central line of inquiry amid the multiple acute territorial crises of the sixteenth and early seventeenth centuries.

As Standaert outlines in chapter 1, several late Ming geographies, encyclopedias, and other compilations extract selected information from, or make reference to, this first genealogy of maps whose production had involved the Jesuits. Less well known, however, are two large maps of the period that also do this. The earliest is the intriguing *Qiankun wanguo quantu gujin renwu shiji* 乾坤萬國全圖古今人物事跡 (Complete map of all countries in the universe, with famous persons and important events then and now; figure 5.7, left).[19] The title's first half refers directly to the 1602 *Kunyu wanguo quantu*, replacing only *kunyu* with *qiankun*, while the second half of the title corresponds with that of Ji Mingtai's map (figure 5.4). The map's overall structure further confirms this latter connection: apart from a twelve-character title, both maps possess significant textual marginalia atop and beneath, containing, respectively, an introductory text and provincial statistics.[20] The map's top-left corner further provides four lines of information regarding its production, the first two attributing its composition to a certain Liang Zhou 梁輈, a teacher from the city of Sizhou 泗州 in Fengyang 鳳陽 Prefecture (Nanzhili Province) who worked at the local school in Wuxi 無錫 (then a county subordinate to Changzhou 常州 prefecture). At least one local gazetteer from Wuxi confirms that a person with this name indeed taught there in the year 1587.[21] The other two lines, carved in a larger font, link its printing to the Nanjing Ministry of Personnel, to a "Zhengyi Hall" 正巳堂, and to a date that can be interpreted as the fall of 1593. A number of prominent scholars have called this date into question, however: the map's introduction mentions the public display in Nanjing of a six-scroll map printed by a European, indicating the map must postdate Ricci's debut in that city in 1595.[22] Close scrutiny of the administrative structures depicted on the central section of the map confirms this: the map refers to both Fenzhou 汾州 and Zunyi 遵義, in the provinces of Shanxi and Sichuan, as prefecture-level cities, a status not accorded them until 1595 and 1601, respectively.

Combining the difficulty as to the date with the map's mention of the Nanjing Ministry of Personnel allows us to shed greater light on its production context. In the early years of the seventeenth century, a key secretary in the ministry was Wu Zhongming 吳中明 (d. 1608), who wrote one of the prefaces found on the 1602 *Kunyu wanguo quantu*.[23] Wu first wrote his preface around 1598 when he asked Ricci to annotate and augment an earlier map, resulting in the creation of the "Nanjing map," as it is referred to in chapter 1, while at least one contemporary source refers to it as the *Shanhai yudi quantu* 山海輿地全圖 (Complete map of mountains, seas, and lands). Wu also presented a map, either the Nanjing map or the 1602 *Kunyu wanguo quantu,* to the public at his official residence soon after, which is perhaps the public display Liang Zhou refers to in the top margin of his map.[24] If this reading is correct, Liang Zhou's map may have originated at the Nanjing Ministry of Personnel during the years immediately following 1598 and must have been completed after 1601, perhaps under the auspices of Wu Zhongming himself.[25]

Zooming in on its contents, we can see that the Liang Zhou map illustrates how Chinese scholars open to incorporating new ideas might have sought to appropriate elements of global geography within the dominant paradigm, centrally emphasizing the hierarchies of Ming administration: Liang Zhou's map stands squarely rooted in the tradition of the aforementioned large commercial maps, bearing strong similarities to Ji Mingtai's map in its symbolic and textual representations of contents (as the second half of the title promises). At the same time, in its extreme margins, at the edges of a squared depiction of the Ming state's administrative hierarchies occupying nearly the entire map, it engages directly with the maps produced by Ricci and his collaborators: more than sixty place-names and annotations, nearly all appearing as islands in the seas to the north, east, and south, were taken directly from the 1602 *Kunyu wanguo quantu* or from the no longer extant but closely related Nanjing map (figure 5.7).[26]

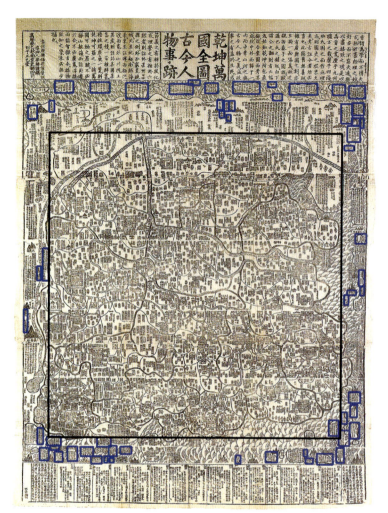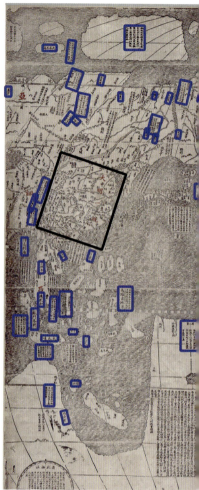

FIGURE 5.7.

Corresponding place-names and descriptions between the 1602 *Kunyu wanguo quantu* (*right*) and Liang Zhou's *Qiankun wanguo quantu gujin renwu shiji* (*left*). Highlighted place-names and brief descriptions from across Asia and the Americas on the former were inserted into the margins of the latter surrounding the familiar squared depiction of Ming state administrative space.

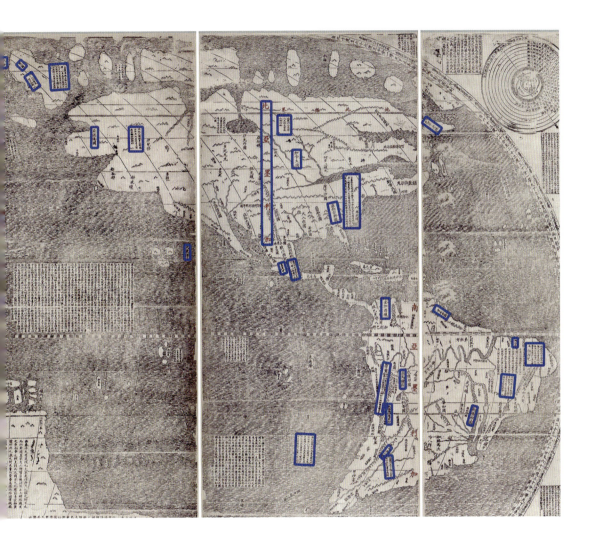

Liang Zhou subscribed to the cosmographical constructs familiar to him: a squared landmass dominated by the central state at the center and surrounded by seas in the four cardinal directions: In the leftmost margins, toward the west, where no seas are depicted, a note confirms "in the west is a large sea [too]." Yet, at the same time, Liang Zhou incorporated elements of the new global worldview propounded by the missionaries and their collaborators. Place-names and annotations are taken directly from the *Kunyu wanguo quantu* and recorded in the margins of the map, including the North Pole, while text found in a small inset on the right bottom margin also emphasizes the global:[27] "This map shows heaven encompasses the earth on the outside. *Heaven is like egg white; the earth is like egg yolk.* The land rests in the middle; water surrounds it on four sides. To the East are the nine *yi* 夷; to the West are the six *rong* 戎; to the South are the eight *man* 蠻; to the North are the five *di* 狄 [non-Chinese peoples]. The ten thousand countries surround them."[28] Considering this short text alongside figure 5.7, we can deduce Liang Zhou's appropriative approach: rather than clashing with the dominant state administrative worldview, expressed in late Ming geographies and large commercial maps, the incoming global geography could serve as an additional layer, thereby *discursively* extending more familiar cosmological constructs. Rather than employing the Jesuit-initiated, projection-based geography or replicating its continental outlines, Liang Zhou chose to remain in the "safe space," so to speak, of the familiar image of Ming geography. The corollary of this strategy linked *qian* with *kun(yu)*, embedding Ming China's state administrative geography, at least in print, within (or perhaps reconnecting it with) a more cosmographical spatial imaginary. This map, in textually incorporating a global spatial imaginary (evinced in the appropriated vocabulary of its title as well as its place-names and annotations), visually retains a more familiar mode of mapping the known world. As such, it continued to inspire later generations, as evinced by a large eighteenth-century map that largely replicates Liang Zhou's arrangement of marginal islands, complete with their place-names and annotations.[29]

Visually Global: The Cao Junyi Map

As Liang Zhou's map must have preceded that of Ji Mingtai by some four decades, their significant similarities suggest a common ancestry.[30] A more direct link, however, connects Ji Mingtai's map with yet another large map, the *Tianxia jiubian fenye renji lucheng quantu* 天下九邊分野人跡路程全圖 (Complete map of all under heaven, the nine frontiers, astral allocations, human traces, and route itineraries; figure 5.8), produced by a certain Cao Junyi 曹君義 only one year after the inception of Ji Mingtai's map. In its symbolic and textual representation of the Ming administration, it constitutes a near-exact copy of Ji's map. The most important difference between the two maps in their depictions of Ming administrative units lies in Cao's reduced annotations, especially those to either side of the squares signifying prefectural cities.[31] Similarly,

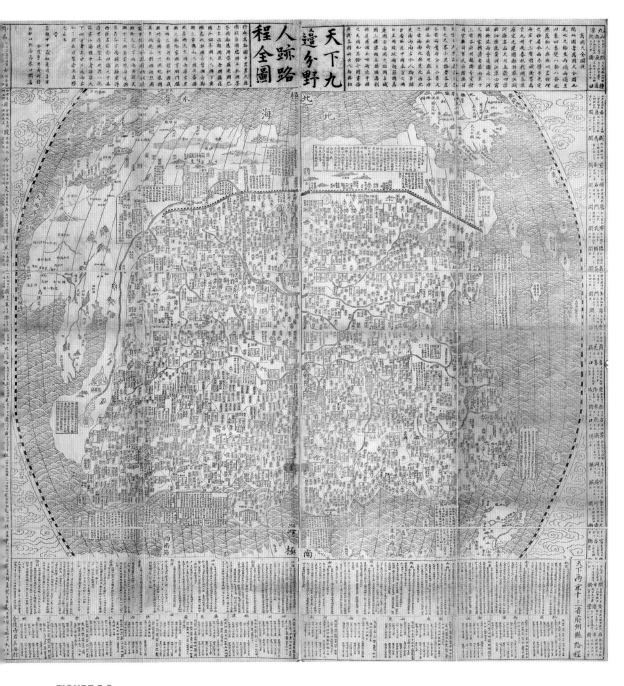

FIGURE 5.8.

Cao Junyi's *Tianxia jiubian fenye renji lucheng quantu* (1644). Attached to the depiction of Ming China (*center*) are the continents of Europe and Africa (*left*) and North and South America as severed islands (*in the top right and bottom right corners*, respectively). Approx. 124 × 126 cm. British Library Board, Maps 60875 (11).

the map contains many orthographic errors and simplifications with regard to place-names. In overall structure and layout, finally, Cao's map possesses additional textual bottom margins, including, below the provincial statistics also found on Ji's map, an extended list of road distances between provincial capitals and, to the left and the right, lists locating adjacent states and important frontier sites.

Far more compelling visually, however, is the space the map reserves beyond the state's confines to depict territories outside its reach: the Ming state appears reduced in size, shaped like a trapezoid, leaving free space to depict the recognizable outlines of Europe and Africa on the left and the (not so recognizable) Americas as two distinct and severed islands on the right, squeezed into the map's top and bottom corners.[32] The map's inclusion of the North and South Poles emphasizes its global geography, as does the frame of curved bar scales on the right and the left that emulates the decimal degrees of latitude found on the maps created by the Jesuits and their collaborators. Moreover, curved vertical lines flattening noticeably toward the map's center mimic the aesthetics (if clearly not the function) of lines of longitude from the Jesuit-initiated maps but do not extend continuously over Ming territories. These eye-catching features of Cao's map have led historians to presume direct descent from a "Ricci map."[33] A detailed analysis of its place-names, however, reveals instead that Cao consulted the world map titled *Wanguo quantu* 萬國全圖 (Complete map of all countries) attributed to Giulio Aleni (1582–1649).[34]

Cao could have encountered the *Wanguo quantu* in either of two distinct formats. First, the map is bound into most extant copies of the *Zhifang waiji* 職方外紀 (Record of everything beyond the administration), essentially a treatise of European world geography coedited by Aleni and Yang Tingyun 楊廷筠 (1563–1627; figure 2.9). As Wang Yongjie discusses in chapter 3, this book was printed in Hangzhou in 1623 and shortly thereafter in Fuzhou. It provides accounts of countries, peoples, customs, and fauna, organized continent by continent. The Hangzhou and Fuzhou editions include six map sheets: the world map under discussion, titled "Wanguo quantu," plus one map apiece depicting the continents of Asia (figure 3.1), Europe, Africa (Libya), and the Americas (figure 3.2), as well as one map depicting the Northern and Southern Hemispheres that also includes small diagrams explaining lunar occultations and solar eclipses.[35]

The second format that presented Aleni's world map to Ming readerships was a separately circulating sheet. The only known Ming print, measuring 63 × 55 cm, is kept at the Kobe City Museum and consists of three parts printed from separate woodblocks (figure 5.9): An introduction titled "Wanguo tu xiaoyin" 萬國圖小引 (Brief introduction to the map of all countries) appears at the top and is authored by Aleni, as confirmed by his personal seal and that of the Jesuit mission (both stamped, not printed). The text introduces global geography as part of a larger cosmology and calls on the reader to consider the relationship between the physical world, the heavens, and the divine:

How big the five continents, how numerous all the countries, even though, compared to the heavens above, they only are tiny spots on the globe. The country I am located in, is only a tiny spot on the five continents; the earth I stand on, is only a tiny spot in this large country. Comparing myself to heaven, what am I? Compared with the Great Lord of the Universe [literally, "of heaven and earth"], what am I? I am just like a tiny spot within a tiny spot, so that I cannot be found anywhere [on the globe]. My body is in the universe, and although it is only a very small spot, a spirit was bestowed onto it by the creator, allowing the self to grasp the universe and to clearly see the True Lord of the universe and of the myriad things. This is what is meant when we say "the human body is a small universe."

This excerpt guides the reader on how to meditate upon the global geography presented immediately below on the maps of the world and the two hemispheres. The blocks used for these maps are identical to those of the Fuzhou edition of the *Zhifang waiji*, further testimony to the centrality of the Fujian printing industry in producing large maps and their close connection to the world of books. This artifact, too, enjoyed a remarkable afterlife: several libraries hold copies of a relatively faithful Qing reprint on which Aleni's seal is printed rather than stamped (figure 2.8).[36] Since Ming-era prints of the *Wanguo quantu* circulated in two distinct formats printed from two different sets of woodblocks, Cao Junyi could have used either as his prototype.

Unlike Liang Zhou, Cao Junyi did not pick and choose among place-names but displayed all those he found on the "Wanguo quantu" in the extended space beyond his rendition of Ji Mingtai's map.[37] Cao's map thus constitutes a faithful imbrication of two entirely different maps—one depicting a flat imperial administrative space, the other depicting a global world. In this light the difference from Liang Zhou's map is remarkable: Liang Zhou takes on the global discursively, in the title and marginal texts, and merely picks and chooses place-names and annotations from the *Kunyu wanguo quantu* or a closely related map, arranging them in the extreme margins as an extra layer. Cao Junyi, on the other hand, unhesitatingly combines the global and imperial worldviews discursively *and* visually. Unlike Liang Zhou, Cao seems to embrace the global geography underlying the maps produced by the Jesuits and their collaborators, even mimicking their aesthetics. This visual aspect encapsulates, almost metaphorically, the mobility of world geographical knowledge and the spatial imaginary underlying the production of Cao's map: a visually global world (although divorced from its geometrical context) encompassed Ming China's imperial geography.

A brief note in the map's top-left corner (alongside Cao's name) describes the map's production context, including its composition in the spring of 1644, and advertises its availability for sale in a shop in central Nanjing (another important node in Ming China's commercial printing industry).[38] As we know that Giulio Aleni, vice-provincial of the Jesuits in China, was then residing in Nanjing, one may suspect

萬國圖小引

造物主化成十二重天而火氣水土四行從輕至重漸次相裹地在天之中圓內德方永不遷移東西南北之名上下中外之分人此從厥所居以定實則無往非中也地與天同一圓體度數相應故舊地心敏規於天天有黃赤二道南北二極冬夏二至經緯之度各三百有六十地圖亦微坎以成然地既形圓則畫之以遂家能像焉是畫之于兩不荒展為長形如削柑皮之苦然天下萬方總分為五大州曰亞細亞曰歐邏巴曰利未亞曰墨瓦蠟泥加又此各州中分為大小萬國不能盡筆也欲迷其大約云天噴五州之大萬國之眾其於上天不過圖中之一點也吾所居之邦又五州之一點也吾之軀足又六邦之一點也今我比天地之點也又為何如乎則我正似黑中之一點而無處可見矣頗我身又往天地難為甚微而一點靈才為造物主所賦則能包佑天地而明天地萬物之真主所謂人身一小天地也信爾以此形軀之至小則何處可生陽倨之見以丹靈心之至大則無可目衆自曉之理試各披前向玩人生天地間夫豈偶然者哉

西海文儒畢敬題

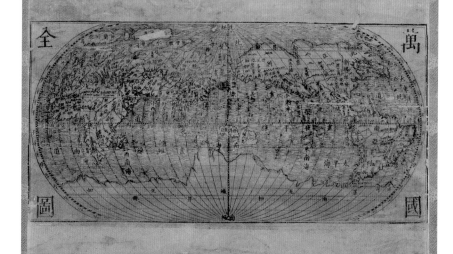

FIGURE 5.9.

(*Opposite page*) The *Wanguo quantu* as a separately printed sheet produced during the Ming era, with introductory text (*top*) signed by Aleni and featuring his personal seal (stamped, not carved). Figure 2.8 is its Qing-era reprint. Approx. 97 × 49 cm. Kobe City Museum.

that the *Wanguo quantu* and/or the *Zhifang waiji* were also sold at this shop. This remains conjecture, although one other link does connect Cao's map to the Jesuit missionaries: the *Novus atlas sinensis,* authored by Martino Martini (1614–1661) and published by Joan Blaeu (1596–1673) in Amsterdam in 1655, includes precisely the provincial statistics and road distances found in the bottom margin of Cao's map.[39] Although it is certainly possible that each independently used some third parent source, the fact that Aleni summoned Martini to Nanjing in the spring of 1644, simultaneous with Cao's map's printing, renders it especially tempting to imagine a meeting of the three men. If indeed they did, theirs might well have been the last collaborative project printed prior to Beijing's fall to the Manchu-Qing armies that summer.

After the Qing conquest, the printing of large separate maps in this tradition was mainly carried out by printers from Suzhou. Wang Junfu 王君甫, a printer in the city, reprinted an almost exact copy of Cao's map in 1663.[40] This presents a remarkable parallel with the Beijing reprint of Ji Mingtai's map in 1679 by Lü Junhan 呂君翰, who belonged to a competing printing family of Suzhou.[41] The link to Suzhou, however, is not the only commonality between the maps of 1663 and 1679. Perhaps even more noteworthy is that both maps circulated in Japan after the turn of the eighteenth century: Itō Tōgai 伊藤東涯 (1670–1736) obtained a copy of the Lü Junhan map in 1705 and reprinted it in Edo sometime between 1750 and 1754,[42] while the Wang Junfu map was reprinted in Kyoto before 1706 (figure 5.10).[43] Max Moerman has recently shown how the Kyoto reprint of Wang Junfu's map even enabled Cao's depiction of South America to migrate onto Hōtan's 鳳潭 (1659–1738) *Nansenbushū bankoku shōka no zu* 南瞻部洲萬國掌菓之圖 (Handy map of all countries of Jambudvīpa, 1710; figure 6.7), a map in the Japanese Buddhist tradition, and thereby onto its many reiterations. This connects two modes of mapping the world: one in the Chinese Catholic tradition as contained within the *Zhifang waiji* and the other in the Japanese Buddhist tradition that harks back to at least a fourteenth-century manuscript.[44]

In all, while Liang Zhou's map appears to be a single attempt at reframing the Ming state administrative worldview discursively by incorporating references to the global textually, Cao Junyi's visually adventuresome compromise with the incoming global geography gave rise to a robust genealogy that proliferated across East Asia. Compared to the world maps initiated by the Jesuits and their collaborators, however, both Liang's and Cao's maps belong to what we could call a secondary, compromise-oriented,

FIGURE 5.10.

Wang Junfu's 1663 map reprinted by Umemura Yahaku 梅村弥白 in Kyoto before 1706 titled *Dai Min kyūhen bankoku jinseki rotei zenzu* 大明九邊萬國人跡路程全圖 (Complete map of human traces and route itineraries in all countries and the nine frontiers of the Great Ming). Approx. 121 × 121.5 cm. Included is its cover (*top-right corner*), carrying the alternative title of *Dai Min ezu* 大明繪圖 (Map of the Great Ming). MacLean Collection, Illinois, MC26634.

genealogy of maps, embracing the global while staying grounded in the familiar worldview centered upon the Ming state. Their further circulation, into the Qing era and across the seas to Japan, illustrates that this secondary genealogy enjoyed a distribution similar to that of the primary genealogy of the maps initiated by the Jesuits and their collaborators.

Mapping the Global in Seventeenth-Century China

One question has occupied center stage in the literature on contact between western Europe and East Asia: Did the "Ricci map" exert a discernable impact on "Chinese cartography?" More often than not, the proffered verdict has been negative: the bright light of "Western science" simply never kindled inside the minds of Chinese intellectuals, or so we are told. Contrariwise, this chapter has illuminated how late Ming intellectuals appropriated the global geography in more ways than one and handed at least two robust genealogies of maps down to future generations across East Asia. When two vastly different modes of mapping the world, both arising from specific print cultures, came into contact at the turn of the seventeenth century, it led to the crossing and blurring of boundaries: Jesuit missionaries and their scholarly collaborators transposed the Renaissance global geography into late Ming intellectual discourses and print cultures, enticing others in turn to push the encompassment of this incoming worldview one step further. One salient format for these diverse mapmaking endeavors was the large commercial map, itself a robust tradition with roots in late Ming China. The resulting family tree illustrates these connections in yet another way: via the nomenclature used in map titles, among which the term *quantu* stands out (figure 5.11).

Even as this chapter has covered a significant part of the diverse encompassment of global geography in seventeenth-century China, it has also illuminated how two maps, both part and parcel of that meeting of worlds, have not received the attention they deserve. This gap is the result of studying an "exchange" between two cultural blocs while implicitly presupposing that the Jesuits were transmitters of superior (European) scientific knowledge.[45] This view neither acknowledges the essential differences between late Renaissance maps and modern cartography nor appreciates the agency of non-European actors. Rather than looking over Europeans' shoulders, therefore, this study built on earlier chapters in this volume and likewise shifted attention to late Ming scholars and their intellectual and material environments. This helps us to appreciate their repackaging of an unfamiliar and global geography so that it accorded better with more familiar discourses and formats. Whereas the Jesuit missionaries and their collaborators achieved this in dialogue, as charted in the first chapters of this volume, other late Ming scholars repackaged the incoming worldview in ways less radical by insisting on centrally retaining the familiar state administrative geography. This view, of a squared central "civilized" (*hua*) state administration surrounded at the

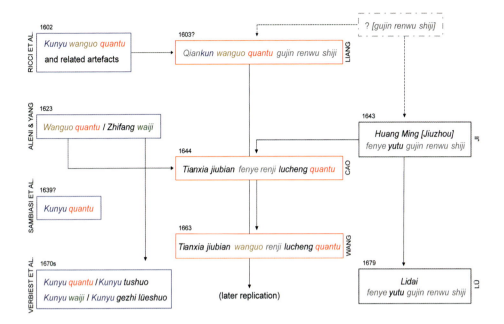

FIGURE 5.11.

The genealogies of maps and works of geography produced in seventeenth-century China and mentioned in this chapter. *Left,* maps and books initiated, attributed to, and coauthored by Jesuit missionaries; *middle,* maps that absorbed elements of global geography without Jesuit involvement; *right,* related maps that did not engage the global. Japanese replications are not included. Colors emphasize links in nomenclature.

four cardinal directions by "non-Chinese/barbarian" peoples, could best appropriate the incoming global geography selectively, as an outer layer circling the square.

This chapter has reconstructed an extended genealogy of maps and investigated different acts in the construction of a global *theatrum,* or "display," of the world as a globe in the context of East Asian scholarly discourses. As such, it has reframed one of the literature's essential questions of whether an imaginary, archetypical "Ricci map" made a lasting impact on Chinese cartography. I contend we have been asking the wrong question and should instead carefully examine the repackaging, in multiple installments, of select elements of Renaissance cosmology and geography for East Asian audiences and ask ourselves what this meant for the scholars engaging with this radically new image of a global world. After all, circling the square, or encompassing global geography into the squared worldview of the late Ming, was a complex endeavor that included the gradual, nonlinear absorption of global elements into preexisting spatial imaginaries.

Appendix

Table 5.1. Chronology of maps

TITLE	DATE	SIZE	DIGITALLY CONSULTED COLLECTION(S)	COMPILER/ PUBLISHER	PLACE
乾坤萬國全圖古今人物事跡 *Qiankun wanguo quantu gujin renwu shiji*	1593 [1603?]	172 × 132	Private collection	Liang Zhou 梁輈	Nanjing
皇明分野輿圖古今人物事跡 *Huang Ming fenye yutu gujin renwu shiji* (manuscript)	1643	134 × 119	Harvard-Yenching Library	Ji Mingtai 季明臺	Nanjing
九州分野輿圖古今人物事跡 *Jiuzhou fenye yutu gujin renwu shiji*	1643	132 × 117	University of British Columbia Library	Ji Mingtai 季名臺	Nanjing
天下九邊分野人跡路程全圖 *Tianxia jiubian fenye renji lucheng quantu*	**1644**	**124 × 126**	**British Library**	**Cao Junyi 曹君義**	**Nanjing**
天下九邊萬國人跡路程全圖 *Tianxia jiubian wanguo renji lucheng quantu*	1663	125 × 123	Harvard-Yenching Library	Wang Junfu 王君甫	Suzhou
歷代分野輿圖古今人物事迹 *Lidai fenye yutu gujin renwu shiji*	1679	135 × 125	Bodleian Library	Lü Junhan 呂君翰	Beijing
大明九邊萬國人跡路程全圖 *Dai Min kyūhen bankoku jinseki rotei zenzu*	ca. 1705	123 × 121	Kyoto University, MacLean Collection	Umemura Yahaku 梅村弥白	Kyoto
歷代分埜之圖古今人物事跡 *Rekidai bun'ya no zu kokin jinbutsu jiseki*	1750	200 × 167	Yokohama City University Library	Katsuragawa Hosan 桂川甫三	s.l.
歷代分埜之圖古今人物事跡 *Rekidai bun'ya no zu kokin jinbutsu jiseki*	1750	179 × 160	University of British Columbia Library	Katsuragawa Hosan with Suharaya Mohē 須原茂兵衛	Edo

Note: Size indications (in centimeters) are from collection catalogues or online databases and may diverge slightly contingent upon how different institutions measured specific maps. Liang's and Cao's maps, central to this chapter, are highlighted in bold.

Notes

The author would like to thank Liu Jie and Sun Lu, history students at the University of Macau, for their help in conducting a first analysis of Ming China's large commercial maps.

1. Through translation, adaptation, and augmentation, greatly affecting how this knowledge reached Renaissance centers of learning. Saliba, *Islamic Science*.
2. This explains why globes were often presented in pairs at the time. See figures 2.4 and 2.5.
3. Chen, "Human Body as Universe."
4. Large separate maps are also extant in manuscript form. A prominent early example is the map, made in 1526, bearing a postscript by Yang Ziqi 楊子器. See Yan, *China in Ancient and Modern Maps,* 96–97. Another is the so-called Wang Pan map at the Bibliothèque nationale de France, Cartes et plans, GE A-1120 (RES). The latter is a Korean copy of a Chinese precursor. See Destombes, "Wang P'an."
5. Cams, "Confusions of Space."
6. Du, "Literati and Spatial Order."
7. Dennis, *Writing, Publishing, and Reading Local Gazetteers,* 22–48.
8. Jin, "Guanyu *Gujin xingsheng zhi tu,*" 56. The only extant version of the *Gujin xingsheng zhi tu* survives in the Archivo General de Indias, MP-Filipinas 5, Seville. It is one of the first Ming maps to have reached Europe.
9. Numbers relating to the administrative structure recorded in the map's top margin, however, suggest it employed not the 1461 version of the *Da Ming yitong zhi* but a later edition or abridged version: the total numbers of prefectures, districts, and counties do not precisely match those in the first edition. Some descriptive information not found in the gazetteer can also be found at the margins. Enoki, "On the Ku-chin hsing-shêng chih t'u," 245.
10. Cheng, *"Guangyu tu" shihua.*
11. The earliest known such "remix" is Zhang Tianfu's 張天復 (1513–1578) *Huangyu kao* 皇輿考 (Study of imperial territories), published in 1557. Other editions appeared in 1577–1578 and 1588.
12. The full title is *Hakluytus Posthumus, or, Purchas his Pilgrimes, Contayning a History of the World, in Sea Voyages, and Lande Travels, by Englishmen and others.* The map appears in chapter 6. Edward Kajdánski was the first to point out the link between the map at Krakow and that inserted into Purchas's work, confirmed by Helen Wallis (Wallis, "Purchas' Maps," 155). Purchas's map of China later appeared, slightly edited, bearing a new title and decorative elements, in the 1655 English edition of Álvaro Semedo's (1585–1658) work titled *The History of That Great and Renowned Monarchy of China* (originally published in Portuguese in 1641).
13. One print, described at length by Wei Yin-Zong and mentioned by Timothy Brook, is in the University of British Columbia's Asian Library. See Wei, "Jianada Yingshu Gelunbiya daxue Yazhou tushuguan"; Brook, *Great State,* 1–14. Tenri University in Nara also holds a printed copy.
14. Wei, "Jianada Yingshu Gelunbiya daxue Yazhou tushuguan," 195.
15. At least two extant copies of the 1679 print survive, one at the Bodleian Library, Sinica 92; the other at Kobe City Museum (Unno, "Han minzoku shakai ni okeru rekishi chizu no hensen," 84). In the title, *lidai* 歷代 (through the ages) replaces *jiuzhou*.

16. The expression *qiankun* in reference to the cosmos or universe appears in the earliest Chinese-language catechism (composed in Zhaoqing), titled *Tianzhu shilu zhengwen* 天主實錄正文 and printed in 1584, as well as in Ricci's earliest Chinese-language astronomical work, *Qiankun tiyi* 乾坤體義.

17. A treatise on maritime defense first printed in 1562, the *Chouhai tubian* 籌海圖編 (Illustrated naval strategy) includes a map titled "Yudi quantu" 輿地全圖 (Complete map of the lands). I am indebted to Elke Papelitzky for this insight.

18. As argued by Huang Shijian, the 1602 map is *in the first place* based on Ortelius's work. On at least three occasions, Ricci gifted editions of the atlas to dignitaries and to the emperor. Huang, "Exploration of Matteo Ricci's World Map."

19. Sotheby's in London auctioned the map in 1988. Its current whereabouts are unknown. Its printing involved at least fourteen woodblocks on seven horizontal pieces of paper (Destombes, "Wang P'an," 245).

20. The first two maps discussed in this chapter do not share these features.

21. *Guangxu Wuxi jinkui xianzhi*, 237.

22. Discussion regarding correct dating of the map began with Funakoshi Akio and Unno Kazutaka (Funakoshi, "Some New Lights," 153–154; Unno, "Concerning a MS Map," 212–213). Both argue, essentially, for a mistake in the composition of the manuscript or in the carving of the date (given on the map in the sexagenary system). See Destombes, "Wang P'an." In this light, 1603 and 1613 are plausible years since both employ *gui* 癸 as the first character in their sexagenary renditions, while the years of 1605 and 1617 also qualify since both employ *si* 巳 as the second character.

23. Wu, from Huizhou, a center of the late Ming production of works of geography, obtained his *jinshi* in 1586. After his first arrival at Nanjing in 1595, Ricci was refused a permit to stay in the city. When Ricci returned to Nanjing, Wu was one of his most important contacts among the city's high elites. Hsia, *Jesuit in the Forbidden City*, 144–145.

24. Tang and Zhou, "Ming dai Li Madou shijie ditu," 304–308. Besides Wu himself, Feng Yingjing 馮應京 (1555–1606) also wrote a preface for the *Kunyu wanguo quantu* (D'Elia, "Recent Discoveries," 128–136). Feng, who, like Liang Zhou, was a native of Sizhou, composed the *Yueling guangyi* 月令廣義 (printed 1602), which includes the same preface by Wu Zhongming. Ricci and Feng met in Beijing, where Feng was imprisoned for denouncing a powerful eunuch (Hsia, *Jesuit in the Forbidden City*, 221).

25. It follows that Funakoshi's suggestion of 1603 or 1605 (see note 22) is most likely correct (Funakoshi, "Some New Lights," 153–154). Timothy Brook argues that the map was a counterfeit (Brook, *Great State*, 3). Brook bolsters his case through reference to a note in the map's bottom-left corner reading "Do not re-engrave" (*Bu xu fanke* 不許翻刻).

26. Annotations often differ slightly in vocabulary and style while nearly always conveying the same content. I am indebted to John Moffett of the Needham Research Institute in Cambridge for his help in tracking down this map.

27. The vocabulary and metaphors also appear in Feng's *Yueling guangyi*.

28. My emphasis. The egg yolk metaphor would have been familiar to Chinese intellectuals, harking back to Zhang Heng's 張衡 (78–139 CE) theory of a revolving spherical heaven,

or *huntian* 渾天, and was frequently used by collaborators of the Jesuits when refuting the theory of a square earth.

29. The Qing-era map does not carry a title and measures 132 × 170 cm. It references Liang Zhou's map directly in its bottom-right corner. A copy of the map is at Oxford, Bodleian Library Sinica 113, https://digital.bodleian.ox.ac.uk/objects/fe07c78b-4d60-490d-84e9-201c996a5f7d/.
30. Possibly dating to the sixteenth century, based on a comparison of administrative units.
31. These annotations on Ji Mingtai's map list each prefecture's historical name, function, and association with famous historical figures.
32. Note that the map assigns the continents no names.
33. Song, "Re-locating the 'Middle Kingdom.'"
34. The 1602 *Kunyu wanguo quantu* presents several place-names slightly differently from the *Wanguo quantu* and depicts a number of continental outlines with marked differences.
35. The two hemispheres, as seen from the North and South Poles, and the diagrams are also found on the 1602 *Kunyu wanguo quantu* and the 1603 *Liangyi xuanlan tu*.
36. The Qing reprint, reproduced in this volume as figure 2.8, largely includes the same contents as the Ming print, with the following exceptions: the last lines of the introductory text were recomposed; the Ming print includes Aleni's personal seal; and the name for China, Da Ming Yitong 大明一統 (Unified Great Ming), was replaced with Da Qing Yitong 大清一統 (Unified Great Qing) on the world map. Interestingly, Da Ming Hai 大明海 (Great Ming Sea; see also figure 1.3), remained unaltered. Further Qing copies can be found at several Italian libraries. See the entry for *Wanguo tu* 萬國圖 in the CCT-Database.
37. His inclusion of the desert strip marked "Da er da" 韃而靼 (Tartars), where the lone character *xi* 細 also stands, confirms this. On the *Wanguo quantu*, the *xi* is part of the continent's name Ya-xi-ya 亞細亞 (Asia), of which the two other characters (which Cao did not copy) span the continent.
38. The note even provides directions to the shop: to the north of Fangkou, at the crossroads with Horse Alley (*Fangkou beilang maxiang kou kaidian* 坊口北廊馬巷口開店). In today's Nanjing, this corresponds to the corner of Shengzhou Road and Zhongshan South Road.
39. Although Cao's map may well have provided Martini these data, it remains possible that Martini and Cao each relied on some no-longer-extant parent source. Although both sets of numbers exhibit minor discrepancies, the near-perfect match for all provincial statistics and road distances is remarkable, especially following a scouring of more than ninety late Ming works of geography for further duplicate data sets, to no avail (Cams, "Displacing China").
40. Small discrepancies include the fact that Wang dropped Cao's mimicking of the graticule.
41. Wang, "Qingdai chuzhongqi zuowei chanye de Suzhou banhua," esp. 19.
42. Wei, "Jianada Yingshu Gelunbiya daxue Yazhou tushuguan," 190–191. It was printed under the title *Rekidai bun'ya no zu kokin jinbutsu jiseki* 歷代分埜之圖古今人物事跡 (Map of astral allocations throughout the ages, with famous persons and important events then and now). Copies survive at the Yokohama City Library and at the University of British Columbia Library, Rare Books and Special Collections.
43. The title's first two characters changed from *Tianxia* to *Da Ming* in the Kyoto imprint. Besides the

reproduced copy kept at the MacLean Collection, further copies are at at several Japanese institutions. Fuchs, "Materialien," 395–396.

44. Moerman, *Japanese Buddhist World Map,* 188–200.
45. Ch'en, "Matteo Ricci's Contribution," 326.

References

Brezzi, Alessandra, Paolo De Troia, Anna Di Toro, and Lin Jinshui, eds. and trans. *Al Confucio di Occidente: Poesie Cinesi in onore di P. Giulio Aleni S.J.* Brescia: Fondazione civiltà Bresciana, 2005.

Brook, Timothy. *The Great State: China and the World.* New York: Harper, 2019.

Cams, Mario. "The Confusions of Space: Reading Ming China's Comprehensive Geographies." *Monumenta Serica* 69, no. 2 (2021): 515–547.

———. "Displacing China: The Martini-Blaeu Atlas and the Late Renaissance Shift in Representations of East Asia." *Renaissance Quarterly* 73, no. 3 (2020): 953–990.

Chen, Hui-Hung. "The Human Body as Universe: Understanding Heaven by Visualization and Sensibility in Jesuit Cartography in China." *Catholic Historical Review* 93, no. 3 (2007): 517–552.

Ch'en, Kenneth. "Matteo Ricci's Contribution to, and Influence on, Geographical Knowledge in China." *Journal of the American Oriental Society* 59, no. 3 (1939): 325–359.

Cheng Yinong 成一農. "*Guangyu tu*" *shihua* 《廣輿圖》史話. Beijing: Guojia tushuguan chubanshe, 2016.

D'Elia, Pascale M. "Recent Discoveries and New Studies (1938–1960) on the World Map in Chinese of Father Matteo Ricci SJ." *Monumenta Serica* 20, no. 1 (1961): 82–164.

Dennis, Joseph R. *Writing, Publishing, and Reading Local Gazetteers in Imperial China, 1100–1700.* Cambridge, MA: Harvard University Asia Center, 2015.

Destombes, Marcel. "Wang P'an, Liang Chou et Matteo Ricci: Essai sur la cartographie chinoise de 1593 à 1603" (An Essay on Chinese Cartography from 1593 to 1603). In *Actes du IIIe colloque international de sinologie, Chantilly 1980: Appréciation par l'Europe de la tradition chinoise à partir du XVIIe siècle,* 47–65. Paris: Les Belles Lettres, 1983.

Du, Yongtao. "Literati and Spatial Order: A Preliminary Study of Comprehensive Gazetteers in the Late Ming." *Ming Studies* 66 (2012): 16–43.

Dudink, Ad, and Nicolas Standaert. Chinese Christian Texts Database (CCT-Database). March 7, 2022. http://www.arts.kuleuven.be/sinology/cct.

Enoki, Kazuno. "On the Ku-chin hsing-shêng chih t'u of 1555." *Memoirs of the Toyo Bunko* 34 (1976): 243–254.

Fuchs, Walter. "Materialien zur Kartographie der Mandjuzeit I." *Monumenta Serica* 1, no. 2 (1935): 386–427.

Funakoshi, Akio. "Some New Lights on the History of Chinese Cartography." *Annual Report of Studies in Humanities and Social Sciences* 19 (1975): 147–170.

Guangxu Wuxi jinkui xianzhi 光緒無錫金匱縣志. 1881. Zhongguo fangzhi jicheng 中國地方志集成. Nanjing: Jiangsu guji chubanshe, 1991.

Hsia, Ronnie Po-Chia. *A Jesuit in the Forbidden City: Matteo Ricci, 1552–1610.* Oxford: Oxford University Press, 2010.

Huang, Shijian. "The Exploration of Matteo Ricci's World Map." In *New Perspectives on the Research of Chinese Culture,* edited by Pei-kan Cheng and Ka Wai Fan, 119–136. Singapore: Springer, 2013.

Jin Guoping 金國平. "Guanyu *Gujin xingsheng zhi tu* zuozhe de xin renshi" 關於《古今形勝之圖》作者的新認識. In *Gujin xingsheng zhi tu yanjiu* 古今形勝之圖研究, edited by Li Yuzhong and José Luis Caño Ortigosa, 51–63. Hsinchu: Qingda renshi zhongxin, 2016.

Kajdánski, Edward. "The Ming Dynasty Map of China (1605) from the Czartoryski Library in Poland." In *Actes du VIIe colloque international de sinology de Chantilly: Échanges culturels et religieux entre la China et l'Occident,* 183–190. Paris: Institut Ricci, 1995.

Mittag, Achim. "'Offensive Expansion' und 'innere Kolonisation'—das Fallbeispiel China." In *Expansionen in der Frühen Neuzeit,* edited by Renate Dürr, Gisela Engel, and Johannes Süßmann, 69–95. Berlin: Duncker and Humblot, 2005.

Moerman, D. Max. *The Japanese Buddhist World Map: Religious Vision and the Cartographic Imagination.* Honolulu: University of Hawaiʻi Press, 2022.

Saliba, George. *Islamic Science and the Making of the European Renaissance.* Cambridge, MA: MIT Press, 2007.

Shirley, Rodney W. *The Mapping of the World: Early Printed World Maps, 1472–1700.* London: Holland Press, 1983.

Song, Gang. "Re-locating the 'Middle Kingdom': A Seventeenth-Century Chinese Adaptation of Matteo Ricci's World Map." In *Mapping Asia: Cartographic Encounters between East and West,* edited by Martijn Storms et al., 185–206. New York: Springer International, 2018.

Szczesniak, Boleslaw. "The Seventeenth-Century Maps of China: An Inquiry into the Compilations of European Cartographers." *Imago Mundi* 13 (1956): 124–126.

Tang Kaijian 湯開建, and Zhou Xiaolei 周孝雷. "Mingdai Li Madou shijie ditu chuanbo shi si ti" 明代利瑪竇世界地圖傳播史四題. *Ziran kexueshi yanjiu* 自然科學史研究 34, no. 3 (2015): 294–315.

Unno, Kazutaka 海野一隆. "Concerning a MS Map of China in the Bibliothèque Nationale, Paris, Introduced to the World by Monsieur M. Destombes." *Memoirs of the Toyo Bunko* 35 (1977): 205–217.

———. "Han minzoku shakai ni okeru rekishi chizu no hensen" 漢民族社會における歷史地図の変遷. In *Tōyō chirigakushi kenkyū: Tairiku hen* 東洋地理学史研究: 大陸編, 58–109. Osaka: Seibundō, 2004.

Wallis, Helen. "Purchas' Maps." In Vol. 1 of *The Purchas Handbook: Studies of the Life, Times, and Writing of Samuel Purchas, 1577–1626,* edited by L. E. Pennington, 145–166. London: Hakluyt Society, 1997.

Wang Zhenghua 王正華. "Qingdai chuzhongqi zuowei chanye de Suzhou banhua yu qi shangye mianxiang" 清代初中期作為產業的蘇州版畫與其商業面向. *Zhongyang yanjiuyuan jindaishi yanjiusuo jikan* 中央研究院近代史研究所集刊 92 (2016): 1–54.

Wei Yin-Zong 韋胤宗. "Jianada Yingshu Gelunbiya daxue Yazhou tushuguan cang *Jiuzhou fenye yutu gujin renwu shiji*" 加拿大英屬哥倫比亞大學亞洲圖書館藏《九州分野輿圖古今人物事跡》. *Mingdai yanjiu* 明代研究 27 (2016): 189–219.

Yan, Ping. *China in Ancient and Modern Maps.* London: Sotheby's, 1998.

PART II

Beyond Ming China: Wider Circulation and Global Pathways

6

World Maps from China Reimagined in Japan

ELKE PAPELITZKY

SEVENTEENTH-CENTURY JAPAN SAW THE RISE OF A flourishing publishing market for maps, including various representations of the world. One popular image of the world was that of the *Kunyu wanguo quantu* 坤輿萬國全圖 (J. *Kon'yo bankoku zenzu*; Complete map of all countries on earth; figure 1.1), which Matteo Ricci (1552–1610), Li Zhizao 李之藻 (1565–1630), and others had printed in Beijing in 1602. Despite a ban on anything relating to Christianity entering Japan from 1630 onward, both the *Kunyu wanguo quantu* and the *Liangyi xuanlan tu* 兩儀玄覽圖 (Mysterious visual map of the two forms, 1603; figure 1.2), as well as books including world maps, reached Japan from China during the seventeenth century, inspiring Japanese mapmakers to craft numerous replicas and new artifacts based on these prototypes in the centuries that followed. Three of the seven known extant prints of the 1602 *Kunyu wanguo quantu* are currently in Japan, and a fourth left Japan only recently.[1] In all, Japan has played an important role in conserving such artifacts from across East Asia, allowing us to reconstruct what became of these depictions of world geography as they moved into a new environment.

Through previous scholarship we have a relatively good grasp of the circulation in Japan of the *Kunyu wanguo quantu* and other world maps made in China, as well as the existence and location of Japanese artifacts using these as their source.[2] However, equally interesting are the processes and methods of creation of the Japanese artifacts. Japanese mapmakers reworked their source material in numerous aspects: materials (e.g., paper/screen/plate/book), format (size), language (Chinese, Japanese, or a mix), and the information contextualizing the maps. Some changed the depiction of particular regions or combined depictions from various sources, not unlike the recombination of material onto the printed maps Mario Cams discusses in chapter 5.

The mapmakers made these changes with their intended audience in mind, targeting different readerships from political elites to common people while, as Cheng Fangyi points out in chapter 4, the choice of format had a profound impact on the way these maps were consumed. This chapter focuses on the interval from the made-in-China artifacts' first arrival in Japan in the early seventeenth century until 1720, when the censorship of Christianity loosened slightly, resulting, together with a flourishing publishing market, in far greater diversification and popularization of world maps.

In China

Scholars in the late Ming took great interest in world geography, an area of knowledge they generally associated closely with history. The *Kunyu wanguo quantu* and *Liangyi xuanlan tu*, on the other hand, mingled world geography with astronomy, displaying information about the earth's sphericity and the heavenly bodies in the map's margins. When Chinese scholars incorporated world maps and adapted Renaissance ideas in their own works, their underlying assumptions varied, so every such work employed the maps slightly differently (see Nicolas Standaert's appendix in chapter 1 for a list of these works).

Feng Yingjing 馮應京 (1555–1606) retained the cosmological context when he placed the "Shanhai yudi quantu" 山海輿地全圖 (Complete map of mountains, seas, and lands; figure 1.6) at the beginning of his almanac *Yueling guangyi* 月令廣義 (Extended meaning of the monthly proceedings, 1602) alongside a star chart, depictions of the planetary spheres, diagrams for calendrical science, and other astronomical and astrological information. Most other Chinese scholars, however, included world maps in books about geography and history or in encyclopedia chapters on geography. The encyclopedia *Sancai tuhui* 三才圖會 (Illustrated compendium of the three powers [i.e., heaven, earth, and humankind], 1609), for example, placed the same map in a section on geography that the *Yueling guangyi* used surrounded by cosmological matters (figure 1.7).[3]

Most Ming scholars located these world maps inside the domain of geography, but they did not agree on their exact purpose and point of view: Should these maps be understood as including China in the wider world, or should they be juxtaposed to a China-centric worldview? For the compilers of the world history and geography book *Fangyu shenglüe* 方輿勝略 (Complete survey of the earth, 1612), a project initiated by Feng Yingjing, the answer was clear.[4] They included a detailed map in two hemispheres (figure 1.5), credited to Ricci, in the second part of their work dealing with the "outer barbarians" (*waiyi* 外夷), which were clearly distinct from the chapters discussing the geography of China at the beginning of the book. The compilers of a subsequent geographical work disagreed. They placed a world map in two hemispheres (using the one from the *Fangyu shenglüe* as their main source) at the very beginning of the book, ahead of a map of China and individual maps of the provinces, thus structuring the maps from largest to smallest and showing China situated within the two-hemisphere map.[5] All this shows that Chinese scholars employed world maps for various purposes, purposes that could shift when incorporating maps into new works.

From China to Japan

Prints of the *Kunyu wanguo quantu* and the *Liangyi xuanlan tu* reached Japan in late 1605 or shortly thereafter, perhaps sent by Ricci himself and taken there by his fellow Jesuits (probably from Beijing to Japan via Macao).[6] Stand-alone world maps and Chinese books containing world maps, however, also entered Japan via other channels. During the Edo period (1603–1867), transmission from China into Japan ran primarily through Nagasaki—due to the Japanese government's strict trading policy, which had banned Portuguese and Spanish traders from entering Japan.[7] In 1630 a ban on books promoting Christianity resulted in the import of books becoming a highly controlled business: censors had to search every arriving book for references to Christianity. In 1685 the ban tightened to include books even mentioning Ricci's name. The discovery of any forbidden passage led to the burning of the relevant pages and the dispatch back to China of both the books and any other trade goods the ship had on board. Restrictions lifted slightly in 1720 to admit any works, even those mentioning Ricci's name, as long as they did not proselytize Christianity. These rules affected not only the importation of books into Japan but also the publication of books there.[8]

The only Chinese book containing a world map that appeared on the list of banned books is Giulio Aleni (1582–1649) and Yang Tingyun's 楊廷筠 (1557–1627) *Zhifang waiji* 職方外紀 (Record of everything beyond the administration, first printed in 1623).[9] The other Chinese books containing such world maps faced a direct threat of censorship upon the stricter ban of 1685.[10] Evidence shows that nearly all of them entered Japan within just a few years of being printed in China, and most arrived by the 1650s at the latest, long before the stricter 1685 rules.[11] Although the *Kunyu wanguo quantu* is not included in any censorship list, two extant prints of the 1602 *Kunyu wanguo quantu* do show clear traces of censoring (see the appendix in chapter 1): the print held by Kyoto University lacks the three Jesuit seals bordering the map. The print held by the James Ford Bell Library has had not only the seals removed but also Ricci's name and references to the Christian God (figures 6.1 and 6.2). Chinese ship captains were well aware of the restrictions and their penalties, suggesting that the merchants removed the references to Christianity. The James Ford Bell Library print might have thus arrived in Japan between 1685 and 1720 when censorship was at its strictest, while the lesser damage to the Kyoto version suggests a date of arrival between 1630 and 1685 or after 1720, when mentioning Ricci was acceptable but more direct references to Christianity were not. Censorship rules directly shaped the circulation of world maps between China and Japan.

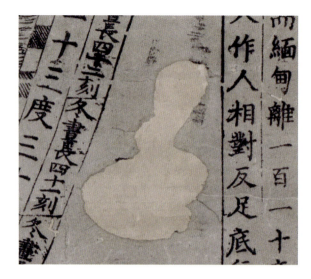

FIGURE 6.1.

A detail of the 1602 *Kunyu wanguo quantu*, showing a damaged section where a Jesuit seal had once been. Main Library, Kyoto University.

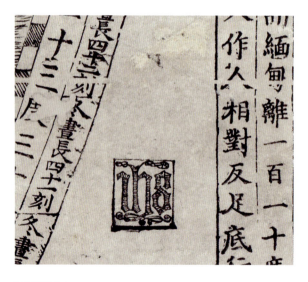

FIGURE 6.2.

The same detail on the intact 1602 print of the *Kunyu wanguo quantu* (compare to figure 6.1; the full image is figure 1.1). Miyagi Prefectural Library, Sendai.

From *Kunyu wanguo quantu* to *Kon'yo bankoku zenzu*: Stand-alone Maps and Globes

After arriving in Japan, many of the world maps, whether included in books or stand-alone, inspired new artifacts ranging from rather faithful replicas to maps significantly altered in materiality and content. In general, mapmakers had two choices: They could produce stand-alone maps (on one or several sheets) or globes, either printed or in manuscript form on paper or on screens, for publication or private consultation. Maps might, alternately, find themselves in books—primarily printed and published. Of course, even maps in the first category were not necessarily stand-alone but often accompanied by other images: pictures of people, maps of Japan, and so on. On such objects, world maps were an *essential* element, whereas maps in books were only one part of a greater whole. In the following section, I will first consider works consisting primarily of a map (or a globe), followed by other works in which maps are merely embedded in larger artifacts.

New configurations could be created not just by drawing new maps but by manipulating the actual print itself, as seen in one of the extant 1602 prints of the *Kunyu wanguo quantu*, now held by the Naikaku Bunko (figure 6.3). This copy conserves only the oval image of the world, neatly omitting the cosmographical framing of the Jesuit seals and most of the references to Ricci. The map had been kept in Nagasaki before the local magistrate (*bugyō* 奉行) had it cut into pieces and then glued onto ten strips of paper. On the backside of these and two additional strips is a colorful manuscript map of East Asia titled *Huangyu tu* 皇輿圖 (Map of imperial territories). In 1734 the local magistrate then gifted the artifact to the shogunal library in Edo, the Momijiyama Bunko 紅葉山文庫.[12] Instead of presenting an image of the world together with cosmographical information, this 1602 print serves to contextualize the much more detailed geography of East Asia on the sheets' backsides. Similar processes of repurposing are also apparent in Japanese manuscripts and commercial publications based on the Chinese prototypes.

Edo-period Japan enjoyed a flourishing market in publishing stand-alone maps. Although a real increase in publishing activity can be seen in the eighteenth century, its origins lie in the seventeenth. The most widely circulating world maps of the time in Japan were titled *Bankoku sōzu* 萬國總圖 (Complete map of all countries), published first in Nagasaki in 1645 and republished in multiple iterations over subsequent decades (figure 6.4). These artifacts combine a world map with images of peoples, drawing from Chinese, Dutch, and Japanese materials including one or more maps similar to the *Kunyu wanguo quantu*.[13] Their size and intended purpose varied from carefully colored objects for decoration to smaller prints targeting a more general public, some of them tiny enough when folded to fit easily inside the sleeve of a kimono to carry around and consult whenever and wherever one wished.[14]

FIGURE 6.3.

The 1602 print of the *Kunyu wanguo quantu* held by the Naikaku Bunko. The map is glued to ten strips of paper and pasted on the back of a manuscript map of East Asia in twelve strips titled *Huangyu tu*. The twelve strips measure approx. 444 × 348 cm when joined together. Each of the twelve strips can be folded into a small booklet. Naikaku Bunko, Tokyo.

FIGURE 6.4.

Bankoku sōzu, 1645 Nagasaki print. Mounted on hanging scrolls. The map (*right*) is accompanied by a second scroll showing images of people (*left*). Each scroll measures 134.5 × 57.6 cm. Moriya-Hisashi Collection, Hiroshima Prefectural Museum of History Collection.

More than twenty large manuscripts titled *Kunyu wanguo quantu* that resemble the 1602 print in many aspects survive in Japan, either as sheet maps or mounted on screens and sometimes even employing gold coloring.[15] Precisely dating most of these maps is unfortunately impossible, although the presence of certain place-names indicates manufacture in the late seventeenth century at the earliest, while those more precisely dateable are, with few exceptions, from the late eighteenth and nineteenth centuries.[16] Probably the best-known copy today, in the Kanō Collection 狩野文庫 at the Tōhoku University Library in Sendai, has appeared as a cover of or illustration in several recent books and even in support of arguments based (supposedly) on the 1602 *Kunyu wanguo quantu*.[17]

While manuscripts close to the 1602 printed *Kunyu wanguo quantu* exist, in each case the Japanese mapmaker altered the map, from making seemingly minor adjustments such as adding Japanese translations of place-names to more obvious modifications like coloring, redrawing coastlines, and changing the information surrounding the map.[18] Most manuscripts retain the cosmological material surrounding the map itself in the 1602 *Kunyu wanguo quantu*. One example of a scholar for whom astronomical information was central was the astronomer Shibukawa Harumi 渋川春海 (1639–1715). He not only possessed a world map (probably one titled *Kunyu wanguo quantu*) but also produced several globes and a world map. The depictions of coastlines on these artifacts, particularly the recognizable squared outline of a protrusion on the northern coastline of the great southern continent of Magellanica, labeled "New Guinea," follow the *Kunyu wanguo quantu*.[19] Harumi paired celestial and terrestrial maps and globes, more centrally emphasizing the duality of geography and astronomy expressed marginally on the *Kunyu wanguo quantu* and exhibiting through his globes what Ricci had described in prefaces on this map: the earth is a sphere and part of a larger whole that includes the celestial world as well.[20]

This composition of the 1602 *Kunyu wanguo quantu*, framing geographical and astronomical information within cosmographical understanding, did not catch on in the Edo-period print market: no known printed world map contains any astronomical references. The *Bankoku sōzu* presents perhaps the most radical departure, depicting not only a world map but also images of ships and an additional sheet showing images of forty-two human pairs from all over the world, an idea inspired from Dutch maps.[21] It exchanged astronomical for ethnographical material, better suiting a curious urban audience. Readers could learn about both the earth and its different peoples, as the introduction emphasized: "Since its beginning, this world has been vast and mankind has been without limits. Countries differ and people are also different. [One can distinguish them according to their] appearances; [there are] big and small ones, [as well as] black and white men and women. The [variegated] shapes are compared and shown [on this map]."[22] Most mapmakers, such as Harame Sadakiyo 原目貞清 in his 1720 *Yochizu* 輿地圖 (Map of the land; figure 6.5), extracted only the oval world map from the *Kunyu wanguo quantu*, without adding new surrounding materials. Only the

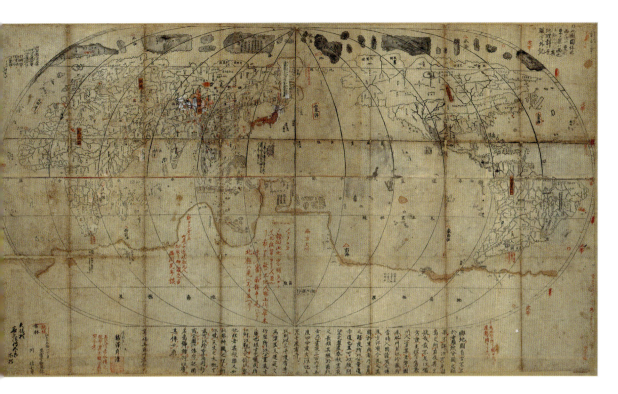

FIGURE 6.5.

Harame Sadakiyo's *Yochizu* (1720). 85.3 × 151.7 cm. This print includes handwritten annotations by Nagakubo Sekisui. Ashida Bunko of Meiji University Library, Tokyo.

geography of the earth interested Sadakiyo, so he omitted the descriptions at the edges of the *Kunyu wanguo quantu*. His map became the model for most large Japanese world maps through the end of the Edo period. Smaller maps either followed Sadakiyo or the idea of the *Bankoku sōzu*, juxtaposing a map with more popular and pictorial materials. They completely lacked the *Kunyu wanguo quantu*'s connection to cosmology.

Japanese mapmakers also used different sources to redraw parts of the coastlines. First, many mapmakers replaced the image of the Japanese archipelago with one showing more place-names and the outlines of the provinces, the latter image widely available in seventeenth-century maps of Japan. The mapmakers also added information regarding the maritime area of the Indian Ocean and of East and Southeast Asian waters, including the imaginary islands of Gold and Silver and several sandbanks throughout the oceanic space. Several mapmakers even changed the coastlines of Southeast Asia, drawing most likely on information from Japanese portolan charts.[23] The *Bankoku sōzu* had already exhibited these revisions in the 1640s, suggesting their incorporation into a prototype created in the first half of the seventeenth century (figure 6.6). While nearly all printed stand-alone world maps published throughout the

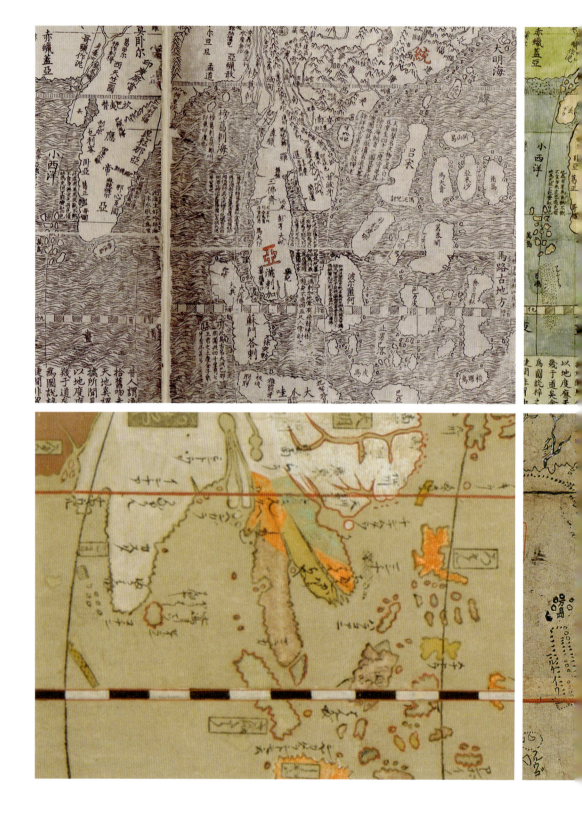

FIGURE 6.6.

A comparison of a section of South and Southeast Asia of the 1602 *Kunyu wanguo quantu* (Miyagi Prefectural Library, *upper left*), a Japanese manuscript replication (Kanō Collection, *upper right*), the 1645 *Bankoku sōzu* (Moriya-Hisashi Collection, *lower left, rotated 90 degrees*), and the *Yochizu* (Ashida Collection, *lower right*). Note the addition of shallow water (marked as dots, e.g., in the Bay of Bengal) on the three latter maps and the revised island coastlines on the lower two maps.

Edo period followed these changes, Japanese manuscripts titled *Kunyu wanguo quantu* employed them far more variably.[24]

The most universal changes the Japanese mapmakers made when using the Chinese source material were also the least visible: in language and script. While the more faithful copies of the *Kunyu wanguo quantu* typically preserved both explanatory texts and place-names in Chinese, most Japanese mapmakers thought it important to give their readership a pronunciation aid for all place-names not in China or Japan, glossing or replacing the Chinese characters with their phonetic equivalent in kana—the Japanese syllabic writing system. However, they generally retained intact all introductory Chinese texts. One exception, a later iteration of the *Bankoku sōzu* published in 1671, supplemented the introductory texts with a Japanese translation, a change that probably contributed to its success. Japanese readings of place-names were far from uniform across the *Bankoku sōzu*, the *Yochizu*, and the manuscript *Kunyu wanguo quantu*, at times reflecting Japanese readings of Chinese characters or transliterations into Japanese from European languages. At different times, multiple people, each with at least working knowledge of a European language, transcribed place-names into Japanese.

All these changes, especially the transliterations and translations, turned these Japanese world maps borrowing from the *Kunyu wanguo quantu* and its cousins into maps of a new kind. The printed artifacts in the seventeenth and early eighteenth centuries bear no hint of the Jesuits' involvement; none mentions Ricci by name. The *Bankoku sōzu* even obscures China's role. Through the translation into Japanese, the 1671 print, especially, was rendered into a fundamentally "Japanese" artifact. The mapmakers intended it to be easy to understand and less scholarly, an aim that was also particularly important for the iterations of the *Bankoku sōzu* in encyclopedias, discussed below.

In contrast to the *Bankoku sōzu*, Harame Sadakiyo's *Yochizu* claims a "Chinese" provenance for his map, stating a man from Quanzhou 泉州 had brought a map to Japan. As Sadakiyo's map includes the usual modifications typical for most Japanese adaptations of the *Kunyu wanguo quantu*—revised coastlines of Japan and Southeast Asia and most place-names expressed in kana—it is unlikely he adapted a Chinese map. Sadakiyo may have tried to obscure its Jesuit origin, in contrast to the geographer Nagakubo Sekisui 長久保赤水 (1717–1801), who used Sadakiyo's map several decades later in producing his own *Chikyū bankoku sankai yochi zenzusetsu* 地球萬國山海輿地全圖説 (Explanation of the complete geographical map of the earth, all countries, mountains, and seas; published in at least two editions between 1785 and 1795). Sekisui identifies the prototype map as the work of a Mr. Li 利氏 (Ricci's last name in Chinese), who had arrived in China and created the map in Beijing in 1601 [*sic*]. This was well in line with most of the more faithful Japanese manuscript *Kunyu wanguo quantu*, which continued acknowledging their Jesuit origin, including Ricci's name and even the seals.[25] We must remember, however, that the manuscripts bearing Ricci's name, like Sekisui's published map, generally postdate 1720 and so avoided stringent censorship.

Buddhist world maps also draw from information derived from Renaissance geographic material. Following a trajectory of maps focusing on the Buddhist continent of Jambudvīpa at least back to the fourteenth century shows that early eighteenth-century Japanese mapmakers supplemented this Buddhist image with material mapping Europe and the Americas. One popular print of these maps was Hōtan's 鳳潭 (1659–1738) *Nansenbushū bankoku shōka no zu* 南瞻部洲萬國掌菓之圖 (Handy map of all countries of Jambudvīpa, 1710; figure 6.7). Conceptually, it resembles the maps Cams discusses in chapter 5 of this volume: India and central Asia (in this case instead of China) at the center surrounded by landmasses in the corners that draw from Renaissance world geography. This map not only resembles the China-centered commercial maps in its layout but draws from the Japanese replica of Wang Junfu's 王君甫 map published in Kyoto before 1706 under the title *Dai Min kyūhen bankoku jinseki rotei zenzu* 大明九邊萬國人跡路程全圖 (Complete map of human traces and route itineraries in all countries and the nine frontiers of the Great Ming; figure 5.10).[26] Through several stages, place-names from the *Zhifang waiji* thus made it onto this Buddhist map of Jambudvīpa, the Buddhist context replacing a Christian one.[27] All these examples of world maps produced in the sixteenth and early seventeenth centuries show that mapmakers drawing from the *Kunyu wanguo quantu*, *Zhifang waiji*, and other material fundamentally transformed their source material, creating new artifacts that visibly and discursively detached them from the prototypes produced in early seventeenth-century China. Similar processes also took place in the case of maps in books, as illustrated next.

Geography within the Encyclopedia: Maps as Illustrations in Books

In Japan, as in China, world maps drawing from Renaissance ideas commonly appeared printed in books. From the late seventeenth century on, fully Japanese replicas of the *Bankoku sōzu* figured prominently in several household encyclopedias (*setsuyōshū* 節用集; figures 6.8 and 6.9).[28] The writing of these books—almost entirely in Japanese with very few Chinese characters—rendered them accessible to a broad readership. Other authors drew more directly from the world maps contained in Chinese books. They produced more scholarly works and translated the Chinese texts into Japanese, although they were still intended to be accessible to a wider audience. In contrast to the *setsuyōshū*, however, these works used more Chinese characters, and in some cases, rather than preparing full translations, the authors only annotated a Chinese text with *kundoku* 訓読 marks (instructions on reading Chinese texts; for a list of these Japanese works, see the appendix). These books are not translations of the Chinese books but independent works that happen to contain maps replicated therefrom. The only apparent exception, at first glance, is the *Wakan Sansai zue* 和漢三才圖會 (Japanese-Chinese *Sancai tuhui,* 1712) by Terajima Ryōan 寺島良安, which presents itself as a

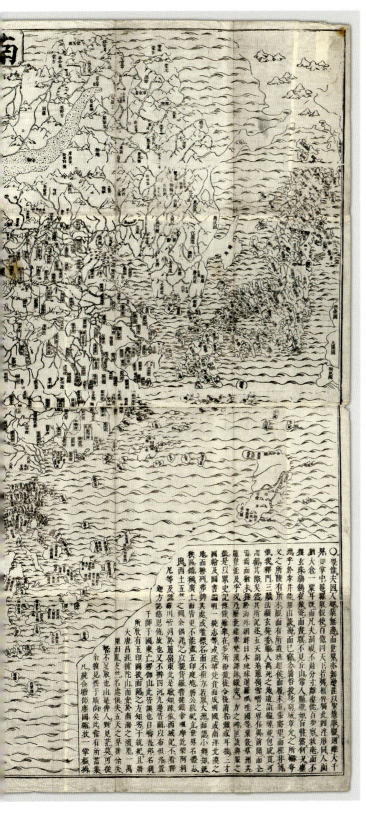

FIGURE 6.7.

Hōtan's *Nansenbushū bankoku shōka no zu*, printed in 1710 by Nagata Chōbei. 113.1 × 142.2 cm. University of British Columbia, Japanese Maps of the Tokugawa Era, G3201.S2 1710 H6.

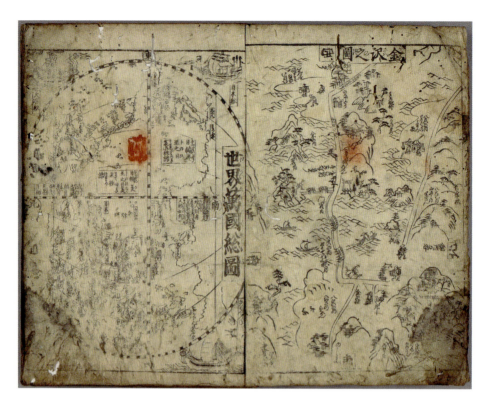

FIGURE 6.8.

The "Sekai bankoku sōzu" included in the *Kashiragaki taisei setsuyōshū: Nigyō ryōten* (1691). Height, 26.5 cm. Waseda University Library, Tokyo.

Japanese version of the *Sancai tuhui*. In reality, Ryōan made significant changes when producing his encyclopedia for the Japanese market and added much information compared to the Chinese work.[29]

While all known printed stand-alone maps revised the coastlines, maps inside books often preserved the coastlines and place-names depicted on the maps they emulated. Even though the books were in Japanese, their maps often kept the Chinese place-names without adding text in kana. Those with revised maps often incorporated changes typical in Japan: glossing the place-names phonetically in Japanese, changing depictions of Japan, and, in one case, adding sandbanks to the oceanic space (figures 6.10 and 6.11).[30]

More substantial changes, however, are evident in a world map titled "Chikyū bankoku ichiran no zu" 地球萬國一覽之圖 (Overview map of the globe and all countries) in an oval shape contained in Nishikawa Joken's 西川如見 (1648–1724) geography *Zōho ka-i tsūshōkō* 増補華夷通商考 (Expanded study of the trade between the civilized and the barbarians, 1708).[31] This map is rather similar to that from the *Sancai*

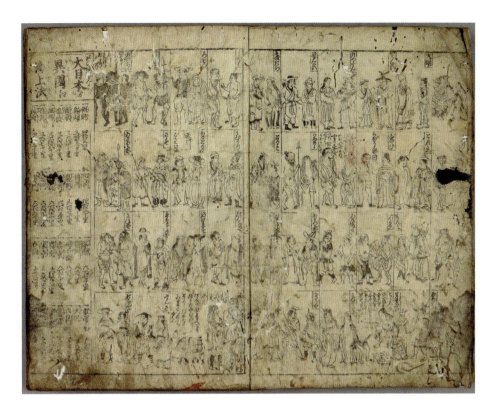

FIGURE 6.9.

Images of people from the *Kashiragaki taisei setsuyōshū: Nigyō ryōten* directly following the world map. Height, 26.5 cm. Waseda University Library, Tokyo.

tuhui (figure 1.7), but it is oval instead of round and includes additional notes (figure 6.12). Jōken used Aleni and Yang Tingyun's *Zhifang waiji* for his description of foreign peoples, so it is likely Jōken combined the *Zhifang waiji*'s world map (figure 2.9) with that from the *Sancai tuhui*, although the continents' simplified shapes and the relatively few place-names make it difficult to tell for certain.[32] One significant addition is the label "New Holland" (Shin Woranda 新ヲランダ) on the southern continent, perhaps the earliest mention of Australia on a Japanese map.[33]

Although many of these Japanese maps underwent few changes to depictions of the coastlines and their overall shape compared to their Chinese predecessors, Japanese books changed the circumstances in which these maps appeared. As in the Chinese books, world maps were sometimes placed at the front to frame subsequent maps, showing that everything to follow was part of the same world,[34] or they illustrated everything that was not China or Japan.[35] As discussed, Chinese books tended to embed the world maps in discussions of geography or, at times, of cosmology and astronomy. While we can identify those contexts in Japanese books as well, a map could easily shift

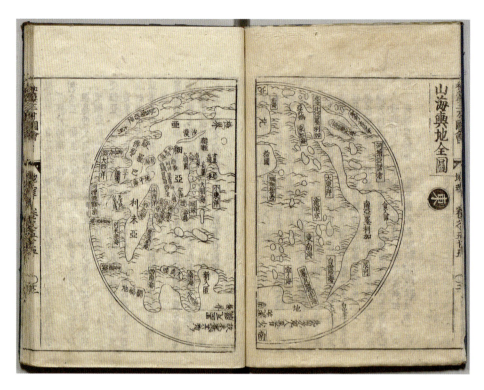

FIGURE 6.10.

The "Sankai yochi zenzu" in the *Wakan Sansai zue* (1712). No Japanese readings were added to the place-names compared to the Chinese map (figure 1.7). Height, 27.1 cm. Naikaku Bunko, Tokyo.

its purpose: a map found in a Chinese book on geography, for example, could appear in an astronomical book in Japan.

In Japan, world maps seem to have been especially important to writers of astronomical books, as evinced by several extant astronomical treatises including such a map.[36] Geography and astronomy were considered closely related, as Nishikawa Joken remarked: "Astronomy, geography, and the study of *yun-ch'i* [*yunqi*] 運氣:[37] these three are inseparable,"[38] and "Geography is a branch of astronomy."[39] Despite these claims, he did not include any terrestrial maps in the books he wrote on astronomy. In his writings, world maps served only geographical functions, and only his world geography *Zōho ka-i tsūshōkō* includes one. Makers of Japanese encyclopedias, like Joken, filed the map within the realm of geography and not that of astronomy. While the *Kunyu wanguo quantu* combined geography and astronomy, in general a map in Japan illustrated *either* geography *or* astronomy despite the area of knowledge's proximity.

Comparing the *Sancai tuhui* with the *Wakan Sansai zue*, which claims descent from the Chinese text, also serves to reveal the differing perceptions of the "Shanhai

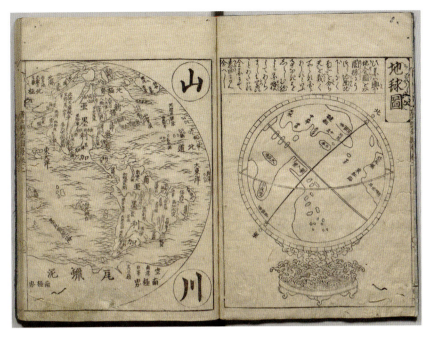

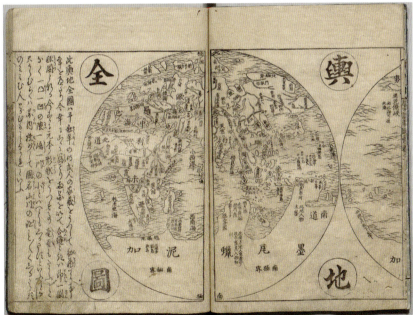

FIGURE 6.11.

The "Sansen yochi zenzu" in the *Morokoshi kinmō zui* (1719) based on the map in the *Fangyu shenglüe* (figure 1.5). Preceding the map is an illustration of a globe to emphasize the sphericity of the earth. Height, 21.5 cm. Naikaku Bunko, Tokyo.

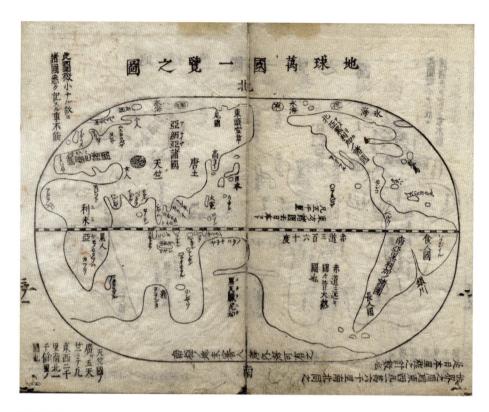

FIGURE 6.12.

World map titled "Chikyū bankoku ichiran no zu" from Nishikawa Joken's *Zōho ka-i tsūshōkō* (1708). Height, 21 cm. Naikaku Bunko, Tokyo.

yudi quantu" involved. As in the *Sancai tuhui*, in the *Wakan Sansai zue* the world map appears at the beginning of a chapter but more generally depicts a section on "earth" (*chi* 地). Following the map is not a further description of the geography of China or of Japan but a section on earthquakes and architecture, followed by a section on mountains. China's geography only comes up several chapters later. Indeed, it appears the map had become relevant to everything even remotely connected to the "earth," not only geography and mapmaking. These examples illustrate each Japanese author's slightly different understanding of the world map's purpose and the ease with which each applied it wherever it was considered relevant.

Unlike several of their Chinese predecessors, none of these sixteenth- and early seventeenth-century Japanese books ascribe the maps' origin as connected to Ricci.[40] The world maps in the *setsuyōshū* contain no comments about their source material. It is doubtful the makers of these *setsuyōshū* even knew of the maps' history, as establishing their provenance was not their concern, and none of the *Bankoku sōzu* mentioned any non-Japanese involvement, Chinese or European. Those authors who consulted the Chinese books may well have known of Ricci's involvement. However, many of the Japanese books, just like Harame Sadakiyo's *Yochizu,* strongly emphasize their content's Chinese origin without considering any European link, such as to Ricci. The titles of many invoke China explicitly, employing terms such as *Ka-i* 華夷 (The civilized and the "barbarian," a Chinese concept for the Japanese), *Wakan* 和漢 (Japan and China), *Morokoshi* 唐土 (the land of the Tang, one way of referring to the Chinese in Edo-period Japan), or references to Chinese dynasties (Min-Shin/Ming-Qing 明清). For these authors, then, not crediting Ricci certainly reflected censorship, even though they knew about the Jesuit's involvement in the Chinese artifacts from which they drew. Arai Hakuseki 新井白石 (1657–1725), for example, was clearly aware of the world maps' connection to the Chinese books because he mentions several of them alongside the *Kunyu wanguo quantu* in his records of interviewing the Jesuit Giovanni Battista Sidotti (1668–1714) in prison in 1709.[41] When Nishikawa Joken's son Nishikawa Seikyū 西川正休 published in 1730 a Japanese version of one of the Chinese books on astronomy that included a world map, the book named ten European "astronomers," including Ricci, Aleni, and other Jesuits.[42] As soon as the Japanese authors were allowed to mention the Jesuits again, they named them as their sources.

Chinese artifacts that incorporated a Renaissance knowledge of geography reached Japan in multiple waves over the seventeenth century, where Japanese mapmakers then started to use them in various ways. They reworked them into every imaginable format: onto expensive and beautiful screens, reproduced fairly faithfully as single- or multi-sheet maps, incorporated into books, and made into globes. The material aspect of the world maps was not static. These processes continued over the course of the Edo period, which saw more of the expensive screens produced. In the late eighteenth century, world maps in two hemispheres were even placed on pairs of ceramic plates.[43] The material combined with the maps, from both the *Kunyu wanguo quantu* and the world maps inside Chinese books, also changed. One mapmaker would remove the astronomical information, while another might add astronomical information, while again others might add new elements altogether absent from the maps in China. This is seen most prominently in the *Bankoku sōzu* with its images of peoples.

The censorship of Christianity inarguably had an impact on Japanese mapmakers and authors. At times they felt compelled to remove any links to Ricci, the results of which are evident especially in the case of the *Bankoku sōzu* and its inclusion in the *setsuyōshū:* the document's translation and recontextualization effectively erased all traces of its European and Chinese links. Many of the authors using these world maps may well have assumed its author as Ricci, but censorship restricted them from mentioning the Jesuit. Their readers may then—quite reasonably—have understood the map as precisely what many such books claimed it to be: "Knowledge from China." In the minds of Japanese readers, the different world maps became European, Chinese, or Japanese representations of a world that all coexisted.

Appendix

World maps printed before 1720 in Japan:

- *Bankoku sōzu* 萬國總圖. Several artifacts with the same title and mostly the same content. Printed in 1645 (Nagasaki; figure 6.4), 1652 (no place), 1668 or earlier (Kyōto, published by Eya Shōbei 絵屋庄兵衛), 1671 (Kyōto, by Hayashi Jizaemon 林次左衛門), as well as several undated prints and manuscripts.
- *Bankoku sōkaizu* 萬國總界圖 by Ishikawa Ryūsen. Editions of 1688 (published in Edo by Sagamiya Tahei 相模屋太兵衛) and 1708 (published in Edo by Suhara Mohei 須原茂兵衛).
- Harame Sadakiyo's 原目貞清 1720 *Yochizu* 輿地圖, published in Edo (figure 6.5).
- Inagaki Kōrō's 稲垣公朗 *Sekai bankoku chikyūzu* 世界萬國地球圖, 1708.
- Hōtan's 鳳潭 (1659–1738) Buddhist world map *Nansenbushū bankoku shōka no zu* 南瞻部洲萬國掌菓之圖, published by Bundaiken Uhei 文臺軒宇平 and later by Nagata Chōbei 永田調兵衞, both dated 1710 (figure 6.7).
- Wang Junfu's 王君甫 China-centered world map published by Umemura Yahaku 梅村弥白 in Kyoto before 1706 under the title *Dai Min kyūhen bankoku jinseki rotei zenzu* 大明九邊萬國人跡路程全圖 (figure 5.10).

Pre-1720 Japanese printed books with world maps:

- The map from the *Sancai tuhui* and *Yueling guangyi* appears in three works, keeping the title of the map "Shanhai yudi quantu"/"Sankai yochi zenzu":
  - Matsushita Kenrin's 松下見林 (1637–1703) *Ron'ō benshō* 論奧辨證 (1665), *jō* 14b–15a, citing the *Sancai tuhui*.
  - Terajima Ryōan's 寺島良安 *Wakan Sansai zue* 和漢三才圖會 (1712), 55.2b–3a (figure 6.10).
  - Baba Nobutake's 馬場信武 *Shogaku tenmon shinanshō* 初學天文指南鈔 (1706), 1.18ab. This map does not have only one source. Islands and labels point to the map in the *Tianjing huowen* 天經或問, while the annotations around the map as well as the title show that Nobutake used either the *Sancai tuhui* or *Yueling guangyi*.
- A map in an oval projection titled "Chikyū bankoku ichiran no zu" 地球萬國一覽之圖 in Nishikawa Joken's *Zōho kai tsūshōkō* 增補華夷通商考 (1708), inserted before the third chapter (figure 6.12). Joken possibly combined information from the map of the *Sancai tuhui* and the world map from the *Zhifang waiji*.
- The two-hemisphere map from the *Huiji yutu beikao quanshu* appears in Maezono Sōbu's 前園噌武 *Min-Shin tōki* 明清鬪記 (1661), keeping the title "Tendozu" 纏度圖.
- The map of the *Fangyu shenglüe* appears in Hirazumi Sen'an 平住專庵 (text) and Tachibana Morikuni's 橘守國 (1679–1748, credited as Naramura Yūzeishi 楢村有税子, illustrations) *Morokoshi kinmō zui* 唐土訓蒙圖彙 (1719), 2.2a–3a (figure 6.11). The map title was changed to "Sansen yochi zenzu" 山川輿地全圖.
- An image of a globe and a section of a map showing the eastern part of Asia, parts of the southern continent, and the western part of North America. The images are probably unrelated:

- *Morokoshi kinmō zui*, 2.1b; titled "Chikyūzu" 地球圖.
- Iguchi Tsunenori's 井口常範 *Tenmon zukai* 天文圖解 (1689), *zu* 5b–6a; map titled "Konten chigizu" 渾天地儀圖.
- Nishikawa Joken's *Nihon suido kō* 日本水土考.

- Maps titled "Sekai bankoku sōzu" 世界萬國總圖 in the following *setsuyōshū* using the 1671 *Bankoku sōzu* as their main source:
  - *Kashiragaki taisei setsuyōshū: Nigyō ryōten* 頭書大成節用集：二行両点 (1691; figures 6.8 and 6.9).
  - *Kashiragaki taisei setsuyōshū* 頭書大成節用集, published by Yorozuya Seibei 万屋清兵衛 (1696).
  - *Kashiragaki zōho taisei setsuyōshū* 頭書増補大成節用集, published by Suharaya Mohei 須原屋茂兵衛 (1698 and 1699).
  - *Hōrin setsuyōji kaitaisei* 宝林節用字海大成, published by Suharaya Mohei (1712).
  - *Kinji setsuyō mukyūsei* 錦字節用無窮成 (1714).

- Maps titled "Bankoku no zu" 萬國之圖 also drawing from the 1671 *Bankoku sōzu* in the following books:
  - An untitled *setsuyōshū* dated 1695 held by the Provincial University of Kumamoto.
  - *Nendaiki Shin-eshō* 年代記新繪抄 (1711).

Notes

This research was supported by and contributes to the European Research Council AdG project TRANSPACIFIC, which has received funding under the European Union's Horizon 2020 Research and Innovation Programme (Grant agreement No. 833143).

1. For a list, see the appendix in chapter 1.
2. Japanese scholars of the twentieth century, especially Aoki Chieko and Ayusawa Shintarō, have pioneered research into the history of the *Kunyu wanguo quantu* in Japan, accessible in part to an English-speaking audience through Unno Kazutaka's contribution to the *History of Cartography* (Aoki, "Mateo Ricci no sekaichizu"; Aoki, "Nihon ni genson suru *Kon'yo bankoku zenzu*"; Aoki, "Wa ga kuni ni genson suru *Kon'yo bankoku zenzu*"; Ayusawa, *Nihon bunkashi jō ni okeru Ri Matō no sekai chizu*; Ayusawa, "Geography and Japanese Knowledge"; Unno, "Cartography in Japan"). Several of the Japanese manuscript copies of the *Kunyu wanguo quantu* are reproduced in Tsuchiura Shiritsu Hakubutsukan, *Sekaizu yūran*.
3. On this map, see Ptak, "Sino-European Map"; Ayusawa, "Getsurei kōgi shosai no Sankai yochi zenzu."
4. Feng Yingjing started the project, but he died before the *Fangyu shenglüe* could be finished. Cheng Bai'er then took over the project, gathered further scholars, and had the book printed. For details, see Papelitzky, "Viejas y nuevas miradas."
5. Pan and Li, *Huiji yutu beikao quanshu*, 1.1b–3a.
6. Ricci mentions in a letter dated May 9, 1605, that Francesco Pasio (1554–1612) had found several of Ricci's works useful and was therefore requesting that he send the "world maps" (in plural)

and additional texts to Japan (Ricci, *Lettere,* 384). Some have misunderstood this as indicating the maps' presence for teaching in Kyoto as early as 1605. See Bernard, *Matteo Ricci's Scientific Contribution,* 70; Huang, "Exploration of Matteo Ricci's World Map," 134. Unno cites Bernard on this issue (Unno, "Cartography in Japan," 404). Huang Shijian mistranslates the letter, claiming that Ricci wrote that he had already sent the maps, while the original Italian reads: "E così adesso vogliono . . . i *Mappamondi*" (And so they [the fathers in Japan] now want the world maps). Although no prints of the *Liangyi xuanlan tu* are extant in Japan today, it surely arrived there as well because Iguchi Tsunenori 井口常範 cites one of Matteo Ricci's prefaces to the *Liangyi xuanlan tu* in his *Tenmon zukai* 天文圖解 (*zu,* 5ab). See also Unno, *Chizu no bunkashi,* 140.

7. W. J. Boot suggests that Kagoshima may have been a second major port of entry (Boot, "Transfer of Learning," 189).

8. Ibid., 193–195; Kornicki, *Book in Japan,* 325–331; Ōba, *Books and Boats,* 40–65.

9. For these lists, see Konta, *Edo no kinsho,* 7–13; Ōba, *Books and Boats,* 46–47, 62. The censorship did not, however, impede the circulation of the *Zhifang waiji,* as evidenced by the many surviving Japanese manuscripts. See chapter 3 in this volume.

10. This is a fate that befell Xiong Renlin's 熊人霖 (1604–1667) *Diwei* 地緯 (Weft of the earth), which was destroyed in 1686 upon arrival in Japan (Ōba, *Books and Boats,* 62).

11. For example, the Owari-Tokugawa family 尾張徳川家 bought the 1623 reprint of the *Tushu bian* now held in the Hōsa Bunko 蓬左文庫 in 1629. See Kyoto University, http://kanji.zinbun.kyoto-u.ac.jp/kanseki?record=data/FAHOUSA/tagged/0960007.dat&back=1. The National Archives of Japan also holds a print of the *Yueling guangyi* formerly owned by Hayashi Razan 林羅山 (1583–1657), indicating the arrival of prints in the first half of the seventeenth century.

12. Aoki, "Wa ga kuni ni genson suru *Kon'yo bankoku zenzu,*" 111; Ōsawa, "Landscape-Style Maps in Early Modern China," 72–73.

13. The coastlines seem, at first glance, to be copied from the *Kunyu wanguo quantu* but, on closer examination, appear more like the coastlines from a two-hemisphere map such as the *Fangyu shenglüe* set into the *Kunyu wanguo quantu*'s oval projection. On this map, see Papelitzky, "Description and Analysis."

14. The 1671 *Bankoku sōzu,* for example, measures only 40 × 56 cm, combining the images of people and the world map on one sheet. When folded together, the booklet measures ca. 7 × 13 cm. For a scan of the map held by the Bavarian State Library, including the cover when folded, see urn:nbn:de:bvb:12-bsb00064977–2.

15. For a list, see Tsuchiura Shiritsu Hakubutsukan, *Sekaizu yūran,* 53. Since this list's compilation, several additional maps have come to light. For a scan of a version using gold held by the Hayashibara Museum of Art, see http://sumiyakenji.xsrv.jp/data/konyo-hayashibara-mus/, n.d.

16. The maps locate the place-name Dongning 東寧, which did not exist before 1664, on Taiwan or on an island south of Taiwan (Aoki, "Nihon ni genson suru *Kon'yo bankoku zenzu,*" 6).

17. For a scan, see *Kon'yo bankoku zenzu,* n.d., http://www.i-repository.net/contents/tohoku/kano/ezu/kon/kon.html. This version's popularity can be explained by its presence in Wikipedia, s.v. *Kunyu wanguo quantu,* October 18, 2022, https://en.wikipedia.org/wiki/Kunyu_Wanguo_Quantu#/media/File:Kunyu_Wanguo_Quantu_(坤輿萬國全圖).jpg. While relatively faithful

to the 1602 *Kunyu wanguo quantu* if the unmistakable change in color is disregarded, it is not identical because it contains the place-name Dongning and several other alterations of oceanic geography typical of Japanese versions.

18. Most of these differences were noted in Aoki, "Nihon ni genson suru *Kon'yo bankoku zenzu*," 5–6.
19. Aoki, "Nihonjin to Kon'yo bankoku zenzu," 10. Aoki bases this on accounts by Harumi's student Tani Jinzan 谷秦山 (1663–1718), who claimed Harumi showed him the map in 1704. His maps, a pair of screens of a celestial and a terrestrial map held in a private collection in Japan, have received little attention. They are reproduced in Oda et al., *Nihon kochizu taisei,* 154–155. A small photograph is available online, http://www.mus-his.city.osaka.jp/news/2018/tenjigae/180530.html, 2018. In contrast to the creation of the Chinese globe discussed in chapter 2 of this volume, Harumi produced globes based only on material sources and did not collaborate with Jesuits.
20. There are conflicting data on Harumi's globes. According to Unno, Harumi created terrestrial globes in 1690 and 1697 (Unno, "Cartography in Japan," 391, 466–467). Utsunomiya Yōjirō, on the other hand, argues that he made a celestial globe in 1697 following three terrestrial globes in 1690, 1692, and 1695 (Utsunomiya, "Nihon chikyūgi seisakushi shūi"). For a detailed study of the 1690 globe, including the techniques of its production, see Utsunomiya, "Jingū Chōko Nōgyō kanzō."
21. Several Japanese world maps combine images of people on screens, probably inspired by the maps by Willem Janszoon Blaeu (1571–1638) that feature engravings by Claes Janszoon Visscher (1587–1652). See Papelitzky, "Description and Analysis," 45–46.
22. For a translation of the whole introduction, see ibid., 40.
23. For examples of such portolan charts, see Nakamura, "Japanese Portolanos."
24. One of the few published examples lacking revised coastlines for Japan and Southeast Asia is Inagaki Shisen's 稲垣子戩 *Kon'yo zenzu* 坤輿全圖 (1802), although it does include the additional sandbanks in the Indian Ocean and Southeast Asian waters. The well-known manuscript *Kunyu wanguo quantu* at the Kanō Collection displays the same coastlines as Shisen's map, while another manuscript held by the Tsuchiura Museum only revises Japan. On Shisen's map, see Kaida, *Zusetsu zōran,* 73–74, 94–95. For a reproduction of the Tsuchiura map, see Tsuchiura Shiritsu Hakubutsukan, *Sekaizu yūran,* 12–13.
25. One exception, a manuscript held by the MacLean Collection, replaces Ricci's name with the generic "A Man from the West" (Seiyōjin 西洋人). This map also curiously changes the title in the map's upper-right corner from *Kunyu wanguo quantu* to *Zhifang waiji tushuo* 職方外紀圖說 (Illustrated explanation of the *Zhifang waiji*). Given that the *Zhifang waiji*—but not the *Kunyu wanguo quantu*—actually appeared listed as a censored book, this is a rather curious choice. For a scan of, and introduction to this map, see Papelitzky, "Remapping the World in Japan."
26. Moerman, *Japanese Buddhist World Map,* 188.
27. Moerman describes other Buddhist maps that used a similar process to enlarge the Buddhist geographical frame. One manuscript map in the Nanba Collection of the Kobe City Museum, for example, takes place-names in Europe from Nishikawa Joken's 1708 *Zōho ka-i tsūshōkō* and the coastlines from a *Bankoku sōzu* (Moerman, *Japanese Buddhist World Map,* 171–175).
28. On *setsuyōshū,* see Kinski, "Treasure Boxes."

29. On the maps in the *Wakan Sansai zue*, see Akin, *East Asian Cartographic Print Culture*, 252–258.

30. For an adaptation of the map from the *Fangyu shenglüe* with these changes, see Hirazumi and Naramura, *Morokoshi kinmō zui*, 2.2a–3a.

31. Nishikawa, *Zōho ka-i tsūshōkō*, inserted before *j*. 3. An earlier version of this text, lacking maps or illustrations, also exists. The term *Ka-i/Hua-yi* in the title refers to the Chinese duality separating the world into a civilized center (China) surrounded by "barbarians" (everyone else). Japanese writers also utilized this concept, even though (in the Chinese view) they themselves would be considered "barbarians." Joken actually makes a distinction between "foreign barbarians" (*gaii* 外夷) and "foreign countries" (*gaikoku* 外國), the latter using the Chinese script (*Zōho ka-i tsūshōkō*, 3.1a). He thus situates Japan in a third category, allowing him to keep the Chinese dichotomy of "civilized" and "barbarian" without having to declare Japan "barbarian."

32. Yachi, "Nishikawa Joken to *Shokuhō gaiki*." Certain place-names, such as Binghai 冰海 (Ice ocean) and Changrenguo 長人國 (Country of Tall People), do not appear on the maps from the *Sancai tuhui* or *Tianjing huowen* but do appear on Joken's map as well as on the *Kunyu wanguo quantu* and, more prominently, on the world map in the *Zhifang waiji*. While this does not demonstrate without a doubt that Joken copied the toponyms from the *Zhifang waiji* rather than from the *Kunyu wanguo quantu*, it is quite likely because we do know Joken had used the *Zhifang waiji*. It is of course also possible that he had access to further maps. The shape Joken gives New Guinea is much closer to that from the *Kunyu wanguo quantu* than that from the *Sancai tuhui* map.

33. On Australia in Japanese world maps, see Morimoto, "Edo-jidai no kochizu ni miru Ōsutoraria." The earliest map showing Australia in Morimoto's list dates to the mid-eighteenth century (ibid., 158).

34. Hirazumi and Naramura, *Morokoshi kinmō zui*, *j*. 2.

35. This is the approach taken by Nishikawa Joken, who included his world map in the section on the non-Japanese, non-Chinese world of his *Zōho ka-i tsūshōkō*. China is included in a separate chapter with its own map (Japan remains unmentioned in this work).

36. Matsushita, *Ron'ō benshō, jō*, 14b–15a; Baba, *Shogaku tenmon shinanshō*, 1.18ab; Iguchi, *Tenmon zukai, zu*, 5b–6a (after *j*. 5).

37. The *yunqi* theory relates to Chinese astrological medicinal knowledge. See Nakayama, *History of Japanese Astronomy*, 112–113.

38. Cited in ibid., 112.

39. Cited in ibid., 110.

40. Cheng Bai'er et al., *Fangyu shenglüe, waiyi*, 1.1.1a; Pan and Li, *Huiji yutu beikao quanshu, fanli*, 5ab; Zhang, *Tushu bian*, 29.35b; Feng, *Yueling guangyi, shoujuan*, 63b. Some prints of the *Yueling guangyi*, however, lack Ricci's signature at the end of the map's introduction. There are at least three different versions of this text, all held by the National Archives of Japan: one of these (call number 291–002) lacks the signature, while the other two (201–001 and 291–003) include it. Version 201–001 includes an additional map after the "Shanhai yudi quantu." The well-known version reproduced in the *Siku quanshu cunmu congshu* lacks both the additional map and the complete explanation of Ricci's map. Removing Ricci's name was likely not censorship, as another print held in Taipei by the National Central Library also omits the name.

41. Matsumura et al., *Arai Hakuseki*, 29. Hakuseki recorded information from these interviews in his

Seiyō kibun 西洋紀聞, completed in 1715 but widely available in Japan only in the eighteenth century's final years due to the belief that Christian matters were too sensitive. Ayusawa, "Geography and Japanese Knowledge of World Geography," 284; Paramore, *Ideology and Christianity,* 105.

42. Nishikawa, *Tenkei wakumon,* "kokin tengakka," 2b.
43. For a reproduction, see Nanba et al., *Nihon no kochizu,* 142.

References

Akin, Alexander. *East Asian Cartographic Print Culture: The Late Ming Publishing Boom and Its Trans-Regional Connections.* Amsterdam: Amsterdam University Press, 2021.

Aoki Chieko 青木千枝子. "Mateo Ricchi no sekaichizu: Nihon he no denrai to juyō" マテオ・リッチの世界地図：日本への伝来とその受容. *Shinika* しにか 6, no. 2 (1995): 31–39.

———. "Nihonjin to Kon'yo bankoku zenzu" 日本人と坤輿万国全図. In Tsuchiura Shiritsu Hakubutsukan, *Sekaizu yūran,* 8–11.

———. "Nihon ni genson suru *Kon'yo bankoku zenzu* shozu ni tsuite" 日本に現存する「坤輿万国全図」諸図について. *Kirishitan bunka kenkyūkai kaihō* キリシタン文化研究会会報 102 (1993): 1–12.

———. "Wa ga kuni ni genson suru *Kon'yo bankoku zenzu* no kanpon ni kansuru ikkōsatsu" 我が国に現存する「坤輿万国全図」の刊本に関する一考察. *Kyūko* 汲古 23 (1993): 100, 107–113.

Ayusawa, Shintarō 鮎澤信太郎. "Geography and Japanese Knowledge of World Geography." *Monumenta Nipponica* 19, no. 3–4 (1964): 275–294.

———. "Getsurei kōgi shosai no Sankai yochi zenzu to sono keitō" 月令廣義所載の山海輿地全圖と其の系統. *Chirigaku hyōron* 地理學評論 12, no. 10 (1936): 899–910.

———. *Nihon bunkashi jō ni okeru Ri Matō no sekai chizu* 日本文化史上に於ける利瑪竇の世界地圖. Tokyo: Ryūbun shokyoku, 1944.

Baba Nobutake 馬場信武. *Shogaku tenmon shinanshō* 初學天文指南鈔. 1706. https://rmda.kulib.kyoto-u.ac.jp/item/rb00028651.

Bernard, Henri. *Matteo Ricci's Scientific Contribution to China.* Translated by Edward Chalmers Werner. Peiping: Henri Vetch, 1935.

Boot, W. J. "The Transfer of Learning: The Import of Chinese and Dutch Books in Tokugawa Japan." *Itinerario* 37, no. 3 (2013): 188–206.

Cheng Bai'er 程百二 et al. *Fangyu shenglüe* 方輿勝畧. 1612. https://www.digital.archives.go.jp/img/4752484.

Feng Yingjing 馮應京. *Yueling guangyi* 月令廣義. 1602. https://nrs.lib.harvard.edu/urn-3:fhcl:4739755.

Hirazumi Sen'an 平住專庵, and Naramura Yūzeishi (Tachibana Morikuni) 楢村有税子 (橘守國). *Morokoshi kinmō zui* 唐土訓蒙圖彙. 1719. http://www.wul.waseda.ac.jp/kotenseki/html/bunko31/bunko31_e0864/.

Huang, Shijian. "The Exploration of Matteo Ricci's World Map." In *New Perspectives on the Research of Chinese Culture,* edited by Pei-kai Cheng and K. W. Fan, 119–136. Singapore: Springer, 2013.

Huang Shijian 黃時鑒, and Gong Yingyan 龔纓晏. *Li Madou shijie ditu yanjiu* 利瑪竇世界地圖研究. Shanghai: Shanghai guji chubanshe, 2004.

Iguchi Tsunenori 井口常範. *Tenmon zukai* 天文圖解. 1689. https://www.wul.waseda.ac.jp/kotenseki/html/i04/i04_03163_0229/.

Kaida Toshikazu 海田俊一. *Zusetsu zōran: Edo jidai ni kankō sareta sekai chizu* 図説総覧:江戸時代に刊行された世界地図. Tokyo: Ars Medica, 2019.

Kinski, Michael. "Treasure Boxes, Fabrics, and Mirrors: On the Contents and the Classification of Popular Encyclopedias from Early Modern Japan." In *Listen, Copy, Read: Popular Learning in Early Modern Japan,* edited by Matthias Hayek and Annick Horiuchi, 70–88. Leiden: Brill, 2014.

Konta Yōzō 今田洋三. *Edo no kinsho* 江戸の禁書. Tokyo: Yoshikawa kōbunkan, 2007.

Kornicki, Peter. *The Book in Japan: A Cultural History from the Beginnings to the Nineteenth Century.* Leiden: Brill, 1998.

Matsumura Akira 松村明, Bitō Masahide 尾藤正英, and Katō Shūichi 加藤周一, eds. *Arai Hakuseki* 新井白石. Tokyo: Iwanami shoten, 1975.

Matsushita Kenrin 松下見林. *Ron'ō benshō* 論奥辨證. 1665. https://rmda.kulib.kyoto-u.ac.jp/item/rb00028668.

Morimoto Mineko 森本峰子. "Edo jidai no kochizu ni miru Ōsutoraria" 江戸時代の古地図に見るオーストラリア. *Eibei bunka* 英米文化 30 (2000): 141–159.

Nakamura, Hirosi. "The Japanese Portolanos of Portuguese Origin of the XVIth and XVIIth Centuries." *Imago Mundi* 18 (1964): 24–44.

Nakayama, Shigeru. *A History of Japanese Astronomy: Chinese Background and Western Impact.* Cambridge, MA: Harvard University Press, 1969.

Nanba Matsutarō 南波松太郎, Muroga Nobuo 室賀信夫, and Unno Kazutaka 海野一隆, eds. *Nihon no kochizu* 日本の古地図. Osaka: Sōgensha, 1969.

Nishikawa Joken 西川如見. *Zōho ka-i tsūshōkō* 増補華夷通商考. 1708. http://www.wul.waseda.ac.jp/kotenseki/html/i13/i13_00581/.

Nishikawa Seikyū 西川正休. *Tenkei wakumon* 天經或問. 1730. https://www.wul.waseda.ac.jp/kotenseki/html/bunko01/bunko01_01597/.

Ōba, Osamu. *Books and Boats: Sino-Japanese Relations in the Seventeenth and Eighteenth Centuries.* Translated by Joshua A. Fogel. Portland, ME: Merwin Asia, 2012.

Oda Takeo 織田武雄, Muroga Nobuo 室賀信夫, and Unno Kazutaka 海野一隆. *Nihon kochizu taisei: Sekaizu hen* 日本古地図大成: 世界図編. Tokyo: Kōdansha, 1975.

Ōsawa, Akihiro 大澤顯浩. "Landscape-Style Maps in Early Modern China: Maps and the Representation of Historical Geography." *Memoirs of the Toyo Bunko* 74 (2016): 61–100.

Pan Guangzu 潘光祖, and Li Yunxiang 李雲翔. *Huiji yutu beikao quanshu* 彙輯輿圖備考全書. 1633. https://www.digital.archives.go.jp/img/4752499.

Papelitzky, Elke. "A Description and Analysis of the Japanese World Map *Bankoku sōzu* in Its Version of 1671 and Some Thoughts on the Sources of the Original *Bankoku sōzu.*" *Journal of Asian History* 48, no. 1 (2014): 15–59.

———. "Viejas y nuevas miradas sobre los 'bárbaros': El *Fangyu shenglüe* 方輿勝略 (1612)." In *Periferias imaginadas: "Bárbaros" en el este asiático desde la antigüedad y a lo Largo de la era imperial,* edited by Ana Carolina Hosne, Paula Hoyos Hattori, and Ignacio Villagrán, Puntarenas, 57–88, Editorial de la Sede del Pacífico, Universidad de Costa Rica, 2023.

Papelitzky, Elke, Katie Osborne, and Jami Biddle. "Remapping the World in Japan." In *Map Chat,* edited by Richard Pegg. 2022. https://www.leventhalmap.org/projects/remapping-the-world-in-japan/html/index.html.

Paramore, Kiri. *Ideology and Christianity in Japan.* London: Routledge, 2009.

Ptak, Roderich. "The Sino-European Map (*Shanhai yudi quantu*) in the Encyclopaedia *Sancai tuhui.*" In *The Perception of Maritime Space in Traditional Chinese Sources,* edited by Angela Schottenhammer and Roderich Ptak, 191–207. Wiesbaden: Harrassowitz, 2006.

Ricci, Matteo. *Lettere (1580–1609).* Edited by Francesco D'Arelli. Macerata: Quodlibet, 2001.

Tsuchiura Shiritsu Hakubutsukan 土浦市立博物館, ed. *Sekaizu yūran: Kon'yo bankoku zenzu to Higashi-Ajia* 世界図遊覧: 坤輿万国全図と東アジア. Tsuchiura: Higashi Nihon insatsu, 1996.

Unno, Kazutaka 海野一隆. "Cartography in Japan." In *The History of Cartography.* Vol. 2, bk. 2, *Cartography in the Traditional East and Southeast Asian Societies,* edited by J. B. Harley and David Woodward, 346–477. Chicago: University of Chicago Press, 1994.

———. *Chizu no bunkashi: Sekai to Nihon* 地図の文化史: 世界と日本. Tokyo: Yasaka shobō, 1996.

Utsunomiya Yōjirō 宇都宮陽二朗. "Jingū Chōko Nōgyō kanzō no iwayuru Shibukawa Harumi saku chikyūgi ni kansuru kenkyū" 神宮徴古館農業館蔵のいわゆる渋川春海作地球儀に関する研究. *Jinbun ronsō* 人文論叢 23 (2006): 29–36.

———. "Nihon chikyūgi seisakushi shūi: Shibukawa Harumi (Yasui Santetsu) seisaku ni kakaru saiko no chikyūgi" 日本地球儀製作史拾遺: 渋川春海（安井算哲）製作に係る最古の地球儀. *Nihon chirigakkai happyō yōshishū* 日本地理学会発表要旨集, 2015, 100176.

Yachi Aya 谷内彩. "Nishikawa Joken to *Shokuhō gaiki: Zōho kai tsūshōkō* wo chūshin ni" 西川如見と『職方外紀』:『増補華夷通商考』を中心に. *Jōchi daigaku bunka kōshōgaku kenkyū* 上智大学文化交渉学研究 6 (2018): 11–23.

Zhang Huang 章潢. *Tushu bian* 圖書編. 1613. http://nrs.harvard.edu/urn-3:FHCL:28553803.

7

From China to Korea

Kim Suhong's Cheonha gogeum daechong pyeollam do

YANG YULEI

Kim Suhong 金壽弘 (1601–1681) produced the *Cheonha gogeum daechong pyeollam do* 天下古今大總便覽圖 (Comprehensive overview map of all under heaven then and now; hereafter *Pyeollam do*) in 1666 (figure 7.1). The *Pyeollam do* is a Sinocentric map depicting China and surrounding regions yet includes several notes tying it to the circulation of geographic knowledge between western Europe and East Asia. The terms "Matteo Ricci" and "Country of Europe" appear north of the Great Wall as if they were place-names. In addition, Kim Suhong's preface refers to information from the *Kunyu wanguo quantu* 坤輿萬國全圖 (Complete map of all countries on earth, 1602; figure 1.1) or *Liangyi xuanlan tu* 兩儀玄覽圖 (Mysterious visual map of the two forms, 1603; figure 1.2).

Author Kim Suhong originated from a well-known branch of the Kim family from Andong 安東 in Gyeongsang Province 慶尚道. His grandfather was Kim Sangyong 金尚容 (1561–1637), known for having committed suicide in Gangwa 江華 city in 1637 during the Manchu-Qing invasion of Korea. Sangyong's brother, Kim Sanghyeon 金尚憲 (1570–1652), was also famous—for protesting against submission to the Qing empire. Belying this family history, however, Kim Suhong did not despise the Qing but was in fact the first Korean scholar (in 1674) to publicly refer to the Chinese state as "Qing" when ridiculing Korean retaliations against it.[1] Kim came into contact with and read works from the Ming and the Qing, including those coauthored by European Jesuits, since several members of his family had visited Beijing as Korean envoys to China and had brought such books back to Korea.[2] When he composed the *Pyeollam do* in 1666, Kim Suhong's official position at the Ministry of Works (Gongjo jeonglang 工曹正郎) put him in charge of matters related to maps.³

Since the *Pyeollam do* is one of the few extant dateable Korean maps, scholars have been paying close attention to it since the 1970s, focusing mainly on the various surviving prints and manuscripts and their characteristics. The first modern scholars to study the map included Kim Yangseon 金良善, A. L. Mackay, and Lee Chan 李燦. All examined the woodblock print in the Korean Catholic Museum of Soongsil (Sungsil) University; Mackay and Lee Chan also discussed several colored manuscripts.⁴ Recent decades have brought further copies to light. Oh Sanghak 吳尙學, Lim Jongtae 林宗台, and I have discussed further printed and manuscript versions kept at the Seoul Museum of History and the Korean National Central Museum. Gari Ledyard emphasizes that Kim's map reflects the close association of map and text as a perennial feature of East Asian cartography.⁵ Oh Sanghak, as well, describes some features of the map and its relationship to aspects of Ming maps, while Lim Jongtae argues that Kim used information from Matteo Ricci (1552–1610) to bolster Confucian ideology.⁶

Each of these authors treated the *Pyeollam do* as representative of Korean mapmaking, generalizing from its characteristics without extensive textual substantiation. In this chapter, by comparing the configurations and contents of each extant copy, I argue that the *Pyeollam do* drew most of its content from maps of a kind popular in Ming China (emphasizing historical geography with the addition of past toponyms) while adding astronomical and geographical information from the *Kunyu wanguo quantu* or *Liangyi xuanlan tu*. In the seventeenth century, prints of these two maps carried from China to Korea captured the interest of intellectuals there (as in China) due to the intriguing geography and worldview they conveyed. Following the *Pyeollam do*'s circulation throughout Korea during the eighteenth and nineteenth centuries, popular Korean atlases incorporated simplified versions. In the process, however, references to information that Kim had taken from the *Kunyu wanguo quantu* or *Liangyi xuanlan tu* were deleted, reflecting coeval Korean (and Chinese) intellectuals' attitudes toward the sort of geographical knowledge that had entered East Asia in the hands of European missionaries.

Content and Extant Versions

As a traditional world map centered on China, Kim Suhong's map mainly displays Ming China's geography in a rectangular shape, exaggerating river systems and important mountains and emphasizing Ming administrative divisions, including provinces, prefectures, and counties. The map also indicates the names of the twenty-eight constellations, which link celestial phenomena to terrestrial ones, a concept known as *fenye* 分野 (astral allocations).⁷ In addition, there are place-names past and present, road distances between certain provinces (or prefectures), and historical figures and cultural sites, as well as the names of several areas and states surrounding Ming China and Joseon Korea. These also include legendary countries from the classical geography *Shanhai jing* 山海經 (Classic of mountains and seas), such as the country of the people with long arms (Changbi Guo 長臂國), the country of the people with long legs (Changjiao Guo 長腳國), and the country of the small people (Xiaoren Guo 小人國).

The woodblock copies of the map contain three paragraphs of text: The first two appear above the map proper, presenting the distances between capitals and between different provinces and prefectures. In the map's left margin, a preface by Kim Suhong states that the arrangement of the twenty-eight constellations on the four sides of heaven accords with the ancient Chinese astronomical treatise *Tianwen zhi* 天文志 (On the heavens). In his preface, Kim also infers that "the celestial bodies are round" from the description of the distances between heaven and earth in the Chinese classical text *Huainan zi* 淮南子 and points out the use of different methods for observing celestial bodies over time. Kim writes that in Matteo Ricci's astronomical studies, a degree divided into sixty parts and one degree on the surface of the earth measured 250 *li* 里, while the Korean scholar Jang Yu's 張維 (1587–1638) *Gyegok manpil* 谿谷漫筆 (Gyegok's literary notes) records one degree as constituting 2,932 *li* on the surface of the earth. In addition, Kim emphasizes that various works of geography record differing distances between various places on the earth's surface, justifying his copying road distances from several sources: in the two paragraphs above the map he used road distances from the Ming state gazetteer *Da Ming yitong zhi* 大明一統志 (Gazetteer of the unified Great Ming, 1461) and the encyclopedia *Tongdian* 通典 (Comprehensive compendium, 801), while for those distances marked on the *Pyeollam do* itself he used a Ming encyclopedia titled *Wanbao quanshu* 萬寶全書 (Complete book of myriad treasures).

Six copies of the *Pyeollam do* are currently extant: four woodblock prints and two colored manuscripts (for a list, see table 7.1). The four woodblock prints are presently at the Christian Museum of Soongsil University (map 1), the Seoul Museum of History (map 2; figure 7.1), the Library of Tenri University (map 3), and the Songam Art Gallery (map 4).[8] Maps 2 and 3 seem to be identical, but all other maps are not. Their key differences include not only their depictions of the Great Wall, the wavy seas, and the mountain symbols, but also their annotations regarding certain mountains and rivers, such as the Amnok (Yalu 鴨綠) and Tumen (Douman 豆滿) Rivers and Baekdu (Baitou 白頭) Mountain. In addition, certain symbols for place-names and the place-names themselves differ, while the typesetting of Kim's preface in maps 2 and 3 deviates from the other two prints. On map 4, the note "reprinted in the year *jiazi* 甲子" (indicating 1684) appears at the end of the preface. In short, the four copies are printed from three different woodblocks, which means the *Pyeollam do* was carved more than once and enjoyed a relatively wide distribution in Joseon Korea.

Two colored manuscript copies also exist, one at the National Museum of Korea (map 5) and the other in a private collection extensively discussed by A. L. Mackay (map 6).[9] The layout of map 5 is markedly different: it includes no title, while Kim's

Table 7.1. Extant prints and manuscripts of the *Pyeollam do* and related maps

NO.	TITLE	SIZE (HEIGHT × WIDTH) (CM)	PRINT OR MANUSCRIPT	COLLECTION PLACE	NOTES
1	*Cheonha gogeum daechong pyeollam do*	approx. 142.8 × 89.5	Print	Christian Museum of Soongsil University	
2	*Cheonha gogeum daechong pyeollam do*	approx. 139.3 × 89.9	Print	Seoul Museum of History	
3	*Cheonha gogeum daechong pyeollam do*	approx. 127 × 96.5	Print	Tenri University Library	Possibly printed from the same blocks as map 2
4	*Cheonha gogeum daechong pyeollam do*	?	Print	Songam Art Gallery	Includes note: "Reprinted in the year *jiazi*" (1684?) 甲子年重刊
5	No title	approx. 144 × 79.5	Manuscript	National Museum of Korea	
6	…*pyeollam yeoji do*	approx. 132 × 84	Manuscript	?	Map discussed by Mackay
7	No title	approx. 110.0 × 77.5	Manuscript	Seoul Museum of History	Source map of Kim Suhong's map
8	No title	approx. 30.0 × 37.6	Manuscript	National Library of Korea	In the atlas *Joseon jidu bu paldo cheonha jido* 朝鮮地圖附八道天下地圖 made between 1666 and 1767
9	No title	approx. 29.6 × 35.3	Manuscript	Tenri University Library	In the atlas *Jido* made between 1666 and 1767
10	"Cheonha Jungguk do"	approx. 37.4 × 30.0	Manuscript	Tenri University Library	In the atlas *Yeoji do* made between 1666 and 1767
11	"Cheonha jido"	approx. 36.5 × 30.0	Manuscript	Yeungnam University Museum	In the atlas *Cheonha jido* made in about the middle of the eighteenth century

preface is at the top of the map rather than on the left side (as on the printed maps), and the paragraphs recording road distances are just below the preface. The manuscript also omits most of the geographical information in the northeast portions of the woodblock editions, particularly such place-names as Wuguo Cheng 五國城, Huanglong Prefecture 黃龍府, Jianzhou 建州, and mountains and rivers such as Baekdu Mountain, the Amur (Heilong Jiang 黑龍江), and Songhua River 松花江, as well as some names of legendary countries from the *Shanhai jing*. The other missing content is the recorded travel distances, which the woodblock prints scatter throughout the provinces. Unfortunately, we cannot consult map 6 at present, complicating a comparison among the manuscript copies. Based on a low-resolution image, however, it appears its title diverges and reads [*Illegible*] *pyeollam yeoji do* 便覽輿地圖 (Overview map of the land) instead, unlike the woodblock editions.[10]

The Origins of Kim Suhong's Map

Scholars have also considered one colored manuscript map, previously in Lee Chan's private collection but currently at the Seoul Museum of History (map 7; figure 7.2),[11] to be a version of the *Pyeollam do*. Close comparison indicates it may indeed constitute an intermediate version between a possible Chinese source and the printed *Pyeollam do*: The map has no title and lacks the preface by Kim. Most of the contents match those of the woodblock copies, but important differences suggest Kim Suhong did not produce it. First, it records Emperor Taizu 太祖 as "Huang Ming Taizu" 皇明太祖 (Taizu of the imperial Ming): Huang Ming was a concept employed by Ming Chinese rather than Koreans, who usually referred to the Ming as *tianchao* 天朝 (heavenly dynasty). Second, the depiction of the Korean Peninsula is quite simplistic, only marking the country as Jizi Guo 箕子國, an old name for Korea, and the astral allocations of *wei* 尾 and *ji* 箕. In addition, it names Jeju 濟州 Island as Danluo country 耽羅國, a name mostly found in Chinese writings (e.g., Xu Jing's 徐兢 twelfth-century text *Gaoli tujing* 高麗圖經, "Illustrated introduction of Goryeo"). No Korean would likely have produced such annotations.

This last map was therefore either a Chinese work or a Korean replication of one, quite possibly the basis for Kim's map and arguably an intermediate version between the Chinese source map and the printed *Pyeollam do*. Further comparison with the six extant copies reveals more differences in detail. Historical figures such as Zhu Xi 朱熹 (1130–1200), Zhou Dunyi 周敦頤 (1017–1073), and Mencius (Meng Ke 孟軻, fourth century BCE), are all labeled with their honorific titles on this manuscript map,[12] while the *Pyeollam do* uses their proper names. Table 7.2 lists further differences in place-names and personal names. A Chinese print might have circulated in Ming China, facilitating its transmission to Korea and enabling Kim Suhong to adapt it, revising information and adding his preface and the two further text segments in order to produce a new artifact: the *Cheonha gogeum daechong pyeollam do*.

Table 7.2: Character differences between map 1 and map 7 in the provinces of Nanzhili and Henan

PROVINCE	MAP 1	MAP 7	NOTE
Nanjing	Bailuzhou 白鷺洲	Baigezhou 白[氵鴿]洲	Place-name, map 1 is correct
	Chang Yuchun 常遇春	Chang Yu 常遇	Personal name, map 1 is correct
	Ming Taizu 明太祖	Huang Ming Taizu 皇明太祖	
	Huqiushan 虎丘山	Hukoushan 虎口山	Mountain name, map 1 is correct
	Jiangdu 江都	Missing	Historical place-name
	Dahu 大湖	Taihu 太湖	Lake name should be Chaohu 巢湖
	Cai Shiji 采石矶	Cai Shijiang 采石江	Personal name, map 1 is correct
Henan	Xinchuan 莘川	Xinzhou 莘州	Historical place-name, map 1 is correct
	Shanzhou 陝州	Shanchuan 陝川	County name, map 1 is correct
	Cheng Hao 程顥	Chengbozi 程伯子	Personal name
	Cheng Yi 程頤	Chengshuzi 程叔子	Personal name
	Xiong'er 熊耳	Yan'er 燕耳	Mountain name, map 1 is correct
	Shao Yong 紹雍	Shaozi 紹子	Personal name

The connection to Chinese maps, although visibly obvious, is not straightforward to trace. Scholars have noted the similarities of Cao Junyi's 曹君義 *Tianxia jiubian fenye renji lucheng quantu* 天下九邊分野人跡路程全圖 (Complete map of all under heaven, the nine frontiers, astral allocations, human traces, and route itineraries, 1644; figure 5.8). They have also argued that the central part of Cao's map appears derived from the *Gujin xingsheng zhi tu* 古今形勝之圖 (Map of advantageous terrain then and now, 1555; figure 10.1), while the peripheral sections borrowed from the *Kunyu wanguo quantu*.[13] However, as Mario Cams shows in chapter 5 of this volume, these maps in fact had no direct relationship: Cao's map instead borrows from the *Wanguo quantu* 萬國全圖 (Complete map of all countries) linked to Giulio Aleni (1582–1649) and Yang Tingyun's 楊庭筠 (1562–1627) *Zhifang waiji* 職方外紀 (Record of everything beyond the administration; figures 2.9 and 5.9) and the *Jiuzhou fenye yutu gujin renwu shiji* 九州分野輿圖古今人物事跡 (Map of astral allocations of the Nine Regions, with famous persons and important events then and now, 1643; figure 5.4) by Ji Mingtai 季明臺.[14] Nonetheless, despite the lack of any traceable direct relation between these maps, the *Pyeollam do*, Cao's map, and the *Gujin xingsheng zhi tu*, as well as Liang Zhou's 梁輈 *Qiankun wanguo quantu gujin renwu shiji* 乾坤萬國全圖古今人物事跡

YANG

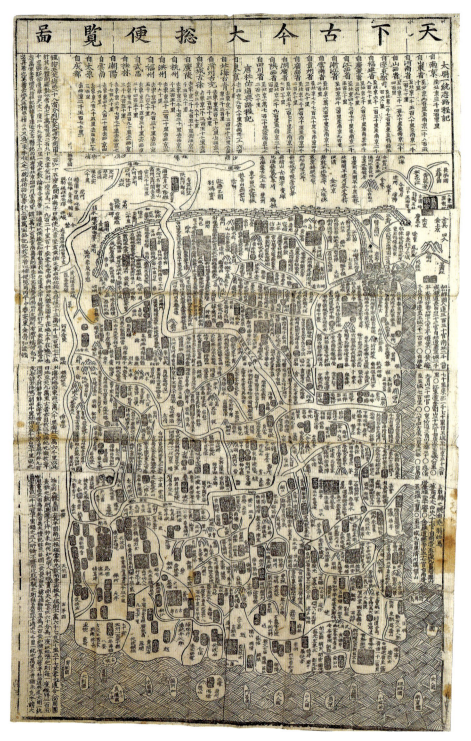

FIGURE 7.1.

Cheonha gogeum daechong pyeollam do (1666). Map 2. 139.3 × 88.9 cm. Seoul Museum of History.

FIGURE 7.2.

Intermediary manuscript copy of the *Pyeollam do*. Map 7. No title. 110 × 77.5 cm. Seoul Museum of History.

(Complete map of all countries in the universe, with famous persons and important events then and now; figure 5.7, left) all share common characteristics, including the Sinocentric layout and the inclusion and emphasis of information of a historical nature. We can therefore consider the *Pyeollam do* a continuation of a certain type of large map popular in late Ming China.

Despite the *Pyeollam do*'s similarities with such large maps, most of which round off China's southeastern coastline, the shape of China on the *Pyeollam do* is more rectangular. This divergence indicates connections to a further format. Illustrated encyclopedias intended for everyday public use known as *riyong leishu* 日用類書 (encyclopedias for daily use) became very popular during the Wanli (1573–1620) and Chongzhen periods (1628–1644). One subset of *riyong leishu*,[15] sometimes generally called *Wanbao quanshu* after their titles, included general maps of Ming China in sections titled "Geography Division" (Diyu men 地輿門), with the figuration of the continent squared very similarly to that on the *Pyeollam do* maps (figure 7.3).

Around thirty-five late Ming editions of *Wanbao quanshu* are extant. Although they include slightly different general maps with varying titles,[16] the maps share the same configurations and contents and include similar expressions and features as the *Pyeollam do*: first, all mark the names of the twenty-eight constellations and match them to provinces and prefectures, as well as mark the names of the ancient twelve *zhou* 州 (states); second, the water systems receive considerable emphasis. However, the *Wanbao quanshu* maps provide far fewer place-names and less text, so they do not appear as dense as the *Pyeollam do*.

The text accompanying the *Wanbao quanshu* provides further clues to the source of the additional place-names on the *Pyeollam do*. Some of the prefectures, counties, road distances, historical place-names, figures, and cultural sites present on the *Pyeollam do,* but not on the maps from the *Wanbao quanshu,* do appear in several chapters from the section on geography (Diyu men) titled "History of Geographical Nomenclature" (Yudi jiyuan 輿地紀原), "Dynastic Capitals through History" (Lidai guodu 歷代國都), "Routes of the Two Capitals and Thirteen Provinces" (Liangjing shisansheng lucheng 兩京十三省路程), and "Government Offices" (Tianxia yamen guanshu 天下衙門官署). In addition, no legendary countries appear in the maps of the *Wanbao quanshu,* while the section on foreigners (Zhuyi/Waiyi men 諸夷/外夷門) introduces geographical features of neighboring countries and regions, including a number of legendary ones. Some of these countries also appear on the *Pyeollam do*. Kim Suhong mentions in his preface to the map that "the route distances in *Wanbao quanshu* were recorded in each province," thus referring explicitly to that type of text. Although examining the many extant editions of *Wanbao quanshu* has yielded no precise match, it is clear that the *Pyeollam do* was based on a Chinese print closely related to the sorts of maps and accompanying texts the genre included.

The *Pyeollam do* also absorbs content from the *Kunyu wanguo quantu* or *Liangyi xuanlan tu*.[17] Kim Suhong recorded the terms "Li Madou" 利瑪竇 (Matteo Ricci) and

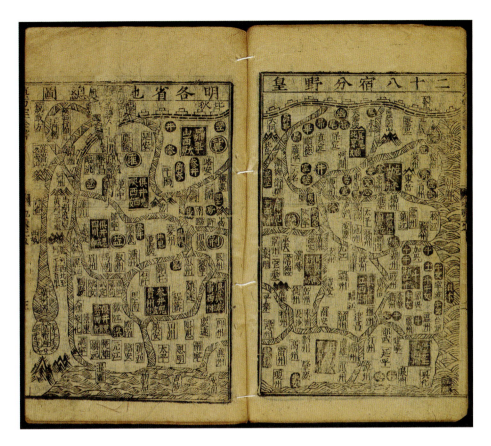

FIGURE 7.3.

"Ershibaxiu fenye huang Ming gesheng diyu zongtu" 二十八宿分野皇明各省地輿總圖 (General terrestrial map of the twenty-eight lodges and their astral allocations of each province of the imperial Ming). In *Miaojin wanbao quanshu* 妙錦萬寶全書. Height of print area, 19.9 cm. Harvard-Yenching Library.

"Ouluoba Guo" 歐羅巴國 (Country of Europe) near Yinshan 陰山 to the north on the map. His preface also quotes from many Chinese classics, such as *Tianwen zhi*, *Huainan zi*, and *Shangshu* 尚書 (Book of documents), as well as textual material coauthored by Jesuit missionaries, in explaining the theory of the spherical heaven:

> The annotations of the "Yao Shun dian" 堯舜典 (part of the *Shangshu*) say the heavens are spherical, half above the earth and half below. There are 90,000 *li* from the earth to the heaven, which is also found in the *Sanwu liji* 三五曆紀 (Calendrical records of the Three Sovereigns and the Five Emperors). Comparing with the number that Dazhang 大章 and Shuhai 豎亥 paced out,[18] the measurement cannot be reconciled, and their differences cannot be explained. In the astronomical studies

of Matteo Ricci, a degree was divided into sixty parts and one degree measured on the surface of the earth was 250 *li*. Jang Yu's *Gyegok manpil* recorded one degree in astronomy as constituting 2,932 *li* on the surface of the earth. The various authors each report the extent of one degree differently. I cannot ascertain who is correct.

The information Kim ascribes to Matteo Ricci appears in one of Ricci's prefaces on the *Kunyu wanguo quantu* and *Liangyi xuanlan tu* in the following way:

> Since the heaven covers the earth, they correspond to each other. Therefore, the heaven has north and south poles, and the earth also has them; heaven is divided into 360 degrees, so is the earth.... Each degree of the earth is 250 *li* wide, so the earth is 90,000 *li* in circumference.

While Kim Suhong could not decide whether Ricci or Jiang Yu was correct, other scholars did not express such doubt. Chinese authors like Liang Zhou and Cao Junyi, who consulted the *Kunyu wanguo quantu* or the "Wanguo quantu" included in the *Zhifang waiji*, naturally received their geographical knowledge through the lens of more familiar geographical concepts, as Cao's preface for the *Tianxia jiubian fenye renji lucheng quantu* shows: "The South Pole, North Pole, Eastern Ocean, and Western Ocean were drawn in the four seas. Their distances, far or near, were all tested and assessed according to descriptions of the *Yitong zhi* (i.e. *Da Ming yitong zhi*), *Shujing* 書經 and *Shanhai jing*." In all, Kim Suhong's map borrowed and synthesized from a wide array of textual sources and maps and connected to a material tradition of large maps produced in late Ming China.

From Map to Atlas: The *Pyeollam do* inside Korean Atlases

During the Joseon dynasty, versions of the *Pyeollam do* also appeared in popular atlases known as *Jidocheop* 地圖帖 or *Jidojang* 地圖帳. These atlases contain between four and forty-six maps.[19] Most common, however, are atlases with thirteen maps, typically beginning with a world map followed by a map of China, a map of Korea, a map of Japan, a map of the Ryukyu Kingdom, and eight maps of the Korean provinces.

Among these, the world maps have attracted the greatest attention, especially the circular "wheel" world maps (apparently unique to Korea) usually titled "Cheonha do" 天下圖 or "Cheonha jido" 天下地圖 (Map of all under heaven; figure 8.1) and further explored in chapter 8 of this volume. Produced from the end of the seventeenth century to the start of the nineteenth, these maps typically not only took pride of place as these popular atlases' first maps but also circulated as stand-alone copies. The main continent occupied the map's center, surrounded by an enclosing sea ring, itself surrounded by an outer ring of land. Beyond this outer land ring appears a further sea ring. At the center of the main continent is Kunlun 昆仑 Mountain, with China located

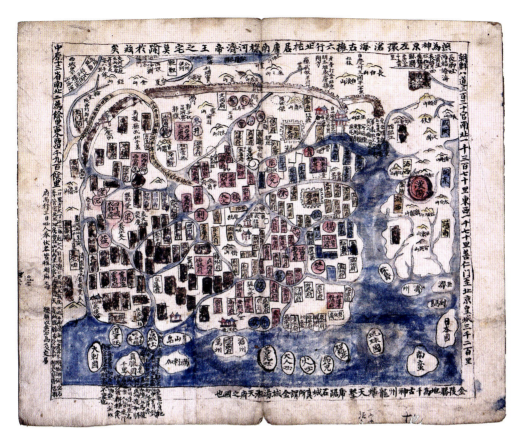

FIGURE 7.4.

"Jungwon sipsamseong do." Map 8, in the atlas *Joseon jido bu paldo cheonha jido*. Approx. 30 × 37.6 cm. National Library of Korea, Seoul.

slightly to its east. It also displays mountains, rivers, and several states and regions surrounding China, such as Hua Mountain 華岳, Heishui 黑水, Chishui 赤水, Korea, Japan, Ryukyu, Siam, and Cambodia. The maps place some of these countries as islands in the enclosing sea ring, but many legendary toponyms are also found in the outer land ring, all of them from the *Shanhai jing*.

At least two atlases contain maps that clearly drew from the *Pyeollam do*. The atlas *Joseon jido bu paldo cheonha jido* 朝鮮地圖附八道天下地圖 (Maps of Joseon with maps of the eight provinces and of all under heaven)—consisting of thirteen maps created sometime between 1666 and 1767 and now in the National Library of Korea—includes a map of China named "Jungwon sipsamseong do" 中原十三省圖 (Map of the thirteen provinces of the Chinese central plains; map 8; figure 7.4).[20] The second is a map titled "Jungwon sipsamseong geup Joseon dodo hapbu" 中原十三省及朝鮮都圖合付 (Combined map of the thirteen provinces of the Chinese central plains and cities of Joseon; map 9) contained in the atlas *Jido* held by the Library of Tenri University in Nara (an atlas with twelve maps, missing the general map of Korea).[21] The maps depict in detail not only China but also Korea (with the country's mountains, rivers, and eight provinces). In the south they reach to the sea; in the north they extend to regions north of the Great Wall such as Dada 韃靼, Changbai Mountain 長白山, Beihai 北海 (Northern Sea), and the Gobi desert. The easternmost extent marks Japan, while the area to the west includes the Yellow River source area with Kunlun Mountain, Tibet (Xifan Guo 西蕃國), and parts of central Asia known to its Chinese and Korean readership as the Western Regions, Xiyu 西域.

Although maps 8 and 9 appear within the atlases as maps of China, they should be read as Sinocentric world maps. Judging from their similarities in content and style (save in the depiction of Korea), these maps were undoubtedly adapted and simplified from Kim Suhong's *Pyeollam do*.[22] They lack its precursor's county-level administrative districts, historical and cultural references (as to certain historical figures), most of its historical place-names, and some of the astral allocations, but map 8 keeps the notes "Country of Europe" and "Matteo Ricci." In addition, all the rivers on both maps interconnect extensively in a way that deemphasizes the Yellow and Yangzi Rivers, reminiscent of the maps in the *Wanbao quanshu*, further evincing the relation of the *Pyeollam do* to the general map of the *Wanbao quanshu*.

Another approach to adapting the *Pyeollam do* can be seen in two further atlas maps. One is also in the Library of Tenri University and titled "Cheonha Jungguk do" 天下中國圖 (Map of China in all under heaven; map 10)[23] in an atlas titled *Yeoji do*, which contains sixteen maps.[24] The second is titled "Cheonha jido" (map 11, a title usually reserved for circular world maps), is enclosed in the mid-eighteenth-century atlas also titled *Cheonha jido* (consisting of fourteen maps), and is held by the Yeungnam University Museum (figure 7.5).[25] They focus on China without mapping Korea and differ from maps 8 and 9 in several ways. They separate the water systems of the Yellow and the Yangtze Rivers, rather than interconnecting them, in way very similar to the *Pyeollam do*. Yet they omit certain details from the *Pyeollam do*: Almost all historical figures are absent, and only a few of the twenty-eight constellation names remain. While maps 10 and 11 retain most of the same foreign countries, as does map 8, they lack both the "Country of Europe" and "Matteo Ricci." These atlases did not adopt the *Pyeollam do* in a consistent way.

These abridged versions of the *Pyeollam do* (maps 8–11) displaced the general map of China in their atlases. The general map of China (figure 7.6) usually included differs from the *Pyeollam do* in terms of configuration—the Yellow and Yangtze Rivers are quite easily distinguished while the southeastern coastline of China is rounded off, unlike its squared shape on the *Pyeollam do*—and in terms of geographical information, lacking both the names of the twenty-eight constellations and the place-names from the *Shanhai jing*. In addition, it includes no trace of geographical information from the *Kunyu wanguo quantu* or *Liangyi xuanlan tu*. The origins of this type of map are not

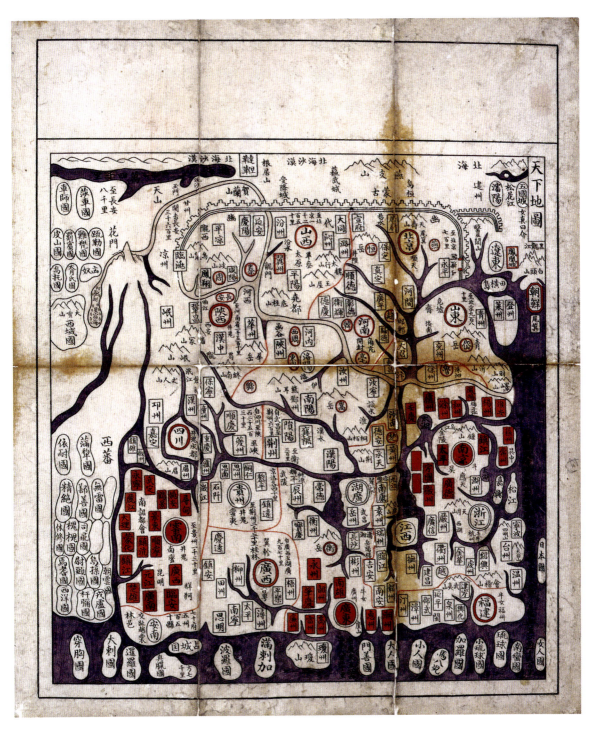

FIGURE 7.5.

"Cheonha jido." Map 11. 19.7 × 11.3 cm. Yeungnam University Museum, Gyeongsan.

FIGURE 7.6.

An example of a typical atlas map of China. "Jungguk do" 中國圖 (Map of China) in the atlas *Yeoji do*. Approx. 35 × 29.5 cm. MacLean Collection, Illinois, MC29648.

yet clear, but judging by their contents, they also belonged to the lineage of Ming maps of China sharing a common ancestor with the *Pyeollam do* (while not directly related). The *Pyeollam do* probably bears fewer examples in its atlas iteration precisely because it appears here as a world map alongside a "Cheonha do" proper, which might have been seen as contradictory.

Kim Suhong's map evolved from a genre of maps prevalent during the sixteenth and seventeenth centuries and shows evidence of connections to the maps in the Ming-era *Wanbao quanshu*. These maps depict the earth schematically and provide historical information and the relative position of places to each other. In the late sixteenth and early seventeenth centuries, these maps, just like a number of late Ming artifacts, such as Cao Junyi's and Liang Zhou's maps, incorporated European astronomical and geographical knowledge in varying degrees without realigning their Sinocentric worldview.

During the seventeenth century, a map of this general kind likely reached Korea, where eager intellectuals desired to reproduce it. Kim Suhong adapted such a map, paying special attention to new astronomical and geographical information from the *Kunyu wanguo quantu* or *Liangyi xuanlan tu,* which he only used to supplement the knowledge system prevalent in Korea, and integrated it into the framework and geographical concepts of his source map produced in China. The *Pyeollam do,* printed a number of times and copied in manuscript form, enjoyed a wide distribution throughout Korea. However, the European astronomical and geographical information it contained attracted little attention, as evinced by its abridged atlas adaptations lacking that information. Indeed, as in China, new knowledge from Europe served primarily as novel exotica to attract readership, rather than to fundamentally alter their understanding of the world.

Notes

1. *Sukjung silrok,* 1.24b.
2. Lee, "Jangdong Gimmun ui munmul suyonglon."
3. Yang, *Nuljaejip,* 1.28a. Kim Suhong also made a map of Korea, the *Joseon paldo gogeum chonglam do* 朝鮮八道古今總覽圖 (Comprehensive overview map of the eight provinces of Joseon, then and now) in 1673.
4. Kim Yangseon first described the woodblock copy in the Korean Christian Museum of Soongsil University as a Ming-style all-under-heaven map. A. L. Mackay stated that two more private handwritten copies existed in addition to the woodblock copy Kim Yangseon introduced, discussing its contents and framing Kim Suhong's map as a junction between the two traditions of naturalistic surveying and of religious cosmology. Lee Chan reproduced the woodblock copy in the Korean Catholic Museum of Soongsil University and his colored manuscript copy (now in the Seoul History Museum). He described the information on the map and emphasized its representative significance as the Korean Ming style of all-under-heaven map. Kim, "Hanguk gojido yeongu cho," 224–225; Mackay, "Kim Su-Hong"; Lee, *Hanguk ui gojido,* 342–343; Lee, *Old Maps of Korea,* 406.
5. Ledyard, "Cartography in Korea," 267–268.
6. Oh Sanghak pointed out the use of Kim's map as a guide to historical geography and emphasized its status as representative of Korean orthodox world maps in the seventeenth century. Lim Jongtae only referred to those marks on the map signifying the cosmic association between heaven and earth. Oh, *Joseon sidae segye jido,* 297–304; Lim, "Matteo Ricci's Maps in Late Joseon Dynasty," 289–290; Yang, "Kim Suhong ui *Cheonha gogeum daechong pyeollam do.*"
7. The twenty-eight constellations, an important concept in China, originated during the Shang and Zhou periods. The constellations divided the heavens into twenty-eight celestial regions for locating astronomical phenomena, each celestial region corresponding to a specific terrestrial realm.
8. The prints at Soongsil University appear reproduced in Lee, *Hanguk ui gojido,* 26; Lee, *Old Maps of Korea,* 26; a low-resolution image is also available at the Encyclopedia of Korean Culture, http://encykorea.aks.ac.kr/Contents/Item/E0056081, the print in Seoul Museum of History, *Lee Chan Collection,* 181, and the print at the Library of Tenri University in Unno, "Chōsen Richō jidai ni ryūkō shita chizuchō," 240.

9. Mackay said the manuscript came from a "rural retreat" without specifying further. Mackay, "Kim Su-Hong."
10. Ibid., 28–29.
11. The manuscript appears reproduced in Lee, *Hanguk ui gojido,* 27; Lee, *Old Maps of Korea,* 27; Seoul Museum of History, *Lee Chan Collection,* 182.
12. That is, respectively, Zhuzi 朱子, Zhouzi 周子, and Mengzi 孟子.
13. Oh, *Joseon sidae segye jido,* 299; Cao et al., *Zhongguo gudai ditu ji,* map 145 (description of map on p. 11).
14. Wei, "Jianada Yingshu Gelunbiya Daxue Yazhou tushuguan."
15. On the *Wanbao quanshu,* see also Wu, *Wanbao quanshu.*
16. See, for example, "Ershibaxiu fenye huang Ming gesheng diyu zongtu" (figure 7.3) or "Huang Ming yitong ershibaxiu fenye diyu zhi tu" 皇明一統二十八宿分野地輿之圖 (Terrestrial map of the unified Ming and the astral allocations of the twenty-eight lodges) in *Wuche bajin* 五車拔錦.
17. These two maps arrived through two Korean tributary missions in 1603 and 1604, respectively (Yang, "Li Madou shijie ditu chuanru Hanguo jiqi yingxiang"). Three Korean adaptations of the *Kunyu wanguo quantu* survive while the Christian Museum of Soongsil University has a 1603 print of the *Liangyi xuanlan tu* (figure 1.2).
18. These were the ministers of the legendary emperor Yu, after whom the name of the *Yugong* 禹貢, the urtext of Chinese geography, was derived.
19. The National Library of Korea contains an atlas with forty-six maps titled *Yeoji do* 輿地圖, while an atlas with only four maps titled *Cheonha do* 天下圖 is in the museum of Yeungnam University.
20. The map itself bears no title, but the distances from south to north and from east to west of the "Jungwon sipsamseong" 中原十三省 appear on the map's left side. The catalogue of the National Library of Korea thus titles it "Jungwon sipsamseong do."
21. The map is reproduced in Unno, "Chōsen Richō jidai ni ryūkō shita
22. The map's depiction of Korea is an abridged adaptation from Kim Suhong's *Joseon paldo gogeum chonglam do.*
23. The map is reproduced in Unno, "Chōsen Richō jidai ni ryūkō shita chizuchō," 248.
24. "Cheonha Jungguk do" is the second map in the atlas. The other maps include "Cheonji do" 天地圖, "Cheonji chongdo" 天地總圖, "Seonggyeong do" 盛京圖 (Map of Shenyang), a map of Korea, eight maps of Korean provinces, a map of Songdo 松都 city, and a map of the Ryukyu Kingdom. The atlas may predate 1767. Unno, "Chōsen Richō jidai ni ryūkō shita chizuchō," 246–250.
25. Compared to map 10, map 11 adds countries in the Western Regions based on Han dynasty (206 BCE–220 CE) knowledge. The circular world map, included as usual as the first map, instead is titled "Taegeuk do" 太極圖 (Map of the supreme ultimate). Its outermost circle consists of a black-and-white pattern reminiscent of the yin and yang pattern known as Taiji 太極 in Chinese or Taegeuk in Korean, hence the map's title. The second map is the "Cheonha jido," followed by a map titled "Yeokdae gukdo chongdo" 歷代國都總圖 (General map of cities through history), the map of the Ryukyu Kingdom, the map of Japan, the map of Korea, and the eight maps of Korean provinces. Here "Yeokdae gukdo chongdo" is the only exception to the abovementioned usual Korean atlas of thirteen maps.

References

Cao Wanru 曹婉如, Zheng Xihuang 鄭錫煌, Huang Shengzhang 黃盛璋, Niu Zhongxun 鈕仲勳, Ren Jincheng 任金城, Qin Guojing 秦國經, and Hu Bangbo 胡邦波, eds. *Zhongguo gudai ditu ji: Mingdai* 中國古代地圖集: 明代. Beijing: Wenwu chubanshe, 1994.

Kim Yangseon. "Hanguk gojido yeongu cho" 韓國古地圖研究抄. In *Maesan gukhak sango* 梅山國學散稿, 215–280. Seoul: Songjeon University Museum, 1972.

Ledyard, Gari. "Cartography in Korea." In *The History of Cartography*. Vol. 2, bk. 2, *Cartography in the Traditional East and Southeast Asian Societies,* edited by J. B. Harley and David Woodward, 235–345. Chicago: University of Chicago Press, 1994.

Lee Chan. *Hanguk ui gojido* 韓國의古地圖. Seoul: Bumwoo, 1991.

———. *Old Maps of Korea*. Translated by Sarah Kim. Paju: Bumwoo, 2005.

Lee Gyeonggu. "Jangdong Gimmun ui munmul suyonglon gwa munye hwaldong." *Hanguk hakbo* 29, no. 3 (2003): 138–167.

Lim, Jongtae. "Matteo Ricci's Maps in Late Joseon Dynasty." *Korean Journal for the History of Science* 33, no. 2 (2011): 277–296.

Mackay, A. L. "Kim Su-Hong and the Korean Cartographic Tradition." *Imago Mundi* 27 (1975): 27–38.

Oh Sanghak. *Joseon sidae segye jido wa segye insik*. Paju: Changbi, 2011.

Sakai, Tadao. "Confucianism and Popular Educational Works." In *Self and Society in Ming Thought,* edited by William de Bary, 331–366. New York: Columbia University Press, 1970.

Seoul Museum of History, ed. *The Lee Chan Collection of Historical Maps*. Seoul: Seoul Museum of History, 2006.

Sukjung silrok 肅宗實錄. Seoul: Guksa pyeonchan wiwonhoe, 1973.

Unno Kazutaka 海野一隆. "Chōsen Richō jidai ni ryūkō shita chizuchō" 朝鮮李朝時代に流行した地図帳. In *Tōyō chirigakushi kenkyū: Tairiku hen* 東洋地理學史研究: 大陸編, 237–265. Osaka: Seibundō, 2004.

Wei Yin-zong 韋胤宗. "Jianada Yingshu Gelunbiya Daxue Yazhou tushuguan zang *Jiuzhou fenye yutu gujin renwu shiji*" 加拿大英屬哥倫比亞大學亞洲圖書館藏《九州分野輿圖古今人物事跡》. *Mingdai yanjiu* 明代研究 27 (2016): 189–219.

Wu Hui-fang 吳蕙芳. *Wanbao quanshu: Ming Qing shiqi de minjian shenghuo shilu* 萬寶全書: 明清時期的民間生活實錄. Taipei: Hua Mulan, 2005.

Yang Seongji 梁誠之. *Nuljaejip* 訥齋集. 1791. Hanguk munjip chonggan 韓國文集叢刊, vol. 9. Seoul: Kyeongin munhuasa, 1988.

Yang Yulei 楊雨蕾. "Kim Suhong ui *Cheonha gogeum daechong pyeollam do* panbun yeongu" 金壽弘의《天下古今大總便覽圖》板本研究. *Journal of the Korean Research Association of Old Maps* 3, no. 1 (2011): 5–18.

———. "Li Madou shijie ditu chuanru Hanguo jiqi yingxiang" 利瑪竇世界地圖傳入韓國及其影響. *Zhongguo lishi dili luncong* 中國歷史地理論叢 20, no. 1 (2005): 91–98.

Yeungnam University Museum, ed. *Hanguk ui yet jido. Dopanpyeon*. Gyeongsan: Yeungnam University Museum, 1998.

8

Utopia and Dystopia

Cheonha do *and the Reception of Renaissance Geography in Late Joseon Korea*

SOH JEANHYOUNG

During the Mongol-controlled Yuan era (1271–1368), a man named Im Seong 林成 is born in Nanjing. As a Chinese, he feels shame living under "barbaric" Mongol rule. One day by chance he meets others who feel the same humiliation, and they decide to overthrow the "barbarian" government together. Before making the attempt, however, they practice divination to ascertain whether they will succeed. The result is hopeless: the Yuan's mandate will endure. The divination also warns that anyone who challenges their rule will destroy themselves.

Im Seong and his friends despair. They decide to leave China and to rebuild its civilization elsewhere. They board a ship in Nanjing, and violent seas and high winds drive them to the eastern seas until they reach some deserted islands, where they anchor off the coast to seek food and water. On the islands they encounter monsters such as giants, foxes with nine tails, and rats that transform into humans. They invade the monsters' territory, overcome their attack, kill them, and so empty the islands.

After sailing more than eighty thousand *li* 里 east from China, Im and his company arrive at the western continent known as Taewon 太原. There they hear that children have been singing a strange prophetic song about men from the West who will come as saviors, unifying Taewon and civilizing its people. They realize all their sufferings on the journey have prepared them to build a civilization on Taewon and begin a war of conquest. In a dramatic twist, people from "the East" turn into "men from the West."

FIGURE 8.1.

A manuscript "Cheonha do," as found in the *Yeoji do*. Approx. 35 × 29.5 cm. MacLean Collection, Illinois, MC29673.

This story appears in the eighteenth-century Korean adventure novel *Taewon ji* 太原誌 (Records of Taewon), authored anonymously.[1] Two ideas of space merge therein. First, for dramatic effect, the author used new geographic information—the earth is a globe. Im Seong and his friends keep going east, not west, but they finally arrive at Taewon, located to the west of China, in the novel's most dramatic scene. Moreover, inspired by older books, the story depicts the space between China (Zhongyuan 中原) and Taewon as full of monsters. The book also describes the various monsters' islands along Im Seong's route to Taewon, which reminds us of the many islands where extraordinary beings lived, as described in the *Shanhai jing* 山海經 (Classic of mountains and seas), a classic Chinese geography that attracted the attention of Korean intellectuals anew in the seventeenth century.[2]

We find a similar intermingling of geographic knowledge of European origin with the traditional idea of space based on the *Shanhai jing* in the unique Korean maps known collectively as *Cheonha do* 天下圖 (Map of all under heaven; figure 8.1).[3]

SOH 207

Cheonha do, sometimes dubbed "Circular *Cheonha do,*" depict the earth as round, contrary to the traditional belief that "heaven is round and earth is square" (*tianyuan difang* 天圓地方), and the continents and islands as filled with strange countries, their names taken from the *Shanhai jing. Cheonha* means "under heaven," implying that the maps' scope encompasses all known regions of the world. The maps' title and their content sparked their readers' imaginations and circulated widely in Korea from the seventeenth through the nineteenth century. This time frame is significant: *Cheonha do* first appeared after the production and circulation of the *Kunyu wanguo quantu* 坤輿萬國全圖 (Complete map of all countries on earth, 1602; figure 1.1),[4] the "Wanguo quantu" 萬國全圖 (Complete map of all countries; figure 2.9) included in the *Zhifang waiji* 職方外紀 (Record of everything beyond the administration, 1623), and the *Kunyu quantu* 坤輿全圖 (Complete map of the earth, 1674) produced at the Qing court by Ferdinand Verbiest (1623–1688) in the early 1670s (figure 5.1). Both the *Kunyu wanguo quantu* and *Kunyu quantu* were reproduced in Korea, where numerous intellectuals transcribed in particular the *Zhifang waiji*'s descriptions of continents and countries.[5]

Cheonha do were one vector of the delivery of new geographic knowledge via such maps in the late Joseon period (1392–1897). Unno Kazutaka insists that *Cheonha do* were linked to the "Shanhai yudi quantu" 山海輿地全圖 (Complete map of mountains, seas, and lands) inserted in Wang Qi's 王圻 (1530–1615) encyclopedia *Sancai tuhui* 三才圖會 (Illustrated compendium of the three powers; figure 1.7). In his view the *Cheonha do,* like the "Shanhai yudi quantu," present the earth as a globe, but unlike the "Shanhai yudi quantu," *Cheonha do* reflect old geographic ideas in a Daoist worldview and must therefore also reflect resistance against the incoming worldview.[6] Bae Wuseong, however, draws the opposite conclusion from his analysis of *Cheonha do.* He claims that Korean intellectuals mentioned the *Shanhai jing* increasingly in the seventeenth century and that they excavated the text to make sense of the new geographic knowledge on their own terms. New geographic knowledge coming into Korea from western Europe via China may therefore have had an impact on the creation of *Cheonha do.* He insists that the detailed explanations in Chinese and the exotic pictures, as well as the map's depictions of such strange countries as that of the one-eyed people (Yimu Guo 一目國) and the legendary Country of Women (Nüren Guo 女人國), are the key to understanding this strange combination of incompatible geographic ideas. *Cheonha do* were one medium to receive new world-geographical ideas from Chinese works via the traditional grammar of East Asian geography.[7]

Since the authors of *Cheonha do* were generally anonymous, their intentions in making such maps are likewise elusive. The maps themselves also provide scant background information. Historians have delineated the apparent features and details of different editions and compared them with other maps of the period but rarely have examined their intellectual context. A lack of understanding of such contexts sometimes leads to unwarranted preconceptions and assumptions in the interpretation of maps.[8] Dismissing the maps' content as a piece of corrupted geographical knowledge or as a crude hybrid are such preconceptions. We must instead interpret *Cheonha do* under the premise that intellectuals and painters, not cartographers, produced them within a web of beliefs situated in the late Joseon period. In the eighteenth and nineteenth centuries, primarily literati and painters both produced and consumed Korean maps. The government sent not cartographers but painters to various areas to "draw" administrative maps, which they could only complete with the aid of local literati.[9]

Most of the local literati had no chance of even seeing the large maps imported from China, such as the abovementioned *Kunyu wanguo quantu* or *Kunyu quantu*. As in China, the people who enjoyed and distributed these maps were not cartographers. We should then consider *Cheonha do* as the result of the reconstruction of a worldview, in this case following the introduction of new depictions of the world from western Europe by way of China. To understand this new or adjusted view of the world, we must relate the maps within a wide range of texts, from treatises by literati to novels, elucidating their web of beliefs. It is also noteworthy that *Cheonha do* were rarely independent works but parts of atlases usually named *Yeoji do* 輿地圖 (Maps of the land).[10] Such atlases generally consist of a *Cheonha do*, a map of China, a map of Japan, a map of Ryukyu, and several maps of Korea. Some of them also contain a narrative history of "Chinese civilization" and information about each country in the atlas.

In reconstructing the intellectual context that gave rise to the *Cheonha do*, I show how the various writings of the literati articulate a desire—not evident before the seventeenth century—to know about the countries beyond the Chinese tributary system. I analyze two cases to show how Korean intellectuals interpreted the incoming maps: Yi Jonghwi's 李種徽 (1731–1797) reading of the *Kunyu wanguo quantu* and Wi Baekgyu's 魏伯珪 (1727–1798) mistaking a *Cheonha do* for the *Kunyu wanguo quantu*. I also explain how hospitality and hostility toward countries outside the Chinese tributary system followed the newly constructed fictional thinking—shaped in part by the incoming geographic knowledge—and then argue that *Cheonha do* reflect both the reception of new geographic knowledge and an extension of the idea of a central Chinese civilization (Zhonghua 中華).

New Geographic Knowledge and Imaginations of Space

In 1719 Japanese translator Amenomori Hōshū 雨森芳洲 (1668–1755) found himself embarrassed when a young Korean diplomat named Shin Yuhan 申維翰 (1681–1753), with whom he was discussing geography, asked him about monsters.[11] Shin was curious whether "people from the West" looked like the monstrous men depicted in the *Shanhai jing*. Amenomori, trying to answer Shin's questions without hurting his feelings, explained that the Dutch and other people from European countries looked physically like Asians, differing only in their costumes and languages.[12] Shin also asked about the Country of Women (Nüren Guo 女國), which he thought was near Japan. Amenomori responded that there was no Country of Women, and no one had even heard about it "for one thousand one hundred years." After finishing their conversation, he noted that before the unification of Japan by Toyotomi Hideyoshi 豊臣秀吉 (1537–1598), monsters and strange countries had existed around Japan.[13]

Shin's knowledge of monsters and strange countries mirrored the contents of the *Shanhai jing*. While Korean intellectuals had rarely even mentioned the *Shanhai jing* until the sixteenth century,[14] interest in the text ran rampant among "rational" neo-Confucian scholars in Korea during the seventeenth century. Their attention to the text paralleled their curiosity about the world beyond the Chinese tributary system. After 1603 both Chinese-language maps produced with the aid of Jesuit missionaries and Chinese encyclopedias such as *Sancai tuhui* and *Fangyu shenglüe* 方輿勝略 (Complete survey of the earth, 1612) began entering Korea, and the geographic descriptions they contained triggered a new spatial imagination.[15]

Giulio Aleni (1582–1649) and Yang Tingyun's 楊廷筠 (1557–1627) *Zhifang waiji,* discussed in this volume in chapters 2 and 3 by Richard A. Pegg and Wang Yongjie, respectively, also served as an important reference work for these intellectuals. Yi Ik 李瀷 (1681–1763), one of the most famous writers of eighteenth-century Korea, quoted the *Zhifang waiji* often in the geography section of his best-selling encyclopedia *Seongho saseol* 星湖僿說 (Insignificant sayings of Seongho). He lent the *Zhifang waiji* to his students and friends, which suggests they transcribed Aleni's text.[16] Yi Ik even wrote a comment to the *Zhifang waiji*:[17]

> Western literati kept going to the end of the Western Ocean but eventually they arrived at the Eastern Ocean. . . . According to what Giulio Aleni mentions in the *Zhifang waiji,* the Great Western Ocean is extremely large and boundless, in the countries of the West they also did not know about the existence of lands across the oceans. More than a hundred years ago, the former bureaucrat Christopher Columbus searched for the lands in the Eastern Ocean. Ferdinand Magellan traveled around the world and arrived at the Chinese continent from the Eastern Ocean. . . . Someone said "how can we trust the Western maps?" However, I will say that they are verifiable.[18]

He argued that "Western people" (*seoyangin* 西洋人) traveled all over the world and understood its geography. Although Korean intellectuals had not witnessed the new geographic information firsthand, they should accept the incoming maps as made on reasonable ground and evidence.[19]

Another intellectual, Yi Gyugyeong 李圭景 (b. 1788, pen name: Oju), quoted from the *Zhifang waiji* extensively. His sources for geographic knowledge were the *Zhifang waiji* and Ferdinand Verbiest's *Kunyu waiji* 坤輿外紀 (Record of everything beyond the earth, 1672). In his enormous work *Oju yeonmun jangjeon sango* 五洲衍文長箋散稿 (Random expatiations of Oju), Yi Gyugyeong quoted the *Zhifang waiji* at least twenty-five times in describing the countries and continents, geographical features, vegetation, climate, and geological phenomena such as volcanoes. He expressed a desire to travel the world after reading books such as Fang Yizhi's 方以智 (1611–1671) *Wuli xiaoshi* 物理小識 (Little notes on the principles of the phenomena) and the *Zhifang waiji*.[20]

A conversation between Yi Uibong 李義鳳 (1733–1801) and Jesuit missionary Ferdinand Augustin von Hallerstein (1703–1771) in 1761 during a Korean envoy's stay in Beijing showcases how Korean literati gained access to the *Zhifang waiji*. Yi Uibong stayed in Beijing as a Korean envoy to China from 1760 to 1761. According to his journal *Bukwonrok* 北轅錄 (Record from beyond the northern gate), Yi met the Jesuit three times at the West Church (Xitang 西堂).[21] Their conversations took the form of written questions and answers, and most of Yi's questions related to geography: the dimensions of the European continent, the number of countries in Europe, the distance between China and Europe, and the European political system. He also learned from Hallerstein how to use a celestial globe (*honcheon ui* 渾天儀) and an astrolabe (*ganpyeong ui* 簡平儀). In turn, Hallerstein asked Yi Uibong if there were catechisms, scientific books, or maps written, translated, and made by Jesuits in Korea. Yi answered that the Korean bureau of astronomy had collected dozens of copies of the *Tianxue chuhan* 天學初函 (First collection on heavenly learning).

The *Tianxue chuhan* is Li Zhizao's 李之藻 (1565–1630) printed collection of Jesuit writings, which includes the *Zhifang waiji*. In one of their meetings, Yi Uibong also spoke to Hallerstein's translator Xu Cheng'en 徐承恩, a descendent of Xu Guangqi 徐光啟 (1562–1633). Xu Guangqi was well known among Korean literati interested in "Western learning" (*xixue* 西學) because he had collaborated on many works included in *Tianxue chuhan*, such as *Jihe yuanben* 幾何原本, the Chinese translation of Euclid's *Elements*. Yi Uibong expressed his pleasure at meeting Xu Guanqi's descendent because he had read the book. Yi Uibong's conversation with Hallerstein and Xu Cheng'en indicates that *Tianxue chuhan* was a crucial source for Korean intellectuals seeking access to books related to "Western learning," including the *Zhifang waiji,* as sources of new geographic knowledge.

As part of the exchange, Hallerstein presented Ferdinand Verbiest's *Kunyu tushuo* 坤輿圖說 (Illustrated exposition on the earth, 1672) to Yi Uibong, who continued to show interest in geography and maps. After reading the *Kunyu tushuo,* Yi praised Verbiest's book, which synthesized the works of Matteo Ricci, Giulio Aleni, Alfonso Vagnoni (1566–1640), and Sabatino de Ursis (1575–1620). He said that the *Kunyu tushuo* also included all the "eccentric" (*i* 異) stories from the *Zhifang waiji,* the key factor behind the book's widespread popularity and citations in Korea. These geographical works entertained Korean intellectuals in a manner comparable to that of popular novels. Xu Xuchen 許胥臣, who wrote a short remark (*xiaoyan* 小言) on the *Zhifang waiji* with Qu Shigu 瞿式穀, had already indicated as much, stating that Aleni and Yang's work wove together the eccentric and the foreign just as the popular *baiguan* novels 稗官小說 did.[22]

Baiguan were low-level officials who collected folktales, legendary stories, myths, and customs from different provinces. Their novels were widely read and written in a style popular among the Korean literati of the eighteenth century.[23] The abundant geographic information, including the strange customs, atmospheric phenomena, and different physical attributes of people in different countries and places, were all exotic, eccentric, and fascinating to the Korean literati, providing them fun and pleasure, as well as a thirst for travel to unknown places. This contextual understanding of the Korean literati's interest in the new works of geography produced in China to some extent explains the creation of *Cheonha do*, a new Korean type of world map. The *Cheonha do*, almost always part of an atlas, became common in Korea in the eighteenth and nineteenth centuries. Strong circumstantial evidence suggests that a new spatial imaginary, constructed following the reception of new geographic knowledge via China, became both popular and widely accepted in Korea.

Reading Maps and Geographical Treatises: Yi Jonghwi's and Wi Baekgyu's Cases

Let us now take a more detailed look at how Korean intellectuals approached the incoming maps and worldview. Yi Jonghwi's and Wi Baekgyu's cases are the most illuminating examples. We know little about Yi Jonghwi, and what we do know comes from his literary works *Susan jip* 修山集 (The complete works of Susan) and *Dongsa* 東史 (History of Korea). Wi Baekgyu was a rural intellectual who had studied under Yun Bonggu 尹鳳九 (1683–1767), a famous conservative scholar in Chungcheong Province 忠淸道. Yi Jonghwi and Wi Baekgyu were neither famous nor influential in the network of literati centered in the capital of Hanyang 漢陽 and its suburbs. They did not know one another personally but shared the idea that the *Kunyu wanguo quantu* was connected to Zou Yan's 鄒衍 (305–240 BCE) theory of nine regions (*da jiuzhou shuo* 大九州說), a connection the Chinese literati had made as well, as chapter 1 of this volume explains. Wi saw a *Cheonha do* and recalled both Zou Yan and Matteo Ricci: "There are nine regions within the small sea and another nine regions beyond them.[24] Matteo Ricci's map originates in [the scholarship of the famous] literatus from the state of Qi [= Zou Yan]."[25] For these intellectuals the *Kunyu wanguo quantu*, or, as they called it, "Matteo Ricci's map," was thus clearly related to Zou Yan's theories, although they also scrutinized the new geographic knowledge in their own ways.

In 1756, Yi Jonghwi received an opportunity to view a replica of the *Kunyu wanguo quantu* in the collection of a certain "ex-minister Yi." The Yi family allowed him to borrow it, and he studied it for three days in a row.[26] After reading the map, he wrote a short introduction to and description of the map he titled "Li Madu nambukgeuk do" 利瑪竇南北極圖 (Matteo Ricci's map of the North and South Poles).[27] The text starts by describing the *Kunyu wanguo quantu*, Asia, Europe, Africa, Magellanica, South America, and North America. According to Yi Jonghwi, Asia consisted of China;

central Asia; East, North, and South "barbarians"; and correspondent to the Buddhist continent of humans, Jambudvīpa (Nanshan Buzhou 南贍部洲).[28] He called Asia a "place" (*difang* 地方) but designated other continents as worlds (*shijie* 世界), such as "the world of Africa" (*Liweiya shijie* 利未亞世界).[29] He then stated that each continent lay between a small sea (*xiaoyang hai* 小洋海) and a big sea (*dayang hai* 大洋海) on the map, equivalent to what Zou Yan calls *bihai* 裨海 (small sea) and *yinghai* 瀛海 (big sea).[30] He concluded that the map could not depict the whole world because it depicted only six continents rather than nine.

The basic narrative of Yi's text helps us to understand how he interpreted and read the map by drawing on existing resources. The most revealing part of the text is not his conclusion but his way of reading. In describing each continent, he chose countries on the continent and wrote down the names. However, as he lacked familiarity with almost any of the place-names indicated, he copied some toponyms that did not designate countries but misapplied them as such. In addition, the order and selection of places in his text seem random and surprising at times. The first names in Europe Yi listed, for instance, are Cumania (a nomadic people),[31] Iceland, Castille, Athens, Crete, and Götaland.[32] He also assumed that the southern part of Southeast Asia belonged to the southern continent of Magellanica.[33] In all, Yi's text and lists illustrate how Koreans read these maps when they first engaged with them without having read texts such as the *Zhifang waiji* or *Kunyu tushuo* (figure 8.2).

The work of Wi Baekgyu, the author of the *Shinpyeon pyoje chando Hwanyeong ji* 新編標題纂圖寰瀛誌 (Record of the world: Newly edited and titled collection of diagrams, 1770; hereafter *Hwanyeong ji*), reveals another approach to the incoming worldview.[34] Manuscript versions of *Hwanyeong ji* show that Wi, who did not have a chance to see a replica of the *Kunyu wanguo quantu,* first mistook a *Cheonha do* for a "Ricci map": he included a *Cheonha do* titled "Li Madu cheonha do" 利瑪竇天下圖 (*Cheonha do* of Matteo Ricci; figure 8.3).[35] Wi Baekgyu's linking of the *Cheonha do* to Matteo Ricci illustrates how people who had never seen the *Kunyu wanguo quantu* or one of its replicas could have associated *Cheonha do* with the missionary.[36] However, Wi's "*Cheonha do* of Matteo Ricci" shows the world in a rectangular shape, whereas most *Cheonha do* are round. There are two possible explanations: He might not have accepted the concept of a round earth, or he might have heard that the "Ricci map" was not circular. In any case, it is certain he had never seen any "Ricci map": unlike Yi Jonghwi, who lived in the capital, Wi was born and lived in Jangheung (Jeolla Province) and had no strong intellectual network, so for Wi to access new information required more time and effort.

Later, sometime between 1795 and 1798, Wi Baekgyu corrected his mistake and replaced the "*Cheonha do* of Matteo Ricci" in the *Hwanyeong ji* with different diagrams and texts. His relative's grandson Wi Yeongbok 魏榮馥 printed this revised version from woodblocks in 1822.[37] The woodblock print, omitting the "*Cheonha do* of Matteo Ricci," makes clear that Wi Baekgyu had read the *Zhifang waiji* and realized Matteo

FIGURE 8.2.

Part of the *Kunyu wanguo quantu*, showing Europe with the place-names referred to in Yi Jonghwi's "Li Madu nambukgeuk do" *highlighted in yellow*. A comparison with the countries described in the *Zhifang waiji*, *highlighted in blue*, shows how Yi randomly chose place-names.

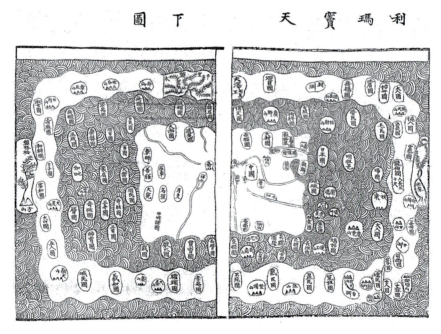

FIGURE 8.3.

"Li Madu Cheonha do," in the fair copy of the *Hwanyeong ji*.

Ricci had not in fact contributed to the "*Cheonha do* of Matteo Ricci." As a replacement, he inserted the "Seoyang jeguk do" 西洋諸國圖 (Map of the countries of the western ocean; figure 8.4), as well as a summary of the *Zhifang waiji* to explain the five continents and their climates, vegetation, cultures, politics, and countries.[38]

The five continents' arrangement in the newly inserted map is significant: from right to left are Asia, Europe, Africa, and America, with Magellanica at the bottom. The map depicts Asia on the right without showing the East Asian countries, such as China, Korea, Japan, and Ryukyu. Wi also annotated the sketch map by indicating the number of countries on each continent. Only the numbers for Asia are missing. In short, for Wi, Seoyang—namely, "the West" found in the title of his work—was a broad concept embracing all countries but China and its tributary states.

It is clear Yi and Wi generally received new geographic information enthusiastically. It is unlikely, however, that the *Kunyu wanguo quantu* and *Zhifang waiji* changed their perceptions of space. If we only read "Seoyang jeguk do" and Wi's summary of the *Zhifang waiji*, we may conclude that Wi accepted the new knowledge and changed his worldview accordingly. However, Wi lists the countries in the *Shanhai jing* in the category of foreign countries.[39] Moreover, examining Yi Jonghwi's other works or Wi Baekgyu's other chapters reveals the complex embeddedness of their writings related to maps and geographical descriptions. They come from a long tradition of thinking about space and are deeply related to a cosmology prevalent in the late Joseon period, with ample references to the *Shanhai jing* and other ancient books.

Korean Literati and the Ming-Qing Transition

The structure of Wi's *Hwanyeong ji* follows the typical order found in East Asian encyclopedias along the three categories of heaven, earth, and humankind.[40] Wi put the diagrams concerning all continents and countries under the "earth" category. New geographic information, including the "Seoyang jeguk do" map, also appeared in this category. Under "humankind," Wi includes chapters with charts and diagrams of Chinese and Korean historical capitals, stories of Confucian sages, wise men's names, birth and death dates, the Chinese and Korean political systems, local products, liturgies, and customs. Preceding all this, however, is an explanation of Shao Yong's 邵雍 (1011–1077) cosmological theory known as *yuanhui yunshi* 元會運世 (cyclical sequence) regarding the sequence and quality of time.

This raises a few crucial questions: Why did Wi start his section on humankind with Shao Yong's cosmology? Why did he treat only Chinese and Korean histories under this category and not those of other parts of the world? Further, why did he *also* discuss Chinese history in the text alongside Korean history? A chart listing era-reign names in the *Hwanyeong ji* supplies one lead. In the earlier versions of the text, Wi named Qing China *hu* Qing 胡淸, "the barbaric Qing." Comparing information on the Qing with that on the previous Ming state shows Wi's contempt for the Qing even

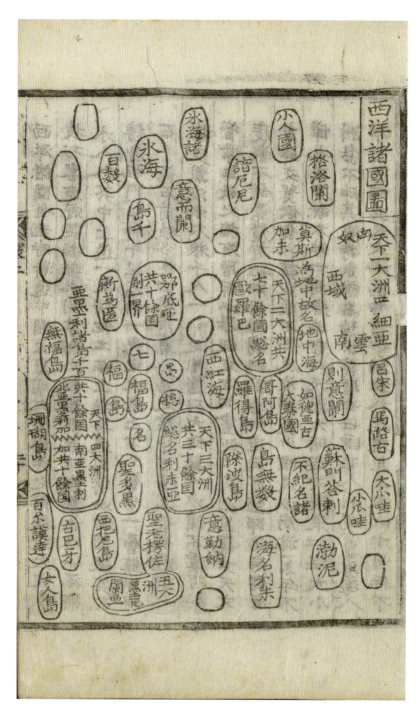

FIGURE 8.4.

"Seoyang jeguk do" in the woodblock print of the *Hwanyeong ji,* 1822. Height of paper, 32 cm. Harvard-Yenching Library.

more clearly. He recorded the Ming emperors' posthumous titles and their era-reign names while omitting all Qing emperors' titles. In the woodblock-printed *Hwanyeong ji*, he removed the character for "barbarian" but still did not add the posthumous names of the Qing emperors. China for Wi was not the Manchu-ruled Qing empire but its Ming predecessor, as well as prior dynasties.[41]

Following the Ming-Qing transition, Shao Yong's cosmology circulated widely in Korea. According to Shao Yong, time had a quality that had become corrupted. To hold off the collapse of the world, a king or emperor must relocate all things to their rightful places. Shao Yong's cosmological time, thought to explain the Manchu-Qing invasion of Ming China, has a strong spatial dimension: the theory predicted a "barbarian" invasion.[42] When Koreans read the *Kunyu wanguo quantu* and *Zhifang waiji* and were thus confronted with the existence of hundreds of countries outside the Chinese tributary system, they could not help recalling Shao Yong's theory: as time progressed, more brutal "barbarians" arose to throw the world into turmoil. Taken to its logical conclusion, the unknown countries of monstrous beings listed and described on these world maps constituted a potential threat to the Korean people. According to the time theory of Shao Yong, this world was collapsing, although an effort to protect civilization could slow the process.[43] For Korean literati like Wi Baekgyu, however, the existence of other continents was not itself a problem so long as the countries and their peoples stayed in their proper places. Trouble began when people moved and invaded the center of civilization, as the Manchu-Qing "barbarians" had done. He thus felt no need to faithfully reproduce a map like the *Kunyu wanguo quantu*. He needed only to know its toponyms' locations relative to one another, a function the "Seoyang jeguk do" performed adequately.

How did the Korean literati overcome what they perceived as the barbaric rule and corruption of central civilization caused by the Qing? An essential idea in both China and Korea was the separation between the "civilized" *hua* 華 and the "barbarian" *yi* 夷. The term *hua* denoted not only "civilized" but also "China." After the "barbarian" Manchu conquered China, many Korean intellectuals regarded Joseon as the last bastion of civilization. Yi Jonghwi, whom we encountered above, went further than other literati in this regard, insisting the Qing had lost their legitimacy as the center of civilization and that Korea was now rightful heir to *hua* civilization. To bolster this claim, Yi tried to prove Korea was civilized and large enough to fulfill this role: Korea had a history comparable to China's; the Korean territories, including Jeju Island, were vast enough to be called Zhonghua (a term literally meaning "central civilization"), as evinced by their diversity of customs and seasons.[44] These ideas matched the new geography found on the *Kunyu wanguo quantu*: the Qing was merely one of many states, and China appeared smaller and thus less important than it had on previous Sinocentric maps. The incoming geography thus bolstered Yi's own idea of a world civilization centered on Korea.

While Yi Jonghwi occupied one extreme of Korean intellectual thought by declaring Korea the new center of civilization, other Korean literati grew fascinated with the idea of the earth as a globe, implying the surface of the earth had no center. On this other extreme stood Hong Daeyong 洪大容 (1731–1783), whose book *Uisan mundap* 醫山問答 (Dialogue at mountain Uimuryeo 毉巫閭, 1766) argued that China was not the center of the world by depicting China's relative location:

> The landmass rotates once a day.... People in Russia regarded Russia as the correct world and Cambodia as the side world. People in Cambodia regarded Cambodia as the correct world and Russia as the side world. Besides, the longitudinal difference between China and Europe is 180 degrees. [Therefore], people in China think China is the correct world and Europe is the inverted world, while people in Europe think that Europe is the correct world, China is the inverted world.... According to their world, they are all the correct world, neither the side world nor the inverted world.... If we look down from heaven, how is there a difference [between civilized and "barbaric" countries]? [It is natural that] people feel familiar with their people, respect their king, defend their country, are comfortable with their customs. The civilized men and the barbarians are the same [in this sense].[45]

Hong Daeyong's argument is progressive but deconstructive for the literati who insisted on the necessity of Zhonghua, a central civilization. For Korean literati in the late Joseon period, a central civilization provided not only a system for relations between states but also the very basis of law and order in the Confucian worldview. However, constructing a worldview with Korea as the center of civilization proved practically impossible: Joseon had suffered Qing invasions in the early seventeenth century and was now a vassal state of Qing China. Although Korean literati did not accept the Qing as the rightful center of civilization, their state had recognized the Qing's ritual and political overlordship.[46] The discordance between ideal and reality and the predicament the literati faced drove them to the idea of a small Zhonghua or small central civilization (*xiao Zhonghua* 小中華) in reference to Joseon.[47] Many of the atlases produced in the late Joseon period actually reflect this concept. They usually consist of four parts: a *Cheonha do* world map, followed by a map of Ming China, a map of Japan, a map of the Ryukyus, and maps of Korea—both of the whole country and of the eight provinces.[48] These atlases thus reveal a premise: China, Ryukyu, Japan, and Korea were part of the civilized world order originally centered in China. The *Cheonha do* world maps in the front of these atlases illustrate Korean intellectuals' expanding perceptions of geography and, at the same time, civilization's relationship to a wider world of peripheral countries.[49]

Yet, although they always functioned as world maps, these *Cheonha do* inserted in Korean atlases did not all look alike. While figure 8.1 shows a common *Cheonha do*, usually the first map in a Korean atlas, the map in figure 8.5, found in another atlas and titled "Cheonha do jido" 天下都地圖 (Map of all cities under heaven), is a replica of the world map included in the *Zhifang waiji* (figure 2.9). Figure 8.6 is of yet another map titled *Cheonha do*, part of an atlas with the title *Gwang yeodo* 廣輿圖 (Extended

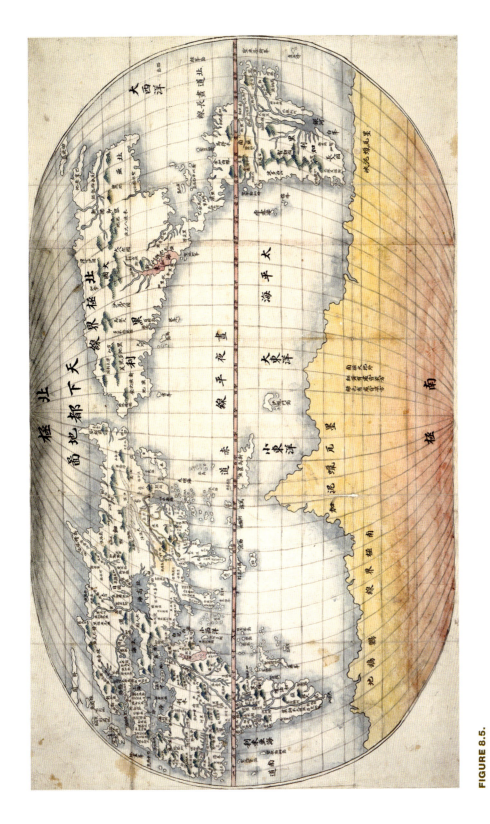

FIGURE 8.5.

"Cheonha do jido" in the *Yeoji do*, late eighteenth century. 60.3 × 103.2 cm. Kyujanggak Institute for Korean Studies, Seoul National University.

FIGURE 8.6.

The manuscript "Cheonha do" as found in the *Gwang yeodo,* late eighteenth century. 36.8 × 28.6 cm. Kyujanggak Institute for Korean Studies, Seoul National University.

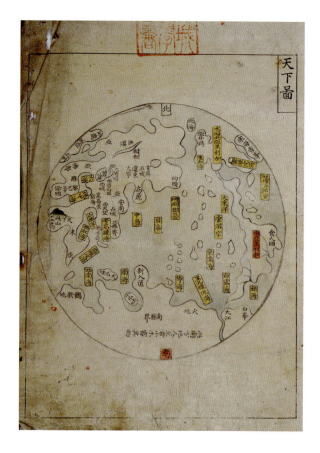

territorial maps) and a replica of the "Shanhai yudi quantu" (figure 1.7). These later two world maps indirectly borrow from Renaissance geographical ideas, while their atlases follow the usual structure of Korean atlases. These maps also show that the title *Cheonha do* could signify different types of world maps.

These *Cheonha do* in atlases thus reflect shifting conceptualizations of the Korea-China relationship following the Ming-Qing transition. All depictions of China produced during the Joseon period confirm this: none ever mentions the Qing but keeps referring to the Ming into the early nineteenth century, as evinced by the *Taeseo hoesa Li Madu Manguk jeondo* 泰西會士利瑪竇萬國全圖 (Complete map of all countries by the emissary of the West Matteo Ricci, 1821; hereafter *Manguk jeondo;* figure 8.7) produced by Ha Baekwon 河百源 (1781–1844). This map, despite the title linking it directly to Matteo Ricci, is also an adaptation of the world map from the *Zhifang waiji.* The map labels China and the sea to its east Dae Myeong 大明 (Ch. Da Ming) nearly two hundred years after the fall of the Ming-Chinese state, undoubtedly a conscious decision because many Korean literati were also bureaucrats, and their family members had been envoys to the Qing court, where they saw the maps and globes that had been produced since the fall of the Ming state (figure 8.8). Some of these, moreover, like

FIGURE 8.7.

Taeseo hoesa Li Madu Manguk jeondo (1821). 81.0 × 131.5 cm. National Library of Korea, Seoul.

FIGURE 8.8.

Detail of *Taeseo hoesa Li Madu Manguk jeondo* (figure 8.7) showing East Asia. China is labeled Da Ming Yitong 大明一統 (Unified Great Ming). National Library of Korea, Seoul.

Verbiest's *Kunyu quantu* and *Kunyu tushuo,* were indeed well known to Korean literati of the late eighteenth and nineteenth centuries, and naturally they indicated that sea as that of the Qing, Dae Cheong Hae 大清海 (Ch. Da Qing Hai). Indeed, one important reason Koreans were able to embrace new geographic knowledge linked to the Jesuits is because they regarded this knowledge as a legacy of the Ming. The premise underlying these maps thus implied that Korea carried on Chinese civilization. Although the Ming had long since collapsed, the tributary system and the order of civilization remained.

Let us return to the story from the novel *Taewon ji* that opened this chapter. Im Seong and his friends reach Taewon after eliminating every monster they encounter on their long journey. After they arrive at Taewon, they start a war, conquer five countries, and unify them. Their qualification for conquering is their status as heirs to the Chinese civilization. No one questions their legitimacy to build an empire on Taewon. After becoming emperor, Im Seong institutes hierarchy, social order, liturgy, and music. The new emperor and his friends bring their families to Taewon, and their lineages last more than a thousand years. Im Seong's construction of a utopian civilization simultaneously connotes violence and anxiety. The exclusion of and discrimination against unknown beings ironically manifest a deep fear of them.

In this chapter I reconstructed the intellectual context of *Cheonha do* in the context of the Korean reception of new geographical ideas by way of China. I showed how weaving new geographic information into a web of existing beliefs affected the spatial imaginaries of Korean literati, finally pushing them to rethink both who they were and their place. The Ming-Qing transition and the Manchu conquest of China resulted in the literati rigidly distinguishing the "civilized" states from the "barbaric" peoples who might invade that space.

Intellectuals and bureaucrats who got to visit China and meet Jesuits in Beijing were more open to intellectual challenges and new information. They even wrote, after reading Euclid's *Elements* or various astronomy books, that Europe also had sages.[50] Literati such as Hong Daeyong even used the new geographic knowledge to deconstruct the very idea of a central Chinese civilization. Others insisted, paradoxically, that Joseon could be the center of civilization because the globe's surface had no center anyway. However, intellectuals with such opinions were relatively few in number. More local elites and less mobile intellectuals struggled with the new geographic information. Although they admitted the world was larger than previously assumed, these Joseon intellectuals shared a common perception of a barbaric outside world threatening the central civilization of which they were, beyond doubt, a part.

Notes

1. Two types of manuscripts of *Taewon ji* are extant: one written in Chinese; the other written in traditional Korean vernacular. The year of the latter's production is unknown. The former, the manuscript in Chinese, includes both the scribe's name, Jo Myeonggyo 曺命教 (1678–1753), and the year he transcribed the book, the year of *byeongin* 丙寅, in this case 1746. This gives the *Taewon ji* a date of composition around the early eighteenth century. For basic information on *Taewon ji*, see Im Chigyun et al., *Taewon ji*. The manuscript in Chinese is in a private collection and that in Korean in the collection of the Hangukhak Jungang Yeonguwon, MF35–204. *Taewon ji* was widely read even by Korea's royal family. It was included in the collection of the royal library, the Nakseon Jae 樂善齋. Prince Sado 思悼世子 (1735–1762)—known for having been executed by his father, King Yeongjo 英祖 (r. 1724–1776)—kept a list of books in which he designated the *Taewon ji* one of his favorites, indicating how the novel had spread in the late eighteenth century. Prince Sado also read Jesuits' books, such as Diego de Pantoja's *Seven Victories* (*Qike* 七克) and Manuel Dias Jr.'s *Shengjing zhijie* 聖經直解. For his booklist, see Yi Seon, *Jina yeogsa hoemobon,* 5a.
2. For Korean intellectuals' renewed interest in the *Shanhai jing,* see Gim, "Joseon sidae ui imul"; Gim, "Joseon hugi minindeul ui *Sanhae gyeong* insik"; and Jeong, "Joseon sidae ui *Sanhae gyeong* suyong yakron."
3. For the relationship between the *Shanhai jing* and *Cheonha do,* see Dorofeeva-Lichtmann, "Mapless Mapping"; Oh, *Joseon sidae segye jido,* 237–294; Lim, *17, 18 segi Jungguk gua Joseon,* 116–135.
4. For the first import of the *Kunyu wanguo quantu,* see Yi, *Jibong ryuseol,* "Jegug bu, 2."
5. Lim, *17, 18 segi Jungguk gua Joseon,* 145. Three Korean manuscript copies of the *Kunyu wanguo quantu* are extant: at the Seoul National University Museum, at the Bongseon Honggyeongsa temple (black-and-white photograph, Seoul National University Kyujangkak collection), and at the Osaka Nanban Bunkakan. For the Korean reception and manuscripts of the *Kunyu wanguo quantu,* see Kyunggi Munhwa Jaedan, *Matteo Richi ui Gonyeo manguk jeondo.* At least ten extant Korean copies of the *Kunyu quantu* are known. Scholars are also aware of at least three replicas of the world map "Wanguo quantu" from the *Zhifang waiji.* The earliest is *Manguk jeondo* 萬國全圖 (Complete map of all countries, 1661) by Bak Jeongseol 朴廷薛 (1612–1693), the next is by an anonymous author in the late eighteenth century and has the title "Cheonha do jido" 天下都地圖 (Map of all cities under heaven; figure 8.5); and the most recent was copied by Ha Baekwon in 1821 (figure 8.7).
6. Unno, "Richō Chōsen ni okeru chizu." Before Unno's work, *Cheonha do* were understood as having originated in China. Unno points out that *Cheonha do*'s origin is Korean, not Chinese, by arguing that their production postdated 1666. For the origin of *Cheonha do,* see Oh, *Joseon sidae segye jido,* 237–250.
7. Bae, *Joseon gwa Junghwa,* 458–483.
8. Regarding preconceptions and assumptions, see Edney, *Cartography,* 65–102.
9. Sivin and Ledyard, "Introduction," 29–31; Yang, "Hanguk, Jungguk, Ilbon," 123–124; Yi, "Joseon hugi Tongjeyeong Hwawon yeongu"; Jeon, "Joseon hugi gunhyeon jido," 112; Jeong, "Joseon hugi hoehwasik gunhyeon jido yeongu."

10. On these atlases or maps, see Yi, "16–17 segi dongram dosik mokpanbon jidochaek."
11. From the fourth month of 1719 to the first month of 1720, Korean diplomatic missions went to Japan to celebrate the inauguration of a new regent. Shin Yuhan wrote a record of his experience in Japan called *Haeyu rok* 海遊錄 (Records of an ocean voyage). The conversation between Amenomori and Shin Yuhan took place in Tsushima. Korean bureaucrats called Amenomori, a translator well known for his fluent Korean, Wusam Dong 雨森東. Amenomori and Shin sometimes communicated by writing so-called brush talk (*bitan* 筆談). Korean and Japanese diplomats and translators usually wrote in Chinese when the theme of conversation was difficult to follow aloud. Their dialogue later found inclusion in "Bu Mungyeon jamnok" 附聞見雜錄 (Additional various records about things heard and seen), a supplement to the *Haeyu rok*.
12. Shin, *Haeyu rok*, vol. 2.
13. Shin Yuhan asked Amenomori about Matteo Ricci. He was also interested in the trade between European countries and Japan at Nagasaki. See Shin, *Haeyu rok*, vol. 2, "Bu Mungyeon jamnok."
14. Bae, *Joseon gwa Junghwa*, 473.
15. Regarding the spread of Chinese encyclopedias in Korea, see Lim, *17, 18 segi Jungguk gua Joseon*, 254–286.
16. Yi, *Seongho jeonhip*, vol. 27, "Dab Hwang Deukbo," *eulmyo*.
17. Yi Ik put "postface" (*bal* 跋) in the title of his text, but its content is more like a book report. The *Zhifang waiji* was possibly transcribed but not reprinted in Korea. Yi Ik habitually added "postface" to his titles. For those titles, see his content in *Seongho jeonhip*, vol. 55.
18. Yi, *Seongho jeonhip*, vol. 55, "Bal *Jigbang oegi*." In the *Zhifang waiji*, Aleni and Yang did not mention Magellan reaching China. Yi Ik perhaps exaggerated Magellan's voyage to persuade other literati to accept the new geographic information. Compare Yi Ik's text with Aleni and Yang, *Zhifang waiji*, 122–124.
19. Yi, *Seongho jeonhip*, vol. 55, "Bal *Jigbang oegi*."
20. Yi, *Oju yeonmun jangjeon sango, gyeongsa pyeon*, vol. 4, "Mulli oegi byeonjeung seol."
21. The following narrative is based on Yi, *Bukwonrok*, vols. 4–5.
22. Aleni and Yang, *Zhifang waiji*, 11.
23. For information on the circulation of *baiguan* novels and other Chinese books in eighteenth-century Korea, see Im, *Hanguk munhaksa ui sigak*; Bak, "Joseon sasindeul i gyeonmunhan bukgyeong yurichang"; Ewha Yeoja Daehakgyo Hanguk Munhwa Yeonguwon, *17, 18 segi dong Asia*.
24. Matteo Ricci and other Jesuits distinguished seas "small sea" or "big sea." This fact made literati recall Zou Yan's "small sea" and "big sea."
25. Wi, *Jonjae jeonseo, ha*, 35.
26. Yi Jonghwi, *Susan jip*, vol. 4, "Li Madu nambukgeuk dogi." It is difficult to identify this ex-minister Yi since Yi Jonghwi merely mentioned "ex-minister Yi" without any further information.
27. Yi, *Susan jip*, vol. 4, "Li Madu nambukgeuk dogi." The text presents an interesting way of reading the *Kunyu wanguo quantu*. Lim Jongtae regards Yi's reading or interpretation as "a mistake," specifically in treating North and South America as distinct continents. For Yi's anecdote and mistake, see Lim, *17, 18 segi Jungguk gua Joseon*, 148–149.
28. Yi, *Susan jip*, vol. 4, "Li Madu nambukgeuk dogi."

29. *Shijie* is a Buddhist concept meaning the universe. In the text, Yi used the concept to invoke Zou Yan's theory.
30. Yi, *Susan jip*, vol. 4, "Li Madu nambukgeuk dogi."
31. Cumania appears as "Gumani" 古禡泥 in Yi's text. He wrote Gumani differently from the *Kunyu wanguo quantu*: Gumani's *ma* is 馬, but Yi wrote Gumani's *ma* as 禡. It is difficult to know whether the difference was intentional or due to the replica he had read containing text from the revised version. Korean literati often used different Chinese characters for place-names and for foreign countries' names. Wi Baekgyu also wrote the countries' names differently from those in the *Zhifang waiji*. For the place-names of the *Kunyu wanguo quantu*, see Huang and Gong, *Li Madou shijie ditu yanjiu*. Thanks to Elke Papelitzky's comment, I could find the differences between Yi's text and the *Kunyu wanguo quantu*.
32. He also wrote Russia and France but seemed not to distinguish countries from other sorts of places.
33. Yi, *Susan jip*, vol. 4, "Li Madu nambukgeuk dogi."
34. According to his preface, he collected Chinese maps, Korean maps, and diagrams. He also confessed that his collection did not cover everything between "then and now" and "heaven and earth," although he titled the book *Hwanyeong* 寰瀛. His modest words contrarily show that the book title means "Everything between old and new, and heaven and earth" and that his intention was to synthesize all the diagrams and maps related to time—cosmogony, history, and Shao Yong's theory of time—and space. For the preface, see Wi, *Jonjae jeonseo, ha*, 33–34. According to Bae, four versions of the *Hwanyeong ji* are extant: two manuscripts, one fair copy version of the manuscript, and the woodblock-printed version. The contents of the four versions are all different. The three manuscript versions include "Li Madu cheonha do." There is no information about when the two manuscripts and the fair copy were exactly made. Wi's first preface, which appears in all versions, just states that he completed the *Hwanyeong ji* in 1770. According to Wi's chronology, he edited the first manuscript in 1758. For a comparison among the versions, see Bae, *Joseon gwa Junghwa*, 488–489. Wi's chronology is contained in *Jonjae jip*, vol. 24. The prefaces and the table of contents of both are contained in *Jonjae jeonseo, ha*, 35–40 and 43–48. For the fair copy version, see Wi, *Jonjae jeonseo, ha*, 43–160. The "*Cheonha do* of Matteo Ricci" reproduced in this chapter (figure 8.3) is from the fair copy version in *Jonjae jeonseo, ha*, 61–62.
35. Wi states in the preface of the first manuscript that he was excited when he saw Ricci's "Gugu ju do" 九九州圖 (Map of the nine [times] nine regions). He claims that he would not denounce the map, even if it was a fake, lest even sea turtles make fun of him for his limited perspective. *Gugu ju* is an alternative way of referring to Zou Yan's nine regions, which to Korean literati represent the entire world.
36. For Wi's mistake, see Lim, *17, 18 segi Jungguk gua Joseon*, 283–286; Bae, *Joseon gwa Junghwa*, 484–493.
37. In 1795, on the king's instructions, Wi gave the fair copy to King Jeongjo (r. 1776–1800). Given that the "*Cheonha do* of Matteo Ricci" was included in the fair copy, we can infer that it was removed between 1795 and 1798, the year of his death.
38. From the lists, it appears that he separated provinces and islands from the countries to which they belonged, treating them independently.

39. Wi, *Shinpyeon pyeoje chando Hwanyeong ji*, 23–28.
40. Wang Qi's *Sancai tuhui* and Yi Ik's *Seongho saseol* were classic encyclopedias that reflected the same order of composition. Wi did not give any title of heaven, earth, and human, so I have divided his monograph according to the order of its contents.
41. Wi, *Jonjae jeonseo, ha*, 160, 345.
42. For Shao Yong's theory and its political meaning, see Soh, "Joseon hugi wang ui gwonwiwa gwonryeok ui gwangye," 48–55. For Shao Yong's philosophy, see Birdwhistell, *Transition to Neo-Confucianism*. For the reception of Shao Yong's philosophy and theory in Korea, see Bak, "Joseon hugi sansuhak"; Jo, *Joseon hugi nakron gye hakpung*.
43. Yi Gyusang 李奎象 (1727–1799), for example, elucidated that the change of *qi* (*qishu* 氣數) had enabled the Qing "barbarians" to occupy China. He warned that as the quality of time fell lower and lower, "barbarians" even more ferocious and undomesticated would rise to conquer China. Yi, *Hansan se go*, "Ilmong go."
44. Yi, *Susanjip*, vol. 12, "Dongsa bongi"; ibid., "Sam Joseon nyeonpyo." For Yi Jonghwi's idea of Zhonghua, see Gim and Jeong, "Joseon hugi jeongtongron"; Jeong, "Joseon hugi saseo e natanan Junghwa juui wa minjok juui"; Jang, "Yi Jonghwi ui Jaguksa insik gwa sojunghwa juui."
45. Hong, *Damheonseo, naejip* vol. 4, "Uisan mundap."
46. People who thought the geographical center corresponded to the center of civilization were anxious about being called "eastern barbarians." The case of Gim Yian 金履安 (1722–1791), a famous scholar and friend of Hong Daeyong, shows this well. One day he had a conversation with an unnamed guest. The guest quoted Hong's words and asked him whether he could possibly accept the premise that a "barbarian" could be civilized. Gim did not agree with this idea and criticized Hong Daeyong's deconstructive thinking. For him, admitting Hong's claim meant accepting the Qing "barbarian." He argued on the basis of old geographic thoughts to maintain civilization and insisted "barbarians" from the periphery of China could never be civilized. The guest then refuted Gim: if he admitted that a person's birthplace was the most important condition for civilizing that individual, Joseon had no chance to be civilized because Joseon people were at best "eastern barbarians." For the conversation between Gim Yian and the anonymous guest, see Gim, *Samsanjae jib*, vol. 10, "Hwa-I byeon."
47. On small Zhonghua, see Yu, *Joseonjo daeoe sasang ui heureum*; Heo, *Joseon hugi junghwaron*; Gim, *Jungguk gwa Joseon*.
48. The order of Japan, Ryukyu, and Korea was changeable.
49. Many of the atlases also served to depict military installations and local administrative agencies. For instance, the atlas *Yeoji do* (National Library of Korea, M古2-1998-49~50) includes a *Cheonha do*, a map of Ming China, and maps of Korea, Japan, and Ryukyu, as well as military maps showing the borders between Korea and the Qing empire in detail.
50. For the attitude of Korean literati toward Western learning, see Roh, "Joseon hugi."

References

Unless stated otherwise, all Korean primary sources were accessed via the database Hanguk Gojeon Jonghab DB, https://db.itkc.or.kr/.

Aleni, Giulio (Ai Rulüe 艾儒略), and Yang Tingyun 楊廷筠. *Zhifang waiji* 職方外紀. Beijing: Zhonghua shuju, 1985.

Bae Wuseong. *Joseon gwa Junghwa: Joseon i kkum kkugo sangsang han segye wa munmyeong*. Paju: Dolbaege, 2014.

Bak Gwonsu. "Joseon hugi sansuhak ui baljeon gwa byeondong." PhD diss., Seoul National University, 2006.

Bak Hyeongyu. "Joseon sasindeul i gyeonmunhan bukgyeong yurichang." *Jungguk hakbo* 45 (2002): 169–188.

Birdwhistell, Anne D. *Transition to Neo-Confucianism: Shao Yung on Knowledge and Symbols of Reality*. Stanford, CA: Stanford University Press, 1989.

Dorofeeva-Lichtmann, Vera. "Mapless Mapping: Did the Maps of the Shan hai jing Ever Exist?" In *Graphics and Text in the Production of Technical Knowledge in China,* edited by Francesca Bray, Vera Dorofeeva-Lichtmann, and Georges Métailié, 217–294. Leiden: Brill, 2007.

Edney, Matthew H. *Cartography: The Ideal and Its History.* Chicago: University of Chicago Press, 2019.

Ewha Yeoja Daehakgyo Hanguk Munhua Yeonguwon, ed. *17, 18 segi dong Asia ui dokseo munhua wa munhwa.* Seoul: Ewha Yeoja Daehakgyo Hanguk munhua yeonguwon, 2004.

Gim Guangnyeon. "Joseon hugi minindeul ui *Sanhae gyeong* insik gua suyong." *Ilbonhak yeongu* 52 (2017): 137–160.

Gim Jeongsuk. "Joseon sidae ui imul mit goemul e daehan sangsangryeok, geu woncheon euroseo ui *Sanhae gyeong* gua taepyeong guanggi." *Ilbonhak yeongu* 48 (2016): 35–56.

Gim Yeongsik. *Jungguk gwa Joseon, geurigo Junghwa.* Seoul: Acanet, 2019.

Gim Yeongsim, and Jeong Jaehun. "Joseon hugi jeongtongron ui suyong gwa geu byeonhwa—Susan Yi Jonghwi ui 'Dongsa' reul jungsim euro." *Hanguk munhwa* 26 (2000): 171–200.

Gim Yian 金履安. *Samsanjae jib* 三山齋集, 1999.

Heo Taeyong. *Joseon hugi junghwaron gwa yeoksa insik.* Seoul: Acanet, 2009.

Hong Daeyong 洪大容. *Damheonseo* 湛軒書, 1939.

Huang Shijian 黃時鑒, and Gong Yingyan 龔纓晏. *Li Madou shijie ditu yanjiu* 利瑪竇世界地圖研究. Shanghai: Shanghai guji chubanshe, 2004.

Im Chigyun, Gang Munjong, Gim Inhoe, Yi Raeho, and O Hwa. *Taewon ji ui jonghapjeok yeongu.* Seoul: Yeokrak, 2018.

Im Hyeongtaek. *Hanguk munhaksa ui sigak.* Seoul: Changjak gua bipyeongsa, 1984.

Jang Yuseung. "Yi Jonghwi ui Jaguksa insik gwa sojunghwa juui." *Minjok munhwasa yeongu* 35 (2007): 40–82.

Jeon Jonghan. "Joseon hugi gunhyeon jido e jaehyeondoen gonggan insik gwa gonggan uisik." *Munhwa yeoksa jiri* 20, no. 2 (2008): 112–126.

Jeong Eunju. "Joseon hugi hoehwasik gunhyeon jido yeongu." *Munhwa yeoksa jiri* 23, no. 3 (2011): 119–140.

Jeong Jaehun. "Joseon hugi saseo e natanan Junghwa juui wa minjok juui." *Hanguk silhak yeongu* 8 (2004): 299–324.

Jeong Jaeseo. "Joseon sidae ui *Sanhae gyeong* suyong yakron—munheon jaryoreul jungsim euro." *Dogyo munhwa yeongu* 47 (2017): 201–230.

Jo Seongsan. *Joseon hugi nakron gye hakpung ui hyeongseong gwa jeongae.* Seoul: Jisik saneopsa, 2007.

Kyunggi Munhwa Jaedan, ed. *Matteo Richi ui Gonyeo manguk jeondo wa Joseon hugi ui segyegwan.* Seoul: Kyungin munhwasa, 2013.

Lim Jongtae. *17, 18 segi Jungguk gua Joseon ui seogu jirihak ihae: Jigu wa daseotdaeryuk ui uwha.* Paju: Changbi, 2012.

Oh Sanghak. *Joseon sidae segye jido wa segye insik.* Paju: Changbi, 2011.

Roh Dae-Hwan. "Joseon hugi 'seohak Jungguk wollyuseol' ui jeongae wa geu seonggyeok." *Yeoksa hakbo* 178 (2003): 113–139.

Shin Yuhan 申維翰. *Haeyu rok* 海遊錄, 1997.

Sivin, Nathan, and Gari Ledyard. "Introduction to East Asian Cartography." In *The History of Cartography.* Vol. 2, bk. 2, *Cartography in the Traditional East and Southeast Asian Societies,* edited by J. B. Harley and David Woodward, 23–31. Chicago: University of Chicago Press, 1994.

Soh Jeanhyoung. "Joseon hugi wang ui gwonwiwa gwonryeok ui gwangye: Hwanggeuk gaenyeom ui haeseok eul jungsim euro." PhD diss., Seoul National University, 2016.

Unno Kazutaka 海野一隆. "Richō Chōsen ni okeru chizu to Dōkyō" 李朝朝鮮における地図と道教. *Tōhō no shūkyō* 東方宗教 57 (1981): 14–36.

Wi Baekgyu 魏伯珪. *Jonjae jeonseo* 存齋全書. Seoul: Geonin munhwasa, 1974.

———. *Jonjae jip* 存齋集, 2000.

———. *Shinpyeon pyoje chando Hwanyeong ji* 新編標題纂圖寰瀛誌. Kyujanggak Collection, 奎5477, 1822.

Yang Bogeong. "Hanguk, Jungguk, Ilbon ui jiriji ui pyeonchan gwa baldal." *Eungyong jiri* 19 (1996): 113–140.

Yeoji do 輿地圖. National Library of Korea Collection M 古2-1998-49~50, n.d.

Yi Gibong. "16–17 segi dongram dosik mokpanbon jidochaek ui Joseon jeondo wa dobyeoldo e daehan yeongu." *Munhwa yeoksa jiri* 26, no. 8 (2014): 20–37.

Yi Gyugyeong 李圭景. *Oju yeonmun jangjeon sango* 五洲衍文長箋散稿, 1959.

Yi Gyusang 李奎象. *Hansan se go* 韓山世稿. National Library of Korea Collection 古, 3647-175, 1935.

Yi Hyeonju. "Joseon hugi Tongjeyeong Hwawon yeongu." *Seokdang nonchong* 37 (2007): 289–327.

Yi Ik 李瀷. *Seongho jeonhip* 星湖全集, 1997.

Yi Jonghwi 李種徽. *Susan jip* 修山集, 2000.

Yi Seon 李愃 (Sado Seja 思悼世子). *Jina yeogsa hoemobon* 支那曆史繪模本. National Library of Korea Collection 한貴古朝, 82-11.

Yi Sugwang 李睟光. *Jibong ryuseol* 芝峰類說, 2000.

Yi Uibong 李義鳳. *Bukwonrok* 北轅錄, 2016.

Yu Geunho. *Joseonjo daeoe sasang ui heureum: Hunghwajeok segyegwan ui hyeongseong gwa Bunggoe.* Seoul: Sungshin Women's University Press, 2004.

9

A Manuscript Map of East Asia Assembled by Jesuits in Nagasaki and Macao

MARCO CABOARA

The circulation of geographic information between western Europe and East Asia in the sixteenth and seventeenth centuries relied on the continually growing commercial and missionary presence of Europeans in the latter region. Much of the impact on the European side, however, centered on the movements of just a few objects, particularly manuscript and printed maps, borne across oceans for studying, copying, and translation, more or less faithfully. This volume addresses several such cases, including the *Gujin xingsheng zhi tu* 古今形勝之圖 (Map of advantageous terrain then and now; figure 10.1) studied by Florin-Stefan Morar, or the Chinese map printed in Fujian that became the model for the first European printed map of China with a Chinese title and outlook, the so-called Purchas map discussed by Mario Cams in chapter 5 (figure 5.3).[1] These maps circulated widely in East Asia and were printed in Chinese. When sent to Europe, such objects only grew intelligible through the mediation of translators and mapmakers able to transpose linguistic and mapmaking conventions.

The manuscript map introduced in this chapter is different (figure 9.1). According to the caption in its bottom-right cartouche, this map of East Asia is a replica—produced in Rome in 1651 and thereafter kept in the Jesuit Archives (ARSI) there—of another manuscript map produced in East Asia and sent to Europe in 1593. Unlike other maps discussed in this volume, it was produced by and for Europeans, more specifically by Jesuit missionaries in Japan and China for the general of the Jesuit Society Claudio Acquaviva (1543–1615) under the sponsorship of the Jesuit visitor Alessandro Valignano (1538–1606).[2] It was certainly not the only manuscript map of the region sent to Rome at the time but, as the caption's author claims, "There is no more precise

FIGURE 9.1.

Manuscript map of East Asia, 1651. 82 × 126 cm. Archivum Romanum Societatis Iesu, Rome.

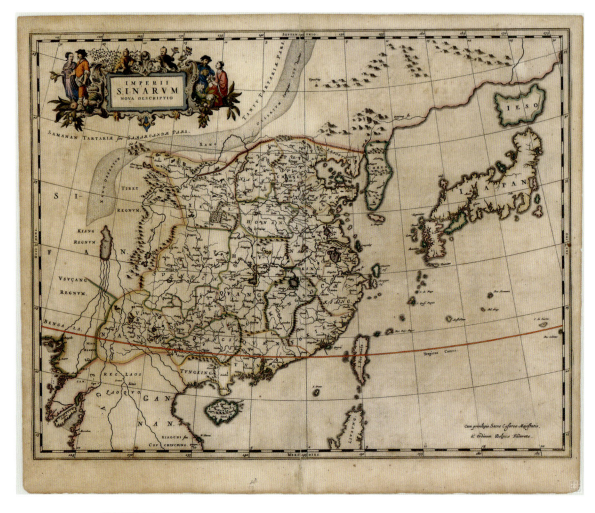

FIGURE 9.2.

"Imperii Sinarum nova descriptio" in the atlas *Novus atlas sinensis,* 1655. Height, 55 cm. Hong Kong University of Science and Technology Library, G2306.S1 M3.

map of China, and especially of Korea and Japan, at least among the ones that came to us here in Europe." This claim certainly has merit: the extant maps of China, based on Chinese artifacts, by the Jesuits Michele Ruggieri (1543–1607, figure 11.1), Michał Boym (1612–1659), and Martino Martini (1614–1661; figure 9.2), the first roughly contemporary with our map's production, depict the Korean Peninsula with far less detail and knowledge of the shape of the coastlines. Before discussing the depictions of the constituent parts of this compound map of East Asia, however, we must first address how this mid-seventeenth-century replica relates to its now lost sixteenth-century prototype.

It was common practice for European mapmakers to amend maps continually, whether printed or in manuscript form, while at the same time preserving the names of the compilers to enhance the maps' authority and commercial appeal. The author of the 1651 cartouche, aware of this and concerned with the appeal of his replica, therefore addresses his audience directly:

> If you want to know how much trust one should have in this map of the kingdoms of China, Korea, and Japan, it should be no other than (the trust) due a map drawn with extreme diligence in his own hands on Chinese paper by an expert in the field [of geography] and sent in the year 1593 to the Very Reverend (Father) Claudio Acquaviva, then Superior General of the Society of Jesus, as it exists in the Professed House of the Society order in this year 1651, when that map has been faithfully converted into this smaller size.

Elsewhere in the cartouche, he explains the first map's rushed production for its voyage to Rome:

> Many locations, especially at the borders of the Kingdom [of China], are missing in the original map, which the author justifies with the sudden departure of the Portuguese ships.[3]

The copyist was thus careful in presenting the map and its text (part of which he seems to have copied verbatim from the 1593 map) as a historical document, copied without updating to preserve its content. At the same time, he also presents the map as a document of ongoing relevance, no mere relic of the past but a map for use and integration with more updated (yet separate) materials, as with China's southern borders, for which the author invites the reader to consult the report of Alexander de Rhodes (1583–1660), missionary in Tonkin. This report was eventually published in Rome in 1650.[4]

Drawing in Japan and Korea

The production of the 1593 map most likely occurred in both Japan and China.[5] Its depiction of China is quite close to other representations of the country—for example, in the Ruggieri maps (investigated in chapter 11 of this volume by Lin Hong). The maps closely follow the depictions of China available to the Jesuits in contemporary printed Chinese works of geography, and the transcriptions of most (but not all) place-names follow the same system of romanization. The ARSI map clearly marks the first two Jesuit missionary stations of Zhaoqing 肇慶 and Shaozhou 韶州 (both in Guangdong Province), the second of which Matteo Ricci (1552–1610) established only after Ruggieri left China, indicating a possible insertion of recent information by Ricci, who was in Macao in 1593 to meet Valignano after he arrived there from Japan.

This study focuses, however, on the Japanese side of the story, centered on the compilation of a map by Valignano, the Jesuit visitor for East Asia, who visited Japan three times, first from July 1579 to February 1582 to reorganize the Jesuit mission in the country entirely. Jesuits had been present in Japan for thirty years, since Francis Xavier (1506–1552) had established the first Christian community in Japan in 1549.[6] Valignano described his experiences during this first visit in the *Sumario de las cosas de Japon* (Compendium of Japan) of 1583.[7] After departing, he arranged for four Japanese youths to accompany him in what was to be the first diplomatic mission from Japan to Europe, to the royal court in Madrid and the papal court in Rome. When he returned (in June 1590, to stay until the end of October 1592)[8] with the title of ambassador of the Portuguese viceroy of India, conveying the four youths back to Japan, he found the country unified under Toyotomi Hideyoshi 豊臣秀吉 (r. 1586–1598; known to him as *kanpaku* 関白, the regent). Japan's elites at the time were eagerly collecting information, geographical and political, to map their own territories and to establish their country's position in the wider world and specifically within East Asia. Gifts brought back from Europe included Abraham Ortelius's (1527–1598) *Theatrum orbis terrarum* as well as other maps, sea charts, an astrolabe, and a terrestrial globe. These and other maps led Japanese scholars and artists to make their own world maps.[9]

Valignano found the country so transformed since his first visit that once back in Macao (in late 1592 or early 1593), he wrote his *Adiciones del sumario de Japon* (Additions to the compendium of Japan), with the purpose of updating his descriptions of Japan and formulating new policy recommendations. On the geography of Japan, he noted:

> Because of the continuous wars that were taking place in Japan, until the *kanpaku* [Hideyoshi], a few years ago, unified it all, there was so little communication between one kingdom and the others, that when I came for the first time to Japan [1579], twenty-two years ago, almost nothing was known about the northern part of the country. But with the conquests that the *kanpaku* made, the country opened up in such a way that when I returned for the second time, in the year 1590, a Portuguese who knew about cosmography named Ignacio Moreira and who came with me to Miyako [Kyoto] made great effort to draw a reliable map of Japan, measuring the precise latitudes of many places he visited, and gathering with great diligence information about most locations. Even though he could not establish secure locations for the places he did not reach himself, as the Japanese are not familiar with the principles of cosmography, so that in the end he could not produce a truly reliable map and description of Japan with all the necessary details. Nevertheless, he produced the best and most accurate map that has been ever made.[10]

The Japanese portion of the 1651 map is probably the closest available approximation to that map, and the cartouche does indeed attribute it to Moreira (figure 9.3).[11]

It thus appears Valignano brought the map of Japan, first produced by Moreira, to Macao in 1592–1593, before its depictions made it onto the lost 1593 map and its extant 1651 replica.

The Japanese side of the story raises a further question regarding the origins of this map's depiction of the Korean Peninsula. Valignano's second stay in Japan coincided with Hideyoshi's order of 1592 to invade Korea, which unleashed a conflict spanning from 1592 to 1598 known as the Imjin War. Military preparations for the invasion over the course of a year included intelligence gathering as to the geography of Korea, China, and the border areas to the north of Korea—where the Jurchen were consolidating their power—possibly reachable from Japan's own northern frontier.[12] This brought into view the territories of Ezo (Hokkaido), inhabited by the Ainu and poorly known by the Japanese government, and raised the question of whether these lands directly adjoined the mainland and were therefore vulnerable to invasion by the Jurchen.[13] Perhaps the most iconic visualization of Hideyoshi's intelligence gathering and territorial ambition is a map drawn onto a fan he supposedly owned, highlighting the Korean capital as well as Beijing and Nanjing (figure 9.4). One side displays a map of

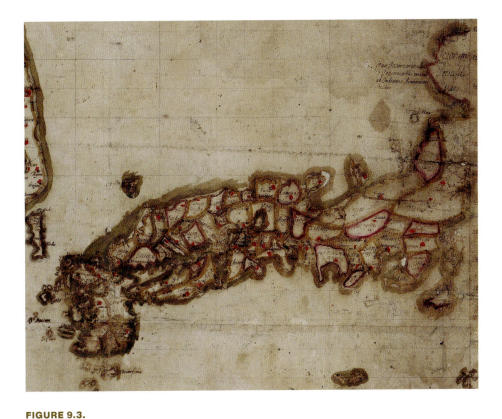

FIGURE 9.3.

Detail of figure 9.1 showing Japan.

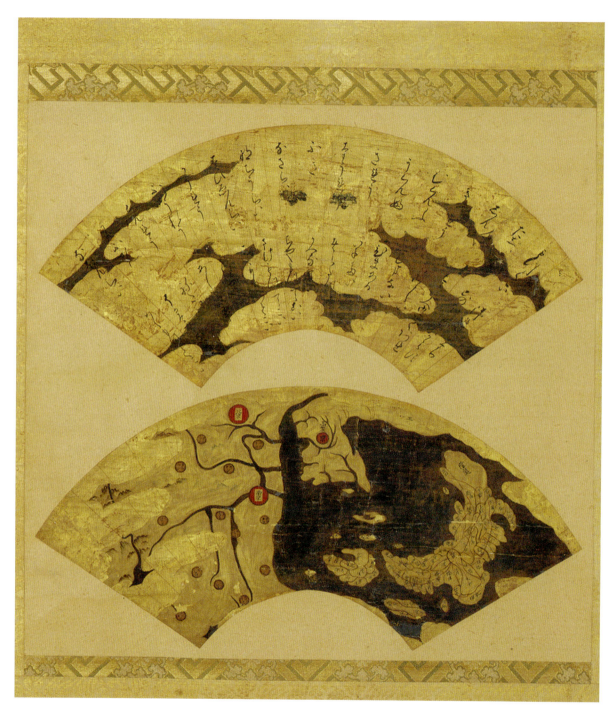

FIGURE 9.4.

A fan originally belonging to Toyotomi Hideyoshi and kept at Osaka Castle. On the top is the side with the "crib sheet"; below is the map of East Asia.

East Asia, combining Chinese and Korean conventions with a local map of the Japanese archipelago. The other contains several Japanese expressions and their Chinese translations—effectively a "crib sheet," possibly to aid Hideyoshi while receiving Ming envoys at his Osaka castle.[14]

The knowledge of Korean geography available in Japan went far beyond the simplistic depiction on the front of the fan. Kawamura Katsunori has convincingly argued that by the mid-sixteenth century, a wide range of Japanese copies of Korean maps, many still preserved in Japanese collections, were in significant production.[15] The Jesuit missionary Luís Fróis (1532–1597), discussing the planning of the invasion of Korea, refers to information and maps of the country available to Hideyoshi at that time and specifically describes a map of Korea with the eight provinces marked in different colors.[16] It would probably have been similar to the Korean portion of the 1593/1651 map under discussion: divided by thick lines into eight blocks showing the eight provinces of Korea under the Joseon state (figure 9.5). Each province block contains several

FIGURE 9.5.

Detail of figure 9.1 showing the Korean Peninsula.

CABOARA   237

symbols marking place-names, each representing a different administrative level, such as red squares for provincial capitals.

Although these features of the 1593/1651 map are based on Korean conventions, several elements attest to the map's production in Japan. First, its depiction of the island of Tsushima points to a Japanese connection, as Korean maps always depicted the island as fairly round and oriented from east to west, while in Japanese maps it appears oriented from north to south and rather elongated, as in this map.[17] Second, at the center of the peninsula appears the name of the country, written as "CORAI" (derived from the name of the Goryeo 高麗 state, 918–1392, commonly used to refer to the country in Japanese), while Koreans would have used the name of the contemporary Joseon 朝鮮 state, a further indicator of Japanese provenance. Last, but not least, Korean military bases—namely, the land units (*peyon* 兵營) and sea units (*suijon* 水營), especially those located in the south and southwest part of the peninsula—may well reflect Hideyoshi's preinvasion intelligence gathering.

The invasion of Korea in turn yielded new geographical knowledge, as Valignano noted in his *Adiciones*:

> Now with this war that the Japanese waged in the last years, invading the kingdom of Korea, many things were discovered that were previously unknown. So, near the northern [= southern?] tip of Japan, which lies to the West, between China and Japan, is situated the kingdom of Korea, which on one side borders with China, to whom Koreans pay allegiance, and on the other borders with the Tartars, known as Orancay [= Jurchen], who inhabit a great extension of land occupying to the North all the longitudinal extension of Japan . . . and between this land and the northern tip of Japan there is another island called Ezo.[18]

Both Ezo and Orankai are important elements of the 1651 replica under discussion, which not only includes the term "Jezorum Insula" (Ezo island) but also provides its Ainu name,[19] "Ainamaxorj," a term corresponding to the Ainu term "Ainu Moshiri" (the Land of Men/the Ainu), its first known occurrence on any map.[20] A similar term, "Ainomoxori," appears in the short "De Yezorum insula," a half-page description of the island also kept at ARSI.[21] According to Josef Schütte, probably either Valignano or Moreira composed the short description "De Yezorum insula" in 1592 or 1593.[22] The unknown author reports gathering information from both Japanese informants and an inhabitant of Ezo who had come for an audience with Hideyoshi when Valignano was there as ambassador of the viceroy of India.[23]

Besides the island of Ezo, the map also depicts a long stretch in the north marked as follows: "Urancanorum gentis incognita regio in orientem tendens" (Unknown region of the people of Orankai stretching toward the East). This feature establishes a strong link with early Japanese world maps, as the presence of the ethnonym "Orankai" to the northeast of Korea is of paramount importance to dating these maps (such as

FIGURE 9.6.

Untitled world map mounted on a six-panel folding screen. Approx. 108 × 216 cm. Jōtoku Temple, Fukui Prefecture.

the Jōtoku temple map shown in figure 9.6) produced in Japan after European models. The term appears first in 1592 when conquering Japanese troops, active in the Jurchen lands beyond Korea's northeastern borders, sent back reports and intelligence on the region.[24] Therefore, although no known historical materials confirm the specific itinerary of the depiction of Korea, it is highly likely it also reached Macao in the hands of Valignano or perhaps as part of Moreira's map of Japan.

In all, the presence of Zhaoqing and Shaozhou, Orankai, and Ezo and its Ainu name, as well as the detailed map of Korea, points to a specific time frame thoroughly consistent with the account given in the cartouche of the 1651 map. The 1651 replica does not incorporate any newly acquired knowledge from the years since 1593, apart from twice mentioning de Rhodes as a further source. Even the account of the Imjin War in the section about Korea remains frozen in time, reflecting the situation as Valignano had understood it in Macao in 1593: "The *kanpaku* [Hideyoshi] sent a huge army to Korea in 1592 which conquered almost the whole kingdom, until in February 1593 China joined forces with Korea and . . . [fought?] the Japanese. They fight their way into the occupied capital city and . . . almost all the others. Of this fight the author of the map writes as follows: 'the result of the fight is uncertain and the ultimate outcome has not reached us.'" With these and similar words, the mapmaker apologizes for the map's imperfections, alluding to the Portuguese ships' abruptly imminent departure. Since time has consumed part of the cartouche (near the edge of the sheet), some sentences are fragmentary, leaving crucial details about locations and dates unclear.

As we may gather from the barely legible text, a map was sent in 1593 to Macao, presumably from Nagasaki. It was then combined in Macao with another map of China and forwarded, in November of the same year, to Goa, whence it proceeded to Rome. Part of the sustained value of the 1651 map, copied more than half a century after its now lost prototype, lay therefore in the fact that it visualized East Asia and its internal structures and conflicts for contemporary Europeans. Japan, Korea, and China all occupied the same frame, reflecting the spatial reality of these early Jesuit missions to the Portuguese Indies: as Ricci himself wrote to Claudio Acquaviva on October 13, 1596, there were great hopes that a settlement, negotiated in part by Christian daimyos from Kyushu, would enable Jesuits from Japan to bring the gospel to China.[25]

FIGURE 9.7.

"Nova et exactissima Sinarum monarchiae descriptio." 32 × 42 cm. Niedersächsische Staats- und Universitätsbibliothek Göttingen, 2 H ITAL I, 62/63 RARA: Taf. 62.

The 1651 Replica and the Giangolini Map

The Imjin War ended not with an opening but with a closure of contact between China and Japan: as Jesuit activities in Japan grew more and more restricted, leading to persecution and finally expulsion, Ricci was allowed to enter Beijing and approach the imperial court. By the time of the copying of the 1651 ARSI map, it was primarily a precious archival document to preserve via faithful copying. The vision of East Asia it presented as the Jesuits had once experienced it—open to penetration—was now just a memory to cherish, even as the map, parts of which remained the most richly detailed depictions of the region in Europe for almost another century, lay unknown to most Europeans.

Finally, the 1593 prototype map, whether the first map or a replica, came to the attention of Carlo Giangolini (1598–1652), an Italian mapmaker now almost forgotten but in his time widely known and well connected to the courts of Castille and Rome, as well as to the Jesuit order. A smaller map from his hands, printed in Rome in 1642 and preserved only in one exemplar titled "Nova et exactissima Sinarum monarchiae descriptio" (New and most precise map of the kingdom of China), bears a clear resemblance to the 1651 replica (figure 9.7). One important difference between the two lies in the differing contents of their northeastern corners. While in the 1642 exemplar Giangolini placed a dedication cartouche there, obscuring the region of the Orankai and the island of Ezo,[26] the 1651 ARSI map's northeastern corner contains a depiction of what are now southern Manchuria and Hokkaido. Despite the obvious connections between the 1651 ARSI map and Giangolini's 1642 exemplar, the latter credited no model and omitted every trace of its missionary origins, even as his generic, outdated annotations about China relied almost exclusively on Jesuit sources.[27]

Notes

A special thanks to Cheng Tsung-jen (Academia Sinica, Taiwan), who collaborated on an earlier version of this paper.

1. Szcześniak, "Seventeenth Century Maps of China"; Kajdanski, "Ming Dynasty Map of China."
2. A visitor was, generally, an official in charge of reviewing or controlling the work of other administrative bodies. As personal delegate of the superior general of the Jesuits in the Indies, Valignano had extraordinarily wide powers to oversee and govern the mission as he saw fit, including to accept or dismiss members from the society, to send members anywhere he judged they might aid a particular mission, to change local superiors, and to implement new mission policies whenever and wherever he deemed necessary. Üçerler, "Alessandro Valignano," 340–341.
3. The ships linking Nagasaki to Macao and Macao to Goa generally left just once a year, so every missive back to Europe had to be ready before casting off.
4. *Relazione de' felici successi della Santa Fede.*
5. On the composite nature of East Asian maps in the era of contact with Europe, see Takahashi, "Birth of New Perspectives through Integration of Origin Maps."
6. Üçerler, "Alessandro Valignano," 346–347.

7. The manuscript was published only in 1594, with the later *Adiciones* (Additions). According to Üçerler, it contains both a summary of his assessment of the situation of the Japanese and of the church there at the end of his first visitation, as well as detailed proposals for resolving the major problems he encountered in the administration of the mission. It is also one of Valignano's most original works. Üçerler, "Alessandro Valignano," 349.
8. Ibid., 349.
9. Unno, "Cartography in Japan," 377.
10. Valignano, *Adiciones,* 384 (author's translation).
11. "When the Viceroy of India sent the Reverend Father Alessandro Valignano to the *kanpaku* as his ambassador, many Portuguese came with him and among them Ignacio Moreira from Lisbon who drew [a map of] the site of the whole country by means of astronomical observations and thanks to information from the best Japanese informants." Not much is known about Moreira besides Valignano's remarks. See a discussion of the available evidence in Schütte, "Ignacio Moreira of Lisbon"; Schütte, "Japanese Cartography at the Court of Florence"; Aihara, "Ignacio Moreira's Cartographical Activities in Japan."
12. Sansom, *History of Japan,* 352–362.
13. Rawski, *Early Modern China and Northeast Asia,* 89–90.
14. Nanba et al., *Old Maps in Japan,* 148; Leca, "Fluttering Ambition."
15. Kawamura, "Kagoshima kenritsu toshokan zō *Chōsen kozu.*"
16. Fróis, *Historia de Japam,* 5.543. See also Walker, *Conquest of Ainu Lands,* 32–33.
17. Ledyard, "Cartography in Korea," 271–272.
18. Valignano, *Adiciones,* 388.
19. The name "Ezo" first appeared in Bartolomeu Velho's map of 1561. See Lach, *Asia in the Making of Europe,* 724–725. On the European mapping of Ezo/Hokkaido, see Boscaro and Walter, "Ezo and Its Surroundings"; De Palma, "Ricerche sulla cartografia di Ezo."
20. Siddle, "Making of Ainu Moshiri."
21. Jap.-Sin. 34, f. 55.
22. Schütte, "Japanese Cartography at the Court of Florence," 41n13.
23. Schilling, "Il contributo dei missionari cattolici"; Cieslik et al., *Hoppō tankenki,* 40; Kodama, *Ainu,* 15. In 1590 Hideyoshi met with Kakizaki Yoshihiro, overlord of Matsumae in southern Hokkaido, resulting in Yoshihiro's investiture in the fief of Ezo; see Harrison, *Japan's Northern Frontier,* 6–8; Walker, *Conquest of Ainu Lands,* 30–32.
24. Unno, "Cartography in Japan," 379; Okamoto, "Desenvolvimento." On the complex issue of the ethnonym "Orankai" and its improper identification with the Jurchen by the Japanese invading army in 1592, see Okamoto, "Desenvolvimento"; Janhunen, "On the Ethnonyms Orok and Uryangkhai."
25. Ricci, *Lettere,* 338–339.
26. Even though an Italian Jesuit missionary, Girolamo de Angelis (1567–1623), had in the meantime explored and produced a map of the island (Boscaro and Walter, "Ezo and Its Surroundings," 85).
27. Even leaving the thoroughly outdated latitude of Beijing at forty-seven degrees: a feature of early Jesuit maps already superseded by the late 1590s. D'Elia, *Fonti Ricciane* 1:13; Caboara, "First Printed Missionary Map of China."

References

Aihara, Ryoichi. "Ignacio Moreira's Cartographical Activities in Japan (1590–1592), with Special Reference to Hessel Gerritsz's Hemispheric World Map." *Memoirs of the Research Department of the Toyo Bunko* 34 (1976): 209–442.

Boscaro, Adriana, and Lutz Walter. "Ezo and Its Surroundings through the Eyes of European Cartographers." In *Japan, a Cartographic Vision,* edited by Lutz Walter, 84–90. Munich: Prestel, 1994.

Caboara, Marco. "The First Printed Missionary Map of China." *Journal of the International Map Collectors' Society* 162 (2020): 6–21.

Cieslik, Hubert, Jeronimo de Angelis, and Diogo Carvalho. *Hoppō tankenki: Genna nenkan ni okeru gaikokujin no Ezo hōkokusho* 北方探検記: 元和年間に於ける外国人の蝦夷報告書. Translated by Yoshitomo Okamoto 岡本良知. Tokyo: Yoshikawa kobunkan, 1962.

D'Elia, Pasquale, ed. *Fonti Ricciane: Storia dell'introduzione del Cristianesimo in Cina.* Rome: Libreria dello Stato, 1942.

De Palma, Daniela. "Ricerche sulla cartografia di Ezo." *Rivista Degli Studi Orientali* 7 (1997): 1–123.

Fróis, Luís. *Historia de Japam.* 5 vols. Lisbon: Biblioteca Nacional, 1976–1984.

Fuchs, Walter. *The "Mongol Atlas" of China, by Chu Ssu-Pen, and the Kuang-yü-t'u.* Peiping: Fu Jen University, 1946.

Harrison, John Armstrong. *Japan's Northern Frontier.* Gainesville: University of Florida, 1953.

Janhunen, Juha. "On the Ethnonyms Orok and Uryangkhai." *Studia Etymologica Cracoviensia* 19, no. 2 (2014): 71–81.

Kajdanski, Edward. "The Ming Dynasty Map of China (1605) from the Czartoryski Library in Poland." In *Actes du VIIe colloque international de sinologie, Chantilly 1992: Échanges culturels et religieux entre la Chine et l'Occident,* 183–190. Paris: Ricci Institute, 1992.

Kawamura Katsunori 河村克典. "Kagoshima kenritsu toshokan zō *Chōsen kozu* no kisai naiyō to sakusei nendai" 鹿児島県立図書館蔵「朝鮮古図」の記載内容と作成年代. *Shin-chiri* 新地理 47, no. 2 (1999): 41–49.

Kodama, Sakuzaemon. *Ainu: Historical and Anthropological Studies.* Sapporo: Hokkaido University School of Medicine, 1970.

Lach, Donald F. *Asia in the Making of Europe.* Vol. 1, *The Century of Discovery.* Chicago: University of Chicago Press, 1994.

Leca, Radu. "Fluttering Ambition: Heteroglossic Geographic Knowledge on a Sixteenth-Century Folding Fan." In *Dialogical Imaginations,* edited by Michael F. Zimmermann. Chicago: University of Chicago Press (forthcoming).

Ledyard, Gari. "Cartography in Korea." In *The History of Cartography.* Vol. 2, bk. 2, *Cartography in the Traditional East and Southeast Asian Societies,* edited by J. B. Harley and David Woodward, 235–345. Chicago: University of Chicago Press, 1994.

Nanba Matsutarō 南波松太郎, Muroga Nobuo 室賀信夫, and Unno Kazutaka 海野一隆, eds. *Old Maps in Japan.* Translated by Patricia Murray. Osaka: Sogensha, 1973.

Okamoto, Yoshitomo 岡本良知. "Desenvolvimento cartográfico da parte Extrema Oriente da Ásia pelos Jesuítas Portugueses em fins do século XVI." *Studia* (Lisbon) 13 (1964): 7–29.

Rawski, Evelyn Sakakida. *Early Modern China and Northeast Asia: Cross-Border Perspectives.* Cambridge: Cambridge University Press, 2015.

Relazione de' felici successi della Santa Fede predicata da' padri della Compagnia di Giesu nel regno di Tunchino. Rome: Giuseppe Luna, 1650.

Ricci, Matteo. *Lettere (1580–1609).* Edited by Francesco D'Arelli. Macerata: Quodlibet, 2001.

Sansom, George Bailey. *A History of Japan, 1334–1615.* Tokyo: Tuttle, 1974.

Schilling, Doroteo. "Il contributo dei missionari cattolici nei secoli XVI e XVII alla conoscenza dell'isola di Ezo e degli ainu." In *Le Missioni Cattoliche e la Cultura dell'Oriente,* edited by Celso Constantini, Pasquale D'Elia, and Georg Schurhammer, 139–214. Rome: Istituto italiano per il Medio ed Estremo Oriente, 1943.

Schütte, Josef. "Ignacio Moreira of Lisbon, Cartographer in Japan, 1590–1592." *Imago Mundi* 16 (1962): 116–128.

———. "Japanese Cartography at the Court of Florence: Robert Dudley's Maps of Japan, 1606–1636." *Imago Mundi* 23 (1969): 29–58.

Siddle, Richard. "The Making of Ainu Moshiri: Japan's Indigenous Nationalism and Its Cultural Fictions." In *Nationalisms in Japan,* edited by Naoko Shimazu, 122–142. London: Routledge, 2006.

Szcześniak, Boleslaw. "The Seventeenth Century Maps of China: An Inquiry into the Compilations of European Cartographers." *Imago Mundi* 13 (1956): 116–136.

Takahashi, Kimiaki 高橋公明. "Birth of New Perspectives through Integration of Origin Maps: The Case of 'Haedong cheguk ch'ongdo.'" *Forum of International Development Studies* 44 (2014): 17–35.

Üçerler, M. Antoni J. "Alessandro Valignano: Man, Missionary, and Writer." *Renaissance Studies* 17, no. 3 (2003): 337–366.

Unno, Kazutaka. "Cartography in Japan." In *The History of Cartography.* Vol. 2, bk. 2, *Cartography in the Traditional East and Southeast Asian Societies,* edited by J. B. Harley and David Woodward, 346–477. Chicago: University of Chicago Press, 1994.

Valignano, Alessandro. *Adiciones del sumario de Japon (1592).* Published together with *Sumario de las cosas de Japon (1583),* edited by Jose Luis Alvarez-Taladriz. Tokyo: Sophia University, 1954.

Walker, Brett L. *The Conquest of Ainu Lands: Ecology and Culture in Japanese Expansion, 1590–1800.* Berkeley: University of California Press, 2001.

10

China Translata

The 1555 Map of Advantageous Terrain Then and Now

FLORIN-STEFAN MORAR

On February 13, 1565, Miguel López de Legazpi (1502–1572) reached the island of Cebu and claimed the island and the entire archipelago of the Visayas for Philip II of Spain (1527–1598). Shortly thereafter, the cosmographer Andrés de Urdaneta (1498–1568), accompanying Legazpi's expedition, discovered a way from Manila across the Pacific to Acapulco in New Spain. This was meant to be the foundation of a trade route directly linking East Asia with the New World, which would fundamentally undercut Portugal's supremacy in the East Asian trade.[1] The Castilians' ambitious plans to dominate the entire Pacific Ocean, however, relied implicitly on securing access to China. It was in the context of early efforts to obtain intelligence about China that the *Gujin xingsheng zhi tu* 古今形勝之圖 (Map of advantageous terrain then and now; abbreviated here as *Xingsheng tu*; figure 10.1) entered the possession of the Castilian crown.[2]

The only known extant print of the *Xingsheng tu* has resided at the Archivo General de Indias (AGI) in Seville since the late sixteenth century. With increased public access to the archives at the beginning of the twentieth century, the map began drawing attention. Brief accounts began emerging from the pens of such scholars as Pablo Pastells, Ettore Ricci, Lothar Knauth, and others.[3] Enoki Kazuo published the first accurate and comprehensive work on the map in 1976.[4] More recently, following the map's restoration, a team of Taiwanese and Spanish scholars issued a new series of studies on various aspects of the map.[5] Through their scholarly contributions, we now know a good deal about the map's origins and general significance, yet the map's most remarkable feature, a series of translations in Spanish inscribed on the map's surface (figures 10.2 and 10.3)

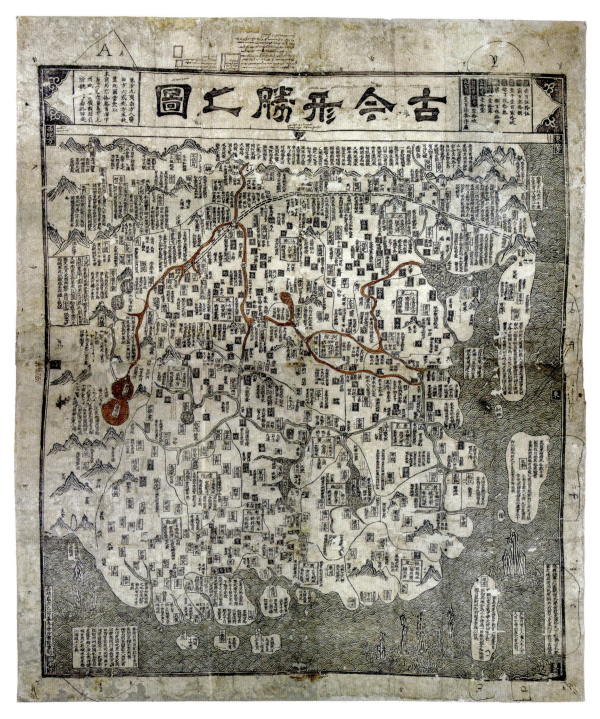

FIGURE 10.1.

Gujin xingsheng zhi tu (1555). 113.8 × 100.8 cm. Ministerio de Cultura y Deporte. Archivo General de Indias, Sevilla, MP-Filipinas, 5.

and on an accompanying document, still remains a worthy topic of research. Who made these translations? How were they made, and what is their import for the significance of the map?

This chapter addresses these questions by locating the *Xingsheng tu* within the broader context of European interactions with Chinese mapping. Prior scholarship has confused the *Xingsheng tu* both with a Chinese map Matteo Ricci (1552–1610) sent from China in 1584 and with the source for Abraham Ortelius's (1527–1598) map of China.[6] These errors, however, are themselves informative. While the map directly relates neither to the Jesuit enterprise in China nor to Ortelius, it exemplifies strategies of dealing with Chinese maps that both the Jesuits and the author of Ortelius's source employed, especially translation. In this chapter I consider the translation of the *Xingsheng tu* comparatively, examining the similarities and differences between its translation and known translations of Chinese maps by Jesuits, such as those of Michele Ruggieri (1543–1607) and Martino Martini (1614–1661). This approach recasts, I believe, our understanding of this map. Historians have sought to show this map's impact upon European maps via direct lines of continuity, a fruitless approach considering this map never circulated outside the AGI, giving rise to specious arguments. The map's significance lies not, however, in its direct influences but in its participation in a broader phenomenon of interactions between western Europe and East Asia.

The signing of the Treaty of Tordesillas in 1494 divided the globe in half, placing the western portion, including large parts of the Americas, under Castilian control, while the Portuguese retained their monopoly over the East Asian trade. When the Castilians started exploring the Pacific Ocean, pushing westward toward East Asia, they problematized that division (consecrated on maps by the drawing of the Line of Demarcation). There is ample evidence that the key strategic goal propelling Miguel López de Legazpi's colonization of the Philippines, the culmination of the Spanish policy of encroaching upon the Portuguese monopoly, was access to China. In a letter from 1569, the Augustinian monk Fray Martín de Rada (1533–1578), a member of Legazpi's expedition, wrote to Philip II: "If your majesty has pretensions over China, which is a large, rich and well-organized country having cities, forts, ramparts even bigger than those of Europe, then it will be necessary first to establish ourselves in these islands. First, because we cannot pass through so many islands and shoals, as China has on its coast with sail ships but with oar ships. Secondly, because in order to conquer a land that big and with so many people it is necessary to have nearby a base of support and relief for any contingency."[7]

To gather intelligence for this ambitious project of conquest, Rada became deeply interested in Chinese culture. In addition to his skills as a cosmographer and mathematician, he was also a talented linguist.[8] During his time in New Spain, he had become fluent in the difficult Otomi (Hñähñu) language, then considered derived from Chinese, and on Cebu he had learned to speak the local dialect. Not long after arriving in Asia, he began compiling a dictionary of Chinese—*Arte y vocabulario de la lengua China*—aided by Chinese merchants from Fujian Province.⁹ Rada's linguistic skills proved crucial to the expedition when Legazpi moved the capital from Cebu to Manila in 1571 to gain the Castilians an outpost near China. Soon after their arrival at Manila, in November 1574, a group of Chinese and Japanese pirates led by Lin Feng 林鳳—known in Castilian documents as Limahon—attacked the settlement.¹⁰ As the Spaniards besieged Limahon, a Ming war junk appeared off the coast. The return of some of Limahon's Chinese prisoners prompted the first exchanges between the Castilian and Chinese officials. Subsequently, Martín de Rada took part in an embassy to Fujian Province. Because Limahon had escaped them, the Castilians could not obtain a settlement on the Fujian coast in the same way the Portuguese had at Macao, but Rada was still able to gather detailed information about China, writing one of the most comprehensive reports of the period, as well as purchasing a substantial number (perhaps a few hundred) Chinese books, many dealing with the sciences.¹¹

It was after Limahon's appearance off the coast of Manila that the governor of the Philippines, Guido de Lavezaris, managed to obtain, through his contacts with Chinese traders from Fujian, a complete and detailed map of China—the *Xingsheng tu*—that he subsequently dispatched to Europe with the aforementioned letter dated July 30, 1574.¹²

The *Xingsheng tu*, a medium-size print (113.8 × 100.8 cm) on a single sheet of Chinese paper, was long believed the work of the imperial censor Yu Shi 喻時, although recently Jin Guoping has convincingly argued that the map's author was more likely a certain Gan Gong 甘宮 from Xinfeng 信豐 County in Jiangxi Province.¹³ This specific surviving edition of the map is a 1555 reprint of Gan Gong's work by the Jinsha Academy 金沙書院 in Longxi County 龍溪縣 of Fujian Province. Besides presenting a complete picture of the known world under heaven (*tianxia* 天下), the narrow purpose of the *Xingsheng tu* was to aid scholarship, enabling the viewer to compare famous historical locations (represented in black) against the current lay of the land (white). In terms of content, the map conforms most to the official *Da Ming yitong zhi* 大明一統志 (Gazetteer of the unified Great Ming; first printed in 1461) while also incorporating information from other sources (e.g., maps) relating to foreign countries like Korea, Japan, and Vietnam.

Scholars have repeatedly sought to demonstrate the map's direct impact on early modern European representations of China, out of which two prevalent strains of confusion presently complicate the literature: first, the identification of *Xingsheng tu* as the source of Ortelius's map of China, *Chinae olim Sinarum Regio nova descriptio*, published for the first time in the 1584 edition of his *Theatrum orbis terrarum* (Display of the lands of the globe) and, second, the belief it was a map the Jesuit Matteo Ricci sent to Europe. Yet both the 1574 letter by Lavezaris and the translation document accompanying the map corroborate its journey from the Philippines. It therefore cannot have been the map to which Ricci referred in his 1584 letter to Bautista Roman.¹⁴ We can equally exclude the possibility that the *Xingsheng tu* was used to compose Ortelius's *Chinae*.

The Ortelius map of China was most likely based on a manuscript map of China sent by his Spanish patron Benito Arias Montano, the confessor of Philip II.[15] This source map was obtained through espionage by the Spanish ambassador to Portugal Juan de Borja (1564–1628). Borja convinced the Portuguese mapmaker Luiz Jorge da Barbuda (ca. 1564–1613) to shift his allegiances to Spain. In 1573 Barbuda left Portugal with a number of maps and Chinese books, accompanying the train of Juan de Borja.[16] While the books and maps made it to Madrid, Barbuda was detained at the border and imprisoned under the accusation of treason until 1579. Barbuda was the author of the map of China published by Ortelius and was credited as such explicitly.[17] Ortelius's map was likely based on one of the maps made by Barbuda brought over from Portugal and not the *Xingsheng tu*, which Barbuda could not have consulted because it arrived in Spain between 1574 and 1576, when he was still imprisoned in Portugal. In short, what we know with certainty about the transmission of the *Xingsheng tu* is that it remained within the confines of the archives of the Council of the Indies as a state secret, unavailable for consultation. Its only possible influence was on a manuscript map Gabriel Tatton made in Madrid in 1609 that displays an outline of the Chinese coasts similar to those on the *Xingsheng tu*, although in light of recent scholarship this connection now appears tenuous.[18]

Since the *Xingsheng tu* had little or no direct impact on early modern European maps, we must seek its significance elsewhere. The print now kept at the AGI in Seville is remarkable, in fact, for the role it played in the process of early modern Europeans' translation of Chinese maps, which included both maps such as that by Ortelius and the Jesuit maps of China. Significant similarities as well as important differences between the translation of the *Xingsheng tu* and those of other Chinese maps merit detailed discussion.

As soon as Guido de Lavezaris (1512–1581) obtained the *Xingsheng tu* in 1574, he recognized the immense usefulness of the important details about China thereon. We read in a letter from that year that he had tasked "an Augustinian with knowledge of Chinese and two Chinese interpreters" with making sense of the map and rendering a translation.[19] The Augustinian in question was most likely Martín de Rada and the two interpreters, probably Lin Bixiu 林必秀 (known to the Castilians under the name Sansay, from "Xiushi" 秀師, Master Xiu) and Chen Huiran 陳輝然, also known as Hernando.[20] The translation of the *Xingsheng tu* was therefore a collaboration between a European with a limited knowledge of Chinese and Chinese translators with a limited knowledge of European tongues. The probable method of translation was oral explanation (*koushu* 口述) along with the writing down of information, a type of collaborative translation we know the Jesuits used both when translating from Chinese—as in their early translations of the Confucian classics—and when translating European books and maps into Chinese.[21] Notably, Matteo Ricci's collaborator Li Zhizao 李之藻 (1565–1630) directly addressed the important role of translation in the making of the *Kunyu wanguo quantu* 坤輿萬國全圖 (Complete map of all countries on earth, 1602; figure 1.1), discussed by Nicolas Standaert in chapter 1 of this volume:

> The foreigners and their rare works, it is not easy to encounter them, and I deplore that his age moves towards decline and that I was unable to complete the translation. This map was recarved by the gentlemen of Baixia [near Nanjing] but the map was small and not detailed. I, with the help of my friends, made six rolls to be put on a screen and in days of leisure I dedicated myself to complete the task. I have done the work of rectifying translations and improved them (*lizheng xiangxu* 厘正象胥), being several times better than the old map, although there are still deficiencies in the names of all the tributary countries. Because of the meaning or the different ways they are called in the past and the present, and the different translations in different dialects, I did not want to transmit that which is doubtful, that which I have myself seen being also not profound.[22]

Li focuses specifically on the names of countries and the effort to translate them, but the process of translation included many other aspects of the map: Ricci's prefaces based on European cosmographical treatises and the commentaries on continents, map features, plants, animals, and peoples. From a certain perspective, we may consider the entire map a translation.

The *Xingsheng tu* also shared much in common with the translations of other Chinese maps in early modern Europe. A form of translation arguably also took place in the case of the first Chinese map translated in Europe under the supervision of the Portuguese historian João Barros (1496–1570). In a letter to the Italian collector Giovanni Battista Ramusio (1485–1557) that was published in the 1563 edition of *Delle navigationi et viaggi*, Barros wrote that he retained "a Chinese slave" who translated for him a number of Chinese works, especially "a book of maps of China printed, as he says in that province."[23] We know little about this educated slave, but it is remarkable that Barros casually mentions somebody originating from China residing in Lisbon.[24] The translated map was likely a source for Ortelius's *Chinae olim Sinarum Regio nova descriptio*, which displays provincial names identical to those Barros gives in his *Décadas da Asia* (compare with table 10.1). Barros's description and Ortelius's map moreover both describe the Great Wall not as one continuous structure but as a number of shorter walls between mountain passes. We cannot be entirely certain, but Barros's map of China (now lost) was possibly created using the *Guang yutu* 廣輿圖 (Extended territorial maps; first published in 1556 or 1557) by Luo Hongxian 羅洪先 (1504–1564) based on earlier work by Zhu Siben 朱思本 (1273–1337). Barros describes the process of making his map as follows: "Before we had this map we have had a book of cosmography in a few volumes, with geographic tables (maps) and commentaries on them in the fashion of the *Itinerario*, in which this wall was not depicted, but it still provided information on it. This book gave us to understand that this wall was not a continuous structure. It only existed in the passes of a chain of very harsh mountains which separate the Chinese and the Tartars. Seeing it depicted [on the map] made us greatly admire it."[25] It is difficult to find any other late Ming publication besides the *Guang yutu* that would match this description.

Translation was equally important for the various Jesuit-initiated projects translating maps of China. While collaboration seems to have been less prominent in these cases, we cannot exclude involvement by Chinese amanuenses. Michele Ruggieri produced the first extensive translation of a late Ming version of the *Guang yutu* titled *Da Ming yitong wenwu zhusi yamen guanzhi* 大明一統文武諸司衙門官制 (System of civil and military titles, positions, and offices of the unified Great Ming, 1586; figures 11.1 and 11.2) using his own extensive Chinese-language skills.[26] The same holds for Joan Blaeu (1596–1673) and Martino Martini's *Novus atlas sinensis* (1655; figure 9.2), based on the *Guangyu ji* 廣輿記 (Records of extended territories) by Lu Yingyang 陸應陽 (1542–1627), and Michał Boym's (1612–1659) maps of China, probably based on a map from the same lineage as the *Xingsheng tu*.[27] All of these maps shared similar translation practices, which the available historical materials allow us to discern to greater or lesser degrees. The *Xingsheng tu* as well as Ruggieri's and Boym's atlases are the most revealing, evincing direct engagement with the Chinese maps' materiality. Ortelius's maps and the Martini-Blaeu atlas, on the other hand, are printed works designed to create an illusion of seamlessness: the original Chinese maps lie hidden beneath the surfaces of these "European" maps of China.

Several noteworthy features distinguish the translation of the *Xingsheng tu*. First, it is selective and embedded into the document via keyed inscriptions: on the margins, large block letters *A* through *H* refer to the more substantial pieces of text rendered in Spanish on a separate document. Translations of the map's title, compass directions, place-names, and a small legend explaining the significance of the squares designating different cities appear on the map itself (figures 10.2 and 10.3). The area of greatest innovation in the translation is in the transliteration from Chinese. Martín de Rada and his collaborators effectively invented an independent system for conveying Chinese characters' phonetic expression. They most likely based this system on the pronunciations in the Fujian Min dialect (*Minnan yu* 閩南語), whence Rada's Chinese collaborators were native. Rada, born in Pamplona, also spoke a dialect of Spanish influenced by Basque with its own phonological idiosyncrasies. Pamplonese inverts voiced and voiceless consonants (e.g., "v" reads as "b"; "Vale!" becomes "Bale!"). This dialogue between dialects affected the renderings of the names of Chinese provinces and of other place-names. Rada translates the map's title, for instance, as "Descripcion de la tierra taybin tunçua o china modernas y antiguas." *Taybin* is here a Fujian dialect version of "Da Ming" 大明 and *tunçua* most likely a rendering of "Zhonghua" 中華, based on phonetic adaptation. These are the common names for China, which Rada in his detailed *Relación* of 1575 identified as the Cathay of Marco Polo.[28] Another example is the syllable *nan* (as in *nan* 南, "south") systematically rendered as *lan*. Nanjing therefore becomes *Lanquiaa*; Henan, *Holan*; and Yunnan, *Yolan*. As table 10.1 illustrates, Rada's translations of the names of provinces contrast with those in João Barros's *Decadas*, the Latinized forms of which became the standard in early modern Europe through the popularity of Ortelius's *Theatrum*. In the case of Barros/Ortelius, the European language used for capturing pronunciations was Portuguese, which readily differentiates the name of Shandong Province from that of Guangdong (translated as "Xanton" and "Cantam," respectively), both of which Rada rendered as "Canton."

The probability remains high that Min dialects also had some influence on early Jesuit translations from Chinese. Paul Fu-Mien Yang has suggested, based on evidence extracted from the Portuguese-Chinese dictionary compiled by Ruggieri, that at least one of Ruggieri's teachers was a speaker of Min dialects, perhaps of Hakka.[29] In any case, Ruggieri went on to create a complete phonological system (exemplified both in his dictionary and in his translations of the *Da Ming guanzhi* incarnation of the *Guang yutu* maps explored by Lin Hong in chapter 11 of this volume).

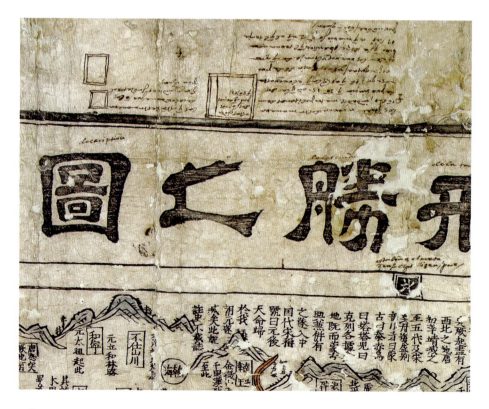

FIGURE 10.2.

Detail from the *Gujin xingsheng zhi tu* (figure 10.1) showing manuscript annotations, including the transcription of terms in the title.

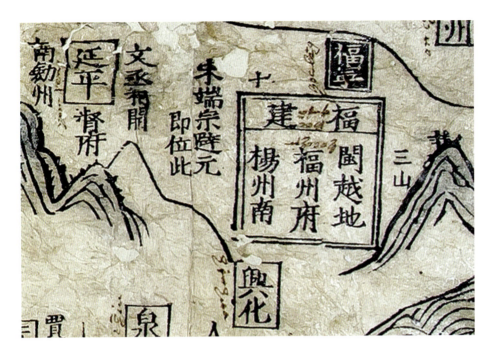

FIGURE 10.3.

Detail from the *Gujin xingsheng zhi tu* (figure 10.1) showing the transcriptions of place-names.

As illustrated in table 10.1, the resultant pronunciations of the names of the fifteen provinces appear nearer those featured by Barros and Ortelius—although, in his manuscript translations, Ruggieri Latinized the provinces' names, rendering the "x" sound in the Portuguese rendering of "Xantung," for example, as "Scianton." It is interesting to compare Ruggieri's translations to those of Martino Martini, who based his rendering of Chinese on the more elaborate transcription rules Ricci began developing as early as 1598 with the musician Lazzaro Cataneo (1560–1640), including a system for the notation of tone marks. Ruggieri and Rada each seem to have ignored this aspect of Chinese phonetics, while Martini, rather than scrupulously employing Ricci's system of tonal notation, still retained the Portuguese transcriptions for the names of a number of provinces: Xantvng (Shandong), Xensi (Shaanxi), Xanci (Shanxi)—even for translations into Latin—while transcribing others according to the method devised by Ruggieri and Ricci (Qvantvng for Canton). Michał Boym's map of China also conforms to the transcription rules Ricci and Ruggieri had set out. His names for provinces are substantially the same as Martini's, save for minor spelling differences: Pekim, Xansi, Xensi, Xantum, Huquam, Nankim, Honam, Cikiam, Fokiem, Quantum, Quamsi, Suciem, Quicheu, Iunnan. This suggests that the China Jesuits had already established a standard form for names of provinces.

Table 10.1. Comparison of the translations of province names in early modern maps and descriptions of China

CHINESE PROVINCES IN THE MING DYNASTY	ORTELIUS, CHINAE, 1584	BARROS, DECADAS III	LINSCHOTEN MAP OF ASIA FROM THE ITINERARIO, 1595	BRITISH LIBRARY MANUSCRIPT MAP, 1609; COTTON MS AUG I II 45	RADA'S RELACIÓN (1) AND XINGSHENG TU (2)	RUGGIERI'S TRANSLATIONS OF THE NAMES OF PROVINCES	NICOLAS SANSON D'ABBEVILLE, LA CHINE ROYAUME	MARTINO MARTINI, NOVUS ATLAS SINENSIS
Guangdong	Cantam	Cantam	Cantam	Quantum	1. Canton 2. canton	Canton	Quantum	Qvantvng
Fujian	Foqviem	Foquiem	Foqviem	Foqvin	1. Hocquien 2. hoc quian	Fuchien	Fichien	Fokien
Zhejiang	Cheqviam	Chequeam	Cheqviam	Cheqvean	1. Chitcan 2. [damaged]	Cechian	Cechian	Chekiang
Shandong	Xanton	Xantom	Missing	Xantvm	1. Canton 2. [unreadable]	Scianton	Sciantum	Xantvng
Nanjing	Nanqvii	Nauquij	Nanqvii	Nanqvin	1. Lanquiaa 2. lan quin	Nanchin	Nanchin	Nanking (Kiangnan)
Beijing (Jingshi)	Qvincii	Quincij	Missing	Paqvin	1. Paquiaa 2. pan quin	Pachin	Pachin	Peking (Pecheli)
Guizhou	Qvichev	Quicheu	Qvichev	Qveichev	1. Kueichou 2. cuy chou	Quejcheu	Queicheu	Qyeichev
Yunnan	Ivnna	Junna	Ivnna	Hivnan	1. Yolan 2. yun lan	Iunnan	Iuonam	Ivnnan
Jiangxi	Qyancii	Quancij	Qviancii	Qviansi	1. Cansay 2. cang çay	Chiansii	Chiamsii	Kiangsi
Sichuan	Svinam	Sujuam	Svcvan & Svinam	Suchuan	1. Susuan 2. çu çu an	Siciuan	Siciuen	Svchven
Huguang	Fvqvam	Fuquam	Fvqvam	Hucqvan	1. Oucun 2. gou cong	Huquan	Huquam	Hvqvang
Guangxi	Qyancii	Cansij	Qvancii	Qvansii	1. Cunsay 2. [damaged]	Quansii	Quansii	Qvangsi
Shaanxi	Xiam cii	Xianxij	Missing	Xiainsii	1. Siamcay 2. cian si	Sciensii	Sciensii	Xensi
Henan	Hona	Honam	Honao	Honan	1. Holam 2. ho lan	Honan	Honan	Honan
Shanxi	San cii	Sancij	Sancii	Xansi	1. Sansi 2. çan si	Sciansii	Sciansii	Xansi

The *Xingsheng tu* is thus an important artifact of European attempts to translate and adapt the Chinese language, reflecting a wider trend in seeking systematic ways to represent Chinese characters through phonetic script—a first crucial linguistic contact between heretofore independently evolved ways of writing.

The translation of the *Xingsheng tu* included transcribing a substantial portion of the Chinese text from various cartouches on the map onto a separate document. Two known manuscripts presently contain these translations. One resides in the AGI (Filipinas 6, r 2, n. 21c) and the other in the Saint Germain collection of the Bibliothèque nationale de France in Paris (Espagnol, 325, 8r–9r; figure 10.4). The two versions of the translation have divergent prefaces. The preface to the Paris version mentions the year 1576, while the AGI version includes no date. From all we know, in 1574 the map accompanied a letter from the governor of the Philippines dated July 30. The year 1576 on the Paris version may well be the date of copying (it is unclear whether in the Philippines or in Spain). The Paris version accompanies a copy of Martín de Rada's *Relación* of China and a few letters by Rada and begins with a passage echoing Lavezaris's letter of 1574: "The Chinese transmitted to this city a print (*ynpresion de molde*) made in their country. It contains a description of the land of China and surrounding islands in many Chinese letters which describe what is painted. We needed to know what the Chinese letter said and the Chinese declared it as interpreters. We put here in writing the meaning of these Chinese letters so that those that see the painting will understand what they say."[30]

The manuscripts also reveal more of the process of translating the map, which entailed considerable collaboration. The three translators likely worked together to decipher the map's content before composing the Spanish text. They keyed their rendition of the meaning of the large blocks of Chinese text using capital letters and probably wrote them out following their process of oral interpretation. Their translation is largely successful, but at one telling point, the Spanish text departs entirely from the original. This is the text marked with the letter *B* (figure 10.5). Here, the Chinese text states:

> Inside this region of the ocean there are countries like Baihua [possibly Batang in Indonesia], Pangheng [Pahang in Malaysia] and many others. They all pay tribute. It is difficult to enumerate them all. Banggela [Bengal] is the largest among them. In India (Xitian) there are the five Indian countries (Yindu Guo). In Eastern India people live through cultivating the land and they mint silver coins. As for the countries of Arabia (Tianfang Guo) their four seasons are all like spring. They use the Muslim calendar, which differs from the Chinese calendar by three days. The country of Medina is of Muslim ethnicity. They have the three versions of the script: the seal script, regular script, and cursive. Nowadays all the countries in the West use these types of script. They have fortified cities with moats and palaces. The natural conditions and social customs do not differ from those of the area of the Yangtze and Huai rivers.

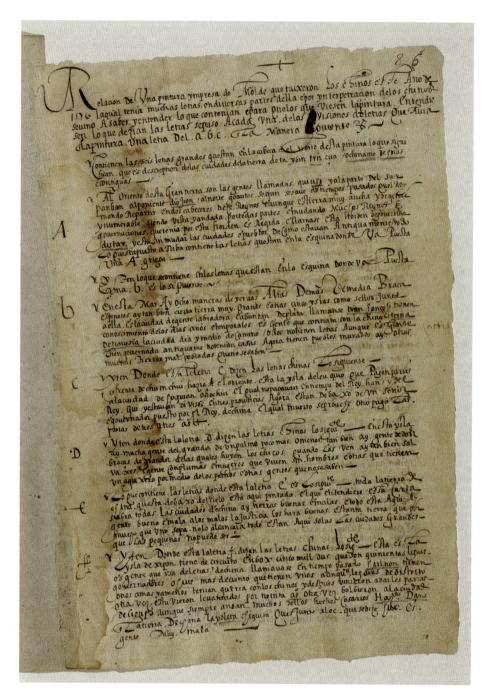

FIGURE 10.4.

The first page of the Spanish translation of the *Gujin xingsheng zhi tu* showing the different keys, labeled A to F. Height, 32.5 cm. Bibliothèque nationale de France. Espagnol, 325, 8r–9r.

The Spanish translation, however, contains a substantially different meaning (for the original Spanish, see the appendix):

> In this sea there are eight kinds of tall grasses over half an arm and thorny. There is also a very large land and another five islands, joined to it like a seal. There is the city where Labradorians live and abounds in silver. It is called "tian hoc cop." They have knowledge of the calendar. It is a people that has trade with China. It takes a day and a half of walking to traverse the city. They do not have letters. It is a well-governed people. In antiquity, they did not have houses. Now they have ramparts. There are also many other lands with more people, which are not known.

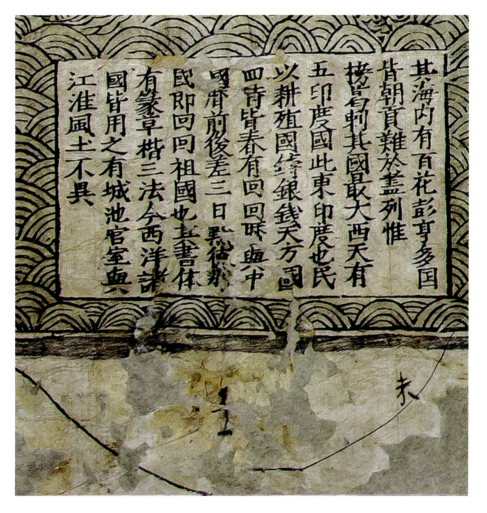

FIGURE 10.5.

Part of the *Gujin xingshengzhi tu* (figure 10.1) keyed with the letter B.

This showcases a breakdown in communication between the Chinese interpreters and the writer of the Spanish text. The mistakes in translation were likely due to the ignorance one might experience when using Chinese characters to convey phonetic values. Baihua 百花 and Pengheng 彭亨 refer to place-names in Indonesia and Malaysia, just as Yindu 印度 refers to India, while the translator focuses exclusively on interpreting the meaning of each character. Batang and Pahang thus become "tall grasses over half an arm and thorny" while Yindu becomes interpreted as "a very large land and another five islands, joined to it like a seal." This largely reflects an inability to match classical Chinese geographic information with Iberian knowledge about well-known places such as India and the Middle East. In contrast, such maps as the *Kunyu wanguo quantu* successfully matched Chinese and European references to places outside China. This was a result of long years of collaboration between Chinese scholars and the Jesuits and access to substantial linguistic and cultural resources. The mistranslations of the *Xingsheng tu* demonstrate a lack both of such resources and of in-depth training for translators.

Unlike other Chinese maps, such as those in the *Guang yutu* atlas by Luo Hongxian, the *Xingsheng tu* neither influenced mapping in Europe nor proved a source for European maps of China. The value of this map becomes apparent, as I have suggested here, in light of the process of translation, which connects it with all the other projects of translating Chinese maps in the early modern period. My effort here has been to discuss these different projects comparatively.

One salient point highlighted throughout this comparison is that the Jesuits were not alone in their approach to translating Chinese and in doing so successfully. While the Jesuits had longer-term exposure to the Chinese language and access to greater resources, it is striking to realize that Martín de Rada and his Chinese collaborators independently devised similar translation strategies. These included developing a system for recording information orally, an entire phonetic system for rendering the values of Chinese characters into European script, and a system of annotation to make the map's topographical and toponymical features intelligible. All of these were shaped by context and by local interactions between Europeans and Chinese in the Philippines.

As I have highlighted, considering translation yields valuable methodological insights. Translation emphasizes interaction rather than mere transmission and discloses negotiations and exchanges at the level of individual actors. Translation is, moreover, a process, not a finished product: its workings undercut the narrative of progress and the positivistic approach to maps. In these ways, the focus on translation can provide a new perspective on the history of exchanges between East Asia and western Europe.

Appendix:
Transcription and Translation of Documents Relating to the *Gujin xingsheng zhi tu* 古今形勝之圖 (Map of Advantageous Terrain Then and Now)

There are currently two manuscripts associated with the *Xingsheng tu*. One is found at the Archivo General de Indias (AGI; Filipinas 6, r 2, n. 21c) in Seville and the other in the Saint Germain collection at the Bibliothèque nationale de France in Paris (Espagnol, 325, 8–9). The two versions differ only with regard to the preface to the translation. The preface of the Paris version mentions the date 1576, while the AGI version does not mention a date. The map was transmitted in 1574 with a letter from the governor of the Philippines on July 30, which is rather specific:

Asimismo embío a V. M. otro papel que hube de los chinos, a donde está figurada de molde toda Ia tierra de la china con vna declaración que hize hazer a algunos intérpretes chinos, la qual declaraçion se hizo mediante vn rreligioso augustino que tiene prinçipios de entender la lengua de los chinos, los quales an quedado de traerme para otro año otras figuras más copiosas y preçesiasas [sic], que embiaré a V. M., siendo dios seruido.

I am sending to Your Majesty another paper which I obtained from the Chinese, where it is depicted in print (figurada de molde) the whole land of China. I also send a declaration which was made by some Chinese interpreters, with the intermediation of an Augustinian monk who understood the fundamentals of the Chinese language. They also promised to send me in another year a more detailed figure, which I will send to Your Majesty.

Carta del gobernador Guido de Lavezaris al rey. Manila, 30 julio de 1574 (AGI, Filipinas, 6, R. 2, N. 21).

The date 1576 of the Paris versions of the documents of translation might be the date when the copy was made. It is unclear whether this was in Spain or in the Philippines. This Paris version is bound together with a copy of Martín de Rada's *Relación* about China and a few letters also by Rada. It is therefore possible that this copy was made and owned by Rada himself.

The transcription provided here is based on the Paris version of the manuscript, which is in better condition. I do mark, however, the minute differences between the two versions where necessary. The transcription follows the original usage of Spanish as it appears in the manuscript. I made no efforts at modernization or inserting accents. The only modification was in dividing the words according to modern usage (e.g., *y en ella* instead of *yenella*). I also provide an English translation for each fragment.

PREFACE OF THE PARIS VERSION

Relacion de una pintura ympresa de molde que truxeron los Chinos este ano de 1576 laqual tenia muchas letras en diversas partes della y [e] por ynterpretacion delos chinos seVino a [A] saber y [e]ntender lo que contenian e para quelos que viesen lapintura entendiesen lo que dezian las letras sepuso a [A] cada una delas divisiones de letras que aVia lapintura una letra del abc La m[M]anera siquiente

Relation of a picture imprinted on paper, which the Chinese brought in this year of 1576, which contains many letters in different parts. For their interpretation some Chinese came and explained what they contained. In order for those who will see the picture to understand what it says, capital letters *ABC* were put in association with each group of Chinese text.

PREFACE OF THE AGI VERSION

Los chinos truseron a esta ciudad una ynpresion de molde ha. en su tierra y en ella estava descripta la tierra firme de la china y algunas yslas a ella comarcanas en muchas lettras chinas que declaravan lapintura. Procurase saver lo que dezian las letras de la pintura y los mismos chinos por ynterpretas lo declararon y ponese aqui la raçon della para q quien vierre la pintura pueda enterder q significan las letras y lo que quieren deaz.

The Chinese transmitted to this city a print made in their country. It contains a description of the land of China and surrounding islands in many Chinese letters which describe what is painted. We needed to know what the Chinese letter said and the Chinese declared it as interpreters. We put here in writing the meaning of these Chinese letters so that those that see the painting will understand what they say.

Main Text Based on the Paris Version

Contienen las seis letras grandes questan en la cabec[ç]a del norte desta pintura lo que significan que es description [descreption] delas ciudades dela tierra de taybin tunçua o china modernas y antiguas.

There are six large letters place in the head of the northern part of this painting, which mean that it is a description of the cities modern and antique of the land of Taibin, Tunçua or China.

Al Oriente desta gran tierra son las gentes llamadas qui uiy y a la parte del sur panban al poniente diojion al norte goautec*. Segun se save de tiempos pasados [que]** el Rey mando departir en dos cabeceres treze Reynos y aunque es tierra muy ancha y de gente ynumbrable *siendo visto y andado [a] por todas partes y [e] mudando muchos Reynos y[e] gouvernaciones [governaciones] que tenia por esta horden es regida e llamasse [llamase] esta [h]**orden de gouvernar distay y esto sin mudar las ciudades y [e] pueblos de como estavan a[A]ntiguamente todo lo quesea puesto ariba contiene las letras que estan en la esquina donde va puesta una A griega.*

To the east of this great land there are the people called "qui uiy," in the South "pan ban," in the West "dijion" and in the North "gotec." According to what is known from times past, the king disposed on dividing the land in two capitals and thirteen kingdoms, this being a widespread land with innumerable people and he having heard, seen and traveled everywhere, changed many previous kingdoms and governances to achieve this and ensure that the land is ruled. This order of governing is called "distay," and it was achieved without moving the people and cities from how they were in antiquity. Everything that was put before is contained in the quadrant where the Greek letter *A* is located.

*AGI manuscript version: gotec
** absent in AGI version

Y en loque contiene e[n] las letras que estan en la esquina donde es a [va] Puesta una B es lo siquiente:

En esta mar ay ocho maneras de yervas Altas Demas Remedia Braca y[e]spinosas ay tanbien cierta tierra muy grande y[e] otras c[ç]inco Yslas como sellos junta aella. Es la ciudad de gente labradora y abundan de plata llamanse tian honcop tienen conoscimiento delos dias anos y[e] temporlaes es gente que contrata con la china terna detravesia la ciudad dia y medio de camino todos no tienen letras. Aunque es Gente bien governada antiguamente notenian casas. Agora tienen pueblos murados ay otras muchas tierras mas pobladas que no se saben.

The letters present in the box where a *B* is placed contain the following meaning:

In this sea there are eight kinds of tall grasses over half an arm and thorny. There is also a very large land and another five islands, joined to it like a seal. There is the city where Labradorians live and abounds in silver. It is called "tian hoc cop." They have knowledge of the calendar. It is a people that has trade with China. It takes a day and a half of walking to traverse the city. They do not have letters. It is a well-governed people. In antiquity, they did not have houses. Now they have ramparts. There are also many other lands with more people, which are not known.

yten Donde es la letera C dizen las letras chinas lo siguiente

en frente [i frente] de chuinchui hazia a l'oriente [el oriente] esta ysla de leuquio que Pagan parias a la ciudad de hoquian o hochiu [hochuy]* el qual nopagavan en tiempo del Rey han y del Rey Qui y estavan divisos entres provincias Agora estan debaxo de un senior [señor] y [e] gouvernador [governador] puesto por el Rey de China y el qual muerto se proveche otro. paga Las parias de tres a tres años.

Where the letter C is located, the Chinese letters say the following:

In front of "chu in chui" there is in the East this island of "Leuquio." They pay tribute at the city of Foquian or Hochiu. They did not pay tribute in the time of the king Han and of the king Qui and was divided among provinces. Now they are under a senior and governor, installed by the king of China, and when he dies he will be replaced by another. He pays tribute every three years.

*AGI version

Yten donde es la letera [letra] D dizen las letras Chinas lo sigui[en]te:

en esta ysla ay mucha gente del grandor de un palmo poco mas o menos tan bien ay gente de dos braças de grandor de las quales huyen los chicos quando los ven ay tanbien salvaj[x]es y[e] gente con plumas y[e] mugeres que viven sin hombres y[e] otras que tienen un aguxero [agusero]* por medio de los pechos y [e] otras gentes que no se saben.

Where there is the letter D, the Chinese text says the following:

On this island there are many people almost as big as a palm, more or less, and there are also people two arm's lengths tall which scare the chickens away when they see them. There are also savages and people with feathers and women who live without men and others that have a perforation in the middle of their breasts and others which are unknown.

*AGI version

Lo que contiene las letras donde esta la letra E es lo sigui[en]te

toda la tierra de China questa debaxo del cielo esta aqui pintada. Lo [el] que entendiere esta carta sabra todas las ciudades de china. ay tierras buenas y[e] males. E todo esta aqui ay gente buena e mala a los malos la justicia los hara buenos. Es tanta tierra que por mucho que uno sepa no lo alcançara todo estan aqui solas las ciudades grandes que las pequeñas no puede ser.

The content of the letters where *E* is placed is the following:

The whole country of China under the heaven is painted here. The one who will understand this map, will know all the cities of China. There are good and bad lands and everything is here. There are good and bad people. The bad people will be made good by justice. There is so much land that no matter how much one person knows, that person will not reach every place. There are described here only the big cities, because the little ones cannot be.

yten Donde esta la letera [letra] f dizen las letras chinas lo sig[uien]te

esta es la ysla de xipon tiene circuito enbox cinco mill dus que son quinientas leguas. Es gente que usa de letras de china. Llamavase en tiempo pasado Hulnon tienen governadores o chuo mas de ciento que tienen unos a cinqu[en]ta leguas de districto [distrito]. otros a mas y menos tienian guerra con los chinos y despues vinieron a darles parias otra vez estuvieron levantados por treinta a[ño]s otra vez bolbieron a la ciudad de lionpo aunque siempre andan muchos dellos hechos corsarios Hale Dano [haciendo dano] a La tierra de china la ysleta chiuita que es junta a ella que sedize que es gente muy mala.

Where the letter *F* is placed, the Chinese letters say the following:

This is the land of "Xipon" and has an area of five thousand diis, which are five hundred leagues. They are people who use the Chinese letters. In the past they were called "Hulnon." They have governors or "chuo," more than one hundred, having one in every fifty leagues district. Some have had war with China and after that came to pay tribute. Other times, they were excused for thirty years and other times returned to the city of "Lionpo." Also, many of them went and became pirates causing great damage to the land of China. The small island which is joined with it is said to have many bad people.

yten En Unas letras Chinas questan en la mar Puestas entres renglones dize lo siguiente tiene por senal le letra g—este golfo se sovia [solía] nevegar e por grandes tormentas que el aya no se navega sino es con gran Rodeo.

The Chinese letters put in the sea between lines the following is said. It is signaled with the letter *G*. This gulf is difficult to navigate and it is not navigated unless with great effort.

Yten las letras chinas donde esta la letra h dize lo sig[uien]te.

Qui suui [qui su hu] fue sbiado a esta tierra de su hermano mayor que se dezia Chicon [Chuycon] despues alçosele con la tierra yntrau [antias] y llamola [llamada] tiasian y Repartola [e repartiola] en quarto [quatro] provincias alqual sele alço Otro tirano que sedezia tob tiau. E puso governadores siendo este viejo vinieron cinco naciones degente e la conquistaron de los quales laganaron los chinos e Repartieron en governaciones de ques y quares tiene de largo de norte sin quatro mil diis que son quatrocientas leguas ye deancho del este y ueste dos mill. tienen letras chinas.

The Chinese letters where *H* is placed say the following:

"Qui suui" was sent to this island by his big brother, who was called Chicon and after that raised it to the land "antias" and called "tiasian" and divided it in four provinces to which another tyrant rose up called [tob tiau] and he installed governors. After he became old, five nations of people came and conquered it. The Chinese obtained it from them and divided it in governances. The land has almost four thousand diis, which are four hundred leagues in breadth from North to South and is two thousand leagues wide from West to East. They use Chinese letters.

Yten La Pintura Ay Unas rayas coloradas que dizen los chinos son Rios que salen de una alaguna. Yl [El] agua della es vermexa e dizese la laguna Suyguan terna cien diis de contorno poco mas. El agua della hierve mucho por la gran furia. Cohque [con que] mana beben della corre mucho el agua navegan hasta [esta] alaguna e los Rios della. En partes y en partes no por la mucha corri[ien]te es muy hondable todo en ancha de quatro leguas por partes navegan los navios grandes con bastimentos.

The painting has some colored rays, which the Chinese call rivers which originate in a lagoon. The lagoon is green and is called "Suyguan." It measures ten diis around, more or less. Its water boils and cooks with great fury. "Cohque mana" drink from it and navigate to its lagoon and rivers. It is floatable in parts and does not have a big current, all four leagues in breath. In some parts it is navigated by large vessels.

Ytem Adelante de las letras que estan junto a la h ay otras letras donde se puso la l letra y dizen lo sigu[ien]te:

Tiene la provincial de Liauton que sta junta ala cerca grande. Del este a ueste mill diis que son cien leguas e de norte son mill e seis cientas.

Behind the letter that are joined with the *H* there are other letters where an *Y* is placed which say the following:

There is the province of Liaoton, which is joined to the great wall. From the East to the West there are one thousand diis, which are one hundred leagues and from the north it is one thousand and six hundred.

Yten en la pintura corre Una Raya de Oriente a Poniente poni[en]te Junto alas Letras Grandes del norte donde dize muralla laqual dizen los chinos divide la tierra de China de tertaria [Tartaria] ocitia. Tiene de longitud mill leguas e de ancho sesenta dies. Antes mas que m[eno]s dealtor terna doze hestados la cerca es de cal y[e] canto tiene torres muy altas que dizen los chinos parescen dende [donde] ariba los hombres muy pequeños.

In the painting there is a line from East to West, joined to the big letters of the North, where it says: a Wall that divides the land of China from the land of "Tartaria ocitia." In terms of length, it is one thousand leagues, and it is sixty diis broad. In terms of height it is more or less twelve estados. The wall is made of lime and stones and has long towers, of which the Chinese say that in comparison, the people seem very little.

Fuera desta Muralla ay gente de guarnicion china al lungo [luengo] de toda la cerca questa a la defense [defensa] delos tartaros para hazer esta muralla tan grande dizen los chinos que de diez hombres que avia en las ciudades sacavan quatro [y an]si acudo alla obra universalmente universalm[en]te toda la tierra e gente de china elligieron lo por defenderse de los tartaros quelos Robaban adelante de la guarnicion Paresce por la pintura Partirse la tierra con unos montes de la otra vada [vanda] delos quales estan los tartaros.

Outside this area, along the whole wall there are the garrisons of the Chinese, which are put there to defend from the Tartars. For making this big wall, the Chinese say that out of every ten people in the cities, they used four and in this way contributed to the work universally the whole land and people of China for defending themselves from the Tartars, who used to rob from the northern garrison. The painting makes it seem that the land is divided by some mountains from the side behind which there are the tartars.

Dentro de la cerca del Reyno de China. Ay tres fortalezas congente de guarnicion cuyos nombres son los siguientes ganbun quan, la otra tayton quan la otra canhay quan y en cade una destas fortalezas dizen los chinos ay quinientos mill hombres de Guerra dizen destas fortalezas tantas cosas los chinos que no se scriben aqui por que no se les puede dar credito.

Behind the enclosure of the reign of China, there are three fortresses with garrisoned peoples, which are named are the following: "ganbun quan," "tayton quan," "canhai quan" and in each of these fortresses, the Chinese say that there are fifteen hundred men of war. Of these fortresses, the Chinese say many things, which cannot be written here because they cannot be believed.

Yten En la pintura ay Unas figuras de letras en quadra las quales lleban por senal (auzes?). Estas son cabecas de Reynos y donde Risiden los visoreyes son quinze provicias—yten dizen los chinos que agora quatro cientos y ochentas salio el Rey de una provicia llamada alanquian y senoreo toda la terra. Y[e] su linase [linaxe] Governo y [e] señores loque aquel gano hasta el dia de oy. Que abra des anos Que murio el Rey llamado leon quen dexo un hijo de treze anos que oy governa llamado Ganlic. desde la ciudad de foquian lugar [marítimo] hasta paquian donde esta la corte Real ay ciento y viente dias de camino por la posta y [e] mudandola posta de legua a legua. Y [e] lo mesmo de donde van los portugueses a llevar baxada al Rey.

In the painting there are some figures of letters inside quadrants. These are capitals of the kingdom and where the viceroys reside are fifteen provinces. The Chinese say that 458 years ago, the king departed from a province called "alanquian" and subjected the whole land. He appointed a government and nobles and this victory lasts until today. Ten years ago, the king named Leonquen died. He had a son thirteen years old, who governs today, whose name is Ganlic. From the city of Foquian, a coastal place, up to Paquian, where the royal court rules, there are 120 days of travel by post, there being a post every league. It is the same distance from the place where the Portuguese sent embassies to the king.

Yten Las tierras chinas que ay en la esquina donde esta le [la] letra y dize lo siquiente:

Ciento y cinq[uen]ta cinco Governadores o huis como ellos llaman ay la tierra de china y estos tienen debaxo de su mandado ciento y cinq[uen]ta magistrados llamados chui otros que siquen a estos llamados quines son mill y ciento y veinte vei[n]te y nueve.

The Chinese letters where the letter Y is placed, say the following:

The land of China has 155 governors, or "huis," as they are called. They all have under them 150 magistrates, called "chui." Others, who follow the latter are called "quines" and are 1,129 in total.

atras [Tras] estos vienen otros llamados huebe que son quatrocientos y noventa y tres. Otros ay subjetos a estos que son dos mill y ochocientos y cinq[uen]ta y quatro ay otros llamados sanuya que son doze. Otros sellaman sanguci son honze otros chianbuci son diez y nueve. Otros se llaman tianquanci, son ciento e setenta y siete. todos estos tienen juridicion sobre los demas naturales de china e son justiciae puestas unos por otros.

Under these last ones, there are others, called "huebe," who are 493 total. There are others subjected to the latter, who are 2,854. There are yet others called "sanuya," 12 in total. Others called "sanguci" are 11, and others "chianbuci" are 19. Others called "tianquanci" are 177. All of these have jurisdiction over the natural divisions of China and are justices put in place one by the other.

Notes

1. Torres López, "Andrés de Urdaneta." A classic on the topic is Schurz, *Manila Galleon*.
2. The map is viewable at AGI, Ministry of Education, http://pares.mcu.es/ParesBusquedas20/catalogo/show/18774.
3. Pastells, "Carta inédita del P. M. Ricci"; Ricci, "Del valore geografico"; Quirino, "Lavezares Map of China." The study of Lothar Knauth is also important (Knauth, "Gu dyin hsing sheng di tu"). A number of other older articles of variable quality exist.
4. Enoki, "On the Ku-chin hsing-sheng chih t'u."
5. Lee and Caño Ortigosa, *Studies on the Map Ku Chin Hsing Sheng Chih Tu*.
6. A first article on the map appeared in the journal *Razon y Fe*, signed simply "L. R." See Pastells, "Carta inédita del P. M. Ricci"; see also Ricci, "Del valore geografico"; Dorofeeva-Lichtmann, "First Map of China Printed in Europe."
7. All translations, unless otherwise indicated, are my own (F-S. M.). AGI, Aud. de Filipinas, July 8, 1569, 79.
8. Cf. Rada's biography by Folch, "Biografía de Fray Martín de Rada," 33–63. See also Boxer, *South China in the Sixteenth Century*, lxvii–xci.
9. Masini, "Chinese Dictionaries."
10. Carta del P. Agustín de Alburquerque comunicando el suceso del corsario Limahón, que había ido contra la isla de Luzón con 70 navíos, AGI, Patro 24 r° 30. For related Chinese documents, see Tang, "Ming Long Wan zhi ji Yue dong juzi Lin Feng shiji xiangkao."
11. Relaçion Verdadera delascosas del Reyno de TAIBIN por otro nombre china y del viaje que ael hizo el muy Reverendo padre fray martin de Rada provinçial que fue delaorden delglorioso Doctor dela yglesia San Agustin. quelo vio yanduvo en la provinçia de Hocquien año de 1575 hecha porelmesmo. BnF 325.9, ff. 15–30. An English translation is in Boxer, *South China in the Sixteenth Century*, 241–311.

12. Lavezaris's letter referring to sending the map is at AGI, Audiencia de Filipinas, 6. For the map, see ff. 204–205. A related document, with Spanish translations of some of the map's text, is at Filipinas 6, R. 2, N. 21. A copy of this document made in 1576 is at BnF 325.9, ff. 8–9.
13. Jin, "New Learnings on the Author," 34.
14. Archivum Romanum Societatis Iesu (ARSI), Jap. Sin. 123, ff. 42v–47r.
15. See the letter of Royal Secretary Zayas to Montano in *Colección de documentos inéditos,* 295, 299. See also Macías Rosendo, *La correspondencia de Benito Arias Montano,* 275–276.
16. Archivo General de Simancas, AGS, Estado, 392r–v, f.185; Royal Library of the Escorial, BME LI.12, f. 251r.
17. The name given by Ortelius is Ludovico Georgio. Cf. *Chinae olim Sinarum regionis, nova descriptio auctore Ludovico Georgio* in Abraham Ortelius, *Theatrum orbis terrarum,* Antwerp, Christophe Plantin, 1584.
18. British Library, Cotton MS Augustus I ii 45. Cf. Skelton, *Explorers' Maps.* Cf. Caboara, "First Printed Missionary Map of China."
19. AGI, Filipinas, 6, R. 2, N. 21.
20. We can deduce this information from the Chinese memorials related to Limahon. See the transcriptions of documents in Tang, "Ming Long Wan zhi ji Yue dong juzi Lin Feng shiji xiangkao," 60. Cf. Li, "'Jiangou' Zhongguo," 30. Further evidence of Rada's role is apparent in the translations of names of provinces, which are consistent with the names in a report Rada wrote after his trip to Fujian Province. See table 10.1 for comparison.
21. Meynard, *Jesuit Reading of Confucius.*
22. See Li Zhizao's preface printed on the *Kunyu wanguo quantu.*
23. Ramusio, *Primo volume & terza editione delle navigationi et viaggi.* The letter appears in the third edition on p. 430A.
24. We know very little of the "Chinese slave" who helped Barros translate the Chinese materials from his *Décadas.* But this person was likely an educated Chinese from Macao or Guangdong Province with knowledge of the official language (*guanfang yu* 官方語). On Chinese living in Europe in the early modern period, see Boxer, "Notes on Chinese Abroad."
25. The full passage from Barros's *Third década:*

    > This wall can be seen in a geographical map of all this land, made by the Chinese, which situates all the mountains, rivers, cities, towns with the names written in their characters. We had this map brought from over there together with a Chinese interpreter and other books which we also have. Before we had this map we have had a book of cosmography in a few volumes, with geographic tables (maps) and commentaries on them in the fashion of the *Itinerario,* in which this wall was not depicted, but it still provided information on it. This book gave us to understand that this wall was not a continuous structure. It only existed in the passes of a chain of very harsh mountains which separate the Chinese and the Tartars. Seeing it depicted [on the map] made us greatly admire it. (Barros, *Terceira década da Asia,* 188–189)

    For a detailed discussion of the connections between Barros, Ortelius, and Luo Hongxian, see Morar, "Connected Cartographies."

26. The edition Ruggieri used was published in 1586. The atlas recopied the maps of the *Guang yutu*, introducing small changes such as updated toponyms and the removal of the grid and of the boundaries between prefectures. This was likely the most widespread blend of the *Guang yutu* circulating in China during the late Ming. See chapter 11 in this volume.
27. Cams, "Displacing China."
28. The document is now at the Bibliothèque nationale de France in Paris, France. *See Relación verdadera de las cosas del reyno de Taibin, por otro nombre China, y del viaje que a el hizo el muy reverendo padre fray Martin de Rada, provincial que fue de la orden de . . . Ste Augustin, que lo vio y anduvo, en la provincia de Hocquien, año de 1575, hecha por el mesmo*. Fonds Espagnol, 325.9 (MF 13184), ff. 15–30.
29. See Yang, "Portuguese-Chinese Dictionary," 189.
30. See the appendix.

References

Barros, João de. *Terceira decada da Asia: Dos feytos que os portugueses fizeram no descobrimento & conquista dos mares & terras do Oriente*. Lisbon: Ioam de Barreira, 1563.

Boxer, Charles Ralph. "Notes on Chinese Abroad in the Late Ming and Early Manchu Periods Compiled from Contemporary European Sources (1500–1750)." *T'ien Hsia Monthly* 9, no. 5 (1939): 447–468.

———. *South China in the Sixteenth Century (1550–1575)*. London: Hakluyt Society, 1953.

Caboara, Marco. "The First Printed Missionary Map of China: *Sinarum Regni aliorumque regnorum et insularum illi adiacentium descriptio* (1585/1588)." *Journal of the International Map Collectors' Society* 162 (2020): 6–21.

Cams, Mario. "Displacing China: The Martini-Blaeu *Novus Atlas Sinensis* and the Late Renaissance Shift in Representations of East Asia." *Renaissance Quarterly* 73, no. 3 (2020): 953–990.

Colección de documentos inéditos para la historia de España. Vol. 41. Madrid: La viuda de Calero, 1862.

Dorofeeva-Lichtmann, Vera. "The First Map of China Printed in Europe [Ortelius 1584] Reconsidered: Confusions about Its Authorship and the Influence of Chinese Cartography." In *Visual and Textual Representations in Exchanges between Europe and East Asia 16th–18th Centuries,* edited by Luís Saraiva and Catherine Jami, 139–169. Singapore: World Scientific, 2018.

Enoki, Kazuo. "On the Ku-chin hsing-sheng chih t'u 古今形勝圖 of 1555." *Memoirs of the Research Department of the Toyo Bunko* 34 (1976): 243–254.

Folch, Dolors. "Biografía de Fray Martín de Rada." *Huarte de San Juan. Geografía e Historia* 15 (2008): 33–63.

Jin Guoping. "New Learnings on the Author of *Ku Chin Hsing Sheng Chih Tu*." In Lee and Caño Ortigosa, *Studies on the Map Ku Chin Hsing Sheng Chih Tu*, 27–44.

Knauth, Lothar. "Gu dyin hsing sheng di tu: El primer mapa histórico chino transmitido al mundo europeo." *Asia: Anuario de estudios orientales* 1 (1968): 99–115.

Lee, Fabio Yu-chung, and José Luis Caño Ortigosa, eds. *Studies on the Map Ku Chin Hsing Sheng Chih Tu*. Hsinchu: Research Center for Humanities and Social Sciences, National Tsing Hua University, 2017.

Li Yuzhong 李毓中. "'Jiangou' Zhongguo: Xibanyaren 1574 nian suo hou da Ming *Gujin xingsheng tu* yanjiu"「建構」中國：西班牙人1574年所獲大明《古今形勝之圖》研究. *Mingdai yanjiu* 明代研究 21 (2013): 1–30.

Macías Rosendo, Baldomero. *La correspondencia de Benito Arias Montano con el presidente de Indias Juan de Ovando: Cartas de Benito Arias Montano conservadas en el Instituto de Valencia de Don Juan.* Huelva: Universidad de Huelva, 2008.

Masini, Federico. "Chinese Dictionaries Prepared by Western Missionaries in the Seventeenth and Eighteenth Centuries." In *Encounters and Dialogues: Changing Perspectives on Chinese-Western Exchanges from the Sixteenth to Eighteenth Centuries,* edited by Wu Xiaoxin, 179–193. Sankt Augustin: Monumenta Serica Institute; San Francisco: Ricci Institute of Chinese-Western Cultural History, 2005.

Meynard, Thierry. *The Jesuit Reading of Confucius: The First Complete Translation of the Lunyu (1687) Published in the West.* Leiden: Brill, 2015.

Morar, Florin-Stefan. "Connected Cartographies: World Maps in Translation between China, Inner Asia and Early Modern Europe, 1550–1650." PhD diss., Harvard University, 2019.

Pastells, Pablo. "Carta inédita del P. M. Ricci con el mapa de la China en 1584." *Razón y Fe* 4 (September–December 1902): 464–477.

Quirino, Carlos. "The Lavezares Map of China (1555)." *Philippine Historical Review* 2, no. 1 (1969): 269–274.

Ramusio, Giovanni Battista. *Primo volume & terza editione delle navigationi et viaggi.* Venice: Nella stamperia de Giunti, 1563.

Ricci, Ettore. "Del valore geografico dei commentarii del P. Matteo Ricci; Icononografia ricciana." In *Atti e memorie del convegno di geografi-orientalisti tenuto in Macerata il 25, 26, 27 settembre 1910 Macerata,* 176–182. Macerata: Premiato Stabilimento Tipografico, 1911.

Schurz, William Lytle. *The Manila Galleon.* New York: E. P. Dutton, 1959.

Skelton, Raleigh Ashlin. *Explorers' Maps: Chapters in the Cartographic Record of Geographical Discovery.* London: Spring Books, 1970.

Tang Kaijian 湯開建. "Ming Long Wan zhi ji Yue dong juzi Lin Feng shiji xiangkao: Yi Liu Yaohui *Dufu shuyi* zhong Lin Feng shiliao wei zhongxin" 明隆萬之際粵東巨盜林鳳事蹟詳考：以劉堯誨《督撫疏議》中林鳳史料為中心. *Lishi yanjiu* 歷史研究, no. 6 (2012): 43–65.

Torres López, Carmen. "Andrés de Urdaneta y el Galeón de Manila." *Revista general de marina* 254 (2008): 235–244.

Yang, Paul Fu-mien. "The Portuguese-Chinese Dictionary of Michele Ruggieri and Matteo Ricci: An Historical and Linguistic Introduction." In *Dicionário Português-Chinês/Pu Han ci dian/Portuguese-Chinese dictionary*/葡漢辭典, edited by John W. Witek, 169–219. San Francisco: Ricci Institute for Chinese-Western Cultural History, 2001.

11

Beyond Translation

Michele Ruggieri's Manuscript Atlas of China

LIN HONG

IN THE LATE 1980S, A MANUSCRIPT ATLAS of China—consisting of one general map, thirty provincial maps of sixteen provinces and regions, and thirty-three pages of geographical descriptions (two pages in Italian and thirty-one in Latin)—reemerged from beneath the dust of centuries in the Archivio di Stato di Roma (figure 11.1; table 11.1). Toponyms and symbols on the maps indicate the locations of several thousand civil and military administrative centers, as well as other settlements. The manuscript's discovery was followed by its publication in facsimile in 1993 after rearrangement by Eugenio Lo Sardo. In 2013 another facsimile edition appeared with the descriptions translated into Chinese.[1]

The manuscript is unsigned. Based on comprehensive analysis of the handwriting, watermarks, annotations of latitude on the general map, and contents and details in the geographical descriptions, Lo Sardo affirmed the manuscript's main producer to be the Jesuit Michele Ruggieri (1543–1607).[2] Lo Sardo also pointed out that the manuscript's production extended from the late sixteenth century into the early seventeenth, ending in the year 1606, a year marked at the end of the included geographical description of Jiangxi Province. Although the atlas remained unpublished until the late twentieth century, as the first provincial atlas of China in a European language it is an important element in the history of bridging the mapping practices of western Europe and East Asia.

During the late sixteenth century, the accumulation of European geographical knowledge of China accelerated, a direct result of the first members of the Society of Jesus, Ruggieri prominent among them, entering inland China. The Portuguese had

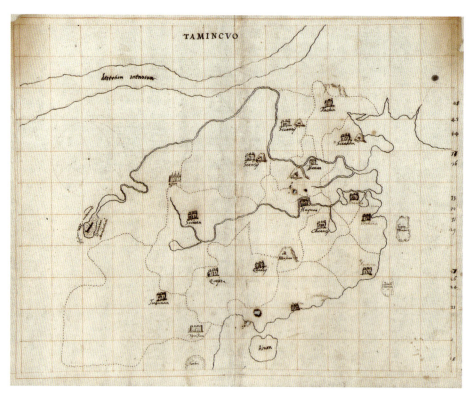

FIGURE 11.1.

The general map of China from Ruggieri's manuscript atlas. 42.5 × 56 cm. Archivio di Stato di Roma.

first reached the southern coasts of Ming China in the 1510s and later settled on the peninsula that came to be known as Macao. In their footsteps, Francis Xavier (1506–1552), one of the founders of the Society of Jesus, arrived at Shangchuan Island 上川島 (offshore from Guangdong Province); in 1573, Visitor of the Missions in the Indies Alessandro Valignano (1539–1606) further promoted missionary work in China, a complex society with a well-organized political system. Valignano advocated for and advanced what modern historians have termed the "accommodation policy": missionaries should be trained in the Chinese classics for cultural accommodation and to seek permission and protection from Chinese authorities. The foundation for his policy lay in Jesuit missionaries' mastering the Chinese language.

Valignano had visited Macao several times but had neither reached beyond its borders with the mainland nor learned the Chinese language; it was Ruggieri who first executed Valignano's plan. Born in Spinazzola (part of the Kingdom of Naples) in 1543, Ruggieri sailed in 1578 for Goa from Lisbon, landing at Macao in the next year, where

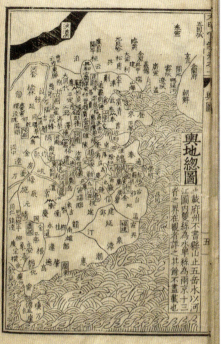

FIGURE 11.2.

The general map of China titled "Yudi zongtu" 輿地總圖 (Complete map of the land) from the 1586 edition of *Da Ming yitong wenwu zhusi yamen guanzhi*. Naikaku Bunko, Tokyo.

he became the first Jesuit missionary to learn Mandarin Chinese. After many attempts, in 1582 Ruggieri finally established the first Christian mission post in China, at Zhaoqing 肇慶 in Guangdong Province, with the help of Francesco Pasio (1554–1612). Following a short stay in Macao, from 1583 onward Ruggieri was able to reside permanently in Zhaoqing, along with Matteo Ricci (1552–1610), who had reached Macao in 1582. From 1585 to 1586, Ruggieri and Antonio de Almeida (1557–1591) left Guangdong Province and traveled to Jiangxi and Zhejiang Provinces in Southeast China to establish new mission stations yet returned without success. In 1587 Ruggieri made new attempts in Guangxi and Huguang Provinces, again in vain.

To strengthen the Jesuit mission in China, then consisting only of one mission station and four missionaries, Valignano decided to dispatch Ruggieri back to Rome to promote a papal embassy to the Ming court. In November 1588, Ruggieri embarked for Europe. He landed at Lisbon in September 1589 and in December reached Madrid, where he presented himself before Philip II (r. 1556–1598). In June 1590, Ruggieri arrived in Rome only to observe the passing of four Popes in rapid succession over sixteen months.[3] Ruggieri's application for a papal embassy failed, and unable to return to East Asia, he eventually passed away on May 11, 1607, in Salerno, near Naples.[4]

Through the so-called accommodation policy, greater access to Chinese materials in both quantity and quality in the 1570s substantially improved European geographical knowledge of East Asia. Prior European writers and mapmakers had used information that navigators had "picked up" while executing their duties. They could not fully exploit their collections of Chinese books and maps due to their limited knowledge of Chinese script. During this period, introductions to the names of provinces and China's general size began appearing in some European books. Maps produced in Europe might contain at most a few dozen Chinese toponyms, and as Florin-Stefan Morar illustrated in chapter 10, their transcription had not been standardized.

From the accommodation policy's onset in the late 1570s, when the Jesuits started learning Chinese, direct and indirect geographical information and observations concerning China began appearing in Europe through letters, reports, and manuscripts, as well as textual expositions and maps produced by Jesuits traveling back to Europe (usually as procurators). One of the key features of this period was the use of Chinese materials, resulting in the considerable growth of Europeans' understanding of China's geography, particularly the complex administrative system. Ruggieri's manuscript atlas is an excellent illustration of the results of the Jesuits' accommodation policy in China. In light of his return to Europe and of the importance of geographical knowledge to the Jesuit mission in China and the European readership at large, Ruggieri kept revising the manuscript maps until his death.

In the decades since the manuscript's rediscovery in Rome, many scholars have studied it from multiple perspectives. A key breakthrough of recent years has been Wang Qianjin's identification of the Chinese work on which Ruggieri relied. Disproving previous identifications of the *Guang yutu* 廣輿圖 (Extended territorial maps; first published in 1556 or 1557) as Ruggieri's key reference, he has shown that Ruggieri in fact used the 1586 edition of *Da Ming yitong wenwu zhusi yamen guanzhi* 大明一統文武諸司衙門官制 (System of civil and military titles, positions, and offices of the unified Great Ming; hereafter *Guanzhi*) for both the maps (figure 11.2) and the descriptions in his manuscript atlas.[5] Based on this atlas-like book, Ruggieri transposed the entire structure of China's administrative geography, including several thousands of cities and settlements, augmented only with fragments of the additional information Jesuits had obtained in China since 1595, such as the location of the new missionary station in Shaozhou 韶州 in Guangdong Province.[6]

At the same time, Ruggieri's mapping work went beyond mere translation. This chapter investigates Ruggieri's process of translation and adaptation of the *Guanzhi* over an extended period. How did Ruggieri extract geographical information from Chinese sources? How did the maps and text in this Chinese geographical work affect Ruggieri's mapping? What are the reasons for the differences between Ruggieri's maps and the Chinese prototypes in the *Guanzhi*? Through systematic analysis of the contents of all the maps, including their toponyms, this chapter differentiates Ruggieri's work into different periods and provides insights into the complex production methods and processes behind his manuscript atlas of China.

The Early Stage: Direct Map Translation from the *Guanzhi*

The atlas contains two maps of the northeastern province of Liaodong. One is a manuscript map in Latin, the other a printed Chinese map titled "Liaodong biantu" 遼東邊圖 (Map of the border region of Liaodong; figure 11.3). The printed page—the only one in this collection—came from Ruggieri's own copy of the *Guanzhi,* a precious witness to the early transmission of Chinese maps into Europe. The Latin map titled "LIAVTVM" copies this Chinese "Liaodong biantu" (figure 11.4). The original size of the "Liaodong biantu" is 22 × 28.5 cm, over which ten horizontal and thirteen vertical red lines form a grid. The *Guanzhi* map bears no such lines; Ruggieri added them purposefully in the course of map translation. The Latin map contains an equal number of lines, even though the sheet of paper is much larger (42 × 56 cm). It is clear Ruggieri used the grid to transpose geographic features and toponyms from the "Liaodong biantu" precisely onto the significantly larger piece of paper, rendering the Latin map almost identical to the Chinese one with regard to the shapes of rivers and coastlines, the positions of mountains, and the location of the Great Wall. Almost all toponyms from the Chinese map appear transliterated and marked in their corresponding positions. Hence, we may consider the Latin map to be a work of translation in a narrow sense, fairly faithful to its Chinese source.

The thirty extant Latin provincial maps cover the sixteen provinces and regions of Ming China, including the two capital territories of Beizhili (the administrative region surrounding Beijing) and Nanzhili (the region surrounding the southern capital of Nanjing), the thirteen provinces, and Liaodong (a special border region governed by a military institution at the time). Some provinces or regions have only one extant map, while others have several. Except for the "Liaodong biantu," the Chinese provincial maps from the copy of the *Guanzhi* owned by Ruggieri are not extant. Nevertheless, we can compare Ruggieri's Latin maps with extant maps from the same 1586 edition of the *Guanzhi* in other libraries. Three more of these Latin maps are identifiably iterations of *Guanzhi* maps: one of the three extant maps of Nanzhili, one of the five extant maps of Guangdong, and the only extant map of Shanxi. On these four early-stage Latin maps, all toponyms are translations from the corresponding Chinese maps and are marked with symbols in two styles—a special symbol for the seats of prefectures, easily recognizable in the maps of the *Guanzhi,* and another for all others.

On the Chinese maps found in the *Guanzhi,* different types of cities and settlements are marked, including the seats of civil administrative regions (most importantly of *fu* 府, "prefectures"; *zhou* 州, "subprefectures"; and *xian* 縣, "counties"), military

FIGURE 11.3.

The printed "Liaodong biantu" included in Ruggieri's collection. 22 × 28.5 cm. Archivio di Stato di Roma.

regions or sites (most importantly, *wei* 衛 and *suo* 所), and a few historical toponyms. However, the *Guanzhi* maps do not use any symbols to distinguish lower-level administrative units. Only prefectural seats are singled out through a rectangle that frames the toponym.[7]

Since toponyms on the Chinese *Guanzhi* maps lack reference to their administrative status, Ruggieri made "creative additions" during this early stage of transposing or translating the maps: he added "ceu" to some of the transliterated toponyms on the Latin maps to highlight the seats of subprefectures known as *zhou*. In most cases, Ruggieri devised his own strategy for determining whether a toponym denoted a *zhou* or not—he guessed that such toponyms always had only one Chinese character as their proper name, to which he added "ceu." For example, "siceu" on the map of Nanzhili was his translation from the "si" 泗 on the map of *Guanzhi*, corresponding to Sizhou 泗州. However, Ruggieri's additions also created many errors because, in fact, the proper names of some *zhou* have two Chinese characters, while those of other administrative units may also have only one Chinese character as their proper names. Regardless of

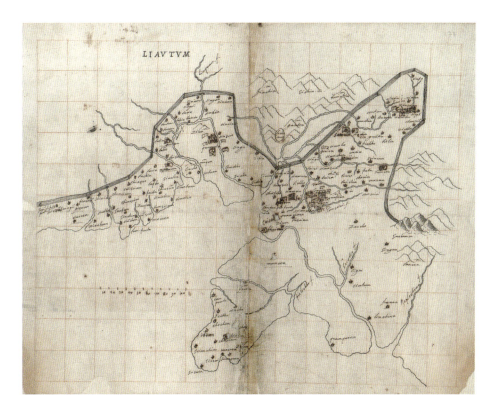

FIGURE 11.4.

The manuscript "Liavtum" included in Ruggieri's collection. 42 × 56 cm. Archivio di Stato di Roma.

these misinterpretations, this close reliance on the maps included in the *Guanzhi* forms the first layer of a journey between two systems of knowledge, one from East Asia, the other from Europe.

Intermission: The Afterlife of the Early-Stage Maps

In 1656 French mapmaker Nicolas d'Abbeville Sanson (1600–1667) compiled and published *La Chine Royaume* within a series of China maps (figure 11.5). The cartouche mentions Ruggieri's work: "This map is but a simplification of another very beautiful, very large, and very particular one, which is in the Cabinet of S.A.R. Monseigneur, the Duke of Orleans. The author Matteo Neroni assures that it was drawn in Rome in 1590. The map was based on four different volumes printed in China, and of which Jesuit Michele Ruggieri gave the translation to Neroni. I can only mark the cities of the first and second rank in this simplified map because there is not enough room for the remaining cities." The "four different volumes" likely refers to the 1586 edition of

FIGURE 11.5.

Nicolas Sanson, *La Chine Royaume,* 1656. 40 × 52 cm. Bibliothèque nationale de France, gallica.bnf.fr.

the *Guanzhi,* which apparently came bound in four separate volumes.[8] The source for Sanson's map, produced in collaboration in 1590 by Ruggieri and the Italian mapmaker Neroni, is now lost. Sanson simplified the 1590 map sixty years later, mainly by reducing the administrative ranks.[9]

The 1590 general map of China is now lost, but we can examine its relationship with Ruggieri's manuscript atlas via Sanson's 1656 map to discover that Neroni pieced the 1590 general map together from Ruggieri's early-stage translated provincial manuscript maps.[10] Toponyms appearing on both Sanson's 1656 map and on the early-stage provincial maps of Ruggieri's atlas invariably have the same spelling and placement. Neither Ruggieri's early translations nor Sanson's map completely marked all military settlements. The relationship between the two is most apparent in the fact that some of the toponyms with the suffix *zhou,* which Ruggieri had wrongly created, reappear unchanged on Sanson's map. Therefore, we can speculate that before Ruggieri and Neroni began to draw the 1590 map in Rome, a full set of early-stage translated manuscript maps—one for each of the sixteen provinces and regions—served as the basis for piecing together a complete general map. Even so, Ruggieri continued his work and later created a different set of provincial maps, which may have contributed to the fact that most of the early-stage maps are now lost.

The Later Stage: Producing the Adapted Maps

Most of the extant provincial maps were made after 1590 and differ markedly from the early-stage translated maps, illustrated best by the maps of Nanzhili, of which an early-stage and two later-stage maps survive.[11] I will compare only two of these: the early-stage map (T63 from the system of numbering adopted in the 2013 facsimile edition), and one later-stage map (T68), which both have the same grid as the aforementioned Chinese and Latin maps of Liaodong.[12] The coastlines, the shapes of rivers and lakes, and the locations of the prefectural seats (*fu*) generally correspond to those on the prototype map from the *Guanzhi*. The biggest difference between the two maps appears in the number and locations of subprefectures (*zhou*) and counties (*xian*). Taking Ningguo Prefecture 寧國府 and the several counties under its jurisdiction as an example, a digital reconstruction of both maps and their Chinese prototypes illustrates this difference (figure 11.6).

Whereas the locations of the counties (*xian*) on the translated map directly follow the map from the *Guanzhi,* those on the later map differ significantly, with several counties and military administrative units (*wei* and *suo*) added and the locations of several counties shifted. Most of these changes illustrate how Ruggieri grappled with the intricacies of the Ming administrative system. One particularly revealing case is Xuancheng County 宣城縣, which Ruggieri positioned next to Ningguo Prefecture 寧國府 on his later map. The toponym "Ningguo Prefecture" represents the prefectural capital, while Xuancheng was a county whose seat was in the same city as the prefecture's capital (known as *fuguo xian* 附郭縣, figure 11.7). The capitals of Ningguo Prefecture and Xuancheng County therefore both designate the same urban space but at different administrative levels. This is only one such example, and changes between the maps concern not only the Chinese administration but also the map's scale (4.5 cm to 50 *miliaria Italica* on the early map and 10.1 cm to 100 *miliaria Italica* on the later map), the symbols of cities and settlements, and the spellings of toponyms (e.g., three characters with the same pronunciation *he* (河, 和, 合) appear as "chho" or "cho" on the early map but as "ho" on the later map).

The *Guanzhi* itself can help explain these differences between the two maps. First published in the early Ming with several later editions, the *Guanzhi* is an administrative guide to the Ming state. The text of the *Guanzhi* mainly includes geographical

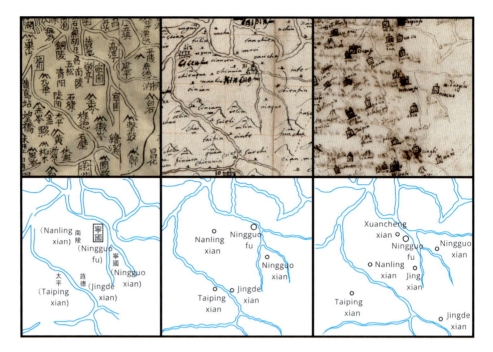

FIGURE 11.6.

Comparison of Ningguo Prefecture 寧國府 as shown on the *Guanzhi* map of Nanzhili (Naikaku Bunko, *left*), the early-stage map (T63) from Ruggieri's collection (Archivio di Stato di Roma, *middle*), and the later adapted map (T68) from the same collection (*right*). The toponyms were adjusted using the current standard Pinyin transcription.

information about the names, locations, and products of each local administrative region or military post. It also contains a set of location data, which, while not providing any information about the locations of the prefectural (*fu*) seats themselves, can help in setting up a relational coordinate system centered on each prefectural seat and, accordingly, can communicate the relative positions of lower-ranking administrative units (*zhou, xian, wei, suo*, etc.) by explicitly stating directions and distances (figure 11.8).[13]

Maps and text in the *Guanzhi* contain somewhat divergent sets of geographical information. The maps in the 1586 edition are based on maps from the 1566 edition of the popular atlas *Guang yutu* but contain a small number of new administrative units.[14] These additions were far from complete, meaning that the situation on the maps in the *Guanzhi* did not present an up-to-date version of the administrative structure of the 1580s. On the other hand, the text of the *Guanzhi* records a much larger number of civil and military administrative units than the maps, reflecting the contemporary administrative structure far more accurately. The text also includes records of military administrative units (*wei* and *suo*) and a complete list of those counties at the same location as

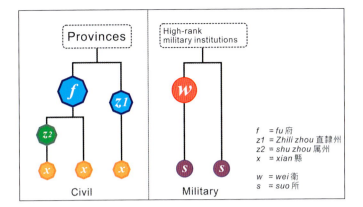

FIGURE 11.7.

This graph displays the basic types of administrative units of Ming China. There are two kinds of subprefectures (*zhou*)—one directly beneath the province (z1) and one administered beneath the prefecture (*fu*; z2). Ruggieri did not distinguish between them.

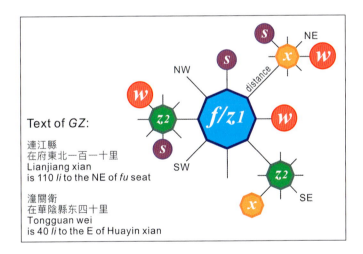

FIGURE 11.8.

Planar polar coordinates in the text of the *Guanzhi*. Orientation is recorded in eight directions. The text does not record the relationship between the provincial capitals and the prefectural and subprefectural seats (f/z1). The locations of military units known as *wei* and *suo* are recorded according to the relative position to the nearest *fu* (f), *zhou* (z1 and z2), or *xian* (x).

the prefectural capitals (the *fuguo xian* mentioned above), which the maps of the *Guanzhi* barely mark—a feature inherited from the *Guang yutu*.

Thus, the discrepancy between the maps and text of the *Guanzhi* can fully account for the differences between Ruggieri's early-stage map of Nanzhili (T63) and its later cousin (T68) apparent from figure 11.6. During the early stage of direct map translation, he referred exclusively to the maps of the *Guanzhi*, but in the later stage, he made full use of the text. Thus, while the early map of Nanzhili marks all administrative units and settlements according to the map from the *Guanzhi*, the adapted map retains the locations of prefectural seats unchanged but adds the lower-ranking civil and military units and settlements—including those not on the *Guanzhi* maps—according to the text (table 11.2; figure 11.9).

Table 11.1. Extant Latin provincial maps

PROVINCE	NUMBER	PROVINCE	NUMBER	PROVINCE	NUMBER	PROVINCE	NUMBER
Guangdong 廣東	T4, 5, 11, 13, 15	Fujian 福建	T17, 19, 21, 23	Zhejiang 浙江	T25, 28	Beizhili 北直隸	T29, 31, 33, 50
Shaanxi 陝西	T34, 35	Shanxi 山西	T39	Shandong 山東	T43	Yunnan 雲南	T47
Sichuan 四川	T49	Guizhou 貴州	T53	Guangxi 廣西	T57	Henan 河南	T59
Nanzhili 南直隸	T63, 65, 68	Huguang 湖廣	T69	Jiangxi 江西	T73	Liaodong 遼東	T77

Note: The numbering follows Jin Guoping (2013).

Table 11.2. A comparison of the distances in Chinese miles (*li*) and orientation given in the text of the *Guanzhi* with the location given on Ruggieri's later map of Nanzhili (T68, Ningguo Prefecture).

COUNTY	NINGGUO	JING	TAIPING	JINGDE	NANLING
Guanzhi text	105 *li* SE	105 *li* S	205 *li* SW	245 *li* S	105 *li* W
T68 orientation	SE	S	SW	SE	SW
T68 converted distance	103 *li* (2.6 cm)	95 *li* (2.4 cm)	217 *li* (5.5 cm)	245 *li* (6.2 cm)	118 *li* (3 cm)

Note: Distances are measured from the map and converted into *li* using the scale found on the map. The slight difference in the orientations of Jingde and Nanling is because Ruggieri's earlier drawing of mountains and rivers had taken their place.

A comparison between the two maps thus shows a shift in Ruggieri's mapmaking. In general, toponyms and symbols on all extant maps fall into two categories, according to the method used for marking settlements. The first simply translates toponyms and symbols from the maps of the *Guanzhi* without altering their locations. The second includes toponyms located according to the text of the *Guanzhi*. Based on these differences, Ruggieri's thirty extant provincial maps fall into three types: translated maps, adapted maps, and a few remaining maps that mix both types, which I consider to be interim maps.

The vast majority of the extant maps, twenty-five, are adapted maps, on which all toponyms are adaptations based on the text of the *Guanzhi*. Only two translated maps, the two early-stage maps of Liaodong and Nanzhili, are extant, both copied directly from the maps of the *Guanzhi*, all toponyms translated while keeping the original appearance.[15] Three interim maps exist—maps of Guangdong and Shanxi and the later-stage map of Nanzhili (T68). The first two maps were originally translated maps, on which Ruggieri subsequently added adapted toponyms based on the text of the *Guanzhi*, overwriting some of the translated toponyms and erasing others or marking them for deletion. The Nanzhili map also contains two layers: one set of toponyms positioned in accordance with practices from the earliest stage of map translation but with handwriting, symbols, and spellings similar to the adapted type, and a second layer with adapted toponyms, following the logic of the text of the *Guanzhi*. These interim maps thus reflect that Ruggieri switched methods in the course of producing his manuscript maps.

Ruggieri's Motivation for Adapting the Maps

The differences between the adapted maps and the 1656 map by Sanson (which may resemble the aforementioned 1590 large map) in terms of spelling rules, locations of cities, and so on indicate that the adaptations on the interim maps and the creation of the adapted maps both occurred after 1590. Ruggieri continued working on the adapted maps until 1606, the year before he passed away.[16] He had spent much time and effort on the adapted maps after 1590, which raises questions about his motivation in continuing his work. As mentioned, it is almost impossible to distinguish the types and administrative levels of the cities and settlements—except those of prefectural seats (*fu*)—on the maps of the *Guanzhi*. The same is true for the translated maps, which follow the symbols and formatting of the toponyms on the *Guanzhi* maps. However, a map that clearly depicted the administrative system would have helped Ruggieri to advocate for the necessity of the accommodation policy because it would have allowed his patrons and superiors to imagine a systematic Christianization of China. To bridge the gap with his translated early maps, Ruggieri needed a complete list of China's settlements with clear classifications. The text of the *Guanzhi* fulfilled this need.

Ruggieri may have tried to check each settlement according to its order in the text of the *Guanzhi* and to find the corresponding toponym on its maps. In the process,

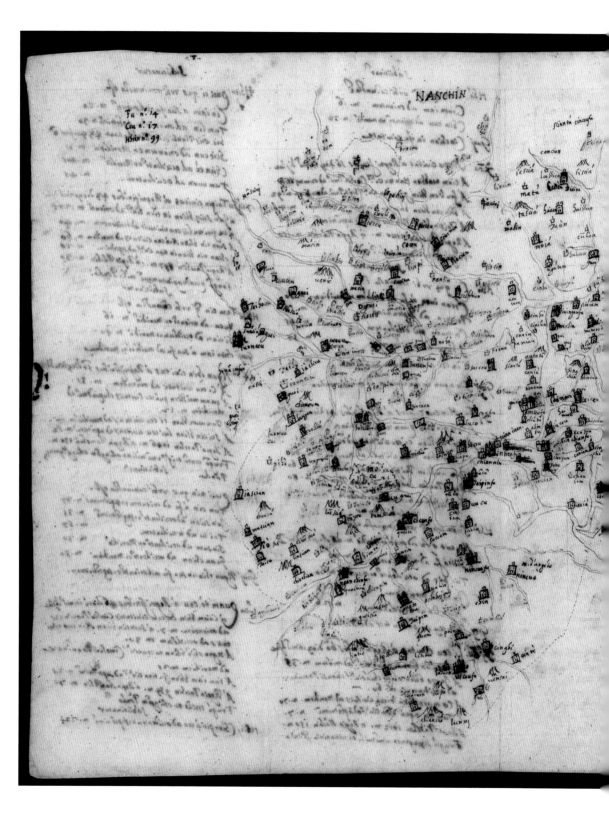

FIGURE 11.9.

One of Ruggieri's maps of Nanzhili (T68). The bottom-right corner features a conversion ruler and scale: 4 Chinese *li* = 1 *miliaria Italica*, and 100 *miliaria Italica* on T68 is measured as 10.1 cm. 44 × 58.5 cm. Archivio di Stato di Roma.

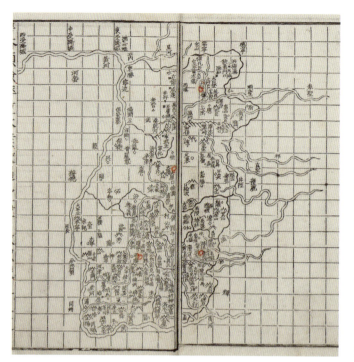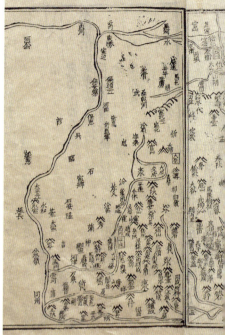

FIGURE 11.10.

Horizontal distortion on the maps of Shanxi in the *Guang yutu* of 1566 (Harvard-Yenching Library, *left*), on the *Guanzhi* of 1586 (Naikaku Bunko, *middle*), and on Ruggieri's map of Shanxi Province (Archivio di Stato di Roma, *right*).

he would easily have found obvious discrepancies between the locations recorded in the text and on the maps. Hence, Ruggieri had to make a choice: either mark the settlements in accordance with the *Guanzhi* maps and his translated maps or relocate the settlements according to the text of the *Guanzhi*. Finally, he decided to trust the text, perhaps because it seemed far more systematic and coherent than the maps.[17] The text also enabled him to present a much more detailed and up-to-date picture of the Ming administration.

As the locations of cities and settlements on the adapted maps differ systematically from those on the prototype maps of the *Guanzhi* and from Ruggieri's early maps, the question arises of whether the adaptations constituted any qualitative improvement. Comparing closely, it quickly becomes clear that Ruggieri's adaptation process resulted in a dubious outcome regarding relative positions between cities and settlements. The reasons for this relate both to the Chinese source itself and to Ruggieri's understanding of it.

Relative locations recorded in the text are less precise than those on the map.[18] Besides the data's inconsistency, moreover, Ruggieri's approach also raises questions.

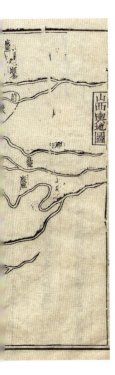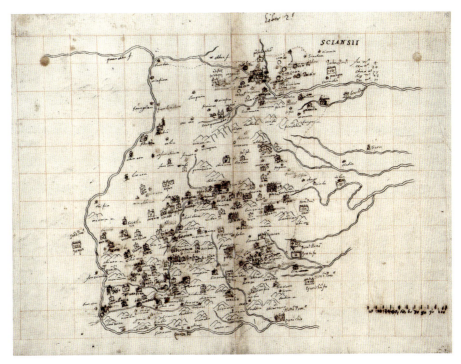

The text describes its orientation through eight directions (figure 11.8). This methodology is far from sufficient when using polar coordinates to mark cities onto provincial maps that cover a relatively large region. Subprefectures and counties distant from prefectural seats especially amplify the negative effect originating from the orientational deviation. Further, distance data in traditional Chinese geographical works generally refer to route lengths rather than straight-line distances, a distinction Ruggieri, it seems, did not recognize when marking the cities, negatively affecting the maps' mathematical foundations.[19] In addition, Ruggieri relied entirely on the provincial outlines of the *Guanzhi* maps, which had introduced a number of differences compared to the source maps taken from the 1566 *Guang yutu* atlas.[20] The maps in the *Guang yutu* contain a grid in which the sides of each square represent a certain distance (in *li* 里). During the reproduction process, the grid was dropped, resulting in the maps of the *Guanzhi* stretching horizontally (figure 11.10). The *Guanzhi* versions also lack the boundary lines between prefectures, as included in the *Guang yutu*. Ruggieri never realized that the maps of the *Guanzhi* were already stretched horizontally. This caused disproportionate length-to-width ratios and strong horizontal distortion of every province. In most cases Ruggieri even enlarged the distortion of the *Guanzhi* maps when converting text-based distances to situate sites on the map.[21]

Another problem Ruggieri faced was the lack of any scale on the maps of the *Guanzhi* due to the absence of a grid. In consequence, the scales he added did not match those of the prototype maps, resulting in problems concerning provinces' relative sizes (e.g., on the adapted maps, according to the scales added by Ruggieri, Yunnan Province is about the same size as Guangxi, whereas in fact the former is much larger than the latter). Comparing Ruggieri's adapted maps with those from the *Guang yutu* easily illustrates the resulting inaccuracies: the distances in the maps in this atlas, unlike those of the *Guanzhi,* can be calculated by using the grid.[22] In addition, the *Guang yutu* more clearly shows the distribution of the subprefectures and counties since it contains prefectural boundaries. Ruggieri set the scale of his manuscript maps in a way that makes the provinces appear either larger or smaller (the latter being more common). First, if the provinces appeared to be larger, Ruggieri's approach of marking locations resulted in the seats of subprefectures and counties being placed in a cluster around each prefectural seat on the adapted maps, with a lot of empty space around each cluster (figure 11.11). The fact that Ruggieri inadvertently stretched his maps even further horizontally only enhanced this effect.

Second, if the provinces appeared smaller, the seats of subprefectures and counties were located farther away from each prefectural seat. As a consequence, the seats of subprefectures and counties belonging to different prefectures are often in "mosaic distribution" on Ruggieri's adapted maps. The boundary lines of prefectures found on the *Guang yutu* but not on the *Guanzhi* maps might have revealed to Ruggieri the limitations of his approach (figure 11.12). On the other hand, since Ruggieri's maps stretched horizontally, this pattern would not have been as obvious as it would have otherwise.

When we return to the question of whether the further adaptations of the early translated maps were worth the effort, we find the answer less straightforward than we might have hoped. Despite the many place-names added (significantly increasing the maps' information content) and the great time and effort devoted to the adapted maps, the distortion increased greatly (reducing their accuracy). This even misrepresented the relationships between the depictions of mountains and rivers and those of cities and settlements. On the adapted maps, while mountains and rivers remained marked according to the maps of the *Guanzhi,* settlements underwent all the adjustments described above, resulting in frequent divergences in relative positions between localities and their natural environs: cities could appear south of rivers when in fact they lay north of them, or cities could appear distant from mountains that were actually rather close. The maps' information on natural and human geography thus no longer constituted an organic whole, at least when compared to the translated maps.

By analyzing Ruggieri's maps in a systematic manner, we can classify the set of manuscripts into three types: translated maps, interim maps, and adapted maps. Certainly, a complete set of translated maps, one for each province and all produced before the drawing of a 1590 large general map in Rome by Ruggieri and Neroni, existed. As we have seen, most maps of this set are now lost, but they are arguably discernable in Nicolas Sanson's printed map.

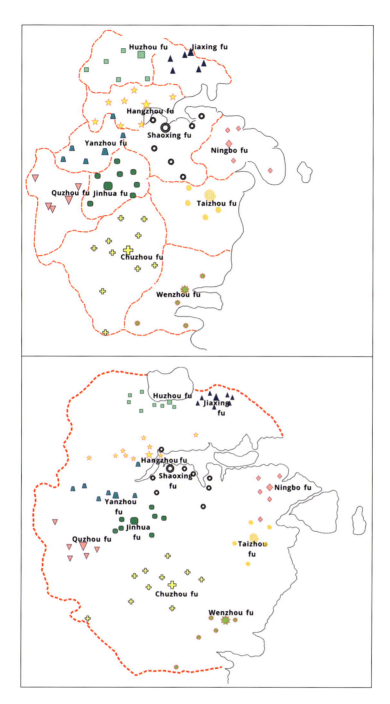

FIGURE 11.11.

Distribution pattern of seats of subprefectures (*zhou*) and counties (*xian*) on the map of Zhejiang Province in the *Guang yutu* (*top*) and on Ruggieri's map of the province (*bottom*).

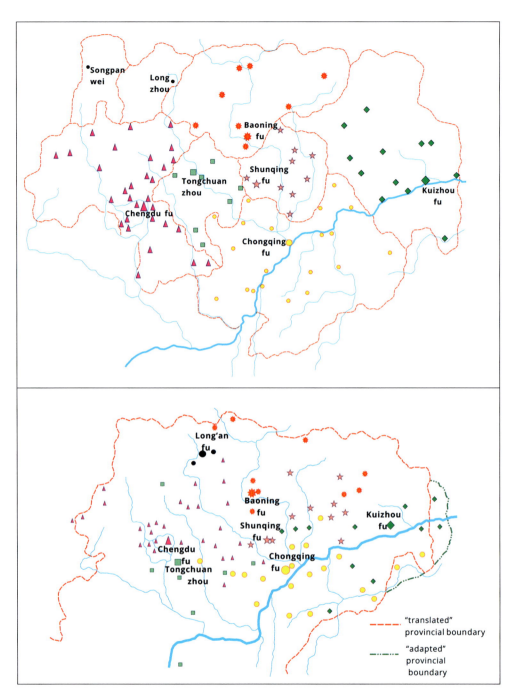

FIGURE 11.12.

Distribution pattern of subprefectures (*zhou*) and counties (*xian*) on the map of Sichuan Province in *Guang yutu* (*top*) and on Ruggieri's map (*bottom*). Note that the town of Long'an was promoted from subprefecture (*zhou*) to prefecture (*fu*) in 1566.

However, Ruggieri did not stop at just translating maps; he endeavored to improve them. Three extant interim maps illustrate Ruggieri's approach vividly. He first added the adaptations to the early-stage translated maps (no earlier than 1590). In contrast to the early and interim maps, however, most extant manuscript maps from Ruggieri's hand are his adapted maps. Compared with the translated maps, the adapted maps mark the administrative hierarchy of toponyms and include a more complete and up-to-date view of the Ming administration. However, the relative locations of the settlements are generally much more distorted than those on the translated maps because Ruggieri followed (but misinterpreted) the information in the text of the *Guanzhi*. Further, many have speculated that Ruggieri's maps remained unpublished due to hostility within the Jesuit order.[23] However, his repeated alterations to the manuscripts suggest another explanation: perhaps the maps simply never met Ruggieri's standards before he passed away.

The detailed classification of the maps into three groups, finally, allows us to understand better the circulation of Ruggieri's maps. A number of people saw and used his maps, especially the translated ones. In 1590 when Ruggieri was in Rome, he must have shown the translated maps to others. At that time he also produced a manuscript map together with Neroni, the only known general map of China to make use of Ruggieri's maps. This 1590 map then served as a source for Italian mapmaker Fausto Rughesi's production of the world maps and maps of Asia about seven years later. In addition, the 1590 manuscript map came into the possession of the Duke of Orleans in the mid-seventeenth century and formed the basis for one of Sanson's China maps printed in 1656. Thus, whereas in 1590 the vast, unified, and orderly Chinese empire depicted might have impressed readers of the translated maps or the larger manuscript map, the more widely circulated Sanson map likely seemed less impressive due to the publication of Martino Martini's (1614–1661) even-more-detailed *Novus atlas sinensis* in the previous year (figure 9.2). In contrast to this wide circulation of works based on Ruggieri's translated maps, the adapted maps of Ruggieri's later years had much less impact. The only record informing us of their circulation is a brief account in the mid-seventeenth century by Jesuit historian Daniello Bartoli (1608–1685), who consulted provincial maps of China in Rome. These included printed maps in Chinese (probably from the *Guanzhi*) as well as Ruggieri's manuscript maps.[24] Thus, even though Ruggieri's maps never saw print, his mapping method, making full use of Chinese maps and geographical books, still made a difference.

During this early stage of the two-way exchanges of maps between East Asia and western Europe, most of the main actors taking Chinese maps to Europe were Jesuit missionaries like Ruggieri. While they made the utmost effort to obtain as much geographical information as possible to enrich their works and to satisfy the curiosity of their readers, their limited knowledge and exposure to books and maps from China resulted in many misinterpretations. In this context, the Chinese materials they used emerge as active factors in knowledge formation: the images and texts themselves influenced the missionaries' practices and approaches.

Notes

1. Lo Sardo, *Atlante della Cina*; Jin, *Atlas of China*.
2. Lo Sardo, "Il primo Atlante della Cina"; Lo Sardo, *Atlante della Cina*; Lo Sardo, "Earliest European Atlas of Ming China."
3. Sixtus V (1521–1590), Urbano VII (1521–1590), Gregorius XIV (1535–1591), and Innocent IX (1519–1591).
4. De Saldanha, "Ruggieri in Europe"; Villasante, "Introducción."
5. Since the maps in the *Guanzhi* were copied from the *Guang yutu*, the maps in these two books are similar—the key reason previous studies identified the *Guang yutu* as Ruggieri's main reference. However, the maps in these two works also differ in many important details.
6. In his first few years after returning to Europe, Ruggieri may have kept in touch with the Jesuits in China—e.g., the geographical description of Guangdong Province reflected the establishment of Shaozhou station in 1589. See Lo Sardo, *Atlante della Cina*, 33; Lo Sardo, "Earliest European Atlas of Ming China," 260.
7. On the maps of the *Guang yutu*, the main source of the *Guanzhi*, detailed legends and normative symbols represent different kinds of settlements, while the maps of *Guanzhi* omit all these symbols.
8. A copy of the 1586 edition of the *Guanzhi*, bound in four volumes, is now held by the Naikaku Bunko.
9. In a detailed essay titled "Considerations sur diverses cartes, & relations de la Chine" in *L'Asie* (1658), Sanson described the 1590 map as displaying three ranks of cities: the seats of prefectures (*fu*), subprefectures (*zhou*), and counties (*xian*). He also cited Ruggieri's introduction to the map in explaining that military governors occupied other cities called *wei* and *suo*. Hence, the 1656 Sanson map marks only prefectural and subprefectural seats, while the 1590 map marked counties as well. Szcześniak translated Sanson's essay into English (Szcześniak, "Seventeenth Century Maps of China," 133–136).
10. Lin, "Yiyi 1590 nian danfu Zhongguo daditu yanjiu," 45–61.
11. The only other province depicted in extant maps from both the early and late stage is Guangdong. However, the early-stage map of Guangdong is overwritten with later modifications, making it unsuitable for comparison.
12. The other later-stage map (T65) contains several hard-to-read toponyms. Moreover, T68 has two layers of toponyms labeled with different symbols, showing Ruggieri's modifications. This section only discusses the upper toponyms on T68.
13. In early editions of the *Guanzhi*, data of this kind mainly originated from the *Da Ming yitong zhi* 大明一統志 (Gazetteer of the unified Great Ming, 1461), while later editions updated their data continuously.
14. Chen, "Luo Mingjian ditu ji de ziliao laiyuan," 57–59.
15. However, a small number of adapted toponyms were added to them later.
16. On the differences between the adapted maps, see Lin, "Luo Mingjian Zhongguo ditu jigao."
17. In the process, he might also easily have discovered his mistakes in misidentifying subprefectures (*zhou*) while making his translated maps.

18. E.g., in the case of Sichuan Province, the province with the greatest number of administrative units, distances for subprefectures and counties are over six times more precise on the map of the *Guanzhi* than in the text.
19. Wang, "Xiancun zui wanzheng," 273–288; Cheng, *"Feikexue" de Zhongguo chuantong yutu*, 215–326.
20. In turn originating from the *Yutu* 輿圖 made in the early fourteenth century and possibly traceable back to general maps of China made in earlier centuries. Thus, the location information contained in the maps of the *Guanzhi* Ruggieri used was passed down from a long tradition of mapping in China. The maps of the 1568 edition of the *Guanzhi* were also based on those from the *Guang yutu*, while the maps in earlier editions of the *Guanzhi*, like the text, were based on the *Da Ming yitong zhi*.
21. Comparing the actual ratios, maps of the *Guang yutu* are more accurate for twelve provinces out of fifteen.
22. Apart from the horizontal stretching of the *Guanzhi* maps, the general relative locations of the toponyms on the *Guanzhi* correspond with those of the *Guang yutu*.
23. Song, "Zhongguo ditu," 118.
24. Lo Sardo, "Earliest European Atlas of Ming China," 260–261.

References

Chen Zongren 陳宗仁. "Luo Mingjian ditu ji de ziliao laiyuan: Yi Fujian tu wei li" 羅明堅地圖集的資料來源—以福建圖為例. In *Luo Mingjian "Zhongguo ditu ji" xueshu yantao hui lunwen ji* 羅明堅《中國地圖集》學術研討會論文集, edited by Yao Jingming 姚京明 and Hao Yufan 郝雨凡, 41–60. Macao: Instituto cultural do Governo da RAE de Macau, 2014.

Cheng Yinong 成一農. *"Feikexue" de Zhongguo chuantong yutu* "非科學"的中國傳統輿圖. Beijing: Zhongguo shehui kexue chubanshe, 2016.

De Saldanha, António Vasconcelos. "Ruggieri in Europe." In Jin Guoping, *Atlas of China by Michele Ruggieri*, 81–87.

Jin Guoping, ed. and trans. *Atlas of China by Michele Ruggieri*. Macao: Instituto cultural do Governo da RAE de Macau, 2013.

Lin Hong 林宏. "Luo Mingjian Zhongguo ditu jigao zhi 'gaichuang xing' tugao de ditu yaosu fenxi" 羅明堅中國地圖集稿之'改創型'圖稿的地圖要素分析. *Guoji Hanxue* 國際漢學, no. 4 (2020): 55–70.

———. "Yiyi 1590 nian danfu Zhongguo daditu yanjiu" 已佚1590年單幅中國大地圖研究. *Zhongguo lishi dili luncong* 中國歷史地理論叢 35, no. 1 (2020): 45–61.

Lo Sardo, Eugenio, ed. *Atlante della Cina di Michele Ruggieri, S.I.* Rome: Istituto poligrafico e Zecca dello Stato, Libreria dello Stato, 1993.

———. "The Earliest European Atlas of Ming China: An Unpublished Work by Michele Ruggieri." In *Images de la Chine: Le contexte occidental de la Sinologie naissante,* edited by Edward J. Malatesta and Yves Raguin, 259–273. Paris: Institut Ricci, 1995.

———. "Il primo Atlante della Cina dei Ming: Un inedito di Michele Ruggieri." *Bollettino della Società Geografica Italiana,* ser. 11, 6 (1989): 423–447.

Song Liming 宋黎明. "Zhongguo ditu: Luo Mingjian he Li Madou" 中國地圖：羅明堅和利瑪竇.

Beijing xingzheng xueyuan xuebao 北京行政學院學報, no. 3 (2013): 112–119.

Szcześniak, Boleslaw. "The Seventeenth Century Maps of China: An Inquiry into the Compilations of European Cartographers." *Imago Mundi* 13 (1956): 133–136.

Villasante, Roberto. "Introducción: Vida de Michele Ruggieri." In *La filosofía moral de Confucio, por Michele Ruggieri, SJ: La primera traducción de las obras de Confucio al español en 1590,* edited by Thierry Meynard and Roberto Villasante, 19–58. Bilbao: Ediciones Mensajero, 2018.

Wang Qianjin 汪前進. "Luo Mingjian bianhui *Zhongguo ditu ji* suoju Zhongwen Yuanshi ziliao xintan" 羅明堅編繪《中國地圖集》所依據中文原始資料新探. *Beijing xingzheng xueyuan xuebao* 北京行政學院學報, no. 3 (2013): 120–128.

———. "Xiancun zui wanzheng de yifen Tangdai dili quantu shuju ji" 現存最完整的一份唐代地理全圖數據集. *Ziran kexue shi yanjiu* 自然科學史研究 17, no. 3 (1998): 273–288.

Postscript

Remapping Map History from East Asia

MATTHEW H. EDNEY

It is a privilege to have been asked to write the postscript to this wonderful collection of essays that pivot about the intersections of early modern western European and East Asian geographical practices. I claim neither expertise in this particular subject matter nor familiarity with the traditions of Sinology and other branches of East Asian studies. Rather, my appreciation for this collection stems, first, from the wealth of new information about significant developments in map history that the essays make accessible to those of us who do not know any East Asian languages and, second, from the structural principles that have motivated the editors in designing the volume; it is the latter that I wish to focus on here. The study of map history has hitherto addressed one of two sets of mapping processes—those of production and consumption—a distinction evident in past studies of the "Ricci maps." Mario Cams and Elke Papelitzky have now created a book that turns attention to a third set of mapping processes, those of circulation, and they plainly demonstrate the benefits of doing so.[1]

Systematic studies of early maps began in the 1830s and 1840s and have followed a series of intellectual threads. One of the very first threads to emerge, an offshoot from the then nascent history of geography and discovery, was a "globalist" map history concerned with using geographical and marine maps as synopses of the geographical knowledge accrued by the societies that made them; a map was defined as much by the information it contained as by its image.[2] Stringing together world maps in chronological sequence was an easy way to demonstrate Europe's steadily increasing knowledge of the world from medieval vagaries, through the "Great Discoveries" and the formation of the modern "Western mind," to the heights of modern cartographic achievements. Globalist map history thus traced the formation of Western civilization and its rise to global imperial dominance. The globalist agenda generally precluded consideration of

Matteo Ricci (1552–1610) and his world maps, which briefly appear in just one of the general histories of mapmaking.[3] Dedicated essays were prepared when these exotic maps were found in or acquired by European and American libraries;[4] these studies all portray Ricci as the agent who effected great change in Chinese mapmaking. Furthermore, the globalist conception of "map" as an archive of geographical information meant that there was only ever *one* "Ricci map" that appeared in eight or more "editions" in China, together with several Korean and Japanese "copies," all descending from the one original work.[5]

A distinct thread of map history emerged later in the nineteenth century to narrate the development of mapmaking as an innately scientific endeavor grounded in the observation and measurement of the landscape. This thread has focused on mapping from the ground up, as it were, which is to say on surveyed maps of properties, places, and regions. This was the intellectual context for Joseph Needham's integration of Chinese and Western practices into an intertwined history of scientific progress.[6] For Needham, Ricci's introduction of late Renaissance cartography into China revived older Chinese mapping practices and was not as innovative as the Eurocentric globalists suggested. Chinese scholars followed a similar emphasis on the surveying and mapping of China and gave little shrift to maps in the Euro-American tradition.[7]

Both of these threads, as well as the several other kinds of map history carried on during the nineteenth and twentieth centuries, emphasized the production of maps, whether in terms of the accumulation of information to be recorded in graphic form or the development of surveying techniques. In about 1980 there emerged a new concern for studying the consumption of early maps. Several interconnected threads of scholarship have studied maps as social instruments and cultural documents by exploring both how and for what purpose they were used and how they were interpreted as symbolic as well as factual works. The resultant "sociocultural" map history has situated maps firmly within the cultures and social institutions that made them. This new scholarship has been remarkably productive and has promoted an interest in matters of mapping and spatiality across the humanities and social sciences.

Cordell D. K. Yee made the crucial sociocultural intervention for the history of mapping in China in the several chapters he wrote for *The History of Cartography*.[8] In line with the larger sociocultural turn, Yee turned the narrative of Chinese mapping from one of scientific development into one of several distinct cultural expressions that were all manifestly different from "Western" mapping. Ricci's maps and the concept of a spherical earth that might be mapped geographically by latitude and longitude were relevant to the work of only a relatively few Chinese intellectuals and did not entail anything close to a complete reformulation of Chinese geographical mapping.[9] Moreover, other kinds of mapping in China, such as the mapping of landscapes and coasts, were quite unaffected by developments within geographical mapping practices.

It is a small but significant step from this argument to realize that there is no such phenomenon as "Chinese cartography" nor, for that matter, "Korean cartography" nor "Japanese cartography." Not all the things that we call maps took the same form or were produced in the same way or were consumed by the same people for similar ends. Rather, there are many ways of making images that conceptualize the world in different ways for different ends. Thus, Thongchai Winichakul also demonstrated that Siamese mapping entailed several distinct traditions of coastal and chorographical mapping before King Chulalongkorn's (1853–1910) extensive reforms after 1870 introduced Western territorial mapping and its associated practices as one plank in his strategy to maintain Siam's independence in the face of British and French imperialism.[10]

It must also be realized that mapping in Europe and the Americas has never constituted a single "Western cartography" either. Empirical investigation reveals the existence of distinct modes of mapping—each comprising a specific constellation of spatial conceptions, representational strategies, and socially mandated functions—within which distinctive kinds of maps are produced and consumed. The identification of mapping modes is very much a heuristic, however, and allowances must be made for the fluidity of the same people working within different modes and for them to bring maps from one mode into another. More precisely, we can trace specific circuits within which maps, in their various forms, circulate between producers and consumers in precise spatial discourses. Each spatial discourse features its own particular combination of representational strategies (verbal, performative, numeric, graphic, constructed). Some spatial discourses are tiny, having a limited circuit, and might be short-lived: one person asking another for directions, with maps made from gestures, verbal instructions, and perhaps a physical sketch that is of use only until the desired destination is reached; alternatively, making a map in manuscript for submission to a governor or emperor to gain interest and favor. Another spatial discourse might be larger and longer-lived—notably, when maps are printed for distribution to some larger body of consumers whose constitution is defined by the manner of publication. Paying close attention to map circulation thus establishes precise social and cultural contexts for specific maps, permitting their meaningful interpretation. The development of and interactions between spatial discourses also provide a mechanism for dealing with change over time without resorting to presumptions of linear cartographic progress.[11]

A key implication of identifying spatial discourses is that when maps move from one into another, as they often do, they become subject to different mapping practices and interpretations. Sumathi Ramaswamy detailed a great example: first, nineteenth-century European scientists hypothesized about lost continents such as Lemuria to explain the modern distribution of isolated populations of flora and fauna, the original land bridges that connected those populations having fallen below the ocean surface; second, the maps that the scientists drew of Lemuria were adopted by New Agey theosophists who populated the lost continents with protohumans in a complex and racially fraught evolutionary history of humanity; third, in the twentieth century, the theosophists' maps were adapted by Tamil nationalists who turned Lemuria into the lost Tamil homeland, creating a powerful nationalistic narrative of loss and nostalgia with which to counter the political domination of southern India by Hindi-speaking peoples from northern India.[12] The movement of the maps of Lemuria from one discourse to another was quite contingent, and in each discourse the maps were thoroughly reinterpreted and redeployed to sustain markedly different ends. In short, each physical translation of a map from one spatial discourse into another necessarily entails a further act of intellectual translation.

The crux of the present book is the circulation of world maps and textual geographies within and between specific spatial discourses in East Asia. The authors eschew the monolithic and incommensurate image of Western and Eastern cultures and instead consider how both sustained geographical discourses through various forms of print, manuscript, and oral communication. What passed between these discourses was not abstract geographical concepts (spherical earth, latitude and longitude) and information (about continents and oceans, coastlines and rivers, countries and cities) but geographical maps and texts whose content could be, and was, repackaged and reinterpreted to meet the needs of the different intellectual communities.

Key to discerning and analyzing circulation and thus the extent of each discourse is its particular assemblage of representational strategies and material forms (text on maps, maps in books, globes, etc.); the translation of maps between discourses requires it to be fitted into a different assemblage. The authors in the present volume all properly pay careful attention to the formation of these assemblages, and several use detailed bibliographical analyses to reveal the nature of specific spatial discourses. Attention to materiality also provides insight into the physical relationship of readers to the maps and texts and therefore into the various conditions and practices by which the maps were consumed. A large multipanel screen bearing text and graphics set within a room specifically as a prompt for intellectual conversation and exchange calls for leisurely examination as readers draw close and read parts of the screen together. A large floor-standing globe offers an incomplete view of the earth, and the consumer must physically turn it to bring new geographical details into view; the globe might also be consumed by scholars together. For less autonomous consumers—notably petitioners, underlings, servants, and perhaps also female relatives—the freestanding screens and globes appear less as things to be interrogated and more as material statements of their owners' status and authority. By contrast, maps in books offer opportunities for individual geographical contemplation, although in a manner structured and guided by the book's organization and sequencing.

The studies collected in this book discern not a single "Ricci Map"—one archive of knowledge reproduced in various editions and formats, even into nineteenth-century Japan—but rather a continual reconfiguration of maps on screens, in books, and as globes that propagated outward from Ricci and his collaborators—notably, Li Zhizao 李之藻 (1565–1630). First are the small number of maps that Ricci produced in several collaborations with Chinese scholars, each to a different end within small circuits motivated more by the politics of gifting and patronage than by a desire for intellectual inquiry. Second, we have the numerous maps that variously reproduced the basic outlines of the "Ricci maps" even as they adapted them to local concerns, such as the early manuscript "figured" maps that ameliorated the images and the later Korean and Japanese adaptations that recast the maps in terms of local concerns over the state of dynastic authority and over the incursions of foreigners. Third are the further geographical works, especially those printed for broader circulation, into which geographical information from Ricci and later western European sources was variously incorporated and realigned to mesh with local aesthetics and ethos, thereby engendering new map forms such as the Korean *cheonha do* that reacted to western European mapping. Throughout, beginning before Ricci, Jesuit missionaries moved some Chinese geographical works into the global circuits by which they acquired, interpreted, and communicated information for their colleagues within the Society of Jesus; the Chinese geographies appeared as exotica to some Jesuits, but others were subject to literal translation.

The flow of maps and books among all of these discourses, and with them the communication and reconfiguration of geographical concepts and information, was contingent on personal interactions and circumstances. No great flood of Western science and data washed over Chinese, Korean, and Japanese intellectuals, as Eurocentric histories suggested. Nor was Western knowledge kept at bay by cultural dams. Rather, geographical things—maps and books—constantly sloshed around like water in small cups and large urns, occasionally spilling over into neighboring vessels. Lines of informational descent are multiple and complex. *Remapping the World in East Asia* advances a nuanced and empirically rich approach to the repeated intercultural interactions and repeated acts of translation and reconfiguration, all occurring in specific local sites of engagement. The result is the creation of many different maps in multiple forms, each revealing extensive and ongoing engagements between East Asia and western Europe. This book demonstrates in no uncertain terms the benefits of remapping map history, of moving beyond the outdated belief in the map-as-archive and of turning the sociocultural concern for the map image toward the study of maps as things and mapping as process.

Notes

1. This outline of different threads of map history is based on my current work in progress, titled *The Map: Concepts and Histories.*
2. Edney, *Cartography,* 55–58.
3. Bagrow, *Die Geschichte der Kartographie,* 188, 361.
4. E.g., Baddeley, "Father Matteo Ricci's Chinese World-Maps"; Wallis, "Influence of Father Ricci on Far Eastern Cartography."
5. Heawood, "Relationships of the Ricci Maps"; D'Elia, "Recent Discoveries"; Day, "Search for the Origins."
6. Needham, "Geography and Cartography," esp. 583–585, 588.

7. Cheng, "Times and Historical Writing."
8. Yee, "Chinese Cartography among the Arts"; Yee, "Chinese Maps in Political Culture"; Yee, "Concluding Remarks"; Yee, "Reinterpreting Traditional Chinese Geographical Maps"; Yee, "Taking the World's Measure"; Yee, "Traditional Chinese Cartography"; separately issued as Yu, *Zhongguo ditu xue shi*.
9. Esp. Yee, "Traditional Chinese Cartography," 170–177.
10. Thongchai, *Siam Mapped*.
11. Edney, "Map History"; Edney, *Cartography*, 26–49; Edney, "Making Explicit the Implicit."
12. Ramaswamy, *Lost Land of Lemuria*.

References

Baddeley, J. F. "Father Matteo Ricci's Chinese World-Maps, 1584–1608." *Geographical Journal* 50, no. 4 (1917): 254–270.

Bagrow, Leo. *Die Geschichte der Kartographie*. Berlin: Safari-Verlag, 1951.

Cheng Yinong 成一農. "Times and Historical Writing: Formation of Historical Writing of Ancient Chinese Cartography and Its Future Diversification" (Shidai yu lishi shuxie: Zhongguo gudai ditu xueshi shuxie de xingcheng yi ji jinhou de duoyuan hua 時代與歷史書寫—中國古代地圖學史書寫的形成以及今後的多元化). Unpublished proceedings of Frontier Forum on Cartographic History and International Seminar on the History of Cartography Translation Project, 571–606. Yunnan University, Kunming, August 24–26, 2019.

Day, John D. "The Search for the Origins of the Chinese Manuscript of Matteo Ricci's Maps." *Imago Mundi* 47 (1995): 94–117.

D'Elia, Pasquale M. "Recent Discoveries and New Studies (1938–1960) on the World Map in Chinese of Father Matteo Ricci SJ." *Monumenta Serica* 20 (1961): 82–164.

Edney, Matthew H. *Cartography: The Ideal and Its History*. Chicago: University of Chicago Press, 2019.

———. "Making Explicit the Implicit, Idealized Understanding of 'Map' and 'Cartography'": An Anti-Universalist Response to Mark Denil." *Cartographic Perspectives* 98 (2022): 51–60.

———. "Map History: Discourse and Process." In *The Routledge Handbook of Mapping and Cartography*, edited by Alexander J. Kent and Peter Vujakovic, 68–79. London: Routledge, 2017.

Harley, J. B., and David Woodward, eds. *The History of Cartography*. Vol. 2, bk. 2, *Cartography in the Traditional East and Southeast Asian Societies*. Chicago: University of Chicago Press, 1994.

Heawood, Edward. "The Relationships of the Ricci Maps." *Geographical Journal* 50, no. 4 (1917): 271–276.

Needham, Joseph. "Geography and Cartography." In *Mathematics and the Sciences of the Heavens and the Earth*, with Wang Ling, 497–590. Vol. 3, *Science and Civilisation in China*. Cambridge: Cambridge University Press, 1959.

Ramaswamy, Sumathi. *The Lost Land of Lemuria: Fabulous Geographies, Catastrophic Histories*. Berkeley: University of California Press, 2004.

Thongchai Winichakul. *Siam Mapped: A History of the Geo-body of a Nation*. Honolulu: University of Hawai'i Press, 1994.

Wallis, Helen M. "The Influence of Father Ricci on Far Eastern Cartography." *Imago Mundi* 19 (1965): 38–45.

Yee, Cordell D. K. "Chinese Cartography among the Arts: Objectivity, Subjectivity, Representation." In Harley and Woodward, *History of Cartography,* vol. 2, bk. 2, 128–169.

———. "Chinese Maps in Political Culture." In Harley and Woodward, *History of Cartography,* vol. 2, bk. 2, 71–95.

———. "Concluding Remarks: Foundations for a Future History of Chinese Mapping." In Harley and Woodward, *History of Cartography,* vol. 2, bk. 2, 228–231.

———. "Reinterpreting Traditional Chinese Geographical Maps." In Harley and Woodward, *History of Cartography,* vol. 2, bk. 2, 35–70.

———. "Taking the World's Measure: Chinese Maps between Observation and Text." In Harley and Woodward, *History of Cartography,* vol. 2, bk. 2, 96–127.

———. "Traditional Chinese Cartography and the Myth of Westernization." In Harley and Woodward, *History of Cartography,* vol. 2, bk. 2, 170–202.

Yu Dingguo 余定國. *Zhongguo ditu xue shi* 中國地圖學史 (*History of Chinese cartography*). Translated by Jiang Daozhang 姜道章. Beijing: Beijing daxue chubanshe, 2006.

Glossary of Titles

This glossary proposes translations for the main artifacts that feature in the chapters of this book. While each of these titles may be translated in several ways, we have striven for consistency in the translation of key concepts and have endeavored to faithfully transpose their literal meanings. Even so, certain terms were closely related and occasionally required an alternative translation depending on their position in the title.

Bankoku sōzu 萬國總圖
Complete Map of All Countries

Beizhi huang Ming yitong xingshi fenye renwu chuchu quanlan 備誌皇明一統形勢分野人物出處全覽
Overview of the Origins of Famous Persons, Astral Allocations, and Topographical Features from the Unified Imperial Ming's Complete Records

Chikyū bankoku sankai yochi zenzusetsu 地球萬國山海輿地全圖説
Explanation of the Complete Geographical Map of the Earth, All Countries, Mountains, and Seas

"*Chikyū bankoku ichiran no zu*" 地球萬國一覽之圖
Overview Map of the Globe and All Countries

Cheonha do 天下圖
Map of All under Heaven

"*Cheonha do jido*" 天下都地圖
Map of All Cities under Heaven

"*Cheonha Jungguk do*" 天下中國圖
Map of China in All under Heaven

Cheonha gogeum daechong pyeollam do 天下古今大總便覽圖
Comprehensive Overview Map of All under Heaven Then and Now

Cheonha gogeum daechong pyeollam yeoji do 天下古今大總便覽輿地圖
Comprehensive Overview Terrestrial Map of All under Heaven Then and Now

Da Ming yitong wenwu zhusi yamen guanzhi 大明一統文武諸司衙門官制
System of Civil and Military Titles, Positions, and Offices of the Unified Great Ming

Dai Min kyūhen bankoku jinseki rotei zenzu 大明九邊萬國人跡路程全圖
Complete Map of Human Traces and Route Itineraries in All Countries and the Nine Frontiers of the Great Ming

Da Ming yitong zhi 大明一統志
Gazetteer of the Unified Great Ming

Daying quantu 大瀛全圖
Complete Map of the Great Ocean

Fangyu shenglüe 方輿勝略
Complete Survey of the Earth

Gonyeo manguk jeondo. See *Kunyu wanguo quantu.*

Guang yutu 廣輿圖 (K. *Gwang yeodo*)
Extended Territorial Maps

Gujin xingsheng zhi tu 古今形勝之圖
Map of Advantageous Terrain Then and Now

Gwang yeodo. See *Guang yutu.*

Huang Ming fenye yutu gujin renwu shiji 皇明分野輿圖古今人物事跡
Map of Astral Allocations of the Imperial Ming, with Famous Persons and Important Events Then and Now

Huntian yishuo 渾天儀說
Exposition on the Armillary Sphere

Hwanyeong ji 寰瀛誌
Record of the World

Jiuzhou fenye yutu gujin renwu shiji 九州分野輿圖古今人物事跡
Map of Astral Allocations of the Nine Regions, with Famous Persons and Important Events Then and Now

Joseon jido bu paldo cheonha jido 朝鮮地圖附八道天下地圖
Maps of Joseon, with Maps of the Eight Provinces and of All under Heaven

Joseon paldo gogeum chonglam do 朝鮮八道古今總覽圖
Comprehensive Overview Map of the Eight Provinces of Joseon Then and Now

"Jungwon sipsamseong do" 中原十三省圖
Map of the Thirteen Provinces of the Chinese Central Plains

"Jungwon sipsamseong geup Joseon dodo hapbu" 中原十三省及朝鮮都圖合付
Combined Map of the Thirteen Provinces of the Chinese Central Plains and Cities of Joseon

Kon'yo bankoku zenzu. See *Kunyu wanguo quantu.*

Kon'yo zenzu. See *Kunyu quantu.*

Kunyu quantu 坤輿全圖 (J. *Kon'yo zenzu*)
Complete Map of the Earth

Kunyu tushuo 坤輿圖說
Illustrated Exposition on the Earth

Kunyu waiji 坤輿外紀
Record of Everything beyond the Earth

Kunyu wanguo quantu 坤輿萬國全圖 (J. *Kon'yo bankoku zenzu*; K. *Gonyeo manguk jeondo*)
Complete Map of All Countries on Earth

Liangyi xuanlan tu 兩儀玄覽圖
Mysterious Visual Map of the Two Forms

"Liaodong biantu" 遼東邊圖
Map of the Border Region of Liaodong

"Li Madu nambukgeuk do" 利瑪竇南北極圖
Matteo Ricci's Map of the North and South Poles

"Li Madu Cheonha do" 利瑪竇天下圖
Cheonha do of Matteo Ricci

Manguk jeondo. See *Wanguo quantu*.

Nansenbushū bankoku shōka no zu 南瞻部洲萬國掌菓之圖
Handy Map of All Countries of Jambudvīpa

Nova et exactissima Sinarum monarchiae descriptio
New and Most Precise Map of the Kingdom of China

Qiankun wanguo quantu gujin renwu shiji 乾坤萬國全圖古今人物事跡
Complete Map of All Countries in the Universe, with Famous Persons and Important Events Then and Now

Rekidai bun'ya no zu kokin jinbutsu jiseki 歷代分埜之圖古今人物事跡
Map of Astral Allocations throughout the Ages, with Famous Persons and Important Events Then and Now

Sancai tuhui 三才圖會
Illustrated Compendium of the Three Powers [i.e., heaven, earth, and human]

"Seoyang jeguk do" 西洋諸國圖
Map of the Countries of the Western Ocean

Shanhai jing 山海經
Classic of Mountains, Seas, and Lands

Shanhai yudi quantu 山海輿地全圖
Complete Map of Mountains, Seas, and Lands

Shanhai yudi tu 山海輿地圖
Map of Mountains, Seas, and Lands

Shinpyeon pyoje chando Hwanyeong ji 新編標題纂圖寰瀛誌
Record of the World: Newly Edited and Titled Collection of Diagrams

"Taegeuk do" 太極圖
Map of the Supreme Ultimate

Taeseo hoesa Li Madu Manguk jeondo 泰西會士利瑪竇萬國全圖
Complete Map of All Countries by the Emissary of the West Matteo Ricci

Taewon ji 太原誌
Records of Taewon

Theatrum orbis terrarum
Display of the Lands of the Globe

Tianxue chuhan 天學初函
First Collection on Heavenly Learning

Tianxia jiubian fenye renji lucheng quantu 天下九邊分野人跡路程全圖
Complete Map of All under Heaven, the Nine Frontiers, Astral Allocations, Human Traces, and Route Itineraries

Tushu bian 圖書編
Compendium of Illustrations and Writings

Wakan Sansai zue 和漢三才圖會
Japanese-Chinese *Sancai tuhui*

Wanbao quanshu 萬寶全書
Complete Book of Myriad Treasures

Wanguo quantu 萬國全圖 (K. *Manguk jeondo*)
Complete Map of All Countries

Wanguo tuzhi 萬國圖志
Maps and Treatises on All Countries

Xinfa suanshu 新法算書
Books on Calculations according to New Methods

Xixue fan 西學凡
Summary of Western Learning

Yochizu 輿地圖 (K. *Yoeji do*)
Map[s] of the Land

Yudi shanhai quantu 輿地山海全圖
Complete Map of Lands, Mountains, and Seas

Yueling guangyi 月令廣義
Extended Meaning of the Monthly Proceedings

Zhifang waiji 職方外紀
Record of Everything beyond the Administration

Zōho ka-i tsūshōkō 増補華夷通商考
Expanded Study of the Trade between the Civilized and the Barbarians

Contributors

NICOLAS STANDAERT obtained his PhD from Leiden University (the Netherlands) in 1984. He is a professor of Sinology at the KU Leuven (Belgium). He has published widely on Sino-European cultural contacts in the seventeenth and eighteenth centuries, including *The Interweaving of Rituals: Funerals in the Cultural Exchange between China and Europe* (University of Washington Press, 2008).

RICHARD A. PEGG is director and curator of Asian Art for the MacLean Collection, an Asian art museum and separate map library located north of Chicago, Illinois. He has written and lectured widely on the visual, literary, cartographic, and martial arts traditions of East Asia, including *Cartographic Traditions in East Asian Maps* (University of Hawai'i Press, 2014).

WANG YONGJIE obtained his PhD in 2014 from Zhejiang University (China) and is an associate professor in the School of History and Culture at Northeast Normal University in Changchun. His research focuses on the history of Sino-European relations and historical geography.

CHENG FANGYI is an associate professor at Sun Yat-sen University (China). He has published widely on the early nomadic history of Eurasia and the history of Sino-Western relations. He is currently working on the history of the Congregational missionaries in Republican China.

MARIO CAMS obtained his PhD from KU Leuven (Belgium) in 2015 and is an associate professor of Chinese studies at KU Leuven. He has published extensively on the role of maps and mapping practices in early modern global connections, including *Companions in Geography: East-West Collaboration in the Mapping of Qing China (c. 1685–1735)* (Brill, 2017).

ELKE PAPELITZKY obtained her PhD from the University of Salzburg (Austria) in 2017 and is currently an associate professor of Chinese history at the University of Oslo (Norway). She has published extensively on the perception of the world of early modern Japanese and Chinese scholars, including *Writing World History in Late Ming China and the Perception of Maritime Asia* (Harrassowitz, 2020).

YANG YULEI studied history and historical geography at Zhejiang University and Fudan University (China), obtaining her PhD in 2005. She is a professor in the School of History at Zhejiang University. Her research interests include the history of Sino-Korean relations, the history of cultural exchanges between western Europe and East Asia, and map history.

SOH JEANHYOUNG obtained her PhD at Seoul National University (Korea) in 2016 and is currently a research fellow at the Institute of Humanities there. She is a political and intellectual historian of early modern East Asia, focusing on political language and rhetoric in the eighteenth and nineteenth centuries.

MARCO CABOARA obtained his PhD from the University of Washington in 2011. He is the head of Special Collections at the Hong Kong University of Science and Technology Library and the author of the first comprehensive carto-bibliography of Western printed maps of China, titled *Regnum Chinae: The Printed Western Maps of China to 1735* (Brill, 2022).

FLORIN-STEFAN MORAR obtained his PhD in the history of science from Harvard University in 2019 and is currently assistant professor at Lingnan University in Hong Kong. His work intersects with translation studies, the history of science, and the history of Sino-Western relations.

LIN HONG holds a PhD in historical geography from Fudan University (China) and is an associate professor in the Department of History at Shanghai Normal University. He is currently leading a project on the cartographic methods and genealogy of early European maps of China (1500–1734), supported by China's National Social Science Fund. His research and publications center on the global history of mapping and cultural exchange and the study of regional historical geography.

MATTHEW H. EDNEY is Osher Professor in the History of Cartography at the University of Southern Maine and director of the History of Cartography Project at the University of Wisconsin–Madison, where he obtained his PhD in 1990. He edited, with Mary Pedley, *Cartography in the European Enlightenment* (University of Chicago Press, 2019). Widely published and broadly interested in the history and nature of maps and mapping practices, his most recent monograph is *Cartography: The Ideal and Its History* (University of Chicago Press, 2019).

Index

Bold page numbers refer to figures and tables.

Acquaviva, Claudio, 229, 233, 240
AGI. *See* Archivo General de Indias
Aleni, Giulio: books brought to China, 98n13; in Fuzhou, 69, 83, 88, 93, 94, 96, 99n24; globe project, 66; in Hangzhou, 69, 96; life of, 69; in Nanjing, 143–145; *Wanguo quantu* text, 142–143; writings, 69, 76n56; *Xixue fan* (Summary of Western learning), 68, 91; *Zhifang waiji* preface, 80, 82, 89, 98n8; *Zhifang waiji* role, 69, 79, 80, 82–83, 91, 93, 96. *See also Wanguo quantu*
Almedia, Antonio de, 273
Amenomori Hōshū, 209–210, 224n11, 224n13
Arai Hakuseki, 179, 185n41
Archivo General de Indias (AGI), 245, 249, 255
ARSI. *See* Jesuit Archives
Asia, maps of, **84**, 142, 171. *See also* East Asia
astronomy: Chinese, 160, 190, 203n11; Chinese books, 179; European, 66, 69, 70, 73, 124, 179, 190, 197–198, 222; Greek, 124; Japanese, 166, 176; Korean, 190, 211
atlases, 98n13. *See also* Korean atlases; *Novus atlas sinensis*; Ruggieri, Michele, manuscript atlas
Ayusawa Shintarō, 6
Baddeley, John F., 6
Bae Wuseong, 208
Bankoku sōzu (Complete map of all countries), **165**; editions, 163, 170; in encyclopedias, 170, 171, 178, 179; images, 166, 179; place-names, 170; publication, 163; size, 182n14; Southeast Asian coastlines, 167, **168–169**
barbarians: Chinese view of foreigners as, 35, 37, 149, 184n31; contrast to civilized, 184n31, 217, 226n46; Japanese view of, 184n31; Mongols seen as, 206; outer, 39, 160; Qing seen as by Koreans, 10, 215–217, 222, 226n43
Barros, João, 250–251, 252, 268n25
Bartoli, Daniello, 291
Behaim, Martin, 57
Beizhi huang Ming yitong xingshi fenye renwu chuchu quanlan (Overview of the origins of famous persons, astral allocations, and topographical features from the unified imperial Ming's complete records), 129, **130**
Blaeu, Joan, 145, 251. *See also Novus atlas sinensis*
Blaeu, Willem Janszoon, 57, 183n21; globe, 59, 60
book market, 8, 9–11, 128, 131
Borja, Juan de, 249
Boym, Michał, 232, 251, 253
British Library (BL) globe, **58**; description, 57, 60; mount, 57, 61; production of, 56, 57, 68, 70, 73; provenance, 73n6; source material, 70; texts, 57, 64–66, **65**
Buddhist world maps, 145, 171, 183n27

calendars: Gregorian, 68; Japanese, 61, 75n28; Ming reforms, 65, 68, 69, 75n28, 98n10
Cao Junyi. *See Tianxia jiubian fenye renji lucheng quantu*
cartography: approaches to history of, 2–5, 295–297; idealization, 103. *See also* mapping practices; maps
Cattaneo, Lazzaro, 66, 253
Chang Yinxu, 34
Ch'en, Kenneth, 4

Cheng Bai'er. See *Fangyu shenglüe*
Cheonha do (Map of all under heaven): association with Ricci, 213; in atlases, 198–200, 209, 218–220; circulation, 208; depiction of round earth, 207–208; intellectual context, 208–212, 218, 222; new geographic knowledge presented in, 208, 209, 213–215, 218–222; scholarship on, 208, 223n6; in *Yeoji do*, **207**
Cheonha gogeum daechong pyeollam do. See *Pyeollam do*
"Cheonha jido" (*Cheonha jido*), 200, **201**, 204n25
China. See Ming China; Qing China; Yuan China
China, maps of: in *Da Ming yitong zhi*, **273**, 274; in encyclopedias, 196; Great Wall in, 250–251, 268n25; by Jesuits, 229, 232–233, 251, 253; in Korean atlases, 199–202, **202**, 218, 220; of Ortelius, 247, 248–249, 250, 251; Portuguese, 249; province name translations, 250, **254**; in *Pyeollam do*, 196; in Ruggieri's manuscript atlas, **272**, 274; by Sanson, 277–279, **277**, 284; translations, 250–258. See also *Guang yutu*; *Guanzhi*
Chinese language: Min dialect, 251, 252; studies by Jesuit missionaries, 247–248, 252–253, 272–273, 274; transcriptions, 253, 274; transliteration, 251, 255, 258
Chinese maps: in books, 38–39, 47–48, 160, 196; chronology, **150**; in Europe, 11–12, 133, 136, 247, 248, 274, 291, 299; European influences, 140, 142, 143, 148–149; genealogy, 145, 148, **149**, 296; in Japan, 145; large, 125, 128–133, 136–137, 140–145, 151n4. See also Chinese world maps
Chinese scholars: collaboration with Jesuits, 65, 66, 68–69, 70, 136, 258; education, 66, 128; geographic information introduced to, 26–27, 35–37, 56, 70, 73, 125; interest in maps and geography, 26–27, 104, 125, 136, 160; *Kunyu wanguo quantu* and, 29, 30, 67; *Liangyi xuanlan tu* and, 29, 67, 107; mobility, 70, 73; relationships among, 34, 128; translations of European books, 68. See also knowledge exchange; Ricci, Matteo, interactions with Chinese scholars; *and individual names*
Chinese world maps, 125, 149, 160–161. See also Chinese maps; Japan, Chinese world maps in

Christianity: Chinese converts, 29, 61, 66–68, 70, 73; Confucianism and, 67; Japanese censorship of, 10, 159, 161, 179; moral code, 1; persecution in China, 66, 69, 83. See also Jesuit missionaries
Clavius, Christopher, 68
communication: confidence in, 37; contact zones, 56, 66, 70; intercultural, 26–27, 35–36, 37–38, 46, 124–125; transmission and reception, 26, 120. See also intertextuality
Confucianism, 1, 37, 67, 189, 210, 218. See also Chinese scholars; neo-Confucianism
contact zones, 56, 66, 70
cosmology: Chinese, 73, 76n59, 136, 140, 215, 217; egg analogy, 65–66, 140, 152n28; European, 69, 149

Da Ming yitong wenwu zhusi yamen guanzhi (System of civil and military titles, positions, and offices of the unified Great Ming). See *Guanzhi*
Da Ming yitong zhi (Gazetteer of the unified Great Ming), 128–129, 151n9, 190, 198, 248, **273**, 274, 292n13
Day, John D., 6
De Christiana expeditione apud Sinas (The Christian expedition among the Chinese), 26–27, 29, 110
D'Elia, Pasquale, 6, 7, 50n31
De Troia, Paolo, 79
de Ursis, Sabatino, 69, 76n57, 80–81, 82, 89, 91, 97, 211
Dias, Manuel, Jr. (Yang Manuo): globe project, 66, 68; in Hangzhou, 83; life of, 69; *Shengjing zhijie*, 223n1; text on globe, 57, 64–66, 73; *Tianwen lüe* (Outline and questions about heaven), 69, 76n53
Dutch traders, 10, 82, 131

East Asia, manuscript map of (1651 copy of 1593 map; ARSI map), **230**–**231**; Italian copy, **240**, 241; map of Japan, 234–235, **235**; map of Korea, 235, 237–239, **237**; production of 1593 map, 229, 233–235, 238–241
Edney, Matthew H., 3, 28, 103, 121n38, 122n41
Enoki Kazuo, 245
Euclid, *Elements*, 68, 211, 222

Europe: colonialism, 3, 247–248, 297; East Asian maps and artifacts in, 11–12, 133, 247, 248, 274, 291, 299; globe production in, 57–60

European maps: Dutch, 166, 183n21; illustrations, 111; in Japan, 166, 234; large, 104–105, 116–117; in Renaissance, 3; updating, 233

European world maps: based on Jesuit maps, 291; brought to China, 26–27, 80–82, 98n13, 104–105, 136; brought to China by Ricci, 31, 50n41, 79–80, 136, 152n18; Chinese translations, 80–82, 88–89; depictions of East Asia, 31; history of, 3, 105, 124, 295–296; in Japan ("Nanban"), 9, 10; by Jesuits, 111, 124–125; large, 105, 107; by Mercator, 31, 105, **106**, 111. *See also* Ortelius, Abraham

Fang Yizhi, *Wuli xiaoshi* (Little notes on the principles of the phenomena), 211

Fangyu shenglüe (Complete survey of the earth), 34, 39, **40–41**, 160, 181n4, 210

Feng Yingjing, 34, 35, 37–38, 45, 152n24. *See also Fangyu shenglüe*; *Yueling guangyi*

Fróis, Luís, 237

Fujian: book market, 8, 131; eunuch tax collector, 81–82, 90–91, 98n12; European maps translated in, 80–82; maps printed in, 128–131, 143; Min dialect, 251, 252; trade networks, 131, 133, 248. *See also* Fuzhou

Fuzhou, 69, 83, 88, 93, 94, 96, 99n24. *See also Zhifang waiji*: Fuzhou edition

Galileo Galilei, 66, 69

Gan Gong. *See Xingsheng tu*

Gao Cai, 81–82, 98n12

geography: Chinese view of earth as square, 35, 73, 76n59, 149, 208; distance data, 190, 198, 280, 286, 287; information in *riyong leishu*, 196; relationship to astronomy, 176; study in Europe, 124

geography books: Chinese, 128, 129, 136, 160–161, 174, 175–176, 210; Japanese, 171, 174–179. *See also Sancai tuhui*

Giangolini, Carlo, "Nova et exactissima Sinarum monarchiae descriptio," **240**, 241

Giles, Lionel, 6

globalist map history, 2, 5, 295–296

globe gores, 57–59, 60, 61, **62**, **63**

globes: celestial, 57, 61, **62**, 73, 211; in China, 57, 61; in Europe, 57–60; in Japan, 61, 74n27, 163, 166, 183nn19–20; materiality, 56–61, 64–66, 298; production, 56–59, 60–61, 74n12; from Qing court, 61, **64**, 74n24; terrestrial, 56–61, **63**, 64–66, **64**, 73. *See also* British Library globe

Gong Yingyan, 6, 104–105, 116

Greuter, Matthäus, globe by, 59–60, **59**

Guang yutu (Extended territorial maps): contents, 129; maps, 129, 280, 292n7, 293n21; popularity, 129; provincial maps, **286**, 287, 288, **289**, **290**; as source for later maps, 250, 269n26, 274

Guanzhi (*Da Ming yitong wenwu zhusi yamen guanzhi*; System of civil and military titles, positions, and offices of the unified Great Ming): compared to Ruggieri's atlas, 275–277, 282, **282**, 286–288; contents, 269n26, 279–282, 286; distance data, 280, 286, 292n13, 293n18; horizontal distortion, **286–287**, 287; maps, 275, **276**, 279, **280**, 282, **282**, 284, 293n18; planar polar coordinates, 280, **281**, 287; Ruggieri's translation, 251, 275, 277–278, 282–283; sources, 293n20

Gujin xingsheng zhi tu (Map of advantageous terrain then and now). *See Xingsheng tu*

Guo Zizhang, 34, 35, 36–37, 52n80, 105

Gwangyeo do (Extended territorial maps), "Cheonha do," 218–220, **220**

Hallerstein, Ferdinand Augustin von, 211

Han Yu, *Yuan Dao* (Essentials of the [moral] way), 37

Hangzhou: globe produced in region, 60–61, 73; Jesuit missionaries in, 7–8, 69, 83; lacquer-making, 60, 73; printers, 7–8, 29, 68, 69, 82, 83; *Zhifang waiji* edition, 83, 88–96, **89**, **92**, **93**, **95**, 97, 142

Harame Sadakiyo, *Yochizu* (Map of the land), 166–167, **167**, **168–169**, 170

Hong Daeyong, 218, 222, 226n46

Hong Weilian (William Hung), 6

Hōtan. *See Nansenbushū bankoku shōka no zu*

Hou Gongchen, 34, 35, 46

Huainan zi, 35, 190, 197

Huang, Cheng, *Xiushi lu* (Records of lacquer décor), 60
Huang Ming fenye yutu gujin renwu shiji (Map of astral allocations of the imperial Ming, with famous persons and important events then and now), 131–133, **132**
Huang Shijian, 6, 104–105, 116
Huangyu tu (Map of imperial territories), 163
Huntian yishuo (Exposition on the armillary sphere), 61; globe gores, **62**, **63**
Hwanyeong ji (*Shinpyeon pyoje chando Hwanyeong ji*; Record of the world: Newly edited and titled collection of diagrams), 213–217, **214**, **216**, 225nn34–35, 225n37, 226n40

Im Seong, 206–207, 222
Imjin War, 9, 235–237, 238, 239, 241
intertextuality: dialogues, 32, 34–39, 46, 52n66; within maps, 31–36; among "Ricci maps," 32, 46; textile metaphor, 39
Intorcetta, Prospero, portrait, 133, **134**, **135**
Itō Tōgai, 145

Jang Yu, *Gyegok manpil* (Gyegok's literary notes), 190, 198
Japan: book market, 11; calendars, 61, 75n28; censorship of Christianity, 10, 159, 161, 179; diplomatic mission to Europe, 234; geography books, 171, 174–179; globes in, 61, 74n27, 163, 166, 183nn19–20; household encyclopedias (*setsuyōshū*), 170, 171, 178–179; Imjin War, 9, 235–237, 238, 239, 241; Jesuit missionaries in, 161, 179, 181n6, 234, 235, 237, 238, 241; *Kunyu wanguo quantu* in, 115–116, 159, 161, **162**; mapmakers, 14n35, 159–160, 163, 166–167, 170–171, 179; maps of, 167, 234–237, **235**, 243n26; Ming envoys in, 237; Momijiyama Bunko, 163; Nagasaki, 10, 161, 163; Spanish traders in, 9
Japan, Chinese world maps in: artifacts influenced by, 9–10, 159–160, 163, 166–167, 170–171, 179; printed, 145; reprints, 145; translated or annotated, 171; transmission channels, 161
Japanese world maps: based on European models, 238–239, **239**; in books, 163, 171, 174–179; 180–181; Buddhist, 145, 171, 183n27; categories, 9–10; ethnographic information, 166, 179; globes, 163, 166, 183nn19–20; Japan in, 167; Jōtokuji, **239**; market, 11; *Nansenbushū bankoku shōka no zu*, 145, 171, **172–173**; place-names and text, 170, 174, 175; Ricci association avoided, 170, 178–179, 183n25; sizes, 163, 182n14; source material, 9–10, 163, 167, 171, 174–176, 178–179, 182n13, 234; stand-alone, 163; titles, 179, 184n31; *Yochizu*, 166–167, **167**, **168–169**, 170. See also *Bankoku sōzu*
Jesuit Archives (ARSI), 229, 238. See also East Asia, manuscript map of
Jesuit missionaries: accommodation policy, 272, 274, 284; annual reports, 82, 98n13; arrival in Ming China, 1, 272–273; astronomical knowledge, 66; churches, 68, 69; collaboration with Chinese scholars, 65, 66, 68–69, 70, 136, 258; Confucianism and, 67; in Hangzhou, 7–8, 69, 83; in Japan, 9, 161, 179, 181n6, 234, 235, 237, 238, 241; Korean envoys and, 211; mission stations, 68–69, 104, 233, 273, 274, 292n6; mobility, 70, 73, 133; publications, 83; study of Chinese language, 272–273, 274; translations by, 249, 251, 252, 253–255; visitors, 229, 234, 241n2, 272. See also knowledge exchange; Ricci, Matteo
Jesuit missionaries, maps by: of China, 232–233, 251, 274; globe projects, 66, 68; intercultural context, 124–125; world maps, 111, 124–125. See also East Asia, manuscript map of; European world maps; Ruggieri, Michele
Jesuits, Chinese, 29, 66–67, 69. See also Li Zhizao; Yang Tingyun
Ji Mingtai. See *Jiuzhou fenye yutu gujin renwu shiji*
Jiaxing, 60
Jido, 199–200
Jin Guoping, 248
Jiuzhou fenye yutu gujin renwu shiji (Map of astral allocations of the Nine Regions with famous persons and important events then and now), **132**; Beijing reprint (1679), 145, 153n42; compared to *Tianxia jiubian fenye renji lucheng quantu*, 140–142, 143, 153n31, 193; shown in Intorcetta portrait, 133, **134**,

135; similarities to *Qiankun wanguo quantu gujin renwu shiji*, 137; title, 133, 136

Joseon jido bu paldo cheonha jido, 199, **199**

Joseon Korea. *See* Korea

Jurchen, 235, 238

Kangnido, 9

Kashiragaki taisei setsuyōshū: Nigyō ryōten, **175**; "Sekai bankoku sōzu," **174**

Kawamura Katsunori, 237

Kim Suhong, 188–189, 203n3. See also *Pyeollam do*

Kim Yangseon, 189, 203n4

Kinda Akihiro, 10

knowledge exchange: complexity, 4–5; in East Asia, 2, 9–11; global, 12; between Jesuits and Chinese scholars, 1, 56, 66–68, 70, 73, 83, 125, 145, 148; material artifacts and, 2, 5–8, 9, 11–12; networks, 7, 12; roles of individuals and cultures, 2, 5, 8. *See also* European world maps; intertextuality

Korea: astronomy, 190, 211; *baiguan* novels, 211–212; book market, 11; diplomats, 209–210, 211, 220, 224n11; geographical knowledge in, 210, 217–218; Imjin War, 9, 235–237, 238, 239, 241; interest in "Western learning," 211; as last bastion of civilization, 217, 218, 222; literati, 209, 210–212, 213–218, 220–222; Manchu-Qing invasions, 188, 218; mapmakers, 14n35; maps imported from China, 11, 209, 210–211; maps of, 203n3, 204n24, 232, 235, 237–239, **237**; painters, 209; relations with China, 10, 218, 220; view of Qing, 10, 188, 215–217, 222, 226n43; *Zhifang waiji* in, 97, 208, 210–212, 215, 217, 218, 220. *See also Cheonha do*; *Pyeollam do*

Korean atlases: *Cheonha do* in, 209, 218–220; *Cheonha jido*, 200, **201**, 204n25; circulation, 11; contents, 198–202, 209, 218, 226nn48–49; *Joseon jido bu paldo cheonha jido*, 199, **199**; maps of China, 199–202, 218, 220; *Pyeollam do* in, 189, 198–200, 202, 203. See also *Yeoji do*

Korean world maps, 9, 189, 190, 198–199, 200. See also *Cheonha do*; *Pyeollam do*

Kunyu quantu (Complete map of the earth; Sambiasi), **114**, 115

Kunyu quantu (Complete map of the earth; Verbiest), 49n16, 111, 125, **126**–**127**, 208, 222

Kunyu wanguo quantu (Complete map of all countries on earth): Chinese editor and sponsors, 29, 30, 67; circulation and influence in Korea, 11, 188, 189, 193, 196–197, 204n17, 208, 212–213, 217; circulation in Japan, 9–10, 11, 159, 161, 163, 166, 184n32; circulation outside China, 9; compared to other maps, 137, **138**–**139**, 140, **168**–**169**, 170; contents, 1–2; copy mounted on screens, 114; extant prints, 6, **22**–**23**, 46–47, 115–116, 159, 161, 163, **164**; figured manuscripts based on, 103, 105–107, **109**, **110**, 111, **112**–**113**, 115, 117; globes based on, 61; goals, 117; Japanese maps inspired by, 166–167, 170, 171, 182n17, 183nn24–25; modern framing, 116, **118**–**119**; prefaces and postscripts, 27–28, 32, **33**, 34, 45, 110–111, 137, 152n24, 249–250; printer, 29, 67; Ricci's text, 34, 52n83, 57, 105, 107, 114, 117, 198, 250; Ricci's work on, 110; scholarship on, 6; size, 30–31, 105, 107, **108**, 110, 111, 120; source material, 152n18; as third map by Ricci and collaborators, 6, 21, 30; title, 30, 136; translation processes, 249–250; Unified Great Ming (Da Ming Yitong), 27, **28**

lacquer-making centers, 60, 73

Lavezaris, Guido de, 248, 249, 255

Ledyard, Gari, 189

Lee Chan, 189, 192, 203n4

Legazpi, Miguel López de, 245, 247, 248

Lévi-Strauss, Claude, 45–46

Li Tianjing, 61, 68

Li Yingshi (Paul), 29, 34, 38, 107

Li Zhizao (Leo): calendar reform efforts, 65, 98n10; collaboration with European Jesuits, 66–67, 68, 69; death, 96; globe project, 66; in Hangzhou, 68, 82–83, 94, 96; *Kunyu wanguo quantu* and, 29, 30–31, 34, 38, 67, 105, 111, 114, 116, 249–250; life of, 68; *Tianxue chuhan* (First collection on heavenly learning), 83, 91, 94–96, 97, 211; translations, 68; *Zhifang waiji* preface, 69, 79–80, 81, 82, 89, 90–91, 94, 104, 114; *Zhifang waiji* role, 94, 96, 97

Liang Zhou, 137. See also *Qiankun wanguo quantu gujin renwu shiji*

Liangyi xuanlan tu (Mysterious visual map of the two forms): Chinese collaborators and sponsors, 29, 67–68, 107; circulation and influence in Korea, 188, 189, 196–197, 204n17; contents, 30; copy mounted on screens, 115; extant prints, **24–25**, 47; figured manuscripts based on, 111; as fourth map by Ricci and collaborators, 6, 21, 30; in Japan, 159, 161; prefaces, 27–28, 30, 31, 32, 34–35, 111, 198; size, 31, 107, **108**; title, 30

Lim Jongtae, 189, 203n6

Lin Feng (Limahon), 248

Liu Baojian, 61

Liu Ning, *Tianxue jijie* (Collected explanations on heavenly studies), 32

Liu Yu, 67

Longobardo, Niccolò (Long Huamin), 57, 64–66, 68–69, 73, 98n13

Lo Sardo, Eugenio, 271

Lu Jiuyuan, 38

Lü Junhan, 133, 145

Lü Tunan, 94

Lu Yingyang, *Guangyu ji* (Records of extended territories), 251

Luo Hongxian. See *Guang yutu*

Ma Duanlin, *Wenxian tongkao* (Comprehensive study of documents), 31

Macao: Jesuits in, 69, 161, 233, 234, 235, 239, 272–273; maps produced in, 240; Portuguese settlement, 248, 272

Mackay, A. L., 189, 190, 203n4

Manchus. See Qing China

Manguk jeondo (*Taeseo hoesa Li Madu Manguk jeondo*; Complete map of all countries by the emissary of the West Matteo Ricci), 220, **221**

mapping practices: commonalities in sixteenth century, 5–6; diversity, 296–297; East Asian, 103–104, 111, 117, 120, 296, 297; scholarship on, 296; Western, 103–104, 140, 142, 143, 148–149, 296, 297

maps: authorship, 28–29, 49n18; circulation and use, 229, 295, 296, 297, 298; compared to globes, 56–57; functions, 44–45, 133, 136; as intercultural communication, 26–27; materiality, 6, 298; modern framing, 116, **118–119**; presenting on screens, 114–115, 116, 117, 120; production process, 30; reception, 116–117, 120; spatial discourses, 297–299; as subjects, 44–45; translation processes, 249–258, 275

Martini, Martino, 247, 253. See also *Novus atlas sinensis*

materiality, 8, 56–61, 64–66, 298

Mercator, Gerard: globes by, 57; world map by, 31, 105, **106**, 111

Miaojin wanbao quanshu, **197**

Ming China: administrative structure, 128, 151n9, 274, 275–276, 279–282, **281**, 288, **289**, **290**; calendar reform, 65, 68, 69, 75n28, 98n10; cultural similarities to Renaissance Europe, 1; envoys to Japan, 237; geography books, 136; intellectual environment, 1, 27; Korean view of, 215–217, 222; lacquer-making centers, 60, 73; province names, 250, 252, 253, **254**; Qing conquest, 10, 133, 145, 217; relations with Korea, 10; relations with Spanish, 248. See also China, maps of; Chinese world maps; *Da Ming yitong zhi*; Jesuit missionaries

Moerman, D. Max, 145, 183n27

Moreira, Ignacio, 234, 238, 239, 243n11

Morokoshi kinmō zui, "Sansen yochi zenzu," **177**

Nagakubo Sekisui, **167**, 170

Nagasaki, 10, 161, 163

Nanjing: book shop, 143–145, 153n38; Jesuits in, 143–145, 152n23; maps printed in, 131–133, 143–145

Nanjing map (1600): Chinese editor, 29; preface, 32, 34, 52n80; as second map by Ricci and collaborators, 6, 21, 30; size, 105, 107; as source for Liang Zhou, 137

Nansenbushū bankoku shōka no zu (Handy map of all countries of Jambudvīpa), 145, 171, **172–173**

Needham, Joseph, 3, 57, 296

neo-Confucianism, 67, 210

Neroni, Matteo, 277, 278, 279, 288, 291

Nestorian stele, 91, 100n31

Nishikawa Joken: on geography and astronomy, 176; *Zōho ka-i tsūshōkō*, 174–175, 176, **178**, 183n27, 184nn31–32, 184n35

Nishikawa Seikyū, 179
"Nova et exactissima Sinarum monarchiae descriptio," **240**, 241
Novus atlas sinensis, 145, 153n39, 232, 251, 291; "Imperii Sinarum nova descriptio," **232**

Oh Sanghak, 189, 203n6
Ortelius, Abraham, *Theatrum orbis terrarum* (Display of the lands of the globe): copies brought to China by Ricci, 50n41, 79–80, 81, 82, 136, 152n18; copy brought to Japan, 234; grid, 70; map of China (*Chinae olim Sinarum Regio nova descriptio*), 247, 248–249, 250, 251; popularity, 105, 252

Pantoja, Diego de, 69, 76n57, 80–81, 82, 89, 91, 97, 223n1
Pasio, Francesco, 181n6, 273
Philip II of Spain, 245, 247, 249, 273
Philippines, 9, 61, 131, 245, 247–248
Portugal: Chinese translator in, 250, 268n24; explorers from, 271–272; mapmakers, 249, 250–251; traders from, 1, 9; Treaty of Tordesillas, 247. See also Macao
print culture, 1, 7–8, 11, 131–133, 143–145. See also book market
Purchas, Samuel, *Pilgrimes*, 129, **131**, 151n12
Pyeollam do (*Cheonha gogeum daechong pyeollam do*; Comprehensive overview map of all under heaven then and now): astronomical information, 189, 190, 203; in atlases, 189, 198–200, 202, 203; composition, 188–189; contents, 188, 189–192; extant print and manuscript copies, 189, 190–192, **191**, **194**; intermediary manuscript copy, 192, **193**, **195**; preface, 188, 190, 192, 196, 197–198; Ricci name in, 188, 190; scholarship on, 189, 203n4, 203n6; source material, 188, 189, 190, 192–193, 196–198, 202–203

Qi Guangzong, 34, 45
Qiankun wanguo quantu gujin renwu shiji (Complete map of all countries in the universe, with famous persons and important events then and now), 38, 136–137, **138–139**, 140, 145, 193, 196

Qing China: conquest of Ming, 10, 133, 145, 217; globe, 57, 61, **64**, 74n24; invasions of Korea, 188, 218; Korean view of, 10, 188, 215–217, 222, 226n43; map printing, 145; relations with Korea, 218, 220
Qu Shigu, 89, 211
Qu Yuan, 76n53

Rada, Martín de, 247–248, 249, 251, 253, 255, 258, 268n20
Ramaswamy, Sumathi, 297
Rho, Giacomo, 61, 69
Rhodes, Alexander de, 233, 239
Ricci, Matteo: astronomical studies, 190, 197–198; atlas and world map brought to China, 50n41, 79–80, 136, 152n18; biography by Aleni, 69, 76n56; Chinese name, 11; death, 68, 69; *De Christiana expeditione apud Sinas* (The Christian expedition among the Chinese), 26–27, 29, 110; European world maps brought to China, 31, 50n41, 79–80, 136, 152n18; on globes, 57; *Jiren shipian* (Ten essays on an extraordinary man), 67; letters, 181n6, 240, 248; map sent to Europe, 247, 248; maps produced with the assistance of, 6–7, 13n24, 21, 27, 30–31; in popular histories, 2–3, 4; portrait, **131**; scholarship on, 295–296; *Tianzhu shiyi* (True meaning of the Lord of heaven), 67; transcription of Chinese, 253; travels around China, 6, 13n24, 69, 104, 152n23, 233, 241; world map displayed by, 26–27, 104–105; in Zhaoqing, 26–27, 104, 233, 273
Ricci, Matteo, interactions with Chinese scholars: maps produced, 7, 28–29, 30–31, 105, 107, 250; personal relationships, 37, 152nn23–24; translations, 67–68
"Ricci maps": authorship, 27–29; evolution, 30–31; genealogy, 298–299; as intercultural communication, 26–27, 31–38, 46; intertextuality, 32, 46; Korean map linked to, 213; origins, 26–27, 28; "Ricci-type" maps in Japan, 9–10; scholarship on, 1, 2, 3–4, 6–7, 26, 148, 295–296; use of term, 2, 6–7, 21, 28, 29, 49n15. See also *Kunyu wanguo quantu*; *Liangyi xuanlan tu*; Nanjing map; Zhaoqing map

riyong leishu (encyclopedias for daily use), 196
Ruan Taiyuan (Louis), 34, 37
Ruggieri, Michele: life of, 272–274; maps of China by, 232, 233, 291; translations by, 247, 251, 252–253, 269n26, 277–278
Ruggieri, Michele, manuscript atlas: adaptation process, 274–275, 276–277, 283, 286–288, 291; attribution, 271; Chinese maps in, 275, **276**; circulation, 291; contents, 271, 275; dates, 271; distortions, 287–288, **287**, **289**, **290**, 291; early-stage translated maps, 275–277, 278–279, 282, 283, 288, 291; interim maps, 283, 288, 291; later-stage maps, 279, 282–283, 286–288, 292n12; Liaodong maps, 275, **276**, 277, 284; map of China, **272**, 274; maps based on, 278–279, 288, 291; Nanzhili maps, 275, 276, 279, **280**, 282, **282**, **284–285**; provincial maps, **282**, 283, 291, 292n11; scholarship on, 274; Shanxi map, 275, 284, **287**; Sichuan map, **290**; source material, 274–275; translated maps, 288; Zhejiang map, **289**
Rughesi, Fausto, 291

Sambiasi, Francesco, 69; *Kunyu quantu* (Complete map of the earth), 111, **114**, 125
Sancai tuhui (Illustrated compendium of the three powers), 171, 174–175, 210; "Shanhai yudi quantu," 39, **43**, 176–178, 208, 220
Sanson, Nicolas d'Abbeville, *La Chine Royaume*, 277–279, **278**, 284, 288, 291, 292n9
Saris, John, 129
Schall von Bell, Johann Adam, 61, 69
Schütte, Josef, 238
screens, maps mounted on, 114–115, 116, 117, 120, 298
Shanhai jing (Classic of mountains and seas): geographic descriptions, 30; influence in Korea, 190, 192, 198, 199, 200, 207–208, 209–210, 215; legendary countries and monsters, 31, 190, 192, 207–208, 209
"Shanhai yudi quantu," *Sancai tuhui*, 39, **43**, 176–178, 208, 220
"Shanhai yudi quantu," *Yueling guangyi*, 39, **42**, 152n24, 160
Shao Yong, 215, 217
Shen Que, 66, 69

Shibukawa Harumi, 61, 166, 183nn19–20
Shin Yuhan, 209–210, 224n11, 224n13
Shinpyeon pyoje chando Hwanyeong ji. See Hwanyeong ji
Siamese mapping practices, 297
Siku quanshu (Complete library of the four treasuries), 80, 83, 96, 97
Sima Qian, 36
Sima Tan, 36
Sinographic sphere, 5, 9, 11, 14n35
sociocultural map history, 296–297
Spain: embassy to Japan, 61, 74n27; explorers from, 245, 247–248; Japanese mission to, 234; Philippines and, 245, 247–248; traders from, 1, 9, 131; Treaty of Tordesillas, 247. See also *Xingsheng tu*
spatial discourses, 297–299
"spiritual traveling" (*woyou*), 45, 117, 122n41
Standaert, Nicolas, 3–4, 13n14, 26
Suzhou, maps printed in, 145

Taeseo hoesa Li Madu Manguk jeondo (Complete map of all countries by the emissary of the West Matteo Ricci; *Manguk jeondo*), 220, **221**
Taewon ji (Records of Taewon), 206–207, 222, 223n1
Tatton, Gabriel, 249
Terajima Ryōan, *Wakan Sansai zue* (Japanese-Chinese *Sancai tuhui*), 171, 174, 176–178, **176**
terrestrial globes. See globes
Theatrum orbis terrarum. See Ortelius, Abraham
Thongchai Winichakul, 297
Tianwen zhi (On the heavens), 190, 197
Tianxia jiubian fenye renji lucheng quantu (Complete map of all under heaven, the nine frontiers, astral allocations, human traces, and route itineraries), 38, 140–145, **141**, 153nn37–39, 193, 198
Tianxue chuhan (First collection on heavenly learning), 83, 91, 94–96, 97, 211. See also *Zhifang waiji*
Tongdian (Comprehensive compendium), 190
Toyotomi Hideyoshi: fan with map, 235–237, **236**; globes and, 61, 74n27; in Hokkaido, 243n23; unification of Japan, 210, 234. See also Imjin War

trade networks, 1, 9, 131, 133, 248
travel: as displacement, 45–46; imaginary (*woyou*), 6, 45, 52n83
Trigault, Nicolas, 26, 66, 83, 104; *De Christiana expeditione apud Sinas* (The Christian expedition among the Chinese), 26–27, 29, 110
Tushu bian (Compendium of illustrations and writings), 39, **44**

Uesugi Kazuhiro, 10
Unno Kazutaka, 6, 208, 223n6

Vagnoni, Alfonso, 211
Valignano, Alessandro: *Adiciones del sumario de Japon* (Additions to the compendium of Japan), 234, 238; East Asian map and, 229, 238, 239; in Japan, 234–235, 238, 243n11; Ricci and, 233; as visitor, 229, 234, 241n2, 272, 273
Verbiest, Ferdinand: *Kunyu quantu* (Complete map of the earth), 49n16, 111, 125, **126–127**, 208, 222; *Kunyu tushuo* (Illustrated exposition on the earth), 211, 222; *Kunyu waiji* (Record of everything beyond the earth), 210
Vermeer, Johannes, *Woman Reading a Letter*, **107**
Wakan Sansai zue (Japanese-Chinese *Sancai tuhui*), 171, 174, 176–178, **176**
Wanbao quanshu (Complete book of myriad treasures), 190, 196, 200
Wang Junfu, map printed by, 145, **146–147**, 171
Wang Pan, 29
Wang Qi. See *Sancai tuhui*
Wang Qianjin, 274
Wang Shen, 83
Wang Yiqi, 91
Wanguo quantu (Complete map of all countries), 69–70, **71**, 142–143, **144**, 145, 153n36, 193
"Wanguo quantu," *Zhifang waiji*, 69–70, **72**, 98n9, 142, 208
Wanguo tuzhi (Maps and treatises on all countries), 80, 98n9. See also Ortelius, Abraham
Wanli emperor, 68, 79–80, 82, 88–89
Wei Jun, *Li shuo huangtang huoshi* (The theories of Ricci are incoherent and deceive the world), 35

Wi Baekgyu, 209, 212, 213. See also *Hwanyeong ji*
Wi Yeongbok, 213
world maps. *See* Chinese world maps; European world maps; Japanese world maps; Korean world maps; maps
Wu Zhongming, 29, 34, 36–37, 137, 152n23
Wylie, Alexander, 75n44, 96

Xavier, Francis, 234, 272
Xie Fang, 79, 98n9, 99n28
Xingsheng tu (*Gujin xingsheng zhi tu*; Map of advantageous terrain then and now), **246**; annotations, 251, **252**, 258; contents, 128–129, 248; extant copy, 129, 245–247, 248, 249; origins, 248–249, 255; potential influence, 193, 248–249; purpose, 248; scholarship on, 245, 247, 248; significance, 247, 249–250, 255, 258; Spanish translations, 245–247, 249, 251–252, **253**, 255–258; text, 128, 151n9, 255, **257**; translation documents, 245–247, 248, 251, 255–258, **256**, 259–267
Xiong Shiqi, 89
Xu Cheng'en, 211
Xu Guangqi, 34, 65, 66–68, 69, 211; *Xinfa suanshu* (Books on calculations according to new methods), 61, 68, 73
Xu Xuchen, 89, 211

Yang Ming, 60
Yang, Paul Fu-Mien, 252
Yang Tingyun: biography by Aleni, 69, 76n56; collaboration with European Jesuits, 66–67, 68, 69; globe projects, 66; *Juejiao tongwen ji* (Collected essays from distant lands), 32; *Zhifang waiji* and, 69, 79, 80, 82, 89, 91, 96, 97, 99n18, 142
Ye Xianggao, 83, 88, 89, 94, 96, 97, 99nn23–24
Yee, Cordell D. K., 4, 104, 296
Yeoji do (Maps of the land): "Cheonha do," **207**, 209, 226n49; "Cheonha jido" (Map of all cities under heaven), 218, **219**; contents, 200, 204n24, 226n49; map of China, 200, **202**, 226n49
Yi Gyugyeong, *Oju yeonmun jangjeon sango* (Random expatiations of Oju), 210–211
Yi Ik, 210, 224nn17–18

Yi Jonghwi, 209, 212–213, 215, 217, 224n27; "Li Madu nambukgeuk do" (Matteo Ricci's map of the North and South Poles), 212–213, **214**, 225n31

Yi Uibong, *Bukwonrok* (Record from beyond the northern gate), 211

Yijing (Book of changes), 67, 136

Yuan China, 60, 129, 206

Yueling guangyi (Extended meaning of the monthly proceedings), 39, 184n41; "Shanhai yudi quantu," 39, **42**, 152n24, 160

Zhang Heng, 65, 152n28

Zhang Huang. See *Tushu bian*

Zhang Wentao, 29, 67–68

Zhang Xie, *Dongxiyang kao* (Study on the eastern and western oceans), 81–82

Zhao Kehuai, 34, 49n15, 52n80

Zhaoqing, Jesuit mission post, 26–27, 104–105, 233, 273

Zhaoqing map (1584): Chinese editor, 29; as first map by Ricci and collaborators, 6, 21, 30; preface, 34; size, 105, 107; title, 13n24

Zhifang waiji (Record of everything beyond the administration): Bodleian Library copy, 94, 96; circulation, 79, 82, 83, 96; circulation in Japan, 88, 97, 171, 175, 182n9, 184n32; circulation in Korea, 97, 208, 210–212, 215, 217, 218, 220; coauthors, 68, 69, 79, 82–83, 89, 91, 97; comparison of editions, 88–96, 97; contents, 8, 69, 76n56, 79, 91, 142; cover pages, 88–89, **89**; Fuzhou edition, 83, 88–96, **89**, **93**, **95**, 97, 99n28, 142, 143; genealogy of Ming-era editions, 83, **86–87**, 88–91, **88**, 94; Hangzhou edition, 83, 88–96, **89**, **92**, **93**, **95**, 97, 142; influence, 70, 83; Japanese ban on, 161; layout, 92–94; maps of continents, **84**, **85**, 142; Naikaku Bunko copy, **72**, 80, **84**, **85**, 94–96, 100n36; prefaces, 69, 79–80, 81, 82, 89–91, **90**, 94–96, 99n28; production and printing, 69, 82–83, 94, 96, 97; reprinting, 79, 83; scholarship on, 79; source material, 79–82, 98n8; Veneranda Biblioteca Ambrosiana copy, **95**; "Wanguo quantu," 69–70, **72**, 98n9, 142, 208

Zhou Wenju, painting attributed to, **115**

Zhou China, 35, 46, 203n11

Zōho ka-i tsūshōkō, 174–175, 176, **178**, 183n27, 184nn31–32, 184n35

Zong Bing, 117

Zou Yan, 36, 212, 213, 224n24

Zuozhuan, 37